THE CLASSICAL
GERMAN ELEGY,
1795-1950

THEODORE ZIOLKOWSKI

# THE CLASSICAL GERMAN ELEGY

## 1795–1950

PRINCETON UNIVERSITY PRESS

COPYRIGHT © 1980 BY PRINCETON UNIVERSITY PRESS

PUBLISHED BY PRINCETON UNIVERSITY PRESS,
PRINCETON, NEW JERSEY
IN THE UNITED KINGDOM: PRINCETON UNIVERSITY PRESS,
GUILDFORD, SURREY

LIBRARY OF CONGRESS CATALOGING IN PUBLICATION DATA WILL
BE FOUND ON THE LAST PRINTED PAGE OF THIS BOOK

PUBLICATION OF THIS BOOK HAS BEEN AIDED BY A GRANT
FROM THE WHITNEY DARROW PUBLICATION RESERVE FUND OF
PRINCETON UNIVERSITY PRESS

CLOTHBOUND EDITIONS OF PRINCETON UNIVERSITY PRESS BOOKS
ARE PRINTED ON ACID-FREE PAPER, AND BINDING MATERIALS ARE
CHOSEN FOR STRENGTH AND DURABILITY

PRINTED IN THE UNITED STATES OF AMERICA BY PRINCETON
UNIVERSITY PRESS, PRINCETON, NEW JERSEY

DESIGNED AND ILLUSTRATED BY LAURY A. EGAN

For Margaret Embry Goldstein
and Samuel Jacob Goldstein
with affection and gratitude

# Contents

# Preface

Somewhat to my surprise, this book has turned out to constitute a chapter in the history of genre. I certainly did not set
out to write a history of the classical German elegy. For a long
time, indeed, it did not occur to me that I was dealing with a
hitherto unrecognized literary form whose history needed to
be written. The book began simply as an essay on Schiller's
"Der Spaziergang," a fascinating poem whose implications, I
felt, had not been exhausted by scholarship and criticism. The
table of contents recapitulates quite precisely the stages of my
preoccupation with that poem.

My effort to understand "Der Spaziergang" prompted me
initially—after I had gone as far as I could with the techniques
of textual analysis and interpretation—to explore some of its
sources. Its title led me, first of all, to look more closely at the
governing motif of the poem—the walk through a landscape
or, more specifically, the climb up a hill or mountain. I soon
discovered that the conventions of nature poetry in general
and of eighteenth-century topographical poetry in particular
could not explain the seemingly self-evident fact that the poet
chooses a mountaintop to engage in his meditations. Before
the mountain could be introduced into a poem as the ideal
locus for philosophical speculation, a major shift had to take
place in the cultural consciousness of eighteenth-century
Europe. Through my study of those developments I came to
regard the mountain as so constitutively central for meditative poetry in the tradition of "Der Spaziergang" that for
some time the working title of this book was "The Poetic
Mountainclimbers."

Although the familiar title "Der Spaziergang" prompted
my exploration of the cultural landscapes of Chapter 2, the
poem's original title, "Elegie," suggested the investigations of
Chapter 3. For in its unique combination of mode and form
Schiller's poem was unlike any other poems calling themselves "elegies" in European literature before 1795. To understand why Schiller chose that specific generic designation it

became necessary not just to survey the history of the European elegy from classical antiquity down to Goethe's "Römische Elegien," but especially to take into account certain important developments in eighteenth-century aesthetic theory, culminating in Schiller's essay "Über naive und sentimentalische Dichtung." Gradually my appreciation of the poem enabled me to identify other works from the same period that resembled "Der Spaziergang" in a more than casual way. That grouping of poems—which by that time I had come to think of collectively as the classical German elegy—led me to ponder the factors underlying the emergence of this specific literary kind at that moment in history. In short, as Chapter 4 indicates, I became convinced that the poems surrounding "Der Spaziergang" represented a general poetic response to the new humanistic conception of *Bildung* and that their characteristics—including setting, mode, and form—were explicitly calculated to enhance the poetic rendering of *Bildung* as experience.

At this point I began to wonder if a literary form regarded as so attractive by the writers of German classicism simply disappeared or whether it had a history that could be traced through following literary generations. The ensuing search persuaded me that the classical German elegy—by which I mean essentially those poems that consciously continued the tradition of "Der Spaziergang"—did indeed constitute an identifiable form that was clearly recognized and appropriated as the basis of poems by many of the finest German writers from Goethe, Hölderlin, and Platen down to Rilke, Trakl, and Bobrowski. Chapters 5 and 6 trace the transmission of that form through the nineteenth century by means of imitation and adaptation. Since generic continuity is preserved only in the totality of all works exploiting any perceived form, it is necessary—if one is writing the history of a genre rather than skipping from masterpiece to masterpiece—to deal occasionally with writers whose achievement is less than epoch-making. I have treated these minor poets as light-handedly as possible and yet with the respect that they deserve for their contribution to the preservation of the genre. It seemed desir-

able, moreover, to show how the new form gradually asserted itself in the chaos of other forms competing for literary
attention at the beginning of the nineteenth century. For the
generic autonomy of the classical German elegy—and indeed
of any genre—can be tested most accurately by contrasting it
with other forms that appear to share some of its characteristics. Finally, it seemed useful to characterize the cultural
aspirations of the elegiac poets in order to make it clear why
they were attracted to this particular genre. Chapter 7 surveys
the brilliant twentieth-century renewal of the classical German elegy, in which imitation and adaptation often are intensified to the point of parody and deformation.

As recent surveys have shown—notably Paul Hernadi, *Beyond Genre: New Directions in Literary Classification* (Ithaca:
Cornell Univ. Press, 1972); Klaus W. Hempfer, *Gattungs-
theorie: Information und Synthese* (München: Fink, 1973); and
Wolfgang Ruttkowski, *Bibliographie der Gattungspoetik für den
Studenten der Literaturwissenschaft* (München: Max Huebner,
1973)—twentieth-century genre theory has been concerned
principally with philosophical questions regarding the on-
tological status of literature. Its speculations and conclusions,
however illuminating these may be for our understanding of
basic types (e.g., epic-lyric-dramatic-didactic), have little
bearing on the definition of such specific literary kinds as the
classical German elegy.

My own methodology, as I have suggested, was motivated
not by theoretical concerns but by the practical exigencies of
interpretation. Essentially it involves a three-stage process
that begins with the analysis of a specific text, then moves to
an exploration of its sources, and finally traces its transmission by means of imitation and adaptation. I would like to
think, however, that the same methodology might be generally applicable to the study of other genres, especially those
that have emerged in the past two centuries at a time when the
reverence for classical generic conventions was breaking
down. In the first place, my procedure—pragmatic in its
methods and historical in its approach—seems to be consistent with the understanding of genre among certain American

critics of recent decades. Thus René Wellek and Austin Warren propose in their *Theory of Literature* (1949): "For the definition of modern genres one probably does best to start with a
specific highly influential book or author, and look for the re-
verberations" (Chap. 17). And E. D. Hirsch, Jr., writes in his
*Validity in Interpretation* (New Haven: Yale Univ. Press, 1967)
that "The best way to define a genre—if one decides that he
wants to—is to describe the common elements in a narrow
group of texts which have direct historical relationships" (p.
110).

In the second place, the focus on specific works enables us
to avoid the hermeneutic circle that involves many students of
genre. Günther Müller stated the classic problem succinctly in
his essay "Bemerkungen zur Gattungspoetik" (*Philosophischer
Anzeiger*, 3 [1929], 136): "It is a dilemma of all historiography
of genres that we seemingly cannot decide what belongs to a
genre without already knowing what is constitutive of the
genre, and that we cannot know what is genre-constitutive
without recognizing this trait or that as belonging to a given
genre." Because I began by looking for poems that resembled
a specific text by Schiller, and not for poems that conformed
to a theoretically defined genre, I was not troubled by the
hermeneutic dilemma.

Two earlier books have dealt specifically with the German
elegy. Friedrich Beissner's *Geschichte der deutschen Elegie* (Berlin: De Gruyter, 1941), a monograph in the great tradition of
German genre histories of the twenties, follows the German
elegy from its beginnings down to the end of the eighteenth
century, stopping roughly where my own pursuits begin. But
Beissner, concerned with cataloguing the entire range of
poems calling themselves elegies, does not pause to define any
such specific type as the classical German elegy. Klaus Weissenberger's *Formen der Elegie von Goethe bis Celan* (Bern:
Francke, 1969) deals with precisely the same period as my
book does and with many of the same poets. But Weissenberger's approach is explicitly ahistorical, and his understanding of the elegy—any poem displaying what he calls the
"principle of antithesis"—is so broad that it encompasses

many elegiac poems that lie well beyond the scope of my definition of the classical German elegy. My book, taking the middle ground between Beissner's largely historical and Weissenberger's largely theoretical approach, seeks to define the classical German elegy as a historically circumscribed literary genre according to criteria derived pragmatically from a representative group of poems.

I hope that the classical German elegy as defined in this book will be received as a useful addition to the taxonomy of German poetry in the nineteenth and twentieth centuries. It is not my ambition, however, to contribute gratuitously to the terminological proliferation that has recently characterized literary criticism. The validity or this, or any, genre should be measured wholly by its effectiveness in the critical apprehension of poetic texts. More generally, I hope that some readers will be persuaded by the conviction implicit throughout the book and explicit in its Conclusion: namely, that the most productive understanding of genre lies somewhere between the extremes of formal categorization and anthropological typology. It is the underlying thesis of this study that genre is not an absolute type but a poetic form that emerges and develops in response to specific historical conditions. Ideally, the history of any genre should become the history of cultural consciousness.

I have been working on this book off and on for more than ten years. During that period my understanding of the material benefited from discussions with several generations of graduate students here at Princeton, to whom I had the opportunity of presenting my ideas in seminars. In 1972, a generous grant from the American Council of Learned Societies supported several months of research in Europe. It is a pleasure to express my gratitude to two colleagues who performed specific favors in connection with these studies: Johannes Anderegg sent me photographs of Schloss Escheberg, which figures importantly in Geibel's life and works, and Maria Tatar obtained for me a copy of the elegies of Ludwig I. Laury Egan deserves special recognition for her perceptive vignettes, which capture the attitudes toward mountains cited in the book and exemplify the paintings that those attitudes inspired. I am again indebted to my friend Jerry Sherwood for an exemplary job of editing, in which tact was combined with rigor and sensibility with common sense. Finally, it is a joy to welcome Saskia, whose arrival coincides auspiciously with the completion of this book.

THEODORE ZIOLKOWSKI
PRINCETON, NEW JERSEY
MAY 23, 1979

THE CLASSICAL
GERMAN ELEGY,
1795-1950

# 1 · THE MODEL: SCHILLER'S MEDITATIVE MOUNTAINCLIMB

Schiller's "Der Spaziergang" was written in September, 1795, and published that fall, in the journal *Die Horen*, under the title "Elegie." As revised for his collected poems of 1800, "Der Spaziergang" consists of one hundred elegiac distichs organized as a framework embracing a meditative core.[1] The poem begins when the poet steps out of his house to greet the nearby mountain, which is bathed in the light of the morning sun:

> Sei mir gegrüßt, mein Berg mit dem rötlich strahlenden
> Gipfel!
> Sei mir, Sonne, gegrüßt, die ihn so lieblich bescheint!

Strolling across the meadows, the poet enters a beech forest, where a winding path leads him up the foot of the mountain. The first part of the framework ends when the poet suddenly emerges from the woods to find himself far up the mountain on a precipice overlooking a broad valley. The view sends him into a rapture of contemplation that takes up almost three-quarters of the poem.

The basic technique underlying the long central meditation could be described as the temporalization of space. As the poet moves along in a virtual trance and gazes down at the landscape, he translates into a historical sequence the countryside, farms, villages, towns, and cities successively exposed to his view. The poem is saved from the dangers of excessive abstraction by the vividly portrayed landscape, which is unified by such devices as the river, mentioned with leitmotivic frequency. The meditation turns out to be a well-organized essay on the rise and fall of Western civilization, from its simplest beginnings down to Schiller's own late-eighteenth-century present. The grand historical movement from natural man to modern man that the poet witnesses as he looks across the open fields to the towers of the distant city is characterized by a dialectical tension. Primitive man, though blissful in his oneness with nature, was limited in his freedom by rigorous laws of nature. Modern man, though liberated by his reason from the iron rule of nature, has cut himself off from that primordial harmony with nature and community with his fellow man. The movement from necessity to freedom, therefore, is paralleled by a counter-movement from unity to alienation. This dilemma produces the cultural pessimism that depresses the observer on his lonely mountain.

More specifically, the landscape suggests to the thoughtful viewer four stages in the development of mankind. First, as he looks down at the fields below, delineated by the river and the road and populated by herds of sheep and cattle, he ponders the lot of natural man, those "happy people of the fields" who, not yet conscious of freedom, are subject to the same strict laws of nature as the very fields they tend:

> Glückliches Volk der Gefilde! noch nicht zur Freiheit
> erwachet,
> Teilst du mit deiner Flur fröhlich das enge Gesetz.
> (ll. 55-56)

As man begins to emerge from this unthinking state of natural harmony—aptly symbolized by the location of his cottage, which is situated in the midst of his fields and protectively embraced by the tree while vines twine around its windows—a series of changes takes place. In this second stage the trees no longer grow at random; instead, stately poplars now line the highway "in ordered pomp," reflecting a society stratified into classes under a single ruler. As village life gives way to urban culture, the fauns of primitive animistic religion retreat into the wilderness, and new gods descend to earth to inhabit temples erected in their honor. The names of the deities as well as the allusion to walled citadels and Spartan warriors suggest that the poet is thinking here of the heroic period of Greek culture, when men were still united by a compelling sense of patriotism and respect for venerable laws and customs:

> Tausend Hände belebt *ein* Geist, hoch schlägt in tausend
> Brüsten, von *einem* Gefühl glühend, ein einziges Herz,
> Schlägt für das Vaterland und glüht für der Ahnen Gesetze,
> Hier auf dem teuren Grund ruht ihr verehrtes Gebein.
> (ll. 75-78)

Gradually, as reason conquers nature in the course of later classical civilization, "man breaks his fetters" (l. 139). In this third stage, as men liberate themselves by means of science and philosophy from the limitations of a simple natural life, the arts, crafts, and trades flourish. But this diversification and specialization is purchased at a considerable price, at first evident only in a certain fragmentation and alienation of the individual, a loss of heroic seriousness, and the substitution of artfulness for natural reality:

> Siehe, da wimmeln die Märkte, der Kran von fröhlichem
> Leben,
> Seltsamer Sprachen Gewirr braust in das wundernde
> Ohr.
> (ll. 115-16)
> Mit nachahmendem Leben erfreuet der Bildner die Augen,
> Und vom Meißel beseelt, redet der fühlende Stein.
> (ll. 123-24)

The dialectical process continues to its inevitable conclusion. As man disencumbers himself wholly of necessity and superstition, he enters a fourth stage in which nothing more is permanent and sacred. The gods vanish, truth disappears from human discourse, law becomes a specter of itself, and even human feeling cannot express itself frankly. The historical panorama closes with the gloomy vision of an utterly dehumanized society that the poet calls a "mummy." He seems to have in mind a period extending from the Byzantine empire all the way to pre-revolutionary France, clinging to the soulless forms of its worn-out institutions. Finally nature, long repressed, claws its way out like a tigress through the bars of its cage, while mankind, driven by rage and misery, seeks its lost nature in the ashes of the city. (The tortuous, and somewhat ungrammatical, sentence of ll. 163-70 presumably refers to the horrors of the French Revolution.)

At this point the poet snaps out of his revery to find that he has reached the top of the mountain that he had greeted, earlier, from the front door of his house. The last twenty-eight lines of the poem, which complete the narrative framework, again describe the landscape immediately surrounding the poet, but the scene contrasts sharply in every detail with the opening framework. The pathless wilderness in which the poet now finds himself has nothing in common with the ordered nature through which he moved at the beginning of the poem (along paths and railed tracks). The lonely eagle suspended against the clouds has replaced the larks and flocks of small birds twittering on the branches of the trees below. The desolation of the mountaintop reflects the desolate state of society at the end of the historical meditation. But as the poem moves to its conclusion, the poet finds consolation and, indeed, a resolution of the seeming predicament posed by his meditations. The awesome decline of mankind, he realizes, was nothing but a nightmare. Nature, which remains constant in the face of all human change, is a reminder that the ancient values are still intact and accessible to anyone who wishes to live by them. After all, the sun that he apostrophized in the second line of his poem is the same sun that shone down upon the Greeks during the most glorious period of their culture:

Und die Sonne Homers, siehe! sie lächelt auch uns.

(l. 200)

On a first reading, the poem so overwhelms us with its wealth of vividly realized details and carries us along so irresistibly with the powerful flow of its narrative that we scarcely pause to appreciate its more subtle poetic qualities. But the second time through, we begin to admire the poem as a work as art rather than as versified cultural history. We ob-

serve, first of all, that we are dealing with a very long poem.
How is it organized? In the absence of any conventional stanzaic pattern or indicated breaks, we must search for some
other principle of poetic organization—one that is inherent in
the text itself. "Der Spaziergang," after all, is a poem and not
an essay. If we pay attention to the language rather than the
sequence of ideas, we note that the poem begins with an apostrophe, uttered while the poet is standing at his front door.
After ten lines, the rhetorical mode suddenly shifts to a description (ll. 11-28) as the poet follows the path across the
fields and up the lower part of the mountain. Once he has
reached his first vantage point, the style switches again: instead of scenic description of the nature immediately surrounding the poet, we get meditations inspired by the landscape seen at a distance. The initial meditation on natural man
is followed by a short apostrophe, which recapitulates the
section:

> Glückliches Volk der Gefilde! noch nicht zur Freiheit
> erwachet,
> Teilst du mit deiner Flur fröhlich das enge Gesetz.
> Deine Wünsche beschränkt der Ernten ruhiger Kreislauf,
> Wie dein Tagewerk, gleich, windet dein Leben sich ab!
> (ll. 55-58)

At this point a pattern begins to become apparent: the central
core of the poem falls into a series of meditations punctuated
at regular intervals by recapitulating apostrophes. The portrayal of man in the stage of heroic culture is concluded by an
apostrophe (ll. 87-100) to the ancient virtues of wisdom, pi-
ety, and courage—virtues whose disappearance is emphasized
poignantly by a switch to the past tense:

> Heilige Steine! Aus euch ergossen sich Pflanzer der
> Menschheit,
> Fernen Inseln des Meers sandtet ihr Sitten und Kunst,
> Weise sprachen das Recht an diesen geselligen Toren,
> Helden stürzten zum Kampf für die Penaten heraus.
> (ll. 87-90)

The succeeding meditative passage, which traces the emergence of the arts and crafts and the concomitant fragmentation of society, ends with an apostrophic exclamation warning man in this third stage of the dangers of unrestrained freedom:

> Seine Fesseln zerbricht der Mensch. Der Beglückte! Zerriss' er
> Mit den Fesseln der Furcht nur nicht den Zügel der Scham!
> Freiheit ruft die Vernunft, Freiheit die wilde Begierde,
> Von der heilgen Natur ringen sie lüstern sich los.
>
> (ll. 139-42)

To be sure, this is not a simple apostrophe like the earlier ones. But it amounts rhetorically to an equally emphatic interruption of the meditative ductus. (Note the exclamation, the optative, and the violent distortion of the meter in line 141.) Like the apostrophes, it expresses the feelings of the observer regarding the situation portrayed in the preceding passage. The rhetorical interruption of pure contemplation is further emphasized by the "Ach" that introduces the reflection on the decline of civilization, which concludes with another lengthy apostrophe (ll. 157-72) on the current misery of mankind and a wish for redemption:

> Deiner heiligen Zeichen, o Wahrheit, hat der Betrug sich
> Angemaßt, der Natur köstlichste Stimmen entweiht,
>
> . . . . . . . . . . . . . . . . . . . .
>
> O, so öffnet euch, Mauren, und gebt den Gefangenen ledig,
> Zu der verlassenen Flur kehr er gerettet zurück!

This final vision is followed, after the poet has come to his senses at the top of the mountain, by another scenic description, and the poem is rounded off by a grand apostrophe to nature (ll. 185-200):

> Bin ich wirklich allein? In deinen Armen, an deinem
> Herzen wieder, Natur, ach! und es war nur ein
> Traum, . . .

The concluding framework, we note, is a mirror image of the first half of the framework, which began with an apostrophe and then went on to the scenic description.

In summary, then, we see that the four logical divisions of the meditative core—natural man, heroic culture, diversified civilization, and corrupted civilization—are set off unmistakably by the rhetorical device of the apostrophe. The astonishing architectonic balance of the poem is strikingly evident if it is exposed diagrammatically:

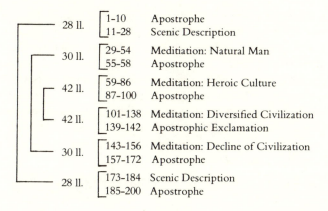

| | | |
|---|---|---|
| 28 ll. | 1-10 | Apostrophe |
| | 11-28 | Scenic Description |
| 30 ll. | 29-54 | Meditiation: Natural Man |
| | 55-58 | Apostrophe |
| 42 ll. | 59-86 | Meditation: Heroic Culture |
| | 87-100 | Apostrophe |
| 42 ll. | 101-138 | Meditation: Diversified Civilization |
| | 139-142 | Apostrophic Exclamation |
| 30 ll. | 143-156 | Meditation: Decline of Civilization |
| | 157-172 | Apostrophe |
| 28 ll. | 173-184 | Scenic Description |
| | 185-200 | Apostrophe |

It would be difficult to imagine a more perfectly structured work of art; yet the neglect of this structure by most critics proves that the organization is neither labored nor obtrusive.[2]

Turning now for a more careful look at the framework, we note further rhetorical devices that reinforce the meaning. In the ten-line apostrophe that opens the poem the poet, who has just escaped from "the prison of his room," gratefully enters the world of nature. As he sets out across the fields, the style shifts to a straightforward narrative description. But the description is characterized by a striking stylistic phenomenon: the language of the next eighteen lines, especially the verbs, emphasizes the fact that the poet is not in control of the situation: he is being acted upon by nature. The meadow "receives" him; the bee· hums about him; the sun's arrow "strikes" him. When he enters the forest, ambrosian night "embraces" him, and a canopy of shady beeches "takes him in." As the winding path "leads" him up the slope, a striking phrase points out that the landscape "gets away" from him in the mystery of the forest:

> In des Waldes Geheimnis entflieht mir auf einmal die
> Landschaft,
> Und ein schlängelnder Pfad leitet mich steigend empor.
> (ll. 23-24)

Finally, when he emerges from the woods, the forest "gives him back" to the blinding radiance of the day. Up to this point the poet has been little more than an object, wholly at the mercy of nature and incapable of detached meditation. His response to nature and reality in these opening lines is totally sensory. His state of passive receptivity is highlighted stylistically by a language that involves all the senses synesthetically. One astonishing distich compresses into two lines images that are auditory, gustatory, visual, olfactory, tactile, organic, and possibly even kinesthetic:

> Deiner Lüfte balsamischer Strom durchrinnt mich
> erquickend,
> Und den durstigen Blick labt das energische Licht.
> (ll. 9-10)

Then, in lines 29-34, an abrupt change in style announces a new situation: suddenly the poet is in charge, both grammatically and sensorially. For the first time in the poem, apart from the purely mechanical first person implicit in the opening apostrophe, the poet speaks as the subject rather than the object of the verbs:

> Endlos unter mir seh ich den Äther, über mir endlos,
> Blicke mit Schwindeln hinauf, blicke mit Schaudern
> hinab.
> (ll. 33-34)

In addition, the images of more intimate sensory perception recede as images of vision take over. The three verbs of seeing in the lines cited immediately above are preceded by the transitional line: "Unab*seh*bar ergießt sich vor meinen *Blicken* die Ferne" (l. 29; my italics). And the succeeding reflection on natural man is introduced by the exclamation "behold!": "Jene Linien, sieh! die des Landmanns Eigentum scheiden" (l. 39).

This striking emphasis on the act of seeing, following the riot of senses dominating the first twenty-eight lines, has several important implications. First, it alerts us to the poet's transition from a passive state, being acted upon by nature, to a state in which for the first time he is able to contemplate nature with detachment. (Incidentally, it also establishes line 29 as the beginning of a new section of the poem since it is there that the shift takes place.) Second, it justifies the mountain as the locus of the poem because it is only when he arrives alone "between the eternal heights and the eternal depths" that he is in a physical position of disengagement suitable for the act of contemplation. Third, the insistence on the sense of sight reminds us that the poet's meditations are neither excessively abstract nor purely visionary but, rather, always attached to a real landscape that provides the constant frame of reference during the poem. In this connection we note that the violent contrasts introduced in this passage—"endlos unter mir . . . über mir endlos"; "hinauf . . . hinab"; "der ewigen Höh und der ewigen Tiefe"—anticipate stylistically the dialectical tension that comes to dominate the poem thematically. Finally, the motif of seeing fulfills a further structural function by emphasizing the organization of the parts.

If we look at the two longest meditative passages—the emergence of heroic culture (ll. 59-86) and the rise of a diversified civilization (ll. 101-39)—we observe that both are punctuated in precisely the same relative position by the exclamation "sieh!"—namely, in the fifteenth line of each section respectively:

Sieh, da entbrennen in feurigem Kampf die eifernden
Kräfte
(l. 73);

> Siehe, da wimmeln die Märkte, der Kran von fröhlichem
> Leben
> (l. 115).

The exclamation "sieh!" occurs only four times in the entire poem: once near the beginning, when the priority of seeing is being established as the sensory mode of the poem; twice more in the middle of the poem, to punctuate lengthy reflective passages and to remind us that we are expected to visualize the scene; and again in the last line:

> Und die Sonne Homers, siehe! sie lächelt auch uns.

But here at the end the word has accumulated such powerful associations that it functions as much more than a conventional exclamation—at least for any reader who has been paying attention to the rhetoric of the poem and not just to the ideas: it has become a sign of consciousness. The poet who beholds the sun at the end has attained a higher level of awareness than he possessed at the beginning, where he was still borne along passively by nature. In the opening apostrophe he merely acknowledged the radiance of the morning sun; here at the end he consciously contemplates the sun as an image of nature's permanence.

Up to this point we have been considering the events in the sequence dictated by the poetic form: a framework embracing a meditative core ($F_1 C F_2$). But if we consider the relationship of the parts in a larger historical context, then we realize that temporally the framework begins at the precise moment when the meditative core ends ($C F_1 F_2$). That is, the vision of human history witnessed by the poet on the mountain (C) ends at a moment in time immediately anterior to the moment at which he steps out of his front door at the beginning of the poem ($F_1$). In the final apostrophe of the meditative core the poet appeals to nature, imprisoned like a tigress behind the bars of a hollow civilization, to awaken. It is hardly an accident that the outer framework ($F_1$) *begins* with the very same image: the poet, emerging from the "prison" of his room to seek lost nature, fulfills the wish expressed in the final apostrophe of the meditative core. The framework, in other words, is not merely a mechanical device: it represents the fulfillment of the entire historical process represented in the poem.

The movement of the poem is therefore not circular, as some critics have argued, but a spiral in several senses: topographically, historically, and psychologically. First, the poet's walk leads him up the mountain, and at the end his gaze is directed farther up, to the eagle and the sun beyond—not back down toward his own house. Second, the movement of history depicted in the poem is clearly progressive and irreversible, not cyclical: there is no suggestion of a return to a Golden Age; the poet's present action fulfills the historical past. Finally, the poet specifically does not return spiritually to some earlier and more primitive state of mind. His "return to nature" is no naive naturism; it is marked by a higher level of consciousness that clearly sets him apart from the "happy people of the fields" and the happy warriors of heroic culture.

We now understand that the walk itself is more than a convention inherited from topographical poetry. The ascent of the mountain symbolizes both the liberation of man from the bonds of natural necessity and the ascent of human consciousness. As he goes up the mountain, the poet emerges from a nature that is overpowering in its domination. At the same time, through the process of reflection he experiences in the course of his walk, the poet attains a level of consciousness at which he is able to be reunited with nature despite the state of liberation he has attained. It is no accident that his sole companion at the conclusion is the eagle which, hovering in lonely space, "links the world to the clouds" (l. 182). It has been pointed out that in Schiller's iconography the bird, and especially the eagle, is a frequent symbol of freedom.[3] But too much emphasis on the conventional emblematic function can obscure the real significance of the eagle in this specific context: it mediates between the earth and the clouds, between reality and the ideal, between necessity and freedom, just as the poet is now enabled to do.

This brings us to a final observation. The ultimate resolution is not attained on the mountaintop. That is where the poet experiences his epiphany, his moment of insight. But the dialectical synthesis is completed when, having returned to his room with the heightened consciousness achieved on the mountain, he sits down and writes the poem about his excursion. For only the aesthetic organization of the entire poem embodies the spiritual equilibrium achieved by the poet and outweighs the cultural pessimism of the meditative core. The poem itself, in other words, becomes a symbolic object: its concinnity of parts is the only adequate image for the spiritual harmony—called *Bildung* by German classicism—achieved by the poet and accessible to humanity as a whole by means of the new consciousness.

Schiller expressed his satisfaction with "Der Spaziergang" in letters to various friends. "I won't deny that I am quite proud of this piece," he wrote to Wilhelm von Humboldt shortly after completing the first version (29 November 1795). "My poetic talent, as you must surely have found, has expanded in this poem: in no other one has the *thought* itself been and remained so poetic; in none other has the mood functioned so wholly as *one* force."[4] It is a critical commonplace that the "thought" informing Schiller's poem is, generally speaking, the thought underlying his letters "Über die ästhetische Erziehung des Menschen," which appeared earlier that year in his journal, *Die Horen.* Indeed, in a very specific sense "Der Spaziergang" can be read as a poetic embodiment, almost a versification, of that treatise, which has as its purpose nothing less than the justification of art in an age of political turmoil. It is unnecessary to recapitulate the entire argument of Schiller's complex and often inconsistent "Letters." But they can clarify our reading of the poem as a symbol of the aesthetic contemplation that contributes to *Bildung.*

The cultural pessimism that motivates Schiller in the early "Letters" produces a vision just as bleak as the nightmare that obsesses the poet near the end of his mountainclimb. "Thus do we see the spirit of the age wavering between perversity and brutality, between unnaturalness and mere nature, between superstition and moral unbelief; and it is only through an equilibrium of evils that it is still sometimes kept within bounds" (Letter 5).[5] Schiller is not speaking theoretically here: he has in mind the very real situation across the Rhine, where a mindless revolutionary mob ("savages") in its struggle with a corrupt aristocracy ("barbarians") is destroying the last vestiges of Western culture. Humanity has reached this impasse through the process already familiar to us from "Der Spaziergang": the fragmentation of the individual by reason. "It was civilization itself which inflicted this wound upon modern man. Once the increase of empirical knowledge, and more exact modes of thought, made sharper divisions between the sciences inevitable, and once the increasingly complex machinery of State necessitated a more rigorous separation of ranks and occupations, then the inner unity of human nature was severed too, and a disastrous conflict set its harmonious powers at variance" (Letter 6). "With the Greeks," Schiller maintains, "humanity undoubtedly reached a maximum of excellence, which could neither be maintained at that level nor rise any higher." If they wished to move to a higher stage of development, they had to surrender their wholeness of being (Letter 6). We recognize here the same predicament portrayed in the poem, in the shift from the second stage (heroic culture) to the third stage (diversified civilization). "When, under Pericles and Alexander, the Golden Age of the arts arrived, and the rule of taste extended its sway, the strength and freedom of Greece are no longer to be found. Rhetoric falsified truth, wisdom gave offence in the mouth of a Socrates, and virtue in the life of a Phocion" (Letter 10). It is Schiller's gloomy conclusion that "however much the world as a whole may benefit through this fragmentary specialisation of human powers, it cannot be denied that the individuals affected by it suffer under the curse of this cosmic purpose" (Letter 6).[6]

If the first part of the "Aesthetic Letters" provides the theoretical basis for the vision of history outlined in the meditative core of "Der Spaziergang," the second part proposes the resolution that is accomplished in the framework of the poem. No matter how much the destiny of mankind may lead us toward fragmentation, Schiller argues, "it must be open to us to restore by means of a higher Art the totality of our nature which the arts themselves have destroyed" (Letter 6). To explain how this ambitious goal of *Bildung* is to be achieved, Schiller speaks of the two drives that motivate men as physical beings and as moral beings: the sensuous drive ("der sinnliche Trieb"), which concerns itself with life and temporal, changing content; and the formal drive ("Formtrieb"), which abstracts from life its timeless shapes and patterns. The historical process of diversification and specialization causes one of these drives inevitably to dominate, thereby producing the "savages" and "barbarians" warring in revolutionary France. To reconcile these two opposing drives Schiller introduces his famous concept of the play-drive ("Spieltrieb"). "To the extent that it deprives feelings and passions of their dynamic power, it will bring them into harmony with the ideas of reason; and to the extent that it deprives the laws of reason of their moral compulsion, it will reconcile them with the interests of the senses" (Letter 14).

It is beauty, according to Schiller, through which the play-drive is engaged. "By means of beauty sensuous man is led to form and thought; and by means of beauty spiritual man is brought back to matter and restored to the world of the senses" (Letter 18). But the organ through which the individual learns to apprehend beauty, is aesthetically liberated, and is enabled to reconcile his physical and moral compulsions is the sense of sight. "As long as man, in that first physical state, is merely a passive recipient of the world of sense, i.e., does no more than feel, he is still completely One with that world; and just because he is himself nothing but world, there exists for him as yet no world. Only when, at the aesthetic stage, he puts it outside himself, or *contemplates* it, does his personality differentiate itself from it, and a world becomes manifest to him because he has ceased to be One with it" (Letter 25). It would be difficult to find a more accurate analysis of the poet's state at the beginning of "Der Spaziergang." "What we actually *see* with the eye is something different from the *sensa-*

*tion we receive*; for the mind leaps out across light to objects. The object of touch is a force to which we are subjected; the object of eye and ear a form that we engender" (Letter 26).[7] Schiller uses the term "aesthetic semblance" to designate nature that originates in man as a perceiving subject in contrast to nature as an alien external force. In the concluding paragraph of the final (twenty-seventh) Letter he asks: "But does such a State of Aesthetic Semblance really exist? And if so, where is it to be found? As a need, it exists in every finely attuned soul; as a realized fact, we are likely to find it, like the pure Church and the pure Republic, only in some few chosen circles, where conduct is governed, not by some soulless imitation of the manners and morals of others, but by the aesthetic nature we have made our own."

In his essay "Über das Erhabene," which was written (though the date of composition is uncertain) as an extension of the "Aesthetic Letters," Schiller carries his thoughts one step further.[8] For he had come to the conclusion that our *Bildung* is complete only if we transcend the beautiful to reach the sublime. In his essay he speaks of "two geniuses" ("Zwei Genien") that nature has given us as companions. One, the spirit of beauty, entertains us, makes us forget the wearying journey through life, and lightens the fetters of necessity. This genius accompanies us up to the point at which we must act as "pure spirits" ("reine Geister") and discard all corporeality in order to perceive truth and duty. At this point the first genius leaves us because his territory is restricted to the realm of the senses, beyond which his earthly wings cannot bear him. But now the second genius appears and transports us across the vertiginous depths. Beauty, as we learned in the "Aesthetic Letters," is an expression of freedom—but of that freedom that we appreciate as human beings living within nature. The power that raises us above nature and liberates us from all corporeal influences is the sublime, which provides us with an egress from the sensory world, within which the beautiful would like to. keep us imprisoned. We see, therefore, that "Der Spaziergang" also represents the poet's progress from beauty to the sublime inasmuch as he escapes, at the conclusion of the poem, the snares of that nature whose beauty he had so profoundly enjoyed at the beginning of the poem. Only at this point has he been fully liberated by aesthetic education and the process of his *Bildung* completed.

Given the significance of "aesthetic semblance" as the mode of resolution, we can now appreciate the importance, for Schiller, of the aesthetic form of his poem. "In a truly successful work of art the contents should effect nothing, the form everything; for only through the form is the whole man affected, through the subject-matter, by contrast, only one or the other of his functions" (Letter 22). Our analysis sought to demonstrate that the poem achieves a perfect concinnity of parts that symbolically exemplifies the balance of freedom and necessity, nature and reason, that constitutes its content. If any doubts remain concerning Schiller's awareness of this startlingly impressive organization, they should be allayed by a comparison of the final revision ("Der Spaziergang"), which appeared in the 1800 edition of Schiller's poems, with the version first published in *Die Horen* ("Elegie"). At the urging of Humboldt, Schiller made a number of changes between the two versions, most of them minor and metrical.[9] However, he undertook several striking revisions that appreciably enhance the balanced structure that we analyzed. The early version of the poem ("Elegie") reveals the following distribution of parts:

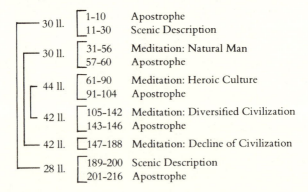

|  |  |  |
|---|---|---|
| 30 ll. | 1-10 | Apostrophe |
|  | 11-30 | Scenic Description |
| 30 ll. | 31-56 | Meditation: Natural Man |
|  | 57-60 | Apostrophe |
| 44 ll. | 61-90 | Meditation: Heroic Culture |
|  | 91-104 | Apostrophe |
| 42 ll. | 105-142 | Meditation: Diversified Civilization |
|  | 143-146 | Apostrophe |
| 42 ll. | 147-188 | Meditation: Decline of Civilization |
| 28 ll. | 189-200 | Scenic Description |
|  | 201-216 | Apostrophe |

The basic distribution of parts is evident here, but the proportions are quite ragged. First, the omission of eight distichs, six of them from the fourth meditation, contributed to the parallelism of the parts and shifted the axis of the poem to the exact center. Second, the fourth meditation was rewritten in such a manner as to produce the characteristic sequence of reflection and apostrophe that marks the first three sections. Finally, Schiller added the exclamation "sieh!" to line 39 (in response to Humboldt's criticism of the verse), thereby reinforcing the motif of vision.

The diagram revealing the encapsulated organization of the poem with its central axis alerts us to a further subtlety expressed by the form. If, in the chiasmic movement from unity to alienation and from necessity to freedom, there is at any point a moment of perfect equilibrium when all the forces are in balance, it should logically come in the middle of the poem, between stages two and three. But the exact center of the poem is a pause between lines. The last words of the first half continue the apostrophe to the Spartan warriors who gave up their lives at Thermopylae "as the law commands":

Ruhet sanft, ihr Geliebten! Von eurem Blute begossen,
   Grünet der Ölbaum, es keimt lustig die köstliche Saat.
                        (ll. 99-100)

For all their heroic culture, these mortals are still very much in thrall to iron law. Yet the very next line contains an allusion to the problematic freedom that increasingly dominates the second half of the poem:

Munter entbrennt, des Eigentums froh, das freie Gewerbe.
                        (l. 101)

In other words, in this dialectically balanced work, the ideal instant of cultural equilibrium slips past unnoticed, between the lines, so to speak—between a heroic age still subject to necessity and a diversified civilization already moving toward unbridled freedom. Through structure alone Schiller can suggest that the Golden Age—the legendary and perfect balance of nature and reason—never existed in reality. This implication is absolutely consistent with everything that we know about Schiller's view of the past as a historian. In his poem "Die Worte des Wahns" he stated explicitly that any naive faith in a Golden Age is one of the three great delusions that plague mankind (along with the belief that happiness is the lot of the noble man and that truth is accessible to human rationality). For the belief in a Golden Age that has already vanished could easily distract us from our true responsibility: to achieve in our own lives through *Bildung* a new resolution of the forces of freedom and necessity. Regardless of what Schiller may have said elsewhere about the Greeks, in the text of his poem perfect harmony is achieved only by the modern poet on the top of his mountain!

Among the mountains that Schiller could see from his house in Jena, admirers of "Der Spaziergang" have singled out two that could have provided the setting for the poem: the Hausberg and the Jenzig. For the view from his front door Schiller may well have had a specific mountain in mind. But the point, interesting as it may be for local historians, is aesthetically irrelevant. First of all, this is no topographical poem: the mountain itself is hardly described. We know that the poet walks through fields of clover edged by alders until he steps into the shade of a beech forest that covers the foot of the mountain. But otherwise the scene is much too general to be pinpointed. The mountain has crags and abysses; the stone is basalt; a rushing torrent tears at the roots of a tree. But apart from these few hints in the framework Schiller is talking not about the mountain itself but about the prospect from the mountain, which he contemplates as he follows a railed path ("ein geländerter Steig") that permits him to indulge his meditative impulse in safety. The mountain, in other words, is neither the goal nor the object of the poem, but its locus; the process of reflection does not begin until the poet is high on the mountain; the moment of insight is achieved at the moment when the poet reaches its summit.

In the second place, the scenes the poet describes cannot be localized to the region around Jena, though certainly Jena may have supplied some of the details that went into Schiller's symbolic landscape. We know that he had a clear visual conception of his imaginary landscape. Wilhelm von Humboldt, who was effusively enthusiastic about the poem—its lucid and lovely organization particularly appealed to him—had only one serious reservation: he felt that Schiller had introduced the road ("die Länder verknüpfende Straße," l. 45) into the poem too soon; a road, he argued, is not appropriate for the age of natural man.[10] Schiller conceded that Humboldt's logic was impeccable. But he justified the presence of the image by arguing that reality, in this case, anticipated the idea. "The road was simply in the scene that had empirically imprinted itself upon my imagination. It will be difficult for me to introduce the road later, and yet I must be as prudent as possible in my use of the sensory objects along which the thought moves. You probably noticed that up to the point where the meditations on corruption begin, I almost always proceed from an external object."[11] But toward the end of the poem, he continues, when he describes the decline of civilization, empirical reality gives way increasingly to pure imagination, with the result that, when the poet awakens from his trance, the desolation of civilization corresponds completely to the desolation of the mountain wilderness.

Even though Schiller assembled in his imagination a symbolic landscape that would adequately embody the thought of the poem, it is generally agreed that he had a specific source for many of the empirical images: the gardens at Hohenheim near Stuttgart, which he visited in 1793 and discussed in his review of Cotta's *Taschenkalender auf das Jahr 1795 für Natur- und Gartenfreunde*.[12] This remarkable establishment surrounding the ducal palace outside Stuttgart was one of the more extravagant manifestations of what came to be known as the "parcomania" of the later eighteenth century. The road leading from Stuttgart to Hohenheim, Schiller writes, amounts to "a tangible history of gardening" ("eine versinnlichte Geschichte der Gartenkunst"). The orchards, vineyards, and gardens that edge the road represent the first beginnings of gardening with no aesthetic ornamentation. Then the stroller walks between the long walls of poplars up to the palace. The rigidity of the formal French gardens is relieved by the so-called English Village behind the palace, and other more exotic scenes: Roman tombs, temples, dilapidated walls, Swiss Alpine huts, gloomy dungeons. Many visitors, Schiller remarks, are unable to comprehend an imagination capable of combining such disparate things into a single whole. But if we imagine that we are looking at a rural colony built on the ruins of an ancient Roman city, the contradiction is resolved and we perceive an ingenious unity. It is the perfect occasion for Schiller's dialectical mentality to go to work. "Rustic simplicity and urban splendor in decline, the two most extreme states of society, border on each other in a poignant manner, and the sober sense of transitoriness vanishes beautifully in the feeling of triumphant life. This happy mixture pours out through the entire landscape a profound elegiac tone that sustains the perceiving observer in a state of vacillation between rest and motion, reflection and enjoyment, resounding long after everything has disappeared."[13] The parallels between the scenes portrayed in the review and those depicted in the poem are obvious. But there is a conspicuous difference in mood. The review describes the scene from the point of view of an observer wholly caught up in the scene he is describing, like the poet in the first part of the framework. In the meditative core of the poem Schiller took the immediate sensations of his trip to Hohenheim and translated them into a more detached mood by shifting the point of view to a site above the scene; he describes the road to Hohenheim as though he were looking down at it from a mountain. Walking along the road from Stuttgart to Hohenheim, he felt that he himself was retracing the steps of history; only from the mountaintop is it possible to contemplate the same process in meditative detachment.

Mindful of Lessing's objections to the dangers and tedium of descriptive poetry, Schiller took conscious pains to avoid them. As he observes in an illuminating review of Friedrich Matthisson's poetry (1794), it is the poet's task "to represent not what *is* but what *happens*; and if he understands his advantage, he will always cling to that aspect of his subject matter that is accessible to a *genetic* description."[14] This review provides, in effect, the theory for the technique that, earlier, we called the temporalization of space: the landscape is depicted not as static but "genetically"—that is, in movement and growth. Schiller goes on to suggest that the poet can bring life into the landscape by peopling it with figures of ancient times—a precise anticipation of his device of populating the valley below with a panorama of figures from the primeval past down to the revolutionary present. But even a genetically active and humanly populated landscape cannot be described as an end in itself. If the poet wishes to lure us out of the turmoil of the world into his natural solitude, he must offer us more than relaxation and escape. "It should be not the longing for rest but the longing for harmony that causes him to weary of art and that endears nature to him."[15] In short, the poet of "Der Spaziergang" may be motivated in the opening lines simply by the desire to escape the wearying conversation of his prison-like room; but ultimately his venture into nature brings him far more than relaxation: it enables him to achieve harmony and the resolution of the tension between necessity and freedom.

This brings us to the walk itself, which Schiller regarded as an image sufficiently important to justify the final title of his poem. In part, of course, the title is simply a descriptive label for what goes on in the poem, and to this extent the poem is related to the topographical poetry of the earlier eighteenth century.[16] But there is ample evidence for the assumption that Schiller regarded the walk—the moment when man betakes himself out of his normal social context in order to encounter nature—as *the* occasion for philosophical meditation, a view that goes back at least to the peripatetic philosophers of classical antiquity.[17] One of his first philosophical essays was entitled "Der Spaziergang unter den Linden" (1782). In his essay "Über das Erhabene," he suggests that many brilliant thoughts and heroic decisions were not produced in a lonely study or in a glittering salon but were born in the course of a walk in the struggle of the sensibility with the powerful spirit of nature.[18] Similarly, in the first sentence of his essay "Über naive und sentimentalische Dichtung" (1795-96) he points out that there are moments in our lives when, disregarding all considerations of reason or taste, we bring a pure love to certain things—animals, plants, landscapes, children—simply because they belong to Nature. "Every finer human being, provided he is not wholly lacking in sensibility, experiences this when he is taking a stroll outdoors, when he is living in the country, or spending time with the monuments of ancient times: in short, whenever in the midst of artificial circumstances and surroundings he is surprised by the sight of simple nature."[19]

Wilhelm von Humboldt was well aware of Schiller's peripatetic inclinations, to which he alludes in his letter on "Der Spaziergang": "In my mind, too, as long as I can remember, ideas have tended to attach themselves to roads, and you may recall that we once talked about this at length in the course of a walk."[20] But by all odds the most spectacular example occurs in a letter that Schiller wrote to his fiancée, Lotte von Lengefeld, in September, 1789—a passage that amounts to an anticipation of the central insight of "Der Spaziergang" six years before the poem was written. The passage begins with a reiteration of the familiar romantic notion that landscape is nothing but a reflection of human consciousness. "I've just come back from a walk. Whether I'm out in the great open spaces of nature or in my lonely room—it's always the same ether in which I move, and the loveliest landscape is merely a lovelier mirror of the ever-constant form. Never before have I felt with such intensity how liberally our soul deals with all creation—how little creation is able to give in return, how it receives everything, everything from the soul."[21] The repetitiveness of nature—for instance, the rising and setting of the sun—would become unbearably tedious, Schiller continues, if our imagination did not constantly invest it with meaning and a soul. But there is a great consolation to be derived from this eternal sameness, he concludes. "How beneficent is this identity, this uniform constancy of

nature. When passion, when inner and outer tumult have buffeted us about long enough, when we have lost ourselves,
then we always find her the same, and we find ourselves in
her. On our flight through life we lay every pleasure that we
have enjoyed, every shape of our mutable being, in her faithful hand, and she restores to us the entrusted goods, well
preserved, whenever we come and demand to have them
back. . . . We owe our whole personality to nature, for if tomorrow she should stand before us transformed, we would
vainly seek our own self of yesterday."[22] It is precisely this
conception of nature as the preserver of enduring qualities
that the poet attains at the end of his walk up the mountain in
"Der Spaziergang." The greatness of Schiller's poem, however, is inherent in the fact that the ideas arise spontaneously
and naturally from a landscape that has an imaginative
reality—it is not a mere abstraction—and in the organization
of the poem, which expresses so much through its very structure that it can leave much unsaid.

For many decades any appreciation of "Der Spaziergang"
*as a poem* was seriously inhibited by the prevailing notion in
German literary theory that a proper lyric poem must be subjective, the expression of an intimate personal experience of
the sort known as *Erlebnis*.[23] There was no room in this
theory for a poem that seemingly amounted to *Gedankenlyrik*
or for a poet who was as obviously as Schiller an *Ideendichter*.
To be sure, scholars regarded the poem as a significant document in the development of Schiller's ideas.[24] But it was only
after the Schiller bicentennial in 1959 that a modest reevaluation of his poetry as *poetry* began to take place.[25] Characteristically, one of the strongest affirmations of the poem has
come from an American scholar of English literature, whose
appreciation of the "greater Romantic lyric" enabled him to
fit Schiller's meditative poem directly into his critical framework. Toward the end of his study of European romanticism
M. H. Abrams writes of "Der Spaziergang": "So many tendencies of the age intersect in this remarkable poem of two
hundred lines that it can serve as a résumé of much that I have

been detailing in this book about design, imagery, and ideas in works of the Romantic imagination."[26] The best of these studies have contributed substantially to our understanding of Schiller's poem as an expression of his ideas, to our appreciation of the poetic merits of the text, and to the location of the poem within the canon of European romantic literature. It is finally being accorded the status that it deserves as one of the major poetic texts of its age.

Yet how much we take for granted when we admire Schiller's masterpiece in these terms! We do not question the simple generic title "Elegie" when it is used to designate a long meditative poem. We calmly accept the fact that it is written in elegiac distichs of great suppleness and expressiveness. We are not even astonished at the circumstance that the poet is standing on top of a mountain, looking down, during the greater part of the poem. We so easily forget that all these things—the mode, the meter, the locus—were exceedingly novel in modern European literature when Schiller combined them for the first time in his poem. And if we do now take them for granted, it is in large measure because Schiller provided the compelling model that successive generations of poets imitated. We have examined certain aspects of Schiller's poem inductively in order to determine its merits as poetry: the success with which the form renders the meaning. But to appreciate the experimental originality of the poem we must now look back in time—to the development of human attitudes toward mountains and to the history of the elegy as genre and as mode.

# 2 · THE SOURCES: THE MOUNTAIN AS IMAGE AND LOCUS

Schiller was by no means the first poet to climb a mountain. On April 26, 1336, the thirty-one-year-old Francesco Petrarch, accompanied by his brother Gherardo, ascended Mont Ventoux and reported the adventure that same evening in a letter to his spiritual adviser, the Augustinian monk Dionigi da Borgo San Sepolcro.[1] Following an exhausting climb the two young men finally reached the topmost peak, where Petrarch stood stunned by the air and the view—*spiritu quodam aeris insolito et spectaculu liberiore permotus*. After letting his thoughts run back over the events of the past ten years, he looked about at the vast landscape extending from the snow-capped Alps to Marseilles and the sea, which was spread out before him in the radiance of the setting sun. If up to this point Petrarch's mood—reflective and ecstatic—is hardly distinguishable from Schiller's, he was not inspired to write an elegy, nor even a sonnet. For suddenly it occurred to him to consult the pocket edition of Augustine's *Confessions* that Brother Dionigi had given him. The volume fell open—quite by chance, he assures us—to a passage in the tenth book: "Men go forth to admire the heights of the mountains and the mighty floods of the sea and the broadest courses of the rivers and the ring of Ocean and the revolutions of the stars; and they abandon themselves." Sobered by this thought, which so precisely described his own state of mind, Petrarch turned his "inner eyes" upon himself—*in me ipsum interiores oculos reflexi*—and did not utter another word until he reached the bottom of the mountain once more. His sense of awe in the face of natural grandeur having been tempered by Augustine's assertion that external reality is diminutive in comparison with the grandeur of the human soul—*nichil preter animum est mirabile, cui magno nichil est magnum*—during the descent he often turned around to look back at the peak, which now seemed minuscule—*vix unius cubiti altitudo*—in comparison with the loftiness of human thought. It was his perplexity at the seeming conflict between experience and tradition that made it impossible for Petrarch to express his sensations in a poem and that prompted him, instead, to sit down and write the now famous letter in which he sought to rid himself of his unseemly enthusiasm for the splendor of nature.

Petrarch's initial reaction to the mountain prospect relates him to Schiller. But his final response is typologically representative of an age that still put authority ahead of experience, that looked to the Bible or one of its exegetes to explain and justify present reality. It was to require over four centuries before European poets could ascend mountains and gaze at the prospect with a vision unblurred by tradition and convention. The process is complicated by the fact that the centuries between Petrarch and Schiller embrace, in European history, a period so eccentric in its attitude toward mountains that it amounts to a cultural aberration.

A reverence for mountains would seem to belong to the most fundamental human experiences.[2] Their awesome height, their grandeur, their aura of mystery and danger have long caused mountains to be associated with deity in the minds of men all over the world. This association has taken two principal forms. In some cultures the mountain itself has been personified and worshipped: in ancient Mexico, China, Tibet, India, Scandinavia, and elsewhere. The most familiar example of a sacred mountain is probably Japan's Mount Fujiyama which was long held to be so inviolable that women were not permitted to venture onto its slopes. The primal tendency toward personification is still evident in the names that have often been bestowed upon mountains, suggesting their human appearance: e.g., the Swiss triumvirate Eiger, Mönch, and Jungfrau. Among other peoples—in Africa, India, Hawaii, pre-Columbian America—the mountain, though not personified, was often revered as the abode of mountain-gods. The Greeks paid homage not only to Mount Olympus, the principal residence of their pantheon, but also to various other mountains—Cithaeron, Helicon, Parnassus, Pelion—that were associated with specific deities. These primal feelings show up even today in the conviction that we can bestow no greater honor upon our leaders than to carve their faces on mountainsides. Related to this reverence of mountains—either personified or as the abode of mountain-gods—is the curious practice among certain ancient peoples of building surrogate mountains—the Babylonian ziggurats (*ziggurat* means, literally, "pinnacle" or "mountain peak") or the Mesoamerican pyramid temples—that replaced mountains as places of worship.

The awe the mountains inspired could assume more terrible aspects, of course, and reverence was easily transformed into fear. Certain mountains—Puy de Dôme in central France or the Brocken in the Harz Mountains of central Germany—became notorious as the meeting place of witches, demons, and evil spirits. The Pilatusberg in central Switzerland, the legendary burial place of Pontius Pilate, enjoyed such ill repute during the Middle Ages that climbing it was long prohibited by fine and imprisonment. This orophobia stems from various associations. In some places, it was the custom to ban the spirits of the dead onto mountains so that they would be unable to harm mortals except those unwise enough to wander into their misty regions. In other places the fear was attached to memories of heathen rituals once practiced in the mountains. It is known, for instance, that quite a few of the quaint mountain chapels in Europe are located on sites consecrated in pre-Christian times to the cult of pagan mountain spirits.

Both responses to mountains—reverence and fear—are evident in the Bible. Mountains provide the location for encounters with deity: it is on Mount Sinai that Moses receives the Table of Laws from Jehovah. But the mountain is also the scene of temptation and sin: Satan leads Jesus up onto a mountain to display the kingdoms of the world and earthly glory. In both Testaments, mountains are identified as places of worship. But they are also notorious as the scenes of terrible sacrifices: Abraham's intended sacrifice of Isaac on the mountain in Moriah prefigures God's sacrifice of Jesus on Mount Golgotha.

Whether regarded as places of law or temptation, of worship or sacrifice, mountains in the Judeo-Christian tradition were not places where one went lightly or unbidden. As result, mountains are not frequently mentioned in medieval literature; and when they do play a role, as in the legend of Tannhäuser and Venus, it is usually a sinister one. But medieval records clearly reflect both attitudes.[3] On the one hand, mountains provided, all over Europe, a favorite location for monasteries because there—close to God and undistracted by intrusions—the monks could seek illumination and hope for epiphany. On the other hand, the mountain ranges—and especially the Alps, which had to be crossed frequently in the course of business, politics, and war—were frequently mentioned in letters and documents as arduous and threatening.

The Judeo-Christian ambivalence toward mountains inevitably showed up in the scholarly commentaries as rabbinical and monastic exegetes applied their subtlety to the biblical texts.[4] It occurred to the interpreters that God was unlikely to have included such terrifying and disruptive elements in his original Creation. This feeling was reinforced by two passages in particular. First, mountains are not mentioned in the Genesis account of the Creation: we first hear of mountains just before the Flood, when God "looked upon the earth, and, behold, it was corrupt; for all flesh had corrupted his way upon the earth" (Gen. 6:12). Second, a familiar passage in the New Testament (2 Peter 3:5-7) implied that "the world that then was, being overflowed with water, perished"; and a different world emerged from the waters of the Flood. On the basis of these passages, it was widely assumed by Christian and Jewish commentators alike that the earth at the time of the Creation, whether it had no hills at all or only very small and regular ones, was much more beautiful than at present and that the mountains as we know them now—vast, awesome, irregular—were a product of the Deluge, a visible reminder of the fact that God cursed the earth because of man's sins. This view, intensified during the Reformation by a widespread hostility toward nature, is summed up by Martin Luther in his commentaries on Genesis.[5] According to Luther, the prelapsarian earth—smooth, lovely, fruitful—began to decay at the time of the Fall; the Flood, marking the climax of that first period of degeneration, produced the mountains.

The widely accepted analogy between the Fall of Man and the decay of the earth accounts for many of the striking images that occur in seventeenth-century poetry, especially in England.[6] John Donne, in "An Anatomy of the World: The First Anniversary" (1611), speaks of mountains as being "but warts, and pock-holes in the face / Of th' earth" (ll. 299-300). James Howell, in his *Familiar Letters* (1621), comparing the Pyrenees with the Alps, wrote that "they are but Pigmies compar'd to Giants, but Blisters to Imposthumes, or Pimples to Warts." Henry More took up the same metaphor in *An Antidote against Atheism* (1652), where "those rudely-scattered Mountains" are seen as "so many Wens and unnatural Protuberances upon the Face of the Earth." And in seventeenth-century German poetry the mountain was frequently cited, in contrast to the *locus amoenus*, as the *locus terribilis* —a dark, dangerous, eerie place suitable only for torment and grief.[7]

The Judeo-Christian view of mountains—that they were produced by the Deluge as a symbol of man's Fall—was often combined in the later Middle Ages with another ancient assumption.[8] According to a Pythagorean tradition the earth was originally not only perfectly smooth but also a perfect sphere. In the *Timaeus*, for instance, Plato relates that the creator "made the world in the form of a globe, round as from a lathe, having its extreme in every direction equidistant from the center, and the most perfect and the most like itself of all figures. . . . This he finished off, making the surface smooth all around for many reasons" (33 b-c). This notion, widespread among classical writers, was passed along by many of the later Fathers of the Church, including Albertus Magnus, Thomas Aquinas, and Vincent of Beauvais.

These two ancient conventions were summed up in 1681

by Thomas Burnet in his controversial and highly influential work, *The Sacred Theory of the Earth* (first published in Latin as *Telluris Theoria Sacra,* and translated into English in 1684). Burnet begins with the proposition "That the Ante-diluvian Earth was of a different form and construction from the present," an assumption that he proves on the basis of Divine Authority.[9] This leads quickly to the second proposition: "That the face of the Earth before the Deluge was smooth, regular and uniform; without Mountains, and without a Sea."[10] "This notion of the *Mundane Egg,* or that the World was *Oviform,* hath been the sence and Language of all Antiquity, *Latins, Greeks, Persians, Egyptians,* and others."[11] Burnet, a Cambridge Platonist, was attempting to reconcile this traditional view with the newest scientific theories of the seventeenth century. As he demonstrates in the diagrams that illustrate his text, the action of gravity gradually caused the elements of the original Chaos to dispose themselves in concentric strata in decreasing order of specific gravity. As the liquid elements separated into heavy and light, they were kept apart by an oily shell produced by surface tension, which caught the dust of the Chaos as it settled, thus producing a smooth layer of fertile earth upon the terrestrial waters. This was the true biblical Paradise. "In this smooth Earth were the first Scenes of the World, and the first Generations of Mankind; it had the beauty of Youth and blooming Nature, fresh and fruitful, and not a wrinkle, scar or fracture in all its body; no Rocks nor Mountains, no hollow Caves, nor gaping Chanels, but even and uniform all over."[12] Up to this point Burnet's geogony is consistent with the leading scientific theories of the day; but he goes on to offer his own explanation for the transformation of the world. The continual summer of Paradise caused the earth to dry out and crack; meanwhile, beneath the surface the waters were steaming from the constant heat and building up a terrific pressure. When the waters finally burst through the fissured earth, this action, Burnet reasoned, had "two great and visible Effects."[13] First, a "Universal Deluge" overflowed the entire broken earth, destroying the pristine Paradise and accounting for the biblical legend of the Flood. Then, "when the Agitation of the Abysse was asswag'd," the present earth emerged from the ruins of the first, with mountains and valleys marring the original "Mundane Egg."

There is no need to summarize the complex and extended controversy that flamed up around Burnet's theory during the following decades.[14] For our purposes it suffices to note its great popularizing effect. Owing at least as much to his sonorous rhetoric as to his ideas, Burnet's influence survived in England well into the nineteenth century. Wordsworth, who read parts of *The Sacred Theory* while he was writing *The Excursion*, intended to publish passages from Burnet along with his notes to that work. Coleridge even toyed with the notion of translating the *Telluris Theoria Sacra* into English blank verse.[15] Burnet's ideas had a delayed but profound effect in Germany, where they were still taken seriously long after they had been discredited in England. Leibniz's account of the Flood in his *Protogaea* (1690) draws heavily on Burnet; but since the treatise was published only posthumously, in 1749, it played no role in the discussion.[16] Zedler's *Universal Lexikon* (1733), the standard German encyclopedia of the period, cautiously synthesized various views, including Burnet's, in the article on mountains: "their Origin can be explained in part from the Creation of the World, in part from Noah's Deluge, but in part from various other Floods."[17] In the 1740's Burnet's ideas were still being incorporated in such scientific works as the cometologies of Johann Heyn and his students, Balthasar Friedrich Kunstmann and Johann Gotthilf Werder.[18]

But it was particularly due to the authority of Johann Christoph Gottsched, professor of Logic and Metaphysics at the University of Leipzig, that Burnet's theory became more widely known outside scientific circles. In the "Theoretical Section" of his ambitious and rather preposterous *Erste Gründe der gesammten Weltweisheit* (1734) Gottsched does not follow Burnet directly. Instead, he refers to William Whiston, whose *New Theory of the Earth* (London, 1696) was an attempt to popularize Burnet and to exploit the contemporary excitement attending Halley's predictions regarding comets. According to Gottsched's confused potpourri of Descartes, Burnet, and Whiston, when man had sinned and thereby shown himself to be no longer worthy of the earth in its blessed pristine state, God sent a comet whose magnetic attraction caused the initially stationary earth to begin revolving about its axis, thus producing "a dreadful alteration."[19] As a result of spinning rapidly, the original globe of the earth was flattened into a more oval shape, acquiring in the process a number of fissures on its surface. The Deluge was caused some years later (in 2346 B.C.) when another comet—identical, Gottsched calculated, with Halley's comet—approached the earth and caused the subterrestrial waters to burst through the fissures and flood the earth. Though Gottsched disagrees at points with Burnet and Whiston, he approves wholeheartedly of their intent: "Namely, to show religious Skeptics that the Teachings of the Scriptures concerning the Origin of the World, the Deluge, and the last Conflagration of the earthly Globe are wholly in accord with Reason, Philosophy, and the new Astronomy."[20]

Epoch-making as the *The Sacred Theory* turned out to be for the struggle between science and theology, another aspect of Burnet's theory had profound implications in the history of aesthetic thought. As a Christian, Burnet was depressed by these "ruins of a broken world" that reminded him of man's sin. As a rationalist he was offended by the incredible confusion of the mountain landscape, which conflicted so sharply with his ideas of symmetry and proportion. Yet when he went abroad in 1671 he discovered, to his surprise and chagrin, that his imagination responded intuitively to the majestic vastness of the looming rubble of the Alps. But Burnet's response is quite different from Petrarch's. To account for the disturbing conflict between reason and imagination, between tradition and experience, Burnet came up with a distinction—in fact, though not in vocabulary—anticipating the later eighteenth-century distinction between the beautiful and the sublime. As Marjorie Hope Nicolson has demonstrated in her analysis of Burnet's vocabulary, the adjectives and epithets that leaped to his mind when he stood before mountains were words that had hitherto been considered appropriate only when applied to God.[21] Inspired by Burnet, men began for the first time in several centuries to regard mountains not simply as a curse on the earth but as a manifestation of Divine Glory.[22] Instead of closing their eyes in disgust as they crossed or skirted the Alps on the Grand Tour, they began to revel in the sensation of awe that they felt as their carriages bore them through the mountains. That this attitude was shared in Germany is shown by the article on "Mountains" in Zedler's *Universal Lexikon*, where the author concedes that some might find mountains ugly while others appreciate the great variety that they present. No one can deny, however, "that the Mountains have something splendid and magnificent about them, and arouse within us lofty Thoughts and Movements of the Spirit, so that we naturally think of God, His Grandeur and Loftiness."[23]

We must be careful to see this gradual shift in a proper perspective. Although the theological-scientific-aesthetic discussion dispelled the ancient beliefs regarding mountains in the minds of certain English thinkers at the beginning of the eighteenth century and gradually prepared the European consciousness to think of mountains as sublime rather than grotesque, it would be a mistake to think that the new attitude spread rapidly or preluded a general stampede in the direction of the Alps. Among many people on the continent, at least, the old notions still prevailed during at least the first half of the century.[24] According to A. Ruchat's *Les Délices de la Suisse* (1714) many people in France still believed that the Alps were inhabited by a wild race of savages with horns and hooves who buried their dead in the ice. (This belief will not strike us as so ridiculous if we remind ourselves that many people still believe in the existence of an Abominable Snow Man in the Himalayas. For most people in the early eighteenth century, the Alps were no less exotic than, for us today, the mountains of Nepal.) A standard German travel guide, J. G. Keyssler's *Neueste Reise durch Teutschland, Böhmen, Ungarn, die*

*Schweiz, Italien und Lothringen* (1740), finds it necessary to describe the lovely houses of the Swiss villages in order to dispel the prevailing notion that there is nothing in these regions but infertile cliffs, rough mountains, constant snow, and gloomy valleys.

Second, although young English gentlemen now reveled in the sublimity of the mountains, the Alps still did not constitute a goal in themselves but merely an event in the course of the Grand Tour. Moreover, these seekers after the sublime were in no sense of the word mountaineers. When Horace Walpole and Thomas Gray set out on the Grand Tour in 1739, they crossed the Alps in a horse-drawn chaise; their most daring venture, the ascent of the Grande Chartreuse, was accomplished in chairs carried by eight men. Men had of course climbed mountains in the past. Indeed, Petrarch was inspired to climb Mont Ventoux by a passage in the *History of Rome* in which Livy describes Philip of Macedon's ascent of Mount Hemus in Thessaly (Mount Balkan in present-day Bulgaria). During a brief wave of Alpinism in the sixteenth century, in fact, some forty-seven lower summits were scaled (e.g., by the Swiss naturalist Konrad Gesner), and the first treatise on the subject was published: Josias Simler's *De Alpibus* (Zürich, 1574).[25] But it would have occurred to no sane person in the seventeenth century to climb a mountain. It is perfectly true that the Baroque consciousness preferred to remain slightly above and apart from nature—to see landscape as a whole rather than to be in the midst of it.[26] This preference produced the typical point of view that can be observed in the literature, painting, and landscape architecture of the age: a slight incline that enables the observer to look out over the surrounding scene. But it is emphatically only a gentle rise, not a towering mountain. It was only toward the end of the eighteenth century, with the ascents of such explorers as the Swiss physicist Horace Benedict de Saussure, the Benedictine monk Placidus à Spescha, and the English adventurer Colonel Mark Beaufoy, that mountain-climbing began in earnest. And it was not until 1857 that this enthusiasm was institutionalized by the establishment of the first Alpine Club in England, followed in close order by clubs in Austria, Germany, Italy, Switzerland and France.

The general public indifference to mountains in Germany during the first two-thirds of the eighteenth century is clearly reflected in the poetry of the period. Barthold Heinrich Brockes preferred to savor his "earthly pleasure in God" in tiny segments of nature: blossoms, grasses, bees, insects, birds, butterflies. Yet although the poet from the North German flatlands was distinctly uncomfortable with mountains, he felt duty-bound to include at least one mountain poem in his monumental didactic catalogue, *Irdisches Vergnügen in Gott* (1721-1748). His poem ("Die Berge," 1724) begins with verses reminding us that even mountains must be regarded as a symbol of God's glory:[27]

> Lasst uns GOtt ein Opfer bringen,
>> Und, Sein' Allmacht zu erhöhn,
> Auch der Berge Bau besingen,
>> Die so ungeheuer schön,
> Daß sie uns zugleich ergetzen,
> Und auch in Erstaunen setzen.
>> Ihre Gröss' erregt uns Lust,
>>> Ihre Gähe schreckt die Brust.

The poem ends with what amounts to an apology for including mountains as an example of the creator's might:

> Sprich, verdienen solche Wercke
>> Nicht einmahl, daß man sie mercke?
>>> Wer's Geschöpfe nicht betracht't,
>>> Schändet seines Schöpfers Macht.

The rhetoric suggests that Brockes is addressing an audience—notably, his fellow-burghers of Hamburg—who might well be astonished to find mountains classified among God's wonders. In fact, the first half of the poem, which cites Burnet and his vision of a shattered world, amounts to a catalogue of horrors:

Wann Burnet der Berge Höhen,
　　Als von der geborst'nen Welt
Rest und Zeichen, angesehen,
　　Und durch Fluth verursacht hält:
Sollt' ihr Schutt fast glaubend machen,
Daß vielleicht die Welt, mit Krachen,
　　Durch die Gluht, schon einst verheert,
　　Und, durch Brand sey umgekehrt.

Indeed, someone who had never before seen a mountain would think, were he suddenly transported to the Alps, that he was in Hell. Yet the second half of the poem amounts to a rationalizing justification for their existence. Even though the peaks are desolate and frightful in appearance, they must be considered beautiful because they are so useful. Within their depths they contain marble, jewels, gold, and other minerals and metals as well as the waters that irrigate the world. In addition, medicinal herbs as well as vineyards thrive on their slopes, which nurture sleek cattle. Brockes is never tempted to climb the mountains; all twenty-one strophes are written from a vantage point safely below. The heights, he says, are so terrifying that even the eye, wearied by much looking, can scarcely scale the peaks. Reading the poem, one senses that Brockes is straining his powers to find a rational justification for an aspect of nature that repels him. He has included the mountains merely as a concession to methodological completeness in his poetic catalogue.

The Swiss poet-scientist Albrecht von Haller was more sympathetically disposed toward mountains than Brockes, but his great poem "Die Alpen" (1729) is not primarily a landscape poem.[28] In fact, more than three hundred of his supple alexandrine verses flow past before he even mentions the mountains as such. For he was less concerned with the mountains than with the sturdy inhabitants who people their valleys; his interest, at least for the first three-fifths of the poem, focuses on society rather than nature.[29] Haller contrasts the peasants of the Bernese Highlands—free, virtuous, reasonable, happy, industrious—satirically with a European civilization in decline. He praises the Alps, first of all, as the barrier that Nature erected to protect these Swiss from the rest of the world.

> Sie warf die Alpen auf, dich von der Welt zu zäunen,
> Weil sich die Menschen selbst die größten Plagen sind.
>
> (ll. 53-54)

When Haller finally gets around to the mountains themselves, his rationalizing bears a distinct resemblance to Brockes' didactic justifications. To be sure, he does not share Brockes' infernal view of the mountains; though, as a scientist, he was no doubt familiar with the Burnet controversy, the rhetoric of a ruined world does not slip into his poem. Yet his own temperament as well as the expectations of his contemporaries are betrayed by his pronounced didacticizing. He appends to his poem a number of learned notes pertaining to the botany and mineralogy of the Alps, and he reminds us constantly how inexhaustibly useful the mountains are:

> Allein der Himmel hat dieß Land noch mehr geliebet,
> Wo nichts, was nöthig, fehlt, und nur was nutzet, blüht:
> Der Berge wachsend Eiß, der Felsen steile Wände,
> Sind selbst zum Nutzen da, und tränken das Gelände.
>
> (ll. 317-20)

Haller, who made a tour of the Alps only a year before writing his poem, does not restrict his point of view to the timorous snail's-eye view assumed by Brockes. But his portrayal of the landscape is qualified in two ways. First, the descriptions are tailored to fit the ten-line strophe he adapted for the poem; as a result, the landscape is exposed in a series of snapshots rather than in a continuous descriptive narrative. Second, these segments of closely observed details are presented from a constantly shifting point of view, so that the central consciousness is unable to develop any sustained speculative argument transcending the segments of landscape themselves. (It is this effect of static description that Lessing criticizes in his famous analysis of Haller's poem in the seventeenth chapter of *Laokoon*.)

"Die Alpen" remains by far the most promising mountain poem of the early eighteenth century—a model to which Schiller looked back from the end of the century. But for at least two reasons Haller's brilliant initiative was not followed up. First, within only a few years he himself forsook poetry for scholarship, rapidly becoming the most learned man of his age. Second, the influence of Gottsched overshadowed Haller's example. Gottsched, as we have seen, shared the seventeenth-century view that mountains were a visible sign of man's Fall. It is hardly surprising, therefore, that in a poem of 1744 he descried with considerable distaste "a new race of misguided bards" who, their breasts chilled by the constant snow, had come to regard the Swiss mountains as their Parnassus and the mountain witches as their Muses. Their rigid verses, Gottsched claims in his own lifeless alexandrines, produce images as cold and ungainly as the ice of the Gotthard:

So starr und ungelenk *St. Gotthards* Eis je war,
Stellt auch ihr steifer Vers, die kalten Bilder dar.[30]

Gottsched's alarm was premature. German literature of the mid-eighteenth century—in contrast to English poetry of the period—is conspicuously lacking in mountain scenery, even when it might most legitimately be expected. By a curious coincidence, the two most representative literary figures of the age—Wieland and Klopstock—were both invited to Switzerland by the critic Johann Jakob Bodmer. Wieland spent seven years in Zürich, but the mountains play no role in his writing—a fact that exemplifies the observation that German anacreontic poetry in general displays a tendency toward the petite, in content as well as form. The poets most characteristic of the years 1750 to 1770 favor a dainty nature with intimate, enclosed landscape rather than towering mountains or wide prospects.[31] When Klopstock visited Zürich in 1750, Bodmer was astonished that he showed no curiosity to see the Alps from near or afar,[32] and his poetry from Switzerland reflects that indifference. For instance, in his great ode "Der Zürcher See" (1750) the landscape is nothing more than a catalyst for the emotions:[33]

Schön ist, Mutter Natur, deiner Erfindung Pracht,
Auf die Fluren verstreut, schöner ein froh Gesicht,
Das den großen Gedanken
Deiner Schöpfung noch einmal denkt.

The Alps, mentioned only once in nineteen strophes, are immediately subordinated to the youths' sentimental hearts:

Jetzt entwölkte sich fern silberner Alpen Höh',
Und der Jünglinge Herz schlug schon empfindender. . . .

And later in his career Klopstock rejected mountains altogether. In his poem "Der Hügel und der Hain" (1767) he argued that hills and mountains might have been perfectly suitable for the poets of Greek antiquity; but the German bard finds his inspiration in Teutonic groves.

Des Hügels Quell ertönet von Zeus,
Von Wodan der Quell des Hains.
Weck' ich aus dem alten Untergange Götter
Zu Gemälden des fabelhaften Liedes auf,

So haben die in Teutoniens Hain
Edlere Züge für mich!
Mich weilet dann der Achäer Hügel nicht,
Ich geh' zu dem Quell des Hains![34]

This poem provided the inspiration for the group of young student-poets in Göttingen who styled themselves, collectively, the Göttinger Hain and whose poetry, which features forest groves and cozy glades rather than elevations, set the tone in the early seventies.[35]

The work that revised the popular European attitude toward mountains was neither scientific, theological, nor aesthetic, but fictional: *La nouvelle Héloïse* (1761). Rousseau's attitude toward mountains was in part an amalgam of current theories of the sublime. Toward the end of Book IV of the *Confessions*, he describes the sensation of beauty spiced with the *frisson* of fear that had come to be identified with the sublime: "What I mean by a beautiful landscape is already sufficiently well known. No landscape of plains, however lovely it

might be, has ever seemed beautiful to my eyes. I require torrents, crags, fir-trees, dark forests, mountains, rough roads to
climb and descend, and precipices alongside to make me
tremble in fear."[36] Unlike Gray and Walpole, who made their
Grand Tour at the end of the decade that Rousseau is talking
about at this point in his autobiography, Rousseau enjoyed
the sensation of walking on foot through the mountains. But,
like the English travelers, he wanted to be assured that he
could savor his terror in relative security. He tells us about a
point on the mountain road to Chambéry, where the way had
been edged with a parapet to prevent accidents. "That enabled
me to look down and to allow myself to be seized by vertigo
at my own whim. The nice thing about my taste for precipit-
ous places is that they make me dizzy, and I enjoy this dizzi-
ness immensely as long as I am safe."[37] It is not only the fact
that he goes by foot that distinguishes Rousseau from the
English travelers. In his works the sensation of the sublime
has been divorced from the divine source that it inevitably
had in earlier writings. Rousseau cultivates the sublime for its
own sake, reveling in his fear and trying to prolong the
ecstasy of vertigo as long as possible.

The mood of the *Confessions* is not so mellow as the mood
that informs Saint-Preux's early letter to Julie, when he has
fled to the mountains at the beginning of *La nouvelle Héloïse*.
Here the mountains are not so much a spiritual rollercoaster
as a refuge to which one flees, on foot and alone, in order to
escape the tribulations of passion and human concern. "Indeed, it is a general impression that all men experience,
though not all of them notice it: atop high mountains, where
the air is pure and thin, one feels a great ease in breathing,
more buoyancy of the body, more serenity of the spirit; one's
pleasures are less consuming, the passions more moderate.
There one's meditations assume a certain grand and sublime
character, in proportion to the objects that move us; a certain
tranquil voluptuousness that has no trace of bitterness or sen-
suality. It seems that by elevating oneself above the abode of
man, one leaves behind all lowly and terrestrial sentiments.
The closer one approaches the ethereal regions, the more the

soul takes on something of their inalterable purity."[38] Rousseau has come far indeed from Petrarch, who felt little serenity on Mont Ventoux and a great deal of guilt. This is the new spirit that captured the century, completely obscuring the conventional view of mountains as symbols of guilt or sin. And this new spirit is one that invades us as we stand atop mountains—not at the bottom looking up. "In short, the spectacle has a certain indefinable magic, a supernatural quality that enraptures the mind and senses. One forgets everything, one forgets oneself, one no longer knows where one is."[39] With Rousseau the sublime has suddenly become lower-case and bourgeois. What was formerly the prerogative of travelers wealthy enough to afford the Grand Tour is now accessible to any wanderer whose legs are sturdy enough to carry him up into the mountains.

As Rousseauism spread across Europe during the last quarter of the century, a new attitude toward the Alps developed. No longer regarded merely as an obstacle on the road to Italy, they became a goal in themselves. In the decades following the publication of *La nouvelle Héloïse* almost every year witnessed the appearance of a new volume of "Letters from Switzerland" or "Travels in the Alps" from well-known pens.[40] The aesthetician C.C.L. Hirschfeld, who achieved European fame with his *Theory of Gardening*, published *Briefe die Schweiz betreffend* (1776), in which he liberally quotes from Haller's poem and records his own sensations of terror in the Alps. The arch-rationalist C. F. Nicolai repeatedly interrupts his twelve-volume *Beschreibung einer Reise durch Deutschland und die Schweiz im Jahre 1781* (1783-96) to talk about the "majesty" of the mountains. G.K.Ch. Storr, in his *Alpenreise im Jahre 1781* (1784-86) compares the wildness of the Alps to the desolation of Ossianic landscapes. One finds *Briefe einer reisenden Dame aus der Schweiz*, by A. H. von Krock (1786), which tell more about the emotions of the "traveling lady" than about the landscape of the Rousseau sites that she visits; as well as D. Plouquet's *Vertrauliche Erzählung einer Schweizerreise im Jahre 1786 in Briefen* (1787), which indirectly suggests the prevailing fad inasmuch as the author, a professor of medicine from Tübingen, finds it necessary to state in his preface that he does not intend to write simply another "sentimental" journey of the currently fashionable variety. The popular novelist Sophie von la Roche presented her public with a *Tagebuch einer Reise durch die Schweiz von der Verfasserin von Rosaliens Briefen* (1787). The dramatist August Wilhelm Iffland published his own *Blick in die Schweiz* (1793), in which he confessed his impulse to "bend my knees before the high altar of Nature." And in 1791 Karl Grosse, who achieved literary fame with his Gothic romance *Der Genius*, brought out two enthusiastic volumes on *Die Schweiz*, which constitute a veritable catalogue of sentimental lore, including Rousseau, the sublime, and freedom. Many of these sentimental journeyers, like Karl Gottlob Küttner in his *Briefe eines Sachsen aus der Schweiz an seinen Freund in Leipzig* (1785-86), used *La nouvelle Héloïse* as a travel guide, tracking down all the scenes of Rousseau's novel. And it was by no means only the Germans who indulged in such sentiments. Christoph Meiners, in his *Briefe über die Schweiz* (1784-90), reported that everywhere he went he found Englishmen, a copy of *La nouvelle Héloïse* in hand, exploring the various locales identified with Rousseau. As a true follower of Rousseau himself, Meiners assures the reader that he intends to describe not only the lakes and the mountains, but also his own sensations as he contemplates them.

The sentimental discovery of mountain landscape brought to the Alps many travelers who could formerly not have afforded such a trip. But even noblemen like the brothers Stolberg, who accompanied Goethe in 1775, left their carriages behind in order to walk in the mountains as their hero had done, to become agitated about freedom, and to recite Homer—in Greek—to the uncomprehending peasants of the Bernese Highlands. Walking, in fact, became a health fad among a sentimental public wearied of the oversophistication of modern civilization. J. G. Ebel, in his *Anleitung auf die nützlichste und genussvollste Art in der Schweiz zu reisen* (1793), points out that walking stimulates the metabolism in a healthful manner. "Hence most foot travelers return from the mountains looking sturdier, livelier, and more active in body and soul."[41]

Whereas at the beginning of the century a few more ven-
turesome travelers had peeked timorously out of their carriage windows for a quick glimpse of the sublime, by the end
of the century countless hikers were swarming over the Alps
and all the lesser mountains of Europe in search of sentimental
experience. The Switzerland that had still been regarded in
1714 either as a rather esoteric delectation for English intellec-
tuals or as the home of half-savage mountain creatures, suddenly became the favorite setting for light opera! The popular
theme of *La Bergère des Alpes* (1766) showed up over and over
again in such works as "The Little Mountaineers" or "The
Huntsman of the Alps." Haydn's *Die Hochzeit auf der Alm*
(1789) preluded a series of similar works with such titles as
Ignaz Walter's *Die Hirten der Alpen* (1794) or Heinrich Christoph Hattasch's *Der ehrliche Schweizer* (1794). The most successful operatic work between *Die Zauberflöte* and *Der Frei-
schütz* was Joseph Weigl's *Die Schweizerfamilie* (1809). Goethe
capitalized knowingly on this fad when he wrote his Singspiel
*Jery und Bätely* (1779), which he characterized as "a little
operetta in which the actors wear Swiss clothes and talk about
milk and cheese."[42] Schiller, of course, was well aware of the
prevailing Swissomania when he wrote his *Wilhelm Tell* at the
beginning of the nineteenth century. And the mountain craze
was not limited to literature and opera. In 1792, Joseph Anton
Koch, painting the first of his monumental Alpine landscapes,
initiated a genre of Swiss mountain painting that extended
across the nineteenth century by way of Wolfgang-Adam
Toepffer, Alexandre Calame, François Diday, Rudolf Koller,
and Maximilian de Meuron, right down to Ferdinand Hodler.
This aesthetic humanization of the mountains, which reduced
them to a scale comprehensible to men, paralleled developments in what has been called "the heroic age of geology."[43]
It was only at this point, for instance, that the first accurate
measurements of mountain heights were made by means of
barometers, replacing the mythic proportions that had formerly been attributed to mountains by fancy and fear.[44]

What we have sketched amounts to nothing less than a radical alteration of consciousness regarding mountains—an alteration that had to take place before Schiller's poet could un-

concernedly climb up his mountain and contemplate the view without being obsessed by Christian guilt, by rationalist disgust, or by other conventional feelings common only a few decades earlier. In "Die Alpen" Haller had talked about the valley-dwellers and their healthy society, virtually ignoring the mountains themselves apart from their utilitarian value. In 1785 his twenty-two-year-old countryman, Johann Gaudenz von Salis-Seewis, homesick for his native Alps, wrote an "Elegie an mein Vaterland," in which he returned in spirit from Paris, where he was serving as an officer in the Swiss Guard, to the mountains of his home.[45] Although he echoes a convention common since Haller by mentioning with chauvinistic fervor the freedom and simple virtues of the happy people, he is obsessed above all with the memory of the mountains themselves, which represent to him the essence of home:

> Vaterland, sei mir gegrüßt! Der hehren Szenen so manche
> Steigt in der grossen Natur schrecklicher Schönheit
> empor:
> Ragende Felsenzinken mit wolkenumlagerter Spitze,
> Welche kein Jäger erklomm, welche kein Adler erflog;
> Blendender Gletscher starre, kristallene Wogen, mit
> scharfen
> Eisigen Klippen bepflanzt, wo, durch umnebelte Luft,
> Schneidenden Zuges, die Gähe hinunter, die wälzende
> Lauwe
> Rollet den frostigen Tod, wo im Wirbel des Nords
> Und im krachenden Donner der tiefaufberstenden Spalten,
> Kaltes Entsetzen und Graun lauschende Wandrer
> ergreift. . . .

Salis-Seewis' poem resembles a poetic travelogue from an aerial point of view—like the occasional comments of an airline pilot pointing out the sights from a cruising jetliner. Flying rapidly across Switzerland, he calls our attention to various landmarks on the route from Paris to his home in the Grisons: we pass over Zürich and its lake, Walenstadt and the Walensee, the Rhaetian Alps, and other points of interest. But the very speed of movement precludes any contemplation or reflection on the mountains.

In 1724 Brockes had stood at the edge of the mountains, peering timidly up at the peaks, in which he reluctantly acknowledged a symbol of God's majesty. In 1790 another poet from the North German plains, Friedrich Matthisson, made the dangerous ascent of the Tour de Mayenne and recorded his feelings in a poem entitled "Der Alpenwanderer."[46] Matthisson pays the conventional tribute to the freedom and virtue of the Alpine inhabitants—"Wo Freiheit in den Hütten / Bei frommer Einfalt wohnt"—but his climb rapidly takes him up to more perilous heights, where such "enchantment" disappears—to a point, he says, where even Haller's muse would have fallen silent. He sees the ruins of another world:

> Wild starren, matt vom Schimmer
>     Der Abendsonn' erhellt,
> Gestürzter Berge Trümmer,
>     Wie Trümmer einer Welt.

Whether Matthisson was aware of Burnet or not, his vocabulary demonstrates the extent to which *The Sacred Theory* had penetrated the poetic consciousness in Germany. As he creeps up the narrow path beside "the ancient Night of Chaos," he senses the presence of death and the terrors of the grave, and like a true apostle of Rousseau he counts every tremor of his spirit:

> Hier dämmern schwarze Gründe
>     Wo nie ein Blümchen lacht,
> Dort bergen grause Schlünde
>     Des Chaos alte Nacht;
> Und wilder, immer wilder
>     Schwingt sich der Pfad empor;
> Bleich wallen Todesbilder
>     Aus jeder Kluft hervor.

It is no accident that Schiller, in his review of Matthisson's poems, singled out "Der Alpenwanderer" along with another mountain poem, "Die Alpenreise," for special praise. In the second poem Matthisson uses several images already familiar to us from "Der Spaziergang"—sun, eagle, prison—to suggest how the mountain inspires the poet as he follows a hunter along precarious mountain paths:

> Ich folge dem Starken! Im Kampf mit Gefahr
> Erhebt sich, wie machtvoll zur Sonne der Aar,
> Der Geist aus kerkernden Schranken
> Zu Göttergedanken.[47]

But in neither poem does Matthisson actually give us the results of his contemplation: he describes the process but not the product. We are still a few years short of Schiller and his meditative mountainclimb. With Matthisson and Salis-Seewis the poet reaches the mountain and joins the eagle, but he is still too exhilarated by the novelty of the experience to devote himself to quiet and detached contemplation.

In the course of the century, then, a conspicuous transformation of views has taken place. Regarded in the seventeenth century as a symbol of man's Fall, reinterpreted by Burnet and his followers as evidence of God's sublimity, justified by early rationalists as useful, mountains were greeted by Rousseau and the sentimental generation as a purifying and serene escape from the passions and ills of civilization. We can now observe a final shift if we consider the circumstances of Goethe's life. When he first went to Switzerland in 1775, the young poet was filled with all the clichés of the new sentimental enthusiasm for mountains. Looking back ironically on the trip in his autobiography, *Dichtung und Wahrheit*, Goethe asks us to imagine "that absolute tendency toward an actual state of natural freedom" in order to understand the young men who regarded Switzerland as the proper place to "idyllicize" their very youthfulness.[48] With his friend Passavant he spent ten days traveling from Zürich up to the Gotthard and back—largely on foot, of course. But he was in such a rush simply to experience the mountains—he speaks of his "longing for those blue mountain heights"[49]—that he found no time for the interests that subsequently occupied him increasingly: geological studies and painting. When an innkeeper offered him a collection of fine crystals, he reports, he was so remote from nature studies that he did not want to load himself down with such mountain products even for a trivial price.[50]

A conspicuous change is evident if we compare the sentimentalism of the trip in 1775 with the well-nigh mystical reverence for mountains, informed by detailed geological knowledge, that characterizes the essay "Über den Granit" (1784). The fact that the essay was inspired by the Harz Mountains is symbolic of the shift of fascination from the Alps specifically to mountains in general. "Sitting on a high naked peak and looking out over a broad expanse, I can say to myself: Here you are resting directly on a foundation that reaches down to the deepest recesses of the earth."[51] Suspended here between the forces of the earth and the close influences of the heavens, he is "elevated to a higher contemplation of nature, and because the human spirit animates everything, an analogy stirs within me whose sublimity I cannot withstand."[52] What Goethe feels on the mountain is not the glory of divinity or the sentiments of his own soul. "I feel the first and firmest beginnings of our existence, I survey the world, its harsher and gentler valleys and its distant fertile pastures, my soul is exalted beyond itself and beyond everything and longs for the heaven that is now so near."[53] Secure on his mountain of granite, Goethe lets his mind pass back across the centuries. He visualizes his peak at a time in the remote past when it was an island in the primal waters. As the tides recede, life begins to emerge on the land below. Then, suddenly, volcanic turmoils bury the inhabitants of the shores. Gazing down at the mountain beneath him, at its mass of seams and gashes, he feels inclined to exclaim: "Here nothing is in its original position, here all is ruins, disorder and destruction."[54] When he returns from the granite peak to his study, he finds a confusing variety of seemingly contradictory explanations in the books of past ages—a clear reference, though no names and titles are cited, to the Burnet controversy. This, Goethe concludes, is the task he has set himself: to bring order into the conflicting theories and to liberate his mind for more far-reaching reflections.

Schiller arrived at a similar association of the mountain

with the sublime, but it is archetypally characteristic that the two men had to approach from diametrically opposite directions in order to reach virtually identical positions. Goethe moves inductively in his short pithy essay from the mountain as a granite-hard geological fact to its appropriateness—indeed, its inevitability—as a locus for large thoughts while Schiller, writing general essays on the nature of the sublime, repeatedly adduces the mountain as an appropriate example to illustrate his thoughts. In the first paragraph of the early essay "Vom Erhabenen" (1793) Schiller attempts a definition: "We call an object *sublime* when our contemplation of it causes our sensory nature to feel its limitations but our rational nature to feel its superiority, its liberation from limitations; *vis à vis* which, in other words, we are physically subordinate but above which we can exalt ourselves *morally*, that is, by means of ideas."[55] It is important to note that Schiller's definition avoids all the associations with deity that were so important to Burnet and his followers. The sublime is no longer evidence of God's presence in nature; instead it is a purely human sensation that reminds man of his moral freedom even in the face of towering physical or natural forces.

Now Schiller repeatedly mentions mountains, and generally heights of all sorts, as examples of the sublime object that inspires sublime feelings in men. In the 1793 essay he cites "an immensely high tower or mountain" as capable of arousing sensations of the sublime.[56] In his "Zerstreute Betrachtungen über verschiedene ästhetische Gegenstände" (1794) he observes that "Heights appear far more sublime than equally great distances," and he points out that mountains, rather than being diminished by the comparison with sky, have the effect of enhancing the height and sublimity of the heavens.[57] In his review of Matthisson's poems (1794) Schiller singled out the device of a walk through the Alps as a singularly effective means of combining the grand and the beautiful in such a manner as to produce the powerful and the sublime.[58] And in his late essay "Über das Erhabene" (1801) he says that man, once he has been liberated by free contemplation from the blind might of natural forces, realizes that "the relatively grand outside of him is the mirror in which he detects the absolutely grand within himself. . . . The sight of unlimited distances and immeasurable heights, the wide ocean at his feet and the greater ocean above him, wrest his spirit from the narrow sphere of the real and the oppressive imprisonment of physical life."[59] (It is superfluous to point out the remarkable coincidence of images between this passage and the opening lines of "Der Spaziergang.")

If the sublime amounts to a sensation of freedom and liberation from the forces of nature, then what could more adequately represent this liberation and reify the notion of sublimity than to put man on top of the mountain, as Schiller did in his poem? As he emerges from his house in the morning, he is exposed to the sublime object in the form of the mountain. When he completes his walk that evening, he has achieved the sensation of the sublime, both physically and morally, by conquering the mountain and liberating himself from the restraining embrace of nature and its beauty. We have seen, in the course of this chapter, that man had to come a long way before Schiller could put his poetic persona on a mountaintop. It was necessary for mountains to lose their ancient associations with sin and ruin, to come beyond their function as a symbol of God's grandeur, and to become both an image of and a locus for the experience of the sublime. And it was necessary for men to lose their fear of mountains to the extent that they were willing and indeed eager to climb them, on foot and alone, to experience this new sensation of the sublime. When Petrarch ascended Mont Ventoux, he was still too much enslaved by ancient conventions to be able to appreciate the sublime vista exposed to his eyes. Haller hiked in his beloved Alps, but his satiric impulses prompted him to portray the model society of the mountain folk while his rationalistic streak caused him to focus pedagogically on the utilitarian aspects of the mountains. Salis-Seewis and Matthisson climbed their mountains, but they found the experience so exhilarating that they had no time left for detached contemplation. Not until Schiller reached the top of his mountain did all the necessary factors come together for the first time to produce a poem in which the experience of sublimity inspired by the mountain is converted in the course of a mountainclimb into the poet's sublime vision of mankind and its history.

We can go a step further. Our survey of mountain literature in German, though by no means complete, is highly representative, including as it does the most conspicuous works of the century and those, moreover, with which Schiller was wholly familiar. We can now see that his poem amounts to a recapitulation of that history. The opening section of the poem, with its catalogue of natural beauties, resembles the works of Brockes and Haller. The "railed path," which enables him to overcome his vertigo and indulge in his contemplations, is identical with the parapet that Rousseau praised. The highest reaches of the mountain, with its eagle, is as desolate and awesome as Matthisson's Alps. But Schiller passes through and beyond all these earlier stages to reach the heights of serene contemplation that Goethe enjoys on his mountain of granite. At every stage, therefore, Schiller is playing with the expectations of mountain poetry and transcending its conventions for his own new purposes. This inversion of conventional motifs is evident at several levels. For instance, the "happy people of the fields, not yet awakened to freedom," take on a different appearance when we relate them to the convention of earlier mountain poetry, from Haller to Matthisson, in which the freedom and natural simplicity of the mountain folk are praised. Schiller has taken the two terms of the original epithet and linked them dialectically: the happy harmony decreases to the extent that freedom increases. It is only when we read Schiller's poem within the conventions of the landscape poetry from which it emerged that we can appreciate its true originality and the ironic play with conventional expectations that characterizes it throughout.

The line that divides novelty from convention is very thin. To see just how quickly the new attitude toward mountains conquered the German cultural consciousness, let us examine in conclusion an essay by the popular moral philosopher,

Christian Garve. An intellectually close relationship bound Schiller to Garve, whose works and translations of various English philosophers had influenced Schiller profoundly and whom Schiller invited to contribute to *Die Horen*. The relationship was reciprocal, however, and Garve's late essay, "Über einige Schönheiten der Gebirgsgegenden" (1798), reads almost like a description of Schiller's "Der Spaziergang."[60]

Garve wrote his essay, he confided, in order to explain on rational grounds his clear emotional sensation: the conviction that mountainous regions are more beautiful than, and generally preferable to, flatlands. Garve spends the first ten pages explaining why a mountain is so interesting to contemplate when one is looking at it from below. A mountainside, he suggests, is like a slab of earth-surface that nature has propped up as on an artist's easel for our convenience: distant objects, which would be lost to our sight on level ground, are clearly exposed on the mountainside. On mountains we see "the wealth of nature put on display."[61] Since the soul lusts for ideas and sensations, Garve continues, it is all the more satisfied by this mountainscape because it sees so much more in a short time. At the same time, the soul demands clarity of disposition. What could be more gratifying than a mountainside where such a wealth of sights is spread before our eyes in the greatest distinctness? All this edifying beauty is enhanced, finally, by the enchanting play of light and shadow that is so much more intense on the mountainside than on a level expanse.

It is a sensation of an entirely different sort when we look down at the valleys from the heights above. "All objects appear reduced in size and yet distinct. Thereby they take on the appearance of fineness and art, becoming more like paintings. . . . This causes the whole, which is perceived all at once, to resemble a painted landscape or a picture in the *camera obscura*."[62] Garve spends several pages working out the analogy between a vista from the mountainside and a painting. In particular, he stresses the movement brought into the landscape by its streams and rivers as well as the articulation of the field by means of the roads.[63] But these more purely aesthetic pleasures decrease the higher one climbs and the more indistinct the objects below become. The satisfaction one receives from looking down from a great height "is more a satisfaction that arises from ideas than one that arises from the sensory view of the objects."[64] For now we are seeing not so much what is actually there as what we know to be there. The man who gradually shifts his gaze from the clearly distinguishable foreground to remote distances experiences a complex series of sensations. Looking down at life from above gives the observer a sense of detachment, of viewing the world *sub specie aeternitatis*. "In general, high mountains are the region for sensations of the sublime; the lower mountains for sensations of the beautiful."[65]

If these thoughts remind us strikingly of Schiller's poem, the following ideas seem to recapitulate Goethe's essay, with a faint reminiscence of Burnet. The mountains, which have the appearance of "extensive ruins left over from the original building of nature," also draw our thoughts to the past. "Nowhere do I see more clearly than in the mountains that things on earth have not always been as they are at present; that the largest and most permanent objects came about and were produced and formed according to certain laws."[66] As a result of all this, mountain regions impress us "more through the contemplation to which they give rise than through the immediate sensations that they stir within us."[67]

Garve's essay sums up the popular response to mountains at the end of the eighteenth century—a response that was enthusiastically adopted by romantic writers in Germany and England and passed along by way of the nineteenth century to the present.[68] But before this new consciousness of the mountain as the appropriate locus for contemplation of the sublime, so laboriously achieved through scientific, theological, and aesthetic controversy, could be fruitful poetically, poetry had to produce a suitable genre to accommodate it.

 # 3 · THE SOURCES: THE ELEGY AS FORM AND MODE

In 1795, the *annus mirabilis* of the German elegy, when the first version of "Der Spaziergang" appeared in *Die Horen*, that same journal contained two other works indispensable for a complete understanding of Schiller's poem. Indeed, Goethe's "Römische Elegien" and Schiller's essay "Über naive und sentimentalische Dichtung" were generally decisive in determining the expectations of the age regarding the elegy as a literary form and as a mode of experience. The significance of these two epoch-making works can be appreciated, in turn, only if they are seen in their cultural context as the result of a historical development.

The term "elegy" is ambiguous to a degree unusual even in a discipline whose terminology is as notoriously inconsistent as literary criticism and poetics. Any reliable dictionary or handbook of literary terms in the major Western languages—e.g., *The American Heritage Dictionary*, the *Oxford Companion to English Literature*, the Larousse, or Merker-Stammler's *Reallexikon der deutschen Literaturgeschichte*—cites two distinct and wholly unrelated meanings under "elegy." One refers to form, or literary kind: an elegy is any poem, regardless of its subject matter, that is written in elegiac distichs. The other refers to subject matter: an elegy is any poem, regardless of its form, that expresses a lament concerning the death of a person or the tragic aspects of life. In English literature, where the elegiac distich exists only as a metrical oddity, the funeral elegy and the more meditative "elegiac" are determined almost entirely by subject matter. Poems that are formally as unlike as Milton's "Lycidas," Gray's "Elegy Written in a Country Churchyard," or Young's "Night Thoughts," are routinely cited as examples of the genre. But in German literature, where the elegiac distich has been widely used since the mid-eighteenth century, the problem is not so simple. Some poems are called elegies for purely formal reasons and others for purely contextual reasons. For instance, Goethe's Marienbad "Elegie" (1823), which would universally be considered typically "elegiac" in mood, uses a six-line strophic form; his poem on such an utterly un-elegiac topic as the metamorphosis of plants is included in his "Elegien und Lehrgedichte" simply because it is composed in elegiac distichs.

This modern terminological ambiguity goes back to an etymological confusion among the Greeks.[1] As late as the fifth century B.C., Greek writers still distinguished between two superficially similar yet etymologically distinct terms: ἔλεγος and ἐλεγεῖον. The term ἔλεγος, popularly but fancifully derived by Alexandrine grammarians from the expression ἒ ἒ λέγειν ("to cry woe! woe!") referred quite generally to any song of mourning or expression of lament regardless of its form. Hence Euripides felt free to call even the mournful song of a bird ἔλεγος (*Iphigenia in Tauris*, 1. 1091). The term ἐλεγεῖον, in contrast, was used to designate a specific metrical form and, by extension, any poem composed in that meter. The elegiac distich, one of the oldest Greek verse forms, consists of a dactylic hexameter followed by a dactylic pentameter, as in Schiller's well-known model:

$$| \acute{x} \quad x|\acute{x} \ x \ x| \ \acute{x} \quad x | \ \acute{x} \qquad x \ | \ \acute{x} \ x \ x| \ \acute{x} \ x|$$
Im Hexameter steigt des Springquells flüssige Säule,
$$| \ \acute{x} \ x \ |\acute{x} \ x \ x| \quad \acute{x} \ \| \acute{x} \quad x \quad x|\acute{x} \ x \quad x|\acute{x} \ |$$
Im Pentameter drauf fällt sie melodisch herab.

Coleridge's translation of Schiller's distich helps us to understand why the form never became popular in English:

In the hexameter rises the fountain's silvery column;
In the pentameter, aye, falling in melody back.

In practice, songs written in elegiac distichs were recited to the accompaniment of the flute—in contrast to lyric poetry, which was sung to the lyre. This circumstance explains

Euripides' allusion to the ἄλυρος ἔλεγος ("unlyrical elegy" or, more literally, "elegy unsuitable for the lyre"; *Iphigenia in Tauris*, 1. 146). For this reason—and because the wild rhythm, so alien to Indo-European ears, was associated with Asiatic cultic celebrations—it is widely assumed that the word ἐλεγεῖον is related etymologically to the Armenian root *elegn* ("flute").

The earliest flute-songs, which can be traced back to eighth-century Ionia, are far from "elegiac" in the commonly accepted sense of the word. The typical setting of these songs is masculine conviviality: a man is talking to a group of friends about war, love, politics, or some other topic of interest to men. The oldest texts, fragments from the seventh century, are primarily martial in subject, ranging from the grim battle songs of the Spartan Tyrtaeus to the campfire anecdotes of Archilochus and Callinus, or erotic, as in Mimnermus' poems about his girl, Nanno. In the sixth century the focus was expanded to accommodate other topics, but the rhetoric remained public. In Solon's hands the elegy became a vehicle for philosophical meditation and political exhortation; Xenophanes employed the distich for speculations on ethics and for social criticism; and Theognis coupled maxims on personal behavior with laments over the decline of aristocratic culture. The distich was also used widely for sepulchral epigrams, but even these epitaphs could hardly be called "elegiac" in the modern sense because they typically assumed the form of exhortations by the deceased to the living, like the famous distich of Simonides that Schiller quotes in "Der Spaziergang":

"Wanderer, kommst du nach Sparta, verkündige dorten,
                                                du habest
Uns hier liegen gesehn, wie das Gesetz es befahl."
                                                (ll. 97-98)

By the fifth century, then, the elegiac distich had emerged as one of the most adaptable poetic forms in Greek literature, used for a variety of purposes ranging from military marches and love songs to philosophical apothegms and sepulchral epitaphs. The popularity of the form was due largely to its metrical characteristics, which place it midway between epic and lyric poetry. While offering a more compact unit than the free-flowing hexameter, the distich provided greater metrical flexibility than the rigid and complex strophic forms of lyric poetry. The elegiac distich was felt to combine the narrative objectivity of the hexameter with the more emotional quality of the pentameter. The elegiac distich can tell a story—a battle episode, an erotic encounter, a mythological tale, a political anecdote—but the story is not told for its own sake, as in the epic; it is adduced to illustrate a general idea or a subjective feeling, as in a lyric poem.

During the Alexandrine period the matter (ἔλεγος) became increasingly identified with the form (ἐλεγεῖον). As a result, it came to be thought that the elegiac distich was the only proper form for the expression of lamentations. This descriptive view had rigidified into a prescriptive formula by the time Horace wrote his *Ars poetica:*

> Versibus impariter junctis querimonia primum,
> Post etiam inclusa est voti sententia compos.
> Quis tamen exiguos elegos emiserit auctor,
> Grammatici certant et adhuc sub judice lis est.
> (ll. 75-78)

Horace reminds us that in his day the scholars were already quarreling about the history of the elegy. But he is quite explicit about its characteristics. The elegiac distich (*versibus impariter junctis*) was originally devised for the purpose of lamentation (*querimonia*); subsequently it was enlarged to include *voti sententia compos*—an obscure phrase that is generally translated as referring to erotic poetry.

Curiously, Horace says nothing further about the genre that flourished so brilliantly during his own lifetime: the Roman love elegy. The Augustan elegists give great praise to Callimachus, Philetas, and other early masters, suggesting the lost glories of the Alexandrine elegy. But it was Catullus, Tibullus, and Propertius who shaped the erotic elegy that was to have a profound influence on modern European literature. (Ovid's *Amores* represent such a sophisticatedly conscious exploitation of the genre that they amount almost to a burlesque.) In contrast to the Greek elegists, whose work has come down to us in fragments and single poems, if at all, the Roman elegists typically arranged their poems in cycles. Although these books can accommodate a variety of moods and situations, they are always unified by the figure of the woman they celebrate. For instance, in Tibullus' two books of elegies the poet presents himself in a number of different roles—as a lover, a friend, a gentleman farmer, a student of Roman antiquities. But in Book I he constantly returns to his love for the faithless Delia, and in Book II he is obsessed with the cruel courtesan Nemesis. It is symptomatic of the genre that we still identify the Roman elegists by the girls to whom they consecrated their works: Catullus' Lesbia, Propertius' Cynthia, and Ovid's Corinna.

For many centuries poets continued to regard the elegy as a genre quite distinct from others,[2] and in accordance with Horace's precept it was reserved principally for lamentation, as in the great elegies to Rome by Hildebert of Lavardin. Eberhard der Deutsche, in his thirteenth-century *Laborintus* (ll. 261-64) specifies that the appropriate form for narratives is the hexameter and for lamentation the elegiac pentameter, while songs of praise use strophic forms:

> Historias habet hexametrum, servitque querelae
> Pentametrum, laudes cetera metra canunt.

But during the so-called *aetas Ovidiana* of the twelfth and thirteenth centuries the elegiac distich became so popular that it was increasingly used for almost any subject matter. Eberhard's own work reveals that the distinctions were becoming blurred, for he used the distich for didactic purposes. Meanwhile, other authors began to use the distich for epic narrative; and the elegiac distich became the standard form around 1150 for the Medieval Latin *comedia* (Matthew of Vendôme, *Milo*; Vitalis of Blois, *Geta*; the anonymous *Babio* and *Pan-*

*philus*). Even when works were written in other meters, the elegiac distich was the conventional form for the personal statements of dedication and preface.

By the end of the Middle Ages, in short, any precise sense of the elegy as a genre had been effaced because the form of the distich had expanded to embrace virtually every extreme of subject matter. This tendency continued in the poetry of Neo-Latin humanism. To be sure, a certain refocusing took place: in contrast to the medieval poets, who still regarded lamentation as the central matter of the elegy, Renaissance Latin poets, following the practice of the Roman poets rather than the prescriptions of Horace, put erotic love into the center of the genre: e.g., the *Amores* (1502) of Konrad Celtis, and the *Basia* (1539) of the Dutch Humanist Johannes Secundus, to whom Goethe felt closely akin. Nevertheless, the elegiac distich continued to encompass such a variety of material that only the form determined the genre, as in the *carmina* of Petrus Lotichius Secundus.

With the emergence of vernacular poetry during the Renaissance the situation changed. During the sixteenth century, to be sure, various poets attempted in different languages to recreate the elegiac distich: Johannes Clajus, Johannes Fischart, and Konrad Gesner in Germany; Antoine de Baïf, Etienne Jodelle, and Pierre de Ronsard in France; and Gabriel Harvey, Edmund Spenser, and Philip Sydney in England. But owing to the metrical difficulty of adapting the classical quantitative meters to modern accentual verse these attempts were rapidly abandoned. Other poets, taking Horace's metrical specification—*versibus impariter junctis*—very literally, sought to achieve the characteristic "elegiac" effect by combining other lines that were unequal in length: e.g., alexandrines alternating with *vers communs*. In general, however, as formal criteria vanished, content became the single means of identifying the elegy in France and England. The term "élégie" first occurred in France in 1505, but during the course of the sixteenth century the term became so fashionable that it was appropriated to designate a wide variety of familiar forms, such as the *épître amoureuse*, that resembled either the Horatian *querimonia* or *voti sententia compos.*[3] In seventeenth-century England it was notably the lamentation that was identified with the elegy.[4] By the end of the century the funeral elegy had become so rampant that it was widely parodied, as in the anonymous *The Mourning Poets* (London, 1695):

> What bulky Heaps of doleful Rhyme I see!
> Sure all the world runs mad with Elegy;
> Lords, Ladies, Knights, Priests, Souldiers, Squires,
>                                         Physicians,
> Beaux, Lawyers, Merchants, Prentices, Musicians,
> Play'rs, Footmen, Pedants, Scribes of all Conditions.[5]

In Germany, in contrast, the characteristic feature of the Baroque elegy was not so much its subject matter as its form.[6] In Martin Opitz's *Buch von der Deutschen Poeterey* (1624), to be sure, the genre is still defined wholly in terms of subject matter: "In elegies were written, originally, only sad matters and then, subsequently, also love affairs, lovers' laments, desire of death, letters, longing for absent ones, accounts of one's own life, and similar things."[7] But this fact stems from the circumstance that Germany was more than a century later than most other countries in adapting classical forms and genres to the vernacular. As a result, when Opitz wrote the first German poetics, he had at his disposal not only the theoretical works of such Renaissance critics as Scaliger but also the practical examples of French and Italian poetry, where the genre was identified by its subject matter. (In Italy, in fact, the form was so negligible that "elegies" were often written in terza rima.) Paradoxically, it was Opitz's practice rather than his theory that affected the development of the genre in Germany. For his own "elegies" he devised a form whose rhythms more closely approximate the classical distich than the rhyming of the French. Opitz's elegiac alexandrines—with alternating feminine and masculine rhymes—retain two characteristics of the distich: the six-beat line in both elements and the alternating acatalectic and catalectic ending. These effects are evident in the opening lines of Opitz's "Beschluss-Elegie":

> Das blinde Liebeswerk, die süße Gift der Sinnen
>   Und rechte Zauberei, hat letzlich hier ein End':
> Es wird das lose Kind, so mich verführen könne,
>   Gott lob, jetzt ganz und gar von mir hinweggewendet.[8]

By the middle of the century Opitz's practice had obscured his theory. When Enoch Hanmann reedited Opitz's poetics (Frankfurt am Main, 1658), he wrote that "Elegies are alexandrine verses in which a feminine and masculine are alternated."[9] The practice of many poets—Johannes Rist, Caspar Ziegler, Christian Hofmann von Hofmannswaldau, and others—substantiated the general observation that the elegy of this period is identifiable by its formal characteristics.

For a variety of reasons the elegy failed to attract the major poets of the Baroque. But during the eighteenth century it became once again one of the most popular literary forms in Europe.[10] In Germany, particularly, its appeal is evidenced by various anthologies, such as Klamer Schmidt's *Elegien der Deutschen* (Lemgo, 1776) and Hans Heinrich Füssli's *Oden und Elegien der Deutschen* (Zürich, 1785). Many volumes by representative poets contain clearly specified examples of the genre, and no issue of a journal is complete without an elegy. Yet, paradoxically, the very popularity of the genre caused it to lose definition, both of form and of subject matter. First, the Baroque elegy continued to exist as a viable form until the end of the century, largely because of the authority of Gottsched, who prefaced his *Versuch einer Critischen Dichtkunst* (1730) with a translation of the *Ars poetica*, rendering Horace's lines as follows:

> Die Elegie war sonst ein Werk der Traurigkeit,
> Allein sie ward hernach zugleich der Lust geweiht.
> Wer sie zuerst erdacht, ist nicht so leicht zu sagen,
> Da die Gelehrten selbst, sich noch darum befragen.

In his extended commentary on this passage Gottsched says that the subject matter "should be composed in a natural and flowing manner, should have a sad content, and consist almost wholly of laments."[11] Although Horace indicated that the original nature of the elegy was expanded to include "jesting and amatory poems," Gottsched opposes the tendency of the late Baroque to restrict the elegy increasingly to erotic poetry. In his consideration of the form, Gottsched first criticizes the French and English for writing poems that are elegies in name and content alone, but not in form. Gottsched is especially contemptuous of the rhyming couplets employed by Marot, Ronsard, Desportes, and Rochester. Opitz did much better for the Germans, he asserts, by creating elegies that, though not identical in form with the Latin distichs, bear at least a close resemblance to them.

Second, around the middle of the century many poets of the Rococo, turning directly back to the model of Catullus, resurrected the animal epicedium as a variety of elegy. The lament over the death of a favorite bird, like Lesbia's sparrow, becomes virtually a subgenre in Anacreontic poetry. We find elegies to sparrows (J.W.L. Gleim), to canaries (Anna Luise Karschin), to quails (Karl Wilhelm Ramler), to doves (Johann Martin Miller), to starlings (Friedrich Matthisson), and to a bevy of other fowl—not to mention pet lapdogs, cats, and sundry other beasts. This trivialization of subject matter was accompanied by a relaxing of the strict Baroque form of cross-rhyming alexandrines. Virtually any couplet consisting of lines of unequal length was felt to be elegiac. The first strophe of Hölty's elegy "Auf den Tod einer Nachtigall" (1771) is representative of the new form:

Sie ist dahin, die Maienlieder tönte,
    Die Sängerin,
Die durch ihr Lied den ganzen Hain verschönte,
    Sie ist dahin!

Sie, deren Ton mir in die Seele hallte,
    Wenn ich, am Bach,
Der durchs Gebüsch im Abendgolde wallte,
    Auf Blumen lag![12]

Third, Friedrich Wilhelm Gotter's translation of Gray's "Elegy Written in a Country Churchyard"—in alexandrine rhymed couplets—introduced still another subject matter into the eighteenth-century German elegy: the melancholy meditation composed in some such isolated spot as a cemetery, a castle ruin, or a battlefield. In 1771, the year that Gotter's translation appeared, Hölty produced elegies inspired by both a country cemetery and a city cemetery. The first strophe of the former leaves little doubt about the source of inspiration:

Mit dem letzten Schall der Abendglocke,
        Die den jungen Maitag
Weinend jetzt zu Grabe läutet, wandle
        Ich in diese Schatten.[13]

Matthisson used an elegiac stanza similar to Gray's for his "Elegie auf einem Gottesacker geschrieben," but he created a different strophe for his "Elegie in den Ruinen eines alten Bergschlosses geschrieben":

Schweigend in der Abenddämmrung Schleier,
        Ruht die Flur, das Lied der Haine stirbt,
Nur daß hier, im alternden Gemäuer,
        Melancholisch noch ein Heimchen zirpt.
Stille sinkt aus unbewölkten Lüften,
Langsam ziehn die Heerden von den Triften,
        Und der müde Landmann eilt der Ruh
        Seiner väterlichen Hütte zu.[14]

C. A. Tiedge selected for his popular elegiac meditations a legend-veiled precipice in the Harz Mountains ("Elegie am Roßtrapp") and the battlefield where Frederick the Great suffered his worst defeat in the Seven Years' War ("Elegie auf dem Schlachtfelde bei Kunersdorf").

Finally, the elegiac distich was gradually refined for use in German poetry[15]—a circumstance that emphatically distinguishes German literature from other European literature. As early as the sixteenth and seventeenth centuries there had been occasional experiments with the distich, but these were in general too sporadic to have any authority. Then, in 1748, the enormous success of Klopstock's *Der Messias*, with its swelling hexameters, undermined the hegemony of alexandrine verse in German literature, which was soon replaced in drama by blank verse and in epic poetry by hexameters patterned after classical models. With Johann Heinrich Voss's widely acclaimed translation of *The Odyssey* in 1781 the hexameter was fully and smoothly naturalized for German versification. In the wake of this success, classically oriented poets began experimenting with other Greek and Latin forms—the Alcaic, Asclepiadean and Sapphic odes as well as the distich. Among the varieties of forms at which Klopstock tried his hand during the fifties and sixties we find occasional poems in distichs. His first of this sort, "Die künftige Geliebte" (1747), in fact, was originally called "Elegie." But despite the allusion to melancholy in the first couplet—

Dir nur, liebendes Herz, euch, meine vertraulichsten
Thränen,
Sing' ich traurig allein dies wehmütige Lied.[16]

—the poem is an elegy only in the formal sense of the word because it contains no real lament. Instead, as the title suggests, it is a speculation about the nature of the girl, presently growing up somewhere, who will become his future beloved. Klopstock's poems in distichs, which stimulated imitation only after they appeared in 1771 in his volume of odes, were metrically quite cumbersome—especially the pentameter. (Note the example just quoted.) During the seventies Voss finally succeeded in writing metrically correct pentameters in German—in such poems as "Die Trennung" (1776) and "An Selma" (1776). And his example was imitated by various poets, such as Kosegarten, who wrote erotic elegies to a chorus-line of girls with names like Agnes, Alma, Ida, Jinny, Minona, and Rosa.[17] In 1783, following various prose versions, K. F. Reinhard published the first translation of a Roman elegist into German distichs. And that same decade witnessed the appearance of other poems in distichs. Salis-Seewis' "Elegie an mein Vaterland" (1785), cited in the preceding chapter, is written in distichs inspired by Voss. As though there were something about mountains that inspired distichs, Friederike Brun also wrote, in 1791, a poem celebrating the Jura range.[18] That same year Matthisson composed an "Elegie an Sophie von Seckendorf und Eleonore von Kalb" in the same form:

> In des einsamen Thales Umschattungen, wo sich der
> Bergquell
> Durch verwachsnes Gesträuch, schäumend vom
> Felsenhang stürzt,
> Weilt' ich im dämmernden Lichte des sinkenden Tages und
> streute,
> In Gedanken versenkt, sterbendes Laub in die Fluth. . . .
> (ll. 1-4)

However, there was still no firm association of the form with the subject matter. In the following year, for instance, Matthisson reverted, for his "Elegien in den Ruinen eines alten Bergschlosses geschrieben" (1786), to the strophic form of the sentimental elegy. And most of the other poems in distichs—by Klopstock, Salis-Seewis, Voss, and a few others—are elegies only in the formal sense of the word.

This, then, was the situation in 1795, when Goethe's "Römische Elegien" and Schiller's essay "Über naive und sentimentalische Dichtung" appeared. For all the popularity of the genre, the elegy had no fixed criteria, of either form or subject matter. An "elegy" could be a poem in cross-rhyming alexandrines, in an elegiac stanza resembling Gray's famous model, in an allegedly "Catullan" strophe of lines unequal in length, or—most recently—even in elegiac distichs. As for subject matter, it could be a threnetic lament, an animal epicedium, a love poem, or a melancholy meditation. Under the influence of Goethe and Schiller, however, the situation changed.

Although a few poets inspired by Klopstock and Voss had been experimenting with elegiac distichs, their poems, appearing sporadically in separate volumes, had little general impact. But the "Römische Elegien," a major work created by Germany's most famous poet and published in one of the foremost literary journals, could not be easily overlooked. It was Goethe's cycle that authoritatively established the elegiac distich as a viable form in German literature.

On June 18, 1788, the thirty-eight-year-old Goethe arrived back in Weimar after a sojourn of almost two years in Italy. The psychic wrench he felt at leaving the eternal city, he reports in the last paragraph of *Die Italienische Reise*, was so "heroic-elegiac" that he wanted to write an elegy to commemorate the occasion. But the vivid recollection of Ovid's famous elegy to Rome, from the *Tristia* (I, 3), intruded into his meditations and prevented him from composing a poem of his own. Determined on his return to Weimar not to sacrifice the sense of spiritual liberation that he had won in Italy and not to relapse into the provincial ways of small-town Germany, Goethe made various changes in his life that alienated many of his former friends and associates. The incident that immediately aroused Frau von Stein and the indignant ladies of Weimar was his liaison with Christiane Vulpius, whom he met four weeks after his return. The rapidity with which he took into his house this simple and devoted young woman of twenty-three suggests that Goethe returned from Italy with the specific intention of finding a mistress as soon as possible. In any case, he was soon eager to give poetic expression to his new domestic happiness, but he had to find a form that would not be flagrantly indiscreet.

In September, Goethe visited his "Urfreund" in Jena, Karl Ludwig von Knebel. Knebel, a lover of the classics who had already tried his hand at various translations, was currently preparing a new prose translation of Propertius. In response to Goethe's intense interest Knebel sent him a fine old Latin edition of the "cloverleaf of poets"[19]—Tibullus, Catullus, and Propertius—and Goethe plunged immediately into their study, renewing an acquaintance that dated back to his schooldays. This re-introduction to the Latin erotic elegists under totally new auspices turned out to be the catalyst that precipitated the poetic treatment of Goethe's Italian years and his new-found love in Weimar. The transposition of his Weimar experience to a Roman setting and the translation of his autobiography into a classical form enabled him to achieve a twofold distance, spatial and temporal, from his experience and to render it with poetic objectivity. Almost immediately, by the end of October, 1788, he began writing occasional poems in distichs that celebrated his love for Christiane as transposed to a Roman setting.[20] In his letters from the period Goethe referred to these poems simply as his "Erotica," and he collected them in an album that he kept under a cast of Raphael's skull.

By April, 1790, when he decided to conclude the collection, he had written at least twenty-four poems in elegiac distichs, which he shared from time to time with a few close friends.[21] Both Herder and Duke Karl August strongly urged him to keep the poems as a private memento, a diary in verse, fearing that a prudish public might be offended by such passages as the one in which the poet recounts how he lay in bed with his beloved, gently scanning his verses with his fingers on her bare back:

> Oftmals hab ich auch schon in ihren Armen gedichtet
>   Und des Hexameters Maß leise mit fingernder Hand
> Ihr auf den Rücken gezählt.Sie atmet in lieblichem
>                                          Schlummer,
> Und es durchglühet ihr Hauch mir bis ins Tiefste die
>                                          Brust.
>                                          (V, 15-18)

Goethe followed this well-meant advice for several years. But when Schiller asked him in 1794 for a contribution to *Die Horen*, he made up his mind to release the poems under the title "Elegien. Rom 1788." He asked Schiller, however, not to let the manuscript out of his hands and to read the poems only to those persons "who have to pass judgment on their admissibility."[22] Of the twenty-two poems he sent—he did not bother to include the two "priapic" poems—he decided before publication to omit two more that contained "objectionable passages."[23] Even Schiller, who felt that the elegies belong among Goethe's finest works, privately found them "lascivious" ("schlüpfrig") and "not entirely respectable" ("nicht sehr decent"). [24] When the issue of *Die Horen* containing the elegies appeared, Schiller sent it to his patron, Duke Friedrich Christian von Augustenberg, along with a cover letter justifying the publication of verses that were perhaps written in too free a tone and that might offend "conventional decency, but not true and natural decency." [25] And he subsequently added a passage to his essay "Über naive und sentimentalische Dichtung"—without mentioning Goethe by name but calling him "the German Propertius"—to clarify the criteria of decency and modesty that govern the naive poet.

Although the reception of the elegies was enthusiastic among liberal spirits—especially the young romantic critics, Friedrich and August Wilhelm Schlegel, were in raptures— the opinion of the minor poet Johann Baptist von Alxinger is probably more typical of the general public reaction. "It was all right for Propertius to boast that he had spent a happy night with his girl. But who can approve when Herr von Goethe practices *con-cubitum* with his Italian mistress before the eyes of all Germany in *Die Horen?*" [26] One contemporary letter reports that "all the respectable ladies are incensed at the bordello-like nakedness" exposed in the elegies. [27] Another claimed that the elegies "outrage morality and, in parts, decency." [28] Schiller was called upon to justify the inclusion of such poems in his journal. [29] And Herder joked that Schiller would have to change the name of his journal from *Die Horen* to *Die Huren.* [30]

It is difficult for modern readers to appreciate the furor of indignation that greeted Goethe's poems—especially in Weimar, where people soon realized that the girl of the poems, even though she was called by an Italian name, looked exactly like Christiane, with her mass of thick dark hair and ringlets curling about her ears. On one level, to be sure, the elegies contain the record of a love affair—a story told with great restraint, with an unusual degree of understanding for the woman's point of view, and with a disarming degree of humor. However, the poems do not amount to a tightly or systematically organized novel in verse form. What we find, rather, are incidents and episodes from a Roman love affair, arranged in a roughly chronological sequence: the poems begin before the poet has even met Faustine, and they end at a point when he fears that the affair is going to be betrayed by gossip—or through his own distichs. In the course of the twenty poems we are provided with a great number of isolated details, which constitute a suggestively complete picture of the affair. Faustine—she is mentioned by name only once—is a young widow with an infant son; her mother countenances the affair because of the material comfort it brings her daughter; and her uncle jealously watches over his niece's virtue. The first-person narrator is a German poet visiting in Italy—an older man who prefers the enjoyment of a secure love rather than the youthful challenge of obstacles:

> Darum macht Faustine mein Glück; sie teilet das Lager
>     Gerne mit mir, und bewahrt Treue dem Treuen genau.
> Reizendes Hindernis will die rasche Jugend; ich liebe,
>     Mich des versicherten Guts lange bequem zu erfreun.
>                                              (XVIII, 9-12)

The affair has brought an unaccustomed degree of prosperity to the simple young Italian woman: new clothes (which arouse the neighbors' envy); better food on the table; and frequent entertainments, such as trips to the opera. For the poet it has provided such a delightful and fulfilling sexual gratification that he cannot restrain himself from constantly tattling. He confides all the details of their love-life to his verses, making involuntary voyeurs of the readers. The couple spends a lot of time in bed, both at his place and hers. He sneaks into her house disguised as a prelate; she creeps to his apartment, betrayed only by the neighbor's barking dog. Under her uncle's watchful eye in an *osteria* she makes an assignation by indicating the hour in a puddle of wine spilled on the table. On another occasion the poet is frightened away from a rendezvous in the vineyards by a scarecrow that he takes to be the uncle. Excited by a parade of harvesters who remind him of ancient fertility rites, he even takes her under a myrtle bush in the countryside.

Yet despite the enchanting vividness of detail, the poems do not constitute an autobiography in verse of Goethe's sex life.

In the first place, it turns out repeatedly that the most charming details—e.g., the rendezvous spelled out in the puddle of
wine—are literary in their origin, borrowed from the poems
of the Roman elegists.[31] In the second place, love is only one
of three large themes in the cycle.[32] The designation
"Erotica" may have been appropriate for the earliest poems
that Goethe placed under Raphael's skull, but he knew full
well what he was doing when he changed the title in *Die
Horen* to "Elegien. Rom 1788" and then, for publication in his
collected poems from 1806 on, to the now familiar title:
"Römische Elegien." For the city of Rome, in all its dimensions, is as meaningful to the poet-narrator as is his mistress.
To this extent the elegies constitute an important chapter in
the history of the infatuation of the modern consciousness
with the eternal city.[33] It is the Rome of classical antiquity
that obsesses the poet, not contemporary Rome or even Renaissance Rome. (Because of his obsession with classical Rome,
Goethe never felt completely at home in Venice, which is so
archetypally a Renaissance city.) We get from the poems an
intimate sense of place, but it is a place delimited by landmarks of antiquity: Ostia, the Flaminian Way, the Capitoline
Hill, Cestius' tomb. Even the poet's apartment is described in
terms of the statues that inhabit it: of Jupiter, Juno, Apollo,
Minerva, Hermes, Bacchus, Cythere—and, of course, "the
splendid son" Priapus (Elegy XI). When he is not with Faustine, the poet is studying the architectural monuments of classical antiquity, reading its authors, recapitulating its history.
Although Faustine belongs entirely, physically and spiritually, to a modern Rome that has nothing to do with classical
antiquity, the poet uses her body in the very act of love-
making to educate himself about the sculpture of classical antiquity:

> Und belehr ich mich nicht, indem ich des lieblichen Busens
>     Formen spähe, die Hand leite die Hüften hinab?
> Dann versteh ich den Marmor erst recht: ich denk und
>                                           vergleiche,
>     Sehe mit fühlendem Aug, fühle mit sehender Hand.
>                                             (V, 7-10)

The principal connection between the city and the love affair—between Roma-Amor of the ancient palindrome—exists in the poet's imagination. When he first arrives in Rome, he apostrophizes the stones of Rome and the *genius loci*, who still remains silent:

> Saget, Steine, mir an, o sprecht, ihr hohen Paläste!
> Straßen, redet ein Wort! Genius, regst du dich nicht?
>
> (I, 1-2)

The *genius loci* who brings the city to life for the poet turns out to be love:

> Eine Welt zwar bist du, o Rom; doch ohne die Liebe
> Wäre die Welt nicht die Welt, wäre denn Rom auch
> nicht Rom.
>
> (I, 13-14)

This connection introduces the third major theme of the cycle: mythology. The principal mythological figure of the poem is predictably Amor himself, who is mentioned in the first poem and the last and cited in half of the poems in between. Rome is "Amor's temple" (I); it is "Amor the Prince" who provides the poet with his Roman asylum from the past that he wants to escape (II); when the lovers are in bed together, Amor tends the lamp and remembers the times when he performed the same service for his "triumvirate"—Catullus, Tibullus, and Propertius (V); it is Amor, "the rascal," who finally loosens the poet's tongue and incites him to confide the account of his love to his distichs (XX). The elegies contain dozens of references to mythological tales, but they are never simply ornamental, as they generally are in Anacreontic poetry. Instead, the allusions have in every case a mediating function: to generalize the contemporary love affair to a point at which it becomes part of the history and culture of Rome. In the third elegy, for instance, the poet cites the examples of various mythic figures—Venus and Anchises, Luna and Endymion, Hero and Leander, Rhea Silvia and Mars—to console Faustine for having yielded so quickly to his desires. He tells her the story of the Eleusinian mysteries as a song of seduction. He summons up the legend of Midas as an analogy to his own compelling urge to speak of his secret love.

The twenty elegies, though all narrated in the first person, do not have a single common pattern. But their organization tends to be quite simple: either bipartite or additive. The poet tells anecdotes and indulges in lengthy meditations; he apostrophizes Rome, various deities, and his absent friends in the North. He chats with his mistress in dialogues; she reproaches him for his insensitivity in a lengthy encapsulated monologue; he records his peregrinations through the city and recounts its history. Yet despite the brilliant variety of forms that characterize them and although the twenty poems do not amount to a closely knit plot, they are wrought into a cycle by means of the consistent elegiac form, the three thematic areas, and a group of recurrent motifs: e.g., the contrast between day and night, past and present, north and south. The growth of the love affair is accompanied throughout by a tension between discretion and gossip, which culminates in the nineteenth elegy, a long mythological narrative concerning the strife between Fama and Amor.

August Wilhelm Schlegel, reviewing the anonymously published "Elegien" in the *Allgemeine Literatur-Zeitung* in 1796, shrewdly foresaw that "the objection will be raised against these poems, with great pomposity, that they are not elegies."[34] For well-nigh two centuries, indeed, scholars have been debating precisely that question. Yet surely only the most provincial pedantry would deny to the poems their proper designation. To be sure, Goethe's elegies are not lamentations—neither in the sense of Horace's *querimonia* nor of the English funeral elegy nor of the Anacreontic epicedia. But to the extent that the erotic distichs of Tibullus and Propertius and Ovid are elegies, Goethe's poems deserve the label as well. For his poems resemble nothing in Western literature so much as the elegy books of his beloved Roman models. Granted, the modest young widow Faustine bears little resemblance to the haughty aristocrats and disdainful *hetaerae* whose wiles and deceits drove Catullus and Propertius to distraction. And Goethe's persona as a sober, mature man differs from the rash youths who generally enunciate the Latin elegies. But otherwise the Latin models provided a great deal—from the form of the elegiac distich, which Goethe learned directly from them rather than from Klopstock and Voss, to the organization of the poems into a cyclical book. Many of the incidents turn out to be a elegiac *topoi*, and on several occasions Goethe paraphrases or quotes lines directly from the Augustan poets. Like his classical models, Goethe also felt free to include a certain didactic element in his elegies: Tibullus inserted antiquarian discourses into his poems, and Propertius had a penchant for philosophical disquisitions. However, these details, which nineteenth-century scholars zealously catalogued, are less important than the general concept.[35] Goethe was not merely assembling a pastiche of passages from the Latin elegists but doing something far more difficult and subtle: he was writing in their style.

The most accurate description of the relationship between Goethe's elegies and the Latin elegies was stated by Schlegel in his review of 1796. He begins by asserting that Goethe's poems constitute a remarkable phenomenon—singular in the history of German and even of modern poetry in general. Germans can now proudly claim that their language offers "the truest poetical re-creations of the Ancients, that it alone can claim original works in the genuine antique style."[36] If the shades of the immortal triumvirate of Roman elegists should return to life, Schlegel concludes, "they would be astonished at this stranger from the Germanic forests, who joins their company after eighteen centuries; but they would gladly concede him a wreath of the same myrtle that greens as freshly for him as once it did for them."[37]

It was Goethe's contribution to conquer the verse form of the elegiac distich for German literature. The earlier isolated cases of its use had smacked of academic exercises—an experiment to be tried once or twice and then dropped again. Here for the first time Goethe succeeded in creating a supple form in which it was possible to write a long poem and to express virtually everything—from the most delicate affairs of the heart to narrative of action and philosophical meditations. Goethe was himself well aware of the effect of the meter. As he remarked years later to Eckermann: If one should translate the content of the "Römische Elegien" into the tone and verse of Byron's *Don Juan*, the effect would be quite "infamous" ("verrucht").[38] The "Römische Elegien" are justified by their classical form, which transports us into a poetic world, over which the standards of decency and morality of modern times have no power of judgment.

Yet for the very reasons that Schlegel cites, Goethe's elegies cannot properly be called "classical German elegies": it would be more accurate to describe them as "Roman elegies in German." This is obviously not an evaluative distinction but a taxonomic one. Goethe's elegies are not better or worse, as a literary kind, than Schiller's elegy. But they are clearly different in conception, and it is pointless to try to understand or to evaluate the one by the criteria of the other. Goethe naturalized an already existing form in German—a huge achievement that no other modern poet had yet managed. In the distich Goethe created the ideal form for all shadings of experience, from the most personal to the most universal—a form, in a word, that could accommodate the extremes of mood that we admired in Schiller's "Der Spaziergang." But he did not reshape the genre of the European elegy in doing so; he did not add a new subgenre to the existing possibilities. Before the classical German elegy could be created, it was necessary to have a suitable elegiac mode for the new elegiac form.

For all that Schiller admired the "Römische Elegien," there was little in Goethe's poems apart from their metrical form to link them to the poem that Schiller first published under the simple generic heading "Elegie." In organization, mood, and subject matter no two works could be more unlike. Yet there are two perfectly valid reasons why both of these masterpieces deserve to be called "elegies." First, they are both elegies in the original *formal* sense of the word: poems in elegiac distichs. Second, both poems are entitled to the label "elegy" by a certain literary tradition. But whereas Goethe finds the justifying source for his poems in *history*—in the works of the Latin elegists—Schiller typically seeks his justification in the *theory* of the genre, as he perfected it in his essay "Über naive und sentimentalische Dichtung." To understand Schiller's essay, however, we need to survey the development of aesthetic theory in the second half of the eighteenth century. For it is not always sufficiently appreciated how extensively Schiller was indebted to his predecessors—the extent, in other words, to which his theoretical writings represent the culmination of a tradition rather than a bold new departure.[39]

As we noted earlier, in 1730 Gottsched followed Horace quite slavishly in his wholly normative definition of the elegy according to criteria of form and subject matter. Zedler's *Universal Lexikon* summarizes the normative view of the elegy that prevailed in the early eighteenth century: it is a *"Carmen"* that consists of alternating hexameters and pentameters, and deals primarily with sorrowful matters ("von betrübten Dingen") although it may sometimes be extended to include other subjects as long as they are not too exalted.[40] Now, at the end of the century, if Schiller had consulted (as he frequently did) Adelung's five-volume dictionary for information on the elegy, he would have found the familiar traditional criteria of content ("Klagegedicht") and form (any poem in distichs). But a third criterion had suddenly appeared: "In a wider sense the elegy, even among the ancients, was a poem dedicated to the gentle sensations of sorrow or joy, especially the amorous sensations of an affection either happy or sad."[41] The fact that a standard reference work included a criterion that occurred in none of the normative poetics from Opitz to Gottsched suggests that a major shift had taken place, a shift indicated by the word "sensation" (*Empfindung*), new in this aesthetic context.

This shift in the definition of the elegy must be seen, in turn, as a specific case within the more general movement from the normative poetics of the early eighteenth century to an increasingly psychological understanding of genre in the second half of the century[42]—from a conception of genre as form and content, in other words, to a conception of genre as mood, from genre as a literary kind to genre as a mode of sensation. During the late seventeenth and early eighteenth centuries thinkers like Locke, Berkeley, and Hume had familiarized in philosophy the sensationist view that the mind is dependent upon the senses for its ideas. Alexander Gottlieb Baumgarten gradually developed the conviction that the sensationist explanation should be extended beyond metaphysics to include art.[43] To designate this "science of sensuous cognition" he coined the term "aesthetics" (from the Greek word meaning "to perceive"), which he then used as the title of his book *Aesthetica* (1750). One of the first thinkers who attempted to adapt the sensationist theory of aesthetics to literary theory was Moses Mendelssohn, whose *Briefe über die Empfindungen* (1755) constitutes a sustained, although often confused, attempt to analyze aesthetic pleasure in terms of the sensations that produce it. It was only in his conclusion that Mendelssohn introduced in passing his analysis of pity as "a mixture of pleasant and unpleasant sensations."[44] Since the brief reference to "mixed sensations" provoked a good deal of misunderstanding, Mendelssohn returned to the subject a few years later in his essay "Rhapsodie oder Zusätze zu den Briefen über die Empfindungen" (1761). At this point Mendelssohn's own thinking had been stimulated further by his reading of Burke's *Philosophical Enquiry into . . . the Sublime and Beautiful* (1757). Burke, whose ideas aroused considerable and immediate interest in Germany, introduces the notion of a "mixed sense of pleasure" to explain such passions as love (e.g., of beauty) and fear (e.g., of the sublime).[45] All pleasure, he argues, is "capable of being mixed with a mode of uneasiness, that is, when an idea of its object is excited in the mind with an idea at the same time of having irretrievably lost it." In agreement with Burke, Mendelssohn explains that our sensations are rarely pure and unmixed. Rather, they are mixtures involving varying degrees of pleasure and pain, satisfaction and dissatisfaction. "This is the nature of our soul! If it cannot differentiate between two emotions that it experiences simultaneously, then it combines them into a phenomenon that is different from both and that bears almost no similarity to them."[46] Pity, he suggests as an example, is a mixed sensation consisting of the love we feel for an object and our discontent at its misfortune. "The mixed sensations have the particular characteristic that they are, to be sure, not so gentle ('sanft') as pure contentment, but they penetrate more deeply into our spirit ('Gemüth') and seem also to maintain themselves longer there."[47]

For Mendelssohn and his friends, Lessing and Nicolai, the theory of mixed sensations was most immediately productive for the analysis of drama and its emotions, namely the Aristotelean catharsis. Their colleague Thomas Abbt, however, soon perceived the implications of the theory for the elegy, a genre that since classical antiquity had lent itself explicitly to the expression of what were now being called mixed sensations: stories of battle told in the safety of the campfire; the celebration of past civic virtue in contrast to present moral decline; the joys of love tinged with the sadness of loss.[48] At the same time, the elegy, having emerged as one of the most fashionable forms of the century, cried out for a satisfactory theoretical interpretation. Abbt's essay on the elegy, which appeared in the *Litteratur-Briefe* in 1762, was occasioned by his review of a volume of Anacreontic love elegies. He begins and ends his comments by attacking that insipid genre. "It is not always possible, without a certain effrontery, to expect the public to listen to an author whining his laments—especially when we are talking about the laments of a lover!"[49] This misconception of the genre, Abbt continues, stems from the fact that most poets have too narrowly limited the range of the elegy. "One might define them [elegies] generally as the sensually perfect description of our mixed sensations."[50] It is their sensual perfection that makes aesthetic objects of them and links them to other poems. But they differ by virtue of their mixed sensations—unlike the ode, for instance, which is the appropriate vehicle for pure sensations of joy. "For the elegiac poet, therefore, there remain only those sensations that are tempered by their opposites: sensations that gradually arise in the soul and not in the storm of violent passion. . . ."[51] Abbt goes on for several pages about the appropriate subjects for elegies. Mixed emotions can be aroused, for instance, by the contemplation of the human condition in general, of a specific society or class, or of a single individual. His discussion of the appropriate circumstances for elegiac sensations reminds us of Schiller's poem: solitude is conducive to the arousal of mixed sensations, as are places like lonely precipices, where the imagining of danger and the consciousness of security are alternately present. But it is above all the mood that produces the elegy: "The soul must be in a state of composure in which neither bitter tears of suffering can be squeezed out nor the deep sigh of fear torn from it nor the rattling sob of melancholy forced from it."[52]

Herder regarded Abbt's psychological theory of literature as such a promising new approach to poetics that he reproduced the entire essay on the elegy in the third volume of his *Fragmente über die neuere Deutsche Litteratur* (1767) under the somewhat misleading title "Von Nachahmung der Lateinischen Elegien," and added a number of annotations in which he qualified certain of Abbt's assertions. Herder is even more explicit than Abbt in distinguishing between the elegy as a literary form and the elegiac as a mode. Maintaining that the pentameter strikes him as forced and harsh in German, he expresses his satisfaction that Abbt does not try to imprison the elegy in any particular metrical form. After all, he says, there can be elegiac odes or elegiac eclogues in a variety of meters.[53] Herder devotes his longest note to disputing the possibility of elegies devoted to the condition of mankind in general, arguing that such speculations tend to move out of the proper realm of the elegy and into the colder regions of philosophical poetry. The personal emotion necessary for the elegy is aroused only by specific cases, not by general reflections.[54] He insists that the proper "residence" of the elegy, in contrast to its more general "territory," is the contemplation of our own condition, and he is especially scornful of the fashionable "Heroides" written in imitation of Ovid. Herder also qualifies Abbt's theory of mixed sensations to a certain extent, insisting that the admixture of fear, anger, terror, and other emotions, must never go so far as to obscure the "gentle feeling" ("das sanfte Gefühl") that is the dominant tone of the elegy.[55]

Herder returned to the notion of mixed sensations in the elegy in his "Torso" *Ueber Thomas Abbts Schriften* (1768). Conceding that mixed sensations—satisfaction and dissatisfaction, love and suffering, joy and sadness—are present initially in human nature, he says that here we have the birth of the elegy: "From the mixture of dejection, which was alleviated by a certain amount of satisfaction—from this mixture the first elegy was wept."[56] However, he cannot agree that just any mixture of sensations provides the source for elegies. For instance, tears of joy are not elegiac, nor tears produced by present misfortune, for the feeling is too immediate and overpowering. Herder concludes that the proper mood for the elegy is sadness diminished by distance. "Not joy and dejection are mixed here; but a gentler dejection is diminished by distance, diminished in such a way that I would prefer to call it a mild sadness."[57]

In a brief passage from his *Kritische Wälder* (1769) Herder summed up his conclusions on the elegy, derived from his reflections on Abbt's essay. Above all, he makes a sharp distinction between form and mode; although he speaks of "the elegy," he is in fact talking about what we would today more precisely call "the elegiac." "Let no one understand under this name that limping monkey which, according to our wise handbooks of poetry, is supposed to be distinguished solely on the basis of its meter; rather, elegy means for me the poetic lamentation ("die klagende Dichtkunst"). Horace's *versus querimoniae* no matter where they are found—in epic or ode, in tragedy or idyll; for any of these genres can become elegiac."[58] And he makes it clear that the elegy is defined not by subject matter but by mode, having its own realm in the human soul, namely "the perceptibility of pain and sadness."[59]

Within two decades the theory of mixed sensations became so familiar that it penetrated into the general reference works. Sulzer's handbook of aesthetics (1771-74) recapitulates the standard information, both historical and normative, in its article on "Elegie." The author discusses the subject matter and the form of the genre, recommending alexandrines for modern languages but noting the gradual naturalization of the elegiac distich in German. And he provides a thumbnail sketch of the history of the genre in classical antiquity. Yet the influence of the age is unmistakable in the statement that "the true character of the elegy seems to consist herein, that the poet is wholly engaged by a gentle emotion of sadness or a gentle joy mixed with much tenderness, and expresses it in an engaging if somewhat chatty manner."[60] All mild passions, he continues, are suitable for the elegy as long as they leave the mind with enough composure to contemplate the subject matter from every aspect. For the elegy is not restricted so precisely to the unity of sensation as is the ode.

We sense clearly how popular the genre and how commonplace the theory of mixed sensations had become by 1775 when we consider J. G. Jacobi's essay "Über die Elegie," which appeared in *Iris*, a literary quarterly he edited. Jacobi's essay, in brief, popularizes and even trivializes the critical discussion of mixed sensations and genres in such a way as to make it easily accessible to the young ladies who constituted the principal audience for his journal. He begins by analyzing the emotions of a young girl who enters a cemetery or a ruined castle in response to an impulse of her heart. "That melancholy, and this smile interrupted by tears, are the content and the expression of the elegy; a favorite genre of poems for our ladies. . . ."[61] Jacobi then asks his readers to imagine a little girl who is called away from a playground where she has been romping happily with her companions and who then returns, several days later, to find the scene empty of the presence and gay voices of her playmates, with no sound but the rustling of the wind in the leaves. "And thus there arises in the poor little abandoned child a mixture of pleasant and unpleasant feelings; the material for a childlike elegy."[62] In the second part of the essay Jacobi provides free prose renditions of passages from Tibullus, Propertius, and Pope to illustrate what he means by poetic elegy. The fact that he does not mention form and that he is content with prose translations of his model elegies implies that formal criteria are unimportant for him. In short, two by now familiar criteria emerge from his essay. The elegy is determined not by subject matter or form but by mode; the mode is produced by mixed sensations.

The chapter on elegy in Eschenburg's widely consulted theory of fine arts (1783), finally, provides a thorough survey of the history and form of the genre in Greek, Roman, and modern literatures. But the theory of mixed sensations has now moved into the first sentence of the first paragraph, which specifically cites Mendelssohn, Abbt, Herder, and Sulzer. "The elegy is a poetic, generally descriptive recitation of mixed sensations, in which pleasant feelings are united with unpleasant ones, and which therefore, in accordance with their nature, are gentle and moderate."[63] Both the nature of the sensations and the manner of their expression distinguishes the elegy from lyric poetry, in which the sensations are unmixed.

It is against this background of familiar aesthetic theory that Schiller's discussion of the elegy in his essay "Über naive und sentimentalische Dichtung" must be read. For Schiller betrays himself as an heir of his age in his tendency to characterize the mode (elegiac) rather than the genre (elegy) and to define the mode by its degree of mixed sensations. The essay falls into three sections of roughly equal length, corresponding to the three installments in which it appeared in *Die Horen* in late 1795 and early 1796. The first section makes the famous typological distinction between "naive" and "sentimental" (that is, "reflective") poets. The second section defines the modes through which sentimental poets can express themselves. The final section amounts to an *apologia pro domo*: Schiller argues that the freedom of the reflective poet more than adequately compensates him for the lack of harmony in his personality; and he generalizes the initial typology to embrace two human types that he calls the realist and the idealist.

It is the second section that is relevant in our context. Naive poets, according to Schiller—he has in mind such figures as Homer, Shakespeare, and Goethe—write out of a sense of unity with nature and the world. The modern poet—and here Schiller also includes the Romans—is no longer at one with nature, for consciousness has interposed itself between him and the world. Unable to accept experience naturally and without mediation, the modern poet *"reflects* on the impression that the objects make upon him."[64] As a result, he is constantly aware of the discrepancy between reality as he experiences it and the ideal as he imagines it. "And the mixed feeling that he arouses will always attest to this double source."[65] It is this state of mixed sensations that accounts for the three principal modes of expression open to the sentimental poet. If the poet, obsessed with the incongruity between the real and the ideal, focuses his attention on the shortcomings of the real world, then he expresses himself satirically. The satire can be either punitive ("strafend") or jesting ("scherzhaft"), but in either case the poet is motivated by the implicit contrast between an imperfect reality and a perfect ideal that he senses. "If the poet opposes nature to art and the ideal to reality in such a way that the representation of the former is preponderant and our pleasure in it becomes the dominant sensation, then I call him *elegiac.*" Like satire, this genre also has two classes. "Either nature and the ideal are an object of grief, if the former is presented as lost and the latter as unattained. Or both are an object of joy in that they are represented as real."[66] In the first case Schiller speaks of the elegy proper, and in the second case of the idyll. (Later in the essay he raises the idyll to full status as one of three principal modes: satire, elegy, idyll.)

Schiller repeatedly stresses the fact that he is talking about modes of sensation rather than poetic kind. "To readers who have a profound understanding of the matter I scarcely need to justify the fact that I am employing the terms satire, elegy, and idyll in a broader sense than is customary. It is by no means my intention to shift the boundaries that previous usage has with good reason established for the satire and elegy as well as the idyll; I am looking exclusively at the mode of sensation ("Empfindungsweise") that prevails in these poetic kinds ("Dichtungsarten"), and it is sufficiently well known

that the mode of sensation does not allow itself to be restricted to the narrow limits of poetic kind."[67] For Schiller as
for Herder, then, the elegiac mode can occur in a variety of
forms. As far as the theory of mixed sensations is concerned,
Schiller had been acquainted with the theory at least since
1779, when he cited Mendelssohn's work in his rejected dissertation, *Philosophie der Physiologie*.

Applying the theory of mixed sensations more specifically
to the anthropological mode of the elegiac, Schiller notes that
"in the elegy, grief may flow only from an enthusiasm
aroused by the ideal."[68] As examples he cites laments over
lost happiness, the vanished Golden Age, the bliss of youth,
and so forth. The subject matter is almost a matter of indifference, for it is not the subject matter in itself but the poet's
response to it that give it poetic dignity. Subject matter becomes suitable for elegiac lament only if it can be enhanced to
a condition at which it represents "moral harmony."[69] "The
elegiac poet seeks nature, but as an idea and in a perfection in
which it has never existed—even if he laments it as something
that was once present and is now lost."[70]

Because of this lofty conception of the elegy, so remote
from the rather trivial notion that had prevailed for so long,
Schiller had reservations regarding a number of contemporary poets whose principal mode is elegiac in his sense. As he
confided to various correspondents, it was one of the most
important purposes of his essay to take to task some of the
more fashionable modern poets for failing to live up to their
noble mission. Rousseau, playing off nature against civilization, is a typical example of the sentimental poet. But Rousseau, Schiller argues, is hampered on the one hand by a tendency toward sentimentalism and on the other by an excessive
intellectual rigor. His poetic works, rather than rising to aesthetic freedom, are either reduced to the expression of passions or else restricted in their grace by conceptual rigor.[71]
Schiller finds similar shortcomings in Haller, Ewald von
Kleist, and Klopstock: in each case, he ascertains, fantasy
tends to replace perception and thought interferes with sensation.

Schiller's approach to the elegy by way of its mode, of course, explains why he does not mention Goethe's "Römische Elegien." (To be sure, he alludes to them without mentioning the title when he discusses the bounds of decency that restrict the naive poet.[72]) For Goethe's poems, according to Schiller's definition, show none of that dissociation of consciousness that characterizes the sentimental modes: the poet is too much at one with his material. If they approach any of Schiller's modes, then it is the idyll and not the elegy.

From Schiller's point of view in late 1794 and early 1795, as he was corresponding with Goethe about the publication of the "Römische Elegien" and working out the plan of his essay, the situation must have looked as follows. Goethe had in one brilliant effort conquered the elegiac distich (ἐλεγεῖον) for German literature, and he himself had worked out a theory of the mode (ἔλεγος) for his general poetic typology. But so far no poetic work adequately exemplified the unification of the two criteria in a modern sentimental model. Goethe's poems were elegiac in form but not in mode; other German poems were elegiac in mode but not in form. It was this act of exemplary unification that Schiller set out to accomplish in the late summer of 1795 when he wrote "Der Spaziergang." His programmatic intent is suggested by the original heading, "Elegie," which in its stark simplicity reminds us of other such normative titles in German classicism as Goethe's "Sonett," "Märchen," or "Novelle." That Schiller had something like a normative model in mind is more than mere guesswork. He spelled out his intentions quite clearly in a letter of November 30, 1795, to Humboldt, which begins by noting that the poem "Das Ideal und das Leben" (originally entitled "Das Reich der Schatten") is nothing but a didactic poem in comparison with the poetic execution of "Der Spaziergang." "I intend to write an *idyll* as here I wrote an elegy. All of my poetic powers are tensing themselves for this effort—to individualize objectively the ideal of beauty and to shape from it an idyll in *my* sense."[73] "In *my* sense"— just as "Der Spaziergang" had been consciously intended as an elegy "in *my* sense."

We can come a bit closer to understanding the achievement of "Der Spaziergang"—specifically, its accommodation of the elegiac mode to an appropriate elegiac form—if we compare it with two other poems from the same period. Schiller had written other "elegies" before "Der Spaziergang." His first published volume of poems contained an "Elegie auf den Tod eines Jünglings" (1781), a typically sentimental funeral elegy in the English manner and strophic form, but not at all "elegiac" in mode. "Die Götter Griechenlands" (1788) is genuinely elegiac in mode though not in its strophic form. There the poet looks back at an idealized classical antiquity from the standpoint of a lifeless, rationalistic modernity, emphasizing the elegiac contrast between past and present with the rhetorical tension between "you" and "we," between "then" and "now":

Da ihr noch die schöne Welt regiertet,
An der Freude leichtem Gängelband
Glücklichere Menschenalter führtet,
Schöne Wesen aus dem Fabelland!
Ach! da euer Wonnedienst noch glänzte,
Wie ganz anders, anders war es da!
Da man deine Tempel noch bekränzte,
Venus Amathusia!

(ll. 1-8)[74]

Similarly, the title of "Das Ideal und das Leben," written only a few months before "Der Spaziergang," suggests the elegiac tension that governs the poem. This tension is brought out skillfully and effectively in the middle section of the poem by a powerful cluster of four pairs of strophes beginning respectively with the words "Wenn" and "Aber": the conditional "if" of reality is relieved each time by an exhortation to seek the ideal:

Wenn ihr in der Menschheit traurger Blöße
Steht vor des Gesetzes Größe, . . .

(ll. 91-92)

Aber flüchtet aus der Sinne Schranken
In die Freiheit der Gedanken, . . .
(ll. 101-102)[75]

In both of these poems the mode is clearly elegiac, inasmuch as nature is lamented as lost and the ideal as still unattained, but neither poem is an elegy in literary kind. In the
first place, neither of the poems is written in elegiac distichs.
But there is a more important and less mechanical criterion:
the presentation of the material is not appropriately elegiac. In
his letter to Humboldt, Schiller had stated that in comparison
with "Der Spaziergang" "Das Ideal und das Leben" is nothing but a didactic poem because of its insufficient poetic
execution. We can try to understand this phrase by looking
more closely at Schiller's criticism of Rousseau, Haller, Kleist,
and Klopstock. In all four cases he reproaches them for excessive abstraction. Rousseau, "goaded at times by passion, at
times by abstraction, rarely or never arrives at the aesthetic
freedom that the poet must assert *vis à vis* his material and
communicate to the reader."[76] Generalizing about the German poets, he says that "they move us through ideas, not
through sensory truth. . . . Involuntarily fantasy intrudes
upon visualization, brain power upon sensation, and one
closes eye and ear in order to sink contemplatively into oneself."[77] Of Klopstock's figures he remarks: "only abstraction
has created them, only abstraction can distinguish among
them. They are good examples for concepts, but not individuals, not living figures."[78] Schiller seems to be reiterating the
view of Herder, who distinguished between elegies and philosophical poems by insisting on the need for a personal element in the true elegy. And it is precisely this personal element that is missing in "Die Götter Griechenlands" and "Das
Ideal und das Leben": the speaker is disembodied; the poems
have neither a clearly defined persona nor an identifiable
locus. In "Der Spaziergang" we have a clear sense of person
and place: we see the poet when he emerges from his house
and when he reaches the mountaintop; we know at every

moment from what vantage point we are looking down at the valley and its spatialized history. The poem is saved from the abstraction of the purely philosophical poem because everything that is thought and said has a direct bearing upon the life and emotions of the poetic persona within the poem. The mode of the two earlier poems is quite close to the "mixed sensations" that govern "Der Spaziergang," but it is never tied to a specific individual and his problematic nature. As a result, both of those poems, "elegiac" though they may be in mode, lack the objectifying individualization necessary to transform them, according to the prescription of Herder and Schiller, from philosophical poems into elegies.

It detracts in no way from the excellence of "Die Götter Griechenlands" and "Das Ideal und das Leben" to say that they are philosophical poems rather than elegies. "Der Spaziergang" is the first poem in which the form of the elegy, which reached its culmination with Goethe's "Römische Elegien," and the elegiac mode, which received its classic formulation in Schiller's essay, are combined into a single exemplary poem. To determine whether or not this single poem became constitutive for an entire subgenre—whether, in other words, "Der Spaziergang" is merely an isolated example or the model for something that may legitimately be called "the classical German elegy"—we now need to look more closely at the works of Schiller's contemporaries.

# 4 · THE GENERIC NORM: THE CLASSICAL GERMAN ELEGY

Schiller himself was not destined to repeat the achievement of "Der Spaziergang." During the years from 1795 to 1799 he composed seven more poems in elegiac distichs—not to mention the scores of satirical epigrams after the fashion of Martial that he and Goethe wrote in 1796 and published under the title "Xenien" in the *Musen-Almanach* for 1797. Yet if we take "Der Spaziergang" as exemplary, not one of the seven poems, however memorable several of them may be, resembles the model in respects other than metrical. In two cases the poems, though "elegiac" in mode, are so short that they suffice only for a quick apodictic statement and not for the kind of meditation that we have come to associate with the elegy. "Die Sänger der Vorwelt" (1795) depends on a genuinely elegiac antithesis between past and present: the poet bemoans the fact that neither the deeds nor the audiences of his own society can inspire poets to works that rival those of the ancients. But the sixteen lines of the poem merely state the problem without developing it meditatively; and the persona of the poet is not sufficiently profiled to engage our interest. The same reservations apply to the magnificent funeral dirge "Nänie" (1799). This gemlike poem is as cold as it is perfect: for its very brevity precludes any meditative leisureliness: we are simply informed, with four mythological examples, that beauty is doomed to perish. No poetic persona to whom this insight might matter is evident in the seven distichs that constitute the poem.

We would have to stretch a point to characterize the other five poems as "elegiac" in Schiller's own sense of the word. "Der Tanz" (1795) has a philosophical theme, but it displays none of the tension between the real and the ideal that Schiller demanded of the elegy. Here a disembodied spectator, identified neither by character nor by location, watches couples moving through the seemingly chaotic paces of a dance; in the second half of the poem he derives the "quiet law" that governs the transformations of the dance—an analogy to life itself. "Der Genius" (1795) sounds like a poetic rendering of the first section of Schiller's essay "Über naive und sentimentalische Dichtung"; but to the extent that the "genius" depicted here is a "naive" poet, still wholly at one with nature although the Golden Age has passed, the poem might more properly be called an idyll than an elegy. "Pompeji und Herkulanum" (1796), a poem inspired by reports of the recently renewed excavations of the two Roman cities, stops after some fifty-six lines of antiquarian description, before any elegiac contrast between past and present emerges. "Die Geschlechter" (1796), a poem often compared to Goethe's verses on the metamorphosis of plants and animals, strikingly anticipates the third of Rilke's *Duineser Elegien*: both poems amount to psychological—indeed, almost psychoanalytical—explanations for the awakening of sexuality and love. But in its pure didacticism the poem lacks all elegiac antithesis. Finally, Schiller himself designated "Das Glück" (1798) as a hymn despite its distichs.[1] Certainly there is little that is elegiac in this paean to Fortuna and to those fortunate mortals who, blessed by the gods, do not need to struggle like ordinary men for their achievements.

In sum, then, the seven poems in elegiac distichs differ in conspicuous respects from the exemplary elegy that Schiller provided in "Der Spaziergang." Notably, they are all much shorter, ranging in length from a mere fourteen lines ("Nänie") to sixty-six lines ("Das Glück"). This brevity has several implications. First, there is little space for the development of any real thought; most of these poems amount to statements rather than meditations. Second, there is little space for the emergence of a narrative persona; as a result, the poems lack the means of linking the general to the specifically individual, as Schiller did in "Der Spaziergang." Moreover, the organization of the poems is less complex; we find in them none of the encapsulation that characterized "Der

Spaziergang." In these poems the speaker is a disembodied voice, as in Schiller's earlier "elegiac" poems in stanzaic form, with no clearly defined persona or locus. All of the poems, of course, are "elegies" in the formal sense. But none of the seven approaches the model of "Der Spaziergang," in which Schiller carefully and consciously adapted the elegiac form to his new theory of the genre. It was left to Goethe to repeat that achievement.

Certainly one of the principal factors underlying the miracle of Weimar culture from 1794 to 1805 was the collaboration and reciprocal stimulation that characterized the friendship between Goethe and Schiller. We have seen one specific example in Schiller's grateful appropriation of the elegiac distich from Goethe's shaping hands. But the process worked both ways. Following his completion of the "Römische Elegien" in 1790, Goethe discarded the form of the elegy, returning to it only once to write "Das Wiedersehen" (1793), an erotic dialogue in elegiac distichs that is quite consistent with the style and manner of the "Römische Elegien." Then, as we have seen, at least three factors rekindled Goethe's interest in the elegy as a literary form: Schiller published the "Römische Elegien" in Die Horen; Schiller provided a theoretical basis for the elegy in his great essay; and Schiller produced a model elegy in the first version of "Der Spaziergang." Almost immediately Goethe returned to the elegy. In May of 1796, he wrote a long poem in elegiac distichs, "Alexis und Dora." And on December 7 of that same year he sent another elegy to Schiller, announcing at the same time his intention to begin "a new book of elegies," which was to express his "longing to make a third trip across the Alps."[2]

Noteworthy as it is, in our context, that the notion of the elegy summoned up in his mind the image of mountains, Goethe did not in fact complete the new book of elegies according to the announced plan. In the various editions of his collected poems from 1800 on, to be sure, Goethe included a section entitled "Elegien II." ("Elegien I" designated the "Römische Elegien.") But of the seven poems that eventually went into that section, most are elegies only in the formal sense of the word, and only one has anything to do with the Alps.[3] We have already noted that the short dialogue "Das Wiedersehen" (1793) resembles the poems in "Römische Elegien," and the same applies to at least two other elegies that Goethe now composed. "Der neue Pausias und sein Blumenmädchen" (1797) is a charming erotic episode narrated in alternating distichs by the poet and his "flowermaid" —an allusion to the circumstance that Christiane Vulpius once worked in a shop making artificial flowers. "Amyntas" (1797) is a symbolic anecdote based on a natural phenomenon Goethe had observed on the way to Switzerland: an apple tree completely strangled by ivy represents the person threatened with destruction by an all-consuming love. The remaining poems are even less "elegiac." In their correspondence Goethe and Schiller consistently referred to the little masterpiece "Alexis und Dora" (1796) as an idyll, and certainly most of the poem, which describes the sudden late-blooming love between a youth and maiden who have grown up in neighboring houses, is characterized by that coincidence of the real and the ideal that Schiller defines as idyllic. The only feature that pushes the poem gently in the direction of the elegiac is its narrative framework: the episode is recollected by Alexis as he sails away from home, plagued by the momentary anxiety that Dora might invite another suitor into her garden during his absence. Yet, in his letters to Schiller, Goethe made it clear that he thought of the poem as an idyll with a faint note of pathos and not as an elegy embracing an idyllic core.[4] The short poem in elegiac distichs entitled "Hermann und Dorothea" (1796) was composed as a dedicatory epistle for Goethe's epic of the same title (1797)—a conventional function of the distich, as we noted earlier. And "Die Metamorphose der Pflanzen" (1798), however revealing it may be in connection with Goethe's thoughts on botany and nature, is an elegy only in the metrical sense of the word. Like "Hermann und Dorothea," it was included in "Elegien II" simply because it was written in distichs.[5] In fact, then, most of the "Elegien II" are not elegies in any non-metrical sense of the word, but epigrammatic poems, didactic poems, and idylls. But the seventh poem that Goethe included among his elegies not only has the Alps as its locus; it is also an exemplary elegy, in form and in mode, according to the model of "Der Spaziergang." As though to underscore the fact, it bore the subheading "Elegie" when it first appeared in Schiller's *Musen-Almanach* for 1799.

If Goethe's first visit to Switzerland in 1775 was a sentimental journey in the spiritual company of Rousseau, and if the second in 1779 was largely a geological expedition under the aegis of Saussure, his third trip, in the fall of 1797, amounted to a much broader experience, thanks to the company of his friend and adviser in affairs of art, Johann Heinrich Meyer. Goethe was fully aware of the different auspices. Gazing at the mountains from Zürich, he reported to Schiller, he recalled the effect that they had produced upon him twenty years earlier. But although the impression as a whole had remained vivid, the parts were blurred. "I felt a remarkable longing to repeat and to amend those experiences. I had become a different person, and therefore the objects also necessarily seemed different to me."[6] This was indeed the case, for on this third trip Goethe was far less preoccupied with his own emotions or with the details of geology. Instead, his interests expanded, as he continued in the same letter to Schiller, to encompass everything from the infertile peaks of the Gotthard to the works of art that Meyer had brought along. After investigating the scientific, geographical, economic, and political circumstances of the Alpine regions, he delved back into their past by means of old chronicles. In short, his attitude toward the mountains during the trip of 1797 was decidedly cultural and meditative, characterized by a mood of detached contemplation.

In the course of this Alpine tour Goethe learned of the death, on September 22, of Christiane Becker, née Neumann, a young actress who had been his particular protégée while he was still acting as director of the Weimar theater.[7] Christiane had enjoyed her greatest triumph in the role of Arthur in Shakespeare's *King John*, and one of her most recent parts had been that of the grace Euphrosyne in Joseph Weigl's operetta

*Das Petermännchen.* "There may be larger talents," Goethe observed shortly after receiving the report of her death, "but for me none that was more endearing. I had long expected news of her death"—she had been suffering from a lung ailment—"and it overtook me in the formless mountains. Lovers have tears in honor of the dead, and poets have rhythms. I hope that I may succeed in writing something in her memory."⁸ This "something" turned out to be the greatest of Goethe's elegies, "Euphrosyne," which he sketched out while still in Switzerland and then completed the following June while visiting Knebel in Jena.

Unlike the "Römische Elegien," a cycle of short poems on different themes and topics, "Euphrosyne" is a sustained composition of one hundred fifty-two lines, based thematically on the putative antithesis between the eternal order of nature and the arbitrary lot of mankind.⁹ The central meditative core is embraced by a framework locating the poetic persona in a landscape. The first-person narrative begins as the weary wanderer is hastening along a mountain path to reach a shepherd's hut in the last light of evening. The valley below and the path itself are obscured although a trace of purple is still visible on the ice-covered peaks of the highest mountains. Suddenly, in a darkened ravine, a rosy cloud appears before the poet's startled eyes and gradually assumes human shape. The poet wonders what goddess or muse is about to reveal herself, but the apparition turns out to be no deity at all.¹⁰ Instead, the shade of the young actress announces itself: "Kennst du mich, Guter, nicht mehr?" (l. 23). From this point on, until the resumption of the framework close to the end, it is her voice we hear. After identifying herself and informing the poet of her demise (ll. 23-34), she shifts to the past tense, recalling the happy days when the poet had coached her in the art of acting (ll. 35-62). She specifically describes the occasion when she rehearsed the scene in *King John* where the child Arthur dies. At this point (ll. 63-96) the narrative voice changes again as Euphrosyne quotes verbatim—"so riefst du"— the words spoken at that time by the poet who, moved by her performance, was stirred to thoughts of death. How impermanent is the fate of man in comparison with the eternal course of Nature!

Alles entsteht und vergeht nach Gesetz; doch über des
Menschen
Leben, dem köstlichen Schatz, herrschet ein schwan-
kendes Los.
(ll. 77-78)

He implored her to live out her young life in full—unlike Shakespeare's Arthur—so that he might witness the ripening of her still unfulfilled talent. Euphrosyne concludes this encapsulated quotation—"Also sprachst du"—with her own reflections on human transcience (ll. 97-119). She has striven to fulfill the poet's hopes, but now that her life and career have been cut short by death, she fears that more impressive talents may blot out the memory of her achievements. Moving gradually back into the present, she ends her speech with an appeal to the poet (ll. 120-40) not to let her descend unsung to the shades of the underworld, for only in poetry can the dead live on:

Laß nicht ungerühmt mich zu den Schatten hinabgehn!
Nur die Muse gewährt einiges Leben dem Tod.

If she has been immortalized in song, she may take her place worthily beside Penelope, Evadne, Antigone, Polyxena, and other "blessed creatures of the tragic art." At this point her voice falters—"Also sprach sie"—and the poet (ll. 141-46) sees Hermes with his staff appear amidst the purple clouds. Then both figures vanish in the swelling mists. When the poet comes to his senses (ll. 147-52), he realizes that he has been on the open precipices all through the night: he sees the rushing torrents beside the slippery path, and he is beset by a sense of grief. But just as his tears begin to flow, he makes out the first flush of dawn on the horizon, and the poem ends with the promise of the new day:

Wehmut reißt durch die Saiten der Brust; die nächtlichen
Tränen
Fließen, und über dem Wald kündet der Morgen sich an.
(ll. 151-52)

Goethe's elegy does not display the same mathematical pre-
cision that we were able to determine in "Der Spaziergang."
(At this point, of course, Goethe was acquainted only with the
unpolished form of "Elegie.") But if we resort again to a diagram we can see that we are dealing with a similarly balanced
structure.[11] Here, of course, the sections are determined not
by an alternation between apostrophe and meditation but by
rhetorical shifts of a different yet equally distinct kind—
notably narrative voice and tense:

| | | | |
|---|---|---|---|
| | 22 ll. | 1-8 | Scenic description |
| | | 9-22 | Mythological vision |
| | 40 ll. | 23-34 | Euphrosyne's announcement (present tense) |
| | | 35-62 | Euphrosyne's recollection (past tense) |
| | 34 ll. | 63-96 | Encapsulated quotation of the poet's words |
| | 44 ll. | 97-119 | Euphrosyne's meditation (past tense) |
| | | 120-140 | Euphrosyne's wish (present tense) |
| | 12 ll. | 141-146 | Mythological vision |
| | | 147-152 | Scenic description |

The diagram enables us to make out a number of features.
First, as in "Der Spaziergang," we find a mirror relationship
between the two parts of the framework. Second, we note the
complex but subtly balanced interplay of tenses in the framework and the meditative core. Finally, we note that the thematic nadir of the poem, the moment of most intense despair,
comes in the middle of the encapsulated quotation when the
poet states that nature proceeds according to immutable laws
whereas man is subject to a vacillating destiny. These lines,
standing in the exact center of the poem (ll. 77-78), constitute
the structural axis around which the entire poem revolves.

Given the thematic contrast between man and nature, it is
fitting that the locus of the poem should be a mountain. We

know from Goethe's essay "Über den Granit" that he regarded mountains as the very fundament of the world, a visual symbol of nature's durability. The elegiac contrast between man's transitoriness and nature's permanence could hardly be brought out more effectively than by having the poet stand on a mountain to encounter the shade of a deceased human being. Within the poem there is no resolution of this elegiac contrast: in fact, the tension is heightened by the fact that the poet's tears in the final distich, signifying his insight into the situation, erupt just at the moment when the sun, in accordance with nature's eternal pattern, begins once more to rise.

Yet the elegy leaves us with no feeling of dejection but with a sense of resolution. We realize, upon putting the text aside, that the poem itself exemplifies the fulfillment of Euphrosyne's wish that she might be immortalized through the means of art: "Nur die Muse gewährt einiges Leben dem Tod." What is viewed as an impossible obstacle *within* the poem is resolved *by means of* the poem. Is this an interior contradiction? Not at all. In the first place, the central passage on the immutable laws of nature and the impermanence of man is not presented as an absolute and irrevocable truth. Contained within the encapsulated quotation, it represents the poet's private view of things—a view, moreover, that he held at some moment in the past but not necessarily still in the present. The whole point of his experience on the mountain is to enlighten him as to the possibility of a resolution through aesthetic means—a resolution that is not quite achieved within the poem (hence the poet's tears in the last distich) but that is attained in the instant the poem is written in fulfillment of Euphrosyne's wish.

Second, we realize that the complicated interplay of temporal levels—the present moment of the framework, the recollected past, the anticipation of the future within the encapsulated quotation—is calculated to blur temporality, to reduce human time to a continuum without past, present, or future. Within the poem, in other words, human time is deprived of its normal successiveness and caused to resemble the eternal time of nature, in which all remains constant. This sense of aesthetic timelessness that is achieved in the course of the poem contrasts sharply with the temporal urgency in which we encounter the poet in the opening lines, where he is rushing along the mountain path. The effect of timelessness and resolution is enhanced, third, by the mythological vision that embraces the meditative core. Euphrosyne is not simply dead; by means of the mythological transition at the beginning and at the end of her speech she is put into the category of such immortals as Hermes and other figures rendered timeless through art. Finally, the very balance of the poem offsets the seeming imbalance discussed within the poem. For this reason the elegy is so carefully organized around the utterance in the middle lines.

On the mountain, then, the poet has been granted a new insight, a privileged experience, that modifies his tragic view of the contrast between man and nature. The mood of despair that thickens from start to finish is counterbalanced by the movement of the sun, which is setting in the opening lines but rising again in the final pentameter. And the description of nature adds to the effect: Goethe does not describe the mountain in any detail. But the few details of the description—the color purple, the cloud, the path, the cliffs, the torrent of water, and the sun—appear in both parts of the framework in such a manner as to enhance the effect of balance. Since Goethe's vision amounts to a personal memory and not, as in Schiller's poem, to the temporalization of an experienced space, the mountain does not function as a point from which the poet looks down upon the scenes below in any literal sense. But its importance is evident in its threefold function. Within the poem it serves as the symbol of nature's permanence, as we have seen. Second, its isolation is necessary to remove the poet from the exigencies of daily life in such a way that he becomes receptive to the epiphany that he witnesses in the apparition of Euphrosyne. Third, its association with the folkloristic belief that the mountain is the abode of spirits—the appropriate place for a mortal to encounter the shade of a loved one who has died but not yet entered the realm of the dead—is necessary to justify the apparition itself.

"Euphrosyne," Goethe's only elegy that is genuinely "elegiac" in Schiller's sense, is so close in organization to "Der Spaziergang" that one might well suspect we are dealing here with another of those amicable rivalries in which the two friends so often engaged during the late nineties (e.g., their epigrams and ballads). Whether by chance or design, they created a model that decisively influenced many poets in following years whenever they attempted to write elegies. Summarizing our findings, we are now in a position to abstract from "Der Spaziergang" and "Euphrosyne" certain common characteristics that I should like to call the generic norm of the classical German elegy. The label seems appropriate because Goethe and Schiller explicitly chose to call these model poems "elegies" and because this model was the only new form of elegy produced during the age of German classicism.

On the basis of the two model poems the classical German elegy would seem to be an extended poem in elegiac distichs, organized as a first-person framework embracing a central meditative core and moving from thematic tension toward resolution. Let us define these criteria in greater detail. The characteristic elegiac tension, a philosophical outgrowth of the traditional mixed sensations, arises from a contrast within the meditative core between two ostensible opposites: the real and the ideal, present and past, freedom and necessity, society and nature, temporality and timelessness—in effect, any duality that obsesses the writer and his times. The elegy is an extended poem because it does not merely state this opposition apodictically: it permits the elegiac tension to emerge fully through meditation. The poetic persona of the framework is introduced initially as still very much enmeshed in the tensions of the poem: when we meet them, Schiller's mountainclimber is still totally dominated by nature and Goethe's poetic "ich" by temporality. But by the time the poetic persona reappears in the concluding part of the framework, it has been elevated through meditation, whose intensity produces a timeless state of entrancement, to a higher level of consciousness at which a resolution is seen as possible: Schiller's poet apprehends the significance of Homer's sun, and Goethe's persona perceives that art can produce an eternity as enduring as the mountain. This moment of revelation or epiphany is symbolized within the poem by a movement toward light: the sun that dominates the final distich in both poems. The growing consciousness of the poetic persona is expressed by its disengagement from the exigencies of daily life and its removal to a location that symbolizes topographically the possibility of detached contemplation. (The aesthetics of the German classical period, as we noted, suggested the mountain as the locus most conducive to the contemplative detachment that characterizes the genre; and we have seen that both Goethe and Schiller had personal reasons for employing the mountain in this function.) The resolution, only anticipated by the persona *within* the poem, is actually accomplished by the delicately balanced organization of the text. The fact that the elegy gets written, in other words, represents the liberation from the tensions and dualities expressed within the poem. Through the act of composition Schiller's poet has escaped the "prison" of contemporary society and Goethe's poet has released Euphrosyne from the constraints of human temporality.

It should be stressed again that we are talking here not about "the elegy," "the elegiac," "the modern elegy" or any other such general category, but only about the genre that we have specifically delimited as "the classical German elegy." Needless to say, the generic norm is understood here not as prescriptive but as descriptive of traits shared—so far, at least—by two representative examples of a given poetic kind. The generic norm, in other words, provides nothing but a useful checklist of criteria that can be used in comparing various works to determine their similarities and differences. Obviously, it is the entire complex of criteria, and no single characteristic, that identifies the genre. As we have repeatedly noted, the elegiac distich by itself is not normative because it is used for so many other poetic kinds, most of which are called "elegies" for purely metrical reasons. The tension of antithesis must be present in the poem, but this tension alone is not constitutive since it characterizes the sonnet as well as the elegy.[12] We cannot have an elegy without a moment of revelation or anagnorisis, but such epiphanies are not limited to the elegy.[13] In fact, the hallucinatory luminous phenomena—called photisms by psychologists—that mark the end of both poems are singled out by William James as a particularly frequent form of sensory automatism accompanying religious conversion.[14] And certainly there are other varieties of poetry involving solitary meditations, on mountains and elsewhere. But when all these characteristics, or at least a significant cluster of them, occur within a single poetic text, then we are dealing with a work that bears a pronounced generic resemblance to the classical German elegy.

It was no doubt inevitable that the new model would be received sympathetically first in the Weimar-Jena circle immediately surrounding Goethe and Schiller. In a certain sense, indeed, the elegy represents the perfect poetic embodiment of the ideals of Weimar classicism—the poetic counterpart of the Bildungsroman. As Emil Ermatinger pointed out, meditative poetry (*Gedankenlyrik*) was the natural response to Kant's philosophical revolution, that separation of self and world that shattered any sense of unity and caused the poet to *reflect* upon his experience rather than to portray it "naively."[15] But this meditative poetry could not become truly "classical" until the meditative core was embraced by a personal framework that put meditation into the service of the *Bildung* that characterized the classicism of Goethe and Schiller. For *Bildung*, in contrast to the erudition prized by earlier generations, implies an ideal of personal cultivation and learning for its own sake. Knowledge and "culture" are valued only to the extent that they contribute to the personal development of the individual. It is this task that the classical German elegy was ideally suited to fulfill since its very structure was conceived in order to demonstrate the anagnorisis achieved by the indi-

vidual through meditation on problems of culture. The point
to be seized upon is this: forms always evolve in response to
the exigencies of the times, and we have noted many sufficient
reasons for the appearance of a genre with the specific characteristics of the classical German elegy in the last decade of the
eighteenth century.

In any case, it is hardly surprising to find imitations of both
"Der Spaziergang" and "Euphrosyne" among the poems of
their talented but wholly unoriginal friend, Karl Ludwig von
Knebel. The situation is not without its ironies. It will be recalled that Goethe was inspired to write his "Römische Elegien" in part by Knebel's prose translation of Propertius.
Knebel, in turn, was so profoundly moved by Goethe's
elegies that he decided "to undertake the difficult task of
elegiac verse in our language," as he put it in the preface to his
distich-translation of Propertius (1798).[16] But the example of
Goethe and Schiller also inspired Knebel to compose a
number of elegies of his own, not to mention scores of epigrams and gnomic verses in elegiac distichs ("Lebensblüthen
in Distichen").[17] Among these eight elegies several are
wholly traditional, as one might reasonably expect from a
student of the classics as familiar with Greek and Latin models
as was Knebel. His elegy on the occasion of Herder's death
("Herders Tod," 1803) is typically threnetic, and his verses on
life's twofold path ("Die Wege des Lebens") are traditionally
gnomic. Yet at least two of Knebel's elegies are unthinkable
without the model of the "twin stars" of Weimar, as he
dubbed his two revered friends.[18]

"Die Wälder" (1799), written as Knebel's response to the
French humiliation of Germany at the congress of Rastatt,
takes as its model "Der Spaziergang," which Knebel presumably knew only in its original version as "Elegie."[19] Knebel's
elegy, to be sure, is much shorter (only 52 lines) and not
nearly so complex in its organization, yet the basic pattern is
clearly evident. As the poem begins, the poet is setting out on
a solitary walk in order to escape the crowded city with its
cares and to recover his soul in communion with nature (ll.
1-6). He briefly recalls (ll. 7-12) the Golden Age when men led

simple happy lives in harmony with nature, undistracted by the pursuit of wealth and ambition and unconstrained by the rules of law and politics:

> Reichthum kannte man nicht, noch der Ehrsucht eiserne
> Schwerter,
> Noch des Gerichtshofs Zwang, noch der Verfolgungen
> Wuth:
> Unter dem eigenen Baum verlebete jeder die Tage,
> Frei, wie die Gegend umher, und wie der Himmel
> beglückt.

Then the poet focuses on the elegiac contrast with the present (ll. 13-28), which displays so little of the order and benefit one would expect from a civilized world:

> In welch andere Zeit hat uns das Schicksal gestoßen!
> Kaum erblick' ich in ihr Ordnung gesitteter Welt.

And he lists the iniquities perpetrated (by the unnamed French) in the name of human rights. Like Schiller, Knebel places the blame on a notion of freedom that has deteriorated into license:

> Freiheit nennt ihr? o ihr, des Lasters gedungene Knechte!
> Wahnsinn und Eitelkeit flimmert von eurem Panier.

At this point (ll. 29-46) Knebel shifts his attention to Germany, for he realizes that servitude can be imposed only on those who are willing to accept it:

> Knechtschaft gebietet man nicht, als dem, der Knechtschaft
> verdienet:
> Welch unwürdiges Loos traf dich, mein mütterlich Land!

The meditative core ends, like Schiller's, with an appeal to his countrymen to liberate themselves from their degrading bondage:

> Reiß der Bande dich los, der seelenschändenden Bande!
> Dränge dich muthig hinan; rette die Ehre der Zeit!

The poet emerges from his trance to find himself once again in the forest (ll. 47-52) where, leaning against the trunk of an ancient oak, he apostrophizes the mountains, which bring him closer to the skies, where a purer air is still preserved:

> Tragt mich näher hinan zu euerem Himmel, ihr Berge!
> Daß ich die reinere Luft athme, der Sümpfe befreit.

Knebel's poem displays all the elements of the generic norm: a personal framework embracing a meditative core; the elegiac tension between past and present; the mountain epiphany. But the imitation remains largely superficial. Neither the locus nor the persona is clearly defined; the contrast between the freedom of the idealized Golden Age and the ignominious servitude of present-day Germany lacks the dialectical tension that lends interest to Schiller's poem; the framework does not really resolve the problem stated in the meditative core, it merely provides an evasion. What we have, in short, is the superficially imitated form of the classical German elegy used as the vehicle for the lament of a former Prussian officer whose dreams for his country, shaped at the court of Frederick the Great, have been sorely disappointed. Yet the poem is of interest because it proves that the generic norm was recognized and imitated at this early date.

Knebel made a second attempt to imitate the generic norm, this time taking Goethe as his model, in a poem entitled "Der Hügel."[20] Again his poem remains as inferior to the model as is the "hill" of his poem to the towering Alpine heights of "Euphrosyne." Again the poet is making his way up the hill to a grove where he has spent many happy hours (ll. 1-20):

> Hier ergehet sich oft im einsamen Irren die Muse,
> Von dem begleitenden Chor ihrer Gesänge geschützt.
> Dahin leit' ich den Fuß. Willkommen, ihr traulichen Orte!
> Und du, sicherer Hain! meinem Verlangen getreu.

This time, however, the poet is in a melancholy mood because, as he grows older, his friends have died and the pleasures of youth no longer gratify him. In the eerie stillness of the hilltop grove he observes a resplendent glitter moving toward him:

Wie still athmet der Hain! Wie leise wallen die Winde!
Welch ein schimmernder Glanz drängt sich vom Hügel
auf mich!

Gradually the rustling of the foliage condenses into a human
voice, and the long central section of the poem (ll. 21-70)
turns out to be an encapsulated monologue by the poet's deceased brother, who committed suicide some years earlier (in
1790) and now returns to bring encouragement to his deso-
lated sibling. First the brother explains his seemingly mysteri-
ous presence. According to his vague pantheism, all being is
inhabited by a single Spirit:

Wisse: das Ganze bewohnt Ein Geist: die innere Flamme
Treibet zu neuer Gestalt immer die Wesen hervor:
Alles belebet sich stets; doch in unterschiedlichem Maße
Hat sich der weckende Hauch durch die Naturen ver-
theilt. . . .

The force that inspirits trees, plants, animals, and human beings does not disappear upon death: the souls of the deceased
seek new homes—in the ether, the oak, the stream. Now,
summoned by his brother's laments, he has returned to serve
his brother with words of wisdom. Don't curse destiny! Venerate the humanity within yourself! Don't strive for ignoble
glory and vain activity! Seek wealth within your own breast!
Love your family and friends! After producing this wisdom
the voice falls silent. In the concluding framework (ll. 71-84)
Knebel beseeches his brother to stay close, but he hears only
the sound of the brook nearby and the stirring of the foliage.
Unaccountably it has become night, and as the distraught
poet departs from the sacred place, he makes out, at the top of
a nearby tree, a blueish light like the St. Elmo's fire sometimes
seen around shipmasts during a storm:

Aber wie nach Gewittern sich zeigt an Spitzen der Masten,
Oder an Thürmen vielleicht, hohes aufglimmendes
Licht:
Bläulich steigt es empor, und steht; ein Wunder den
Menschen,

> Und ein bedeutender Wink ihres noch künft'gen
> Geschicks!
> Also sah ich am Gipfel des Baums die steigende Flamme,
> Als ich, verwirrt in der Nacht, wich von dem heiligen
> Ort.

At this point we realize that the entire apparition is based on an unusual natural phenomenon: a case of corposant that Knebel no doubt actually witnessed and used as the basis for his poem. Yet the labored rationalization of the apparition seems entirely out of proportion with the platitudes brought forth by the brother's spirit—a sort of homespun trivialization of the beliefs of classical humanism. Despite the triviality of the use to which it is put, however, the pattern is again unmistakable: the lonely wanderer on the hillside encounters the shade of someone who was dear to him; the apparition is produced by an effect of nature; the reflective core consists of the meditations of the shade.

Knebel's slavish imitation of the generic norm as manifested in "Der Spaziergang" and "Euphrosyne" is ample evidence of the fact that the form was recognized and copied almost immediately—that its suitability for the needs of German classicism was quickly appreciated. But Knebel's poems are typically epigonal efforts because the significance and dignity of their subject matter in no way justifies the expectations of the genre. For an imaginative use of the generic norm, an appropriation so bold that it chafes against the restrictions of the norm from the start, we must look away from the circle of intimates in Weimar and Jena to an ambitious younger admirer of Goethe and Schiller.

On August 22, 1797, while stopping in Frankfurt on his way to Switzerland, Goethe received a visit from Friedrich Hölderlin, which he reported the following day in a letter to Schiller. The twenty-seven-year-old poet, whom Goethe had already met casually, struck him as being somewhat depressed and sickly—small wonder in view of the tensions in the Gontard household, where Hölderlin was acting as tutor.

But intellectually he reminded Goethe of Schiller: "He approached various matters in a manner that betrayed your school."[21] This notion of a spiritual kinship between the two Swabians would hardly have come as a surprise to either of them. Only two months earlier Hölderlin had submitted two poems to Schiller for publication in his *Musen-Almanach*—"Der Wanderer" and "An den Aether"—but Schiller had promptly forwarded them to Goethe, saying that he was unable to formulate "a pure judgment" about them.[22] "Frankly," he confided, "I found in these poems much of my own former self, and it is not the first time that the author reminded me of myself. He has a violent subjectivity, which is combined with a certain philosophical spirit and profundity."[23] A year later, in one of his most anguished letters, Hölderlin admitted to Schiller that he was "sometimes engaged in a secret battle with your genius in order to preserve my freedom against it, and the fear of being dominated wholly by you has often prevented me from approaching you with an untroubled spirit."[24]

The story of Hölderlin's development as a poet and thinker is in no small measure the record of his struggle to come to grips with Schiller. The various "hymns" he wrote during his student years at Tübingen—to immortality, to freedom, to humanity, to beauty, to the muse and various "geniuses"—clearly remind us in their mood as well as their strophic form of such poems by Schiller as "Die Götter Griechenlands." Schiller's ambivalent attitude toward Hölderlin, whom he encouraged and yet kept warily at a distance, can be attributed to a generational misunderstanding. The younger poet represented, in Schiller's eyes, a stage of his own development, a "violent subjectivity" that he had managed to overcome by means of supreme personal discipline.

When we read Schiller's analysis of the sentimental poet, riven by the conflict between the real and the ideal, it is almost as though Schiller had had the anguished Hölderlin in mind—a tormented soul who was long unable to attain the aesthetic freedom that, in Schiller's view, liberated the sentimental poet from his predicament and who was ultimately driven into madness by the tensions that wracked his spirit. Unlike either Goethe or Schiller, Hölderlin was by disposition a fundamentally elegiac poet—one, that is, who lived in a constant awareness of the chasm between present reality and a vanished ideal. This elegiac tone is evident in most of his poems, including those employing non-elegiac forms. The ode "Sonnenuntergang," for instance, depicts the plaintive mood of the poet whose rhapsodic intoxication by the sounds of Apollo is qualified by the knowledge that the *deus absconditus* has now departed this world to dwell among "pious peoples" who still venerate him:

Wo bist du? trunken dämmert die Seele mir
    Von aller deiner Wonne; denn eben ists,
        Daß ich gelauscht, wie, goldner Töne
            Voll, der entzückende Sonnenjüngling

Sein Abendlied auf himmlischer Leier spielt';
    Es tönten rings die Wälder und Hügel nach.
        Doch fern ist er zu frommen Völkern,
            Die ihn noch ehren, hinweggegangen.[25]

Along with his Tübingen classmates, Hegel and Schelling, Hölderlin shared that Swabian proclivity for philosophical speculation that also characterized Schiller. If his poems sometimes suffer from an excessive burden of thought, it is precisely the "philosophical profundity" noted by Schiller that informs his greatest works. This tendency toward abstraction, especially in a young poet, bothered Goethe. When he read the two poems that Schiller had sent along, he observed that the natural scenes were "painted neither through sensory nor through inner visualization."[26] This weakness is exemplified by "Der Wanderer." The poem begins with the poet standing alone in the African desert and, in the second strophe, in polar wastes. But neither landscape is described: instead, as Goethe astutely remarked, they are characterized by what is not there: no shady forests, no melodic brooks, no herds at babbling wells, no sun-filled groves. "The poet has a serene view of nature," Goethe concluded, "with which he seems to be acquainted only through tradition."[27] In his subsequent interview with Hölderlin, Goethe advised the younger man to write shorter poems and to choose subjects with greater human interest.

Goethe's assessment, though predictable, was not entirely fair. In fact, Hölderlin had a profound and intimate love of nature, especially the landscape of his native Swabia, which he knew at first hand. It was his method of depiction that bothered Goethe. Although nature and landscape play an important role in Hölderlin's poetry, the world is never laid out and exposed as systematically as in Goethe's and Schiller's poems. Instead it becomes curiously interiorized. The poetry is dense with images, but for that very reason perhaps the parts rarely coalesce into an organized landscape.[28] This tendency is clearly evident in the six major elegies Hölderlin composed from the fall of 1799 to the spring of 1801: "Menons Klagen um Diotima" (and its first version, entitled simply "Elegie"), "Der Wanderer" (based on a preliminary version of 1797), "Der Gang aufs Land," "Stuttgart," "Brot und Wein," and "Heimkunft."[29] All these poems amount to a celebration of nature, a fact that emerges with particular vividness if we consider as a group the four Swabian elegies, which display a remarkably similar pattern: in each case the speaker is a wanderer, who pays homage to the loveliness of the Swabian countryside, always observed from an elevation. In both versions of "Der Wanderer" the poetic persona returns from the African deserts and arctic wastes to take up a position on a hillside from which he can overlook the "blessed valley of the Rhine" and recall the sights and scenes of his childhood. In "Stuttgart" the poet makes a journey of the imagination to his hometown of Lauffen am Neckar, where he greets his friend Siegfried Schmid, whom he escorts back through the autumn landscape to Stuttgart, which is depicted as the center toward which the youths of Swabia descend from the surrounding hills and mountains:

> Groß ist das Werden umher. Dort von den äußersten
> Bergen
> Stammen der Jünglinge viel, steigen die Hügel herab.
> (Str. 4)

"Heimkunft," as the title suggests, portrays Hölderlin's own return from the Alps of Switzerland to the "land of my birth."[30] And even "Der Gang aufs Land," though fragmentary, betrays the same basic pattern: together with his friend Landauer, the poet walks up into the hills surrounding Stuttgart to celebrate the consecration of a new country inn, which is being built on a spot that affords a spectacular view of the surrounding countryside:

> Nämlich droben zu weihn bei guter Rede den Boden,
> Wo den Gästen das Haus baut der verständige Wirt;
> Daß sie kosten und schaun das Schönste, die Fülle des
> Landes,
> Daß, wie das Herz es wünscht, offen, dem Geiste gemäß
> Mahl und Tanz und Gesang und Stuttgarts Freude gekrönt
> sei,
> Deshalb wollen wir heut wünschend den Hügel hinauf.
> (Str. 2)

These four lesser elegies display the pattern—a wanderer ascending a hill to contemplate the landscape—that occurs with interesting variations in Hölderlin's two greatest elegies, "Menons Klagen um Diotima" and "Brot und Wein." "Menons Klagen," if we discount the original version of "Der Wanderer" (1797), is the earliest of Hölderlin's elegies. The poem deserves particular attention because of its normative value: the first version, written in the fall of 1799, was called simply "Elegie." Now, if we stop to ask what precedents Hölderlin would have had in mind, in 1799, for his understanding of the genre, the answer suggests itself immediately: Schiller and Goethe. The rare occasions when Hölderlin speaks specifically of the elegy as a genre make it clear that his conception is quite close to Schiller's. A letter he wrote to his friend Neuffer on July 3, 1799—that is, only a few weeks be-

fore he began writing "Elegie" and the other major elegies—
is particularly noteworthy. It begins by reasserting the high
degree of consciousness with which Hölderlin approached his
writing: "I examine the feeling that leads me to this or that, to
satisfy myself that the form I have chosen does not contradict
the ideal and, especially, the material that it treats."[31] As an
example Hölderlin discusses the elegy, which he regards as a
subsidiary form of the tragic since both deal primarily with
the ideal. The principal difference is that the elegy treats such
"sentimental" material as love and that it does not rigorously
exclude what Hölderlin calls "the fortuitous" ("das Akziden-
telle"). As soon as we realize that, by "the fortuitous," Hölderlin means exactly what Schiller understands under "the
real," we see that we are dealing with a sentimental form that
contrasts the real and the ideal with primary emphasis on the
latter—a definition clearly based on Schiller's essays and not
on traditional theories of the elegy of mixed sensation.

It is more than a *bon mot* to suggest that "Menons Klagen"
resembles "Euphrosyne" as it might have been written by
Schiller. Although Hölderlin's vision of the elegy was qualified primarily by the theory of his mentor, Schiller, the
example of Goethe's poem was quite fresh in Hölderlin's
mind as he wrote, for "Euphrosyne" had recently appeared as
the first item in Schiller's *Musen-Almanach für das Jahr 1799*,
which also included two poems by Hölderlin. More specifically, "Menons Klagen" uses the apparition of a deceased girl
as the occasion for a philosophical discourse after the fashion
of Schiller.

The "Diotima" of Hölderlin's title was, in real life, Susette
Gontard, the wife of the Frankfurt banker in whose home
Hölderlin was the resident tutor from the end of 1795 until
the fall of 1798. Susette was not so much the model as, rather,
the embodiment of the feminine ideal that Hölderlin associated with the name borrowed from Plato: in many poems and
especially in his novel *Hyperion* he celebrated the figure of the
woman who awakens in man, through the power of love, a
sense of eternal being. Susette did not die until 1802; in fact,
even after Gontard's suspicions drove Hölderlin away, he and

Susette continued to correspond and to see each other occasionally during the very months while he was writing his
elegy. It was only poetically, therefore, that she was portrayed
as being dead—unlike Christiane Becker-Neumann. In Hölderlin's poem, moreover, there is no trace of biographical circumstances, as in Goethe's elegy. In fact, in the earlier version
of the poem ("Elegie") Diotima's name is mentioned neither
in the title nor in the text; and it was inserted only a single
time in the final version.[32]

The elegy—and for the present I am speaking of the final
version—consists of 130 lines divided into nine strophes of
roughly equal length: 14 lines each except for strophe 5 (12
lines), strophe 7 (12 lines), and stophe 9 (22 lines). Strophe 1
exposes us to the poet's elemental grief: we are not at first told
why, but we see him wandering disconsolately through the
world, like a wounded animal, restlessly seeking a tranquillity
that he never finds. His total enmeshment in physical reality,
his inability to achieve the distance necessary for meditation,
is indicated by the same device Schiller used at the beginning
of "Der Spaziergang"—violent assault by sensory images:

Nicht die Wärme des Lichts, und nicht die Kühle der Nacht
hilft,
Und in Wogen des Stroms taucht es die Wunden
umsonst.
Und wie ihm vergebens die Erd ihr fröhliches Heilkraut
Reicht, und das gärende Blut keiner der Zephyre stillt, . . .

The second strophe, which begins with an address to the gods
of death, hints at the reason for his grief: a profound personal
loss. Yet toward the end of the strophe the poet apostrophizes
his own soul which, despite the implacability of death, feels a
sudden sensation of bliss:

und lächeln muß ich und staunen,
Wie so selig doch auch mitten im Leide mir ist.

This shift of mood anticipates the third strophe, which constitutes an extended address to the "images of a brighter time":

the last line, finally, cites the name of Diotima, the source and symbol of all his past bliss. The fourth strophe evokes the specific happiness of the days when he and Diotima strolled through the world, as content as "affectionate swans." But this brief moment of recollected bliss gives way, in the last lines, to a sense of meaninglessness as the poet, returning to the present, realizes that he has lost Diotima, the "eye" through which he had viewed the world. The fifth strophe expresses the poet's utter despair: he feels that his sinews are lamed by a curse ("es lähmet ein Fluch mir / Darum die Sehnen"), and the skies weigh down upon him like prison walls ("wie Gefängniswände, der Himmel / Eine beugende Last über dem Haupte mir hängt!"). In his present despondency even the plants of the fields and the singing birds bring him no tranquillity, for they merely remind him of all he has lost. The sixth strophe begins in a more reflective mood. The poet wonders if there are no prayers that can bring back his youth, if there is no path leading back into the past:

Sonst mir anders bekannt! o Jugend, und bringen Gebete
Dich nicht wieder, dich nie? führet kein Pfad mich
zurück?

Will he be like those godless feasters who fell into a deep sleep that will last until "the power of a miracle" enables them to walk upon the earth again? This faint hope of a miracle prepares the way for the seventh strophe, in which the apparition of Diotima appears, speaking of "higher things." In the eighth strophe the poet realizes that Diotima, whom he calls "the Athenian," does still "blossom and repose amongst the roses of the year"—that joy is immortal if only one has the sense to apprehend it. The last strophe, finally, brings "the singer's prayer" and his decision to continue living. For he has understood at last that it is his mission to proclaim an eternal realm of love and beauty that may be shared by all who enter it through an act of the imagination—a realm where poetry becomes truth, where spring is eternal, and where the soul is reborn to a new and higher existence:

Wo die Gesänge wahr, und länger die Frühlinge schön sind,
Und von neuem ein Jahr unserer Seele beginnt.

The disposition of the strophes, which is startlingly close to
the pattern of "Euphrosyne," shows that we are dealing once
again with the typical encapsulated structure of the classical
German elegy: the poetic persona, initially obsessed by his
own grief, is led through the process of meditation to a higher
level of consciousness at which the seeming disparity between
the real and the ideal, between temporality and timelessness,
is resolved by the intense light of illumination represented by
Diotima:

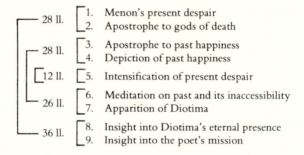

|  |  |  |
|---|---|---|
| 28 ll. | 1. | Menon's present despair |
|  | 2. | Apostrophe to gods of death |
| 28 ll. | 3. | Apostrophe to past happiness |
|  | 4. | Depiction of past happiness |
| 12 ll. | 5. | Intensification of present despair |
| 26 ll. | 6. | Meditation on past and its inaccessibility |
|  | 7. | Apparition of Diotima |
| 36 ll. | 8. | Insight into Diotima's eternal presence |
|  | 9. | Insight into the poet's mission |

This scheme is somewhat oversimplified for the sake of comparison with the generic norm. In fact, the transitions between the parts begin *within* the strophes and not between
them. But we will postpone further discussion of that point
until we take up Hölderlin's theory of poetry.

On the conceptual level "Menons Klagen" is an elegiac
meditation on the relationship between a lost past and a meaningless present; but on another level it is also a *sacre du printemps*, for its imagery recites a myth of annual regeneration.[33]
Throughout the poem, from the first strophe to the last, we
see signs of an awakening nature: the air becomes warm and
fragrant; the plants begin to grow and the birds to sing; the
repeated use of such words as *blühen* and *grünen* hints at processes going on in the earth. Particularly conspicuous in this
context are images of fluidity, which suggest the thawing of
ice, the flowing of waters, the rising of sap. These images of

vernal nature are counterposed against an entirely different set
of images that designate the poet: images of rigidity. Thus in
the second strophe the gods of death "hold fast the van-
quished man" ("und fest habt den bezwungenen Mann");
they compel him to live "in constraint" ("im furchtsamen
Banne"), where he dreams "in an iron sleep" ("im eisernen
Schlaf"). In the fifth strophe the poet's limbs are "lamed" by
a curse; he sits "unfeeling" ("fühllos") and "mute" ("stumm");
his very tears are "cold"; the sun is "cold and infertile"; and
the skies weigh upon him like the walls of a prison. These few
examples—there are many others—reveal that in the imagery
of the poem a struggle is going on between freedom and constraint, between spring and winter—in nature as well as man.
It is only in the last lines that the two tensions are resolved in
the bold genitive metaphor that combines the human and the
natural into the synthesizing harmony of "a year of our soul"
("ein Jahr unserer Seele"). In other words, the thematic
resolution—the poet's recognition of Diotima's message of
love—releases him from the rigid constraints that have hampered him, enabling him to undergo spiritually the same rejuvenation that nature celebrates in its annual rite of spring.
The images tell us what the conceptual vocabulary of the
poem does not spell out: that the poet's despair actually stems
from his alienation from nature. We see this, for instance, in
the sequence of animal images used from the first strophe to
the last. When he was with Diotima he felt wholly at one with
nature; they were like "affectionate swans." But in his isolation from her he is like a wounded animal ("das getroffene
Wild"), harassed and without peace. It is only at the end that
"the bleeding pinions" ("die blutenden Fittige") are healed.
Menon's relationship to Diotima, in other words, is the
spiritual odometer measuring his movement out of his youthful harmony with nature through a period of despairing
alienation back into the vision of a new unity.

This vision of humanization is one of Hölderlin's most
compelling themes. Close to the beginning of his novel
*Hyperion*, the hero writes to his friend Bellarmin: "Like a
spirit that finds no peace on the Acheron, I return to the de-

serted regions of my life. Everything ages and is rejuvenated. Why are we excluded from the lovely cycle of nature? Or does it apply to us also?"[34] Expanding that thought in a fragmentary introduction to his novel, Hölderlin outlined a three-stage sequence progressing from a naive harmony with nature through alienation to a new and higher unity.[35] Human existence, he writes, has two poles: a "condition of highest simplicity" ("Zustand der höchsten Einfalt"), in which man is unconsciously at one with nature; and a "condition of highest culture" ("Zustand der höchsten Bildung"), where he again achieves this unity through the exercise of consciousness. At these extremes man is at the heart of nature, its center. But during the interval when he is moving from the state of unconscious harmony to conscious unity, he follows what Hölderlin calls "the eccentric course" ("die exzentrische Bahn"). This is precisely the process that we can observe in "Menons Klagen." In his youth, he and Diotima enjoyed a "condition of highest simplicity"; after her death he suffers the alienation of the "eccentric course" until, finally, a moment of anagnorisis enables him to perceive the "condition of highest culture." As presented in the poem, of course, the stages come in a different sequence to suit the demands of the elegiac structure: we first meet Menon during his period of alienation; his recollection of the condition of highest simplicity is interrupted by another violent attack of alienation, amounting to anomie (strophe 5). It is only when he realizes in his epiphany (strophe 6 and 7) that he cannot go back to his lost youth but must press forward to a higher stage of consciousness that the resolution becomes possible.

This conception of life as a movement away from the center of nature and then back again bestows particular significance upon the image of the "path" that runs through Hölderlin's works.[36] In particular, this path represents the appropriate locus for the "wanderer" who turns up as the poetic persona in all his elegies. If we look again at "Menons Klagen," we see that the entire poem is unified by the motif of the path and associated images of movement, as Menon wanders through the three stages of his life and consciousness. In the opening distich the poet's despair is suggested by the fact that, in his search, he has tried every path in vain:

Täglich geh ich heraus, und such ein Anderes immer,
Habe längst sie befragt, alle die Pfade des Lands; . . .

The remainder of the strophe develops this image of the aimless wandering of the spirit ("hinauf irret der Geist und hinab") in the analogy of the wounded animal, "fleeing" and "driven" through the forests. The first strophe, whose restless verbs exemplify the "eccentric course," stands in sharp contrast to the peacefulness of the "condition of highest simplicity" represented in strophes 3 and 4. The third, an apostrophe, consists almost wholly of substantives: the poet speaks of "silent paths of the grove, witnesses of heavenly bliss." Temporality that "rages" past is set in opposition to the timeless tranquillity of the blissful lovers:

so tost droben vorüber die Zeit
Über sterblichem Haupt, doch nicht vor seligen Augen,
Und den Liebenden ist anderes Leben geschenkt.

The verbs that describe the movement of the lovers in strophe 4 are all calm: *ruhen, wallen, wandeln*. It is only at the end of the strophe, when the poet recalls his loss, that the "eccentric" verb *irren* ("to go astray") appears.

In the first four strophes, then, the pattern is established. The youthful "condition of highest simplicity" is characterized by paths where the lovers stroll in peace and harmony with nature; the "eccentric course" is described as aimless wandering through a pathless and hostile nature. It is perfectly consistent for the poet to wonder, at the beginning of the sixth strophe, if there is no path that can lead him back ("führet kein Pfad mich zurück?"). He has not yet realized that human development must lead forward to a higher stage of consciousness, not back to the innocence of lost youth. The seventh strophe begins with a curiously inverted image: the poet recalls Diotima's death, a "parting of the way": it is not said, however, that Diotima ascended to a higher level; rather, the poet "sank" from the heights of their previous harmony:

> Aber o du, die schon am Scheidewege mir damals,
> Da ich versank vor dir, tröstend ein Schöneres wies, . . .

He begins to realize that he has been seeking her in the wrong place ("in der Irre") and that, without the proper attitude of mind, the paths of the earth remain "lifeless" ("matt"):

> Denn so lange, so lang auf matten Pfaden der Erde
> Hab ich, deiner gewohnt, dich in der Irre gesucht, . . .

In truth, as he sees in strophe 8, Diotima still walks as before; the word used to describe her gait is *wandeln* ("stillherwandelnd"), which occurs twice elsewhere in the poem to designate the movement of the blessed—in the condition either of highest simplicity or of highest culture. The last strophe introduces for the first time the image of the mountain—but it is a wholly interiorized mountain toward which the poet has been moving. The state of youthful simplicity is described as the time when the poet stood with Diotima "on the sunny heights" ("auf sonniger Höhe"). In his "eccentric course" he has fallen away from those heights. It is appropriate, therefore, that the attitude of highest culture is to be found on the "silvery mountains of Apollo" ("silbernen Bergen Apollons"), where dazzling radiance is combined with the sublime perspective of great height. Once again, unity with nature and highest reflective consciousness are sought on mountains:

> Großes zu finden, ist viel, ist viel noch übrig, und wer so
> Liebe, gehet, er muß, gehet zu Göttern die Bahn.

At the end of the poem the poet is still condemned to an earthly existence: it is his mission to remain below and proclaim the existence of the higher state. He cannot yet attain the mountains of Apollo, "where the eagles, the constellations, the messengers of the Father, the muses are, whence heroes and lovers come," for that is the prerogative of those who have already achieved immortality. But through an act of the imagination he can achieve that mountain view, that sense of unity and detached reflection, even while still on earth. As a result, when the land begins to thaw and the gardens to blossom, he too is able to rejoice, for his anagnorisis has lifted his soul to the level at which it reflects nature in the eternal cycle of rejuvenation.

We see, then, that "Menons Klagen," like "Euphrosyne" and "Der Spaziergang," is also built around a walk. But it is an interiorized and symbolic walk that leads the poet from the paths of youth through the labyrinthine confusions of the "eccentric" course up to the peaks of consciousness, as he proceeds from the darkness of despair to the radiance of anagnorisis. Hölderlin's vision of individual development from an initial state of simple harmony through alienation to a higher unity closely parallels Schiller's theory of history as set forth in "Der Spaziergang" and elsewhere. In fact, the philosophy of history as a triadic rhythm, which is as old as the Greeks and which underlies various contemporary views of history (e.g., Christianity and Marxism), was quite common among thinkers of the later eighteenth century.[37] But Hölderlin is remarkable to the extent that he attempted to discover a means of translating this view of history with absolute consistency into poetic form. His study of the Greek classics led him to believe, as he wrote in the notes to his translation of *Oedipus Rex*, that there is a "calculable law" of poetic effects[38]—a law he set out to demonstrate through his theory of "tonal modulation."[39] It is unnecessary for our purposes to go into all the complexities of his controversial theory, but a few words should suffice to adumbrate the main points.

According to Hölderlin, each of the three stages of human development—whether of the individual or of the society—has its own appropriate mode of experience. The stage of simple harmony, which he calls "naive," is characterized by pure sensation ("Empfindung"). The "eccentric course," variously labeled as "energetic" ("energisch") or "heroic," is characterized by passion or profound emotion ("Leidenschaft"). The highest level of consciousness, which Hölderlin calls "ideal," is characterized by the power of imagination ("Phantasie"). Now a simpler thinker might possibly expect these three modes of experience to precipitate themselves in three basic poetic genres: lyric, epic, and tragic. But Hölderlin's mind works according to a subtler dialectic. The underlying disposition of an individual, or a nation, tends to express itself by means of its "opposite." In the sequence naive-heroic-ideal-naive-heroic-ideal-etc., which recurs according to an inevitable cycle determined (as we have already seen) by psychology and history, the "opposite" is always two steps further along the scale than its basic disposition. A "naive" disposition strives for an "ideal" manner, a "heroic" one produces a "naive" effect, and so forth. In a letter to his friend Boehlendorff, Hölderlin tried to clarify his meaning by reference to the Greeks.[40] Nothing is more difficult, he says, than to utilize our inherent national disposition. Thus the Greeks—and Hölderlin reached this startling conclusion seventy years before Nietzsche in *Die Geburt der Tragödie*—were by nature inclined to a "sacred pathos" ("heiliges Pathos"—that is, they were heroic by disposition); but they excelled in "Junonian sobriety" ("Junonische Nüchternheit"—that is, naive sensation) because they had to work to achieve an effect so alien to their basic disposition. By analogy, every successful poem is, according to Hölderlin's literal understanding of the term, a "metaphor" because it translates its meaning, its governing impulse (which Hölderlin calls its "Grundton") into an objective correlative that expresses a totally different mood (which he calls its "Kunstcharacter").

Every poem begins with a tension between its basic tone ("Grundton") and its more conspicuous artistic effect ("Kunstcharakter"). In order to resolve this tension the poet must take his poem through a series of "tonal modulations" consisting typically of seven stages. In his essay on "Wechsel der Töne" Hölderlin provides elaborate charts to illustrate the possibilities of modulation. Disregarding the subtleties of the theory, let us emphasize the fact that each strophe must modulate in such a manner that its "basic tone" begins to emerge even while the initial "artistic effect" still predominates, and this "basic tone" then becomes the dominant "artistic effect" of the following strophe, which has in turn a new "basic tone." For instance, a "tragic" poem—that is, one generated by a basic impulse of ideal imagination—would instinctively go to the opposite extreme of heroic passion in order to find the adequate artistic effect. (Accordingly, the reader's initial reaction to the poem would be heroic.) But even during the first strophe the basic impulse would tend to assert itself, becoming dominant and providing the artistic effect for the second strophe. After the third modulation the poem reaches a turning-point ("Katastrophe"), following which the order is reversed in such a manner that the artistic effect now determines the basic mood of the following strophe. By the time the full sequence of seven modulations has been carried through, the resolution of the initial tension has been achieved in Hölderlin's sense, as in the following model:

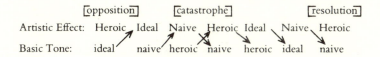

Not many of Hölderlin's poems perfectly fit the ideal scheme of seven modulations. The model sequence of modulations outlined above is the basic elegiac sequence since, for Hölderlin, the elegy is a form of the tragic mode. Therefore, it accurately describes the tonal modulations in "Menons Klagen" if we regard strophes 1 and 2 and strophes 6 and 7 as one stage each. Yet even if it cannot be clearly determined in the case of most poems which sequence of modulations is in effect, there are at least three compelling reasons why an acquaintance with the theory of tonal modulation is necessary for a full appreciation of Hölderlin's poetry. First, it is only through the theory that we can evaluate Hölderlin's magnificent enterprise of converting a philosophy of history into a theory of poetry. This authorial intention might not be particularly relevant for some of Hölderlin's poems, but it assumes a particular significance in his elegies since the elegy is by tradition a meditative poem frequently focusing specifically on the philosophy of history. Second, it forces us to acknowledge how systematically and consciously Hölderlin worked on the realization of his poetry: we meet him in a capacity of poet as maker to a degree virtually unmatched until the twentieth century. Finally, it highlights the fact that for Hölderlin the essence of poetry lay in the interplay of moods and sensations—not in maintaining a single consistent tone. More specifically, the theory helps us to understand the changes that Hölderlin made when he revised his original "Elegie" into the final version of "Menons Klagen um Diotima."

When we turn to "Elegie" after an analysis of "Menons Klagen," we note first of all that the elegiac structure stands out in much sharper relief here than in the revision. The poem has fewer lines, and it is divided into six, rather than nine, strophes in such a way that the breaks correspond quite precisely to the mood of the strophes:

|          |          |         |                     |
|----------|----------|---------|---------------------|
| 22 ll.   | 1-12     |         | Present despair     |
|          | 13-22    |         |                     |
| 28 ll.   | 23-50    |         | Past bliss          |
| 22 ll.   | 51-72    |         | Present despair     |
| 24 ll.   | 73-96    |         | Diotima's apparition |
| 20 ll.   | 97-116   |         | Poet's mission      |

In this version, moreover, the nadir of despair ("und lähmet ein Fluch nicht / Mir die Sehnen, und wirft, wo ich beginne, mich weg?") comes in the exact middle of the poem (ll. 57-58) and not slightly off-center. This clear disposition of the parts, which is close to the elegiac structure of "Der Spaziergang" and "Euphrosyne," is intentionally effaced in the revised version of the poem. Since according to the theory of tonal modulation no strophe should be dominated exclusively by a single tone (bliss, despair, ideal resolution), Hölderlin shifted the strophic divisions, cutting and adding lines in such a way that the sharp differences between the moods were blurred. For instance, in "Elegie" the third strophe ends with the depiction of naive bliss and the fourth begins on an utterly unanticipated note of despair:

Unter trautem Gespräch, im hellen Seelengesange,
So im Frieden mit uns kindlich und selig allein.

[4]
Ach! wo bist du, Liebende, nun? Sie haben mein Auge
    Mir genommen, mein Herz hab ich verloren mit ihr.
Darum irr ich umher, und wohl, wie die Schatten, so muß
                                                      ich
    Leben und sinnlos dünkt lange das Übrige mir.

But in "Menons Klagen" the abrupt shift in mood is avoided
by moving the four lines to the end of the preceding strophe
so that the new strophe represents not a break but a continuation of the preceding mood.

Aber das Haus ist öde mir nun, und sie haben mein Auge
    Mir genommen, auch mich hab ich verloren mit ihr.
Darum irr ich umher, und wohl, wie die Schatten, so muß
                                                      ich
    Leben, und sinnlos dünkt lange das Übrige mir.
                        [5]
Feiern möcht ich; aber wofür? und singen mit Andern,
    Aber so einsam fehlt jegliches Göttliche mir.

The basic tone emerges toward the end of the strophe and becomes the dominant artistic effect of the succeeding strophe.
The following chart should make the changes clear: in virtually every case the shifting or addition of lines can be attributed to Hölderlin's effort to efface sharp contrasts and to enhance the effect of tonal modulation:

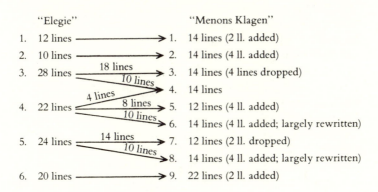

| "Elegie" | | "Menons Klagen" | |
|---|---|---|---|
| 1. | 12 lines ⟶ | 1. | 14 lines (2 ll. added) |
| 2. | 10 lines ⟶ | 2. | 14 lines (4 ll. added) |
| 3. | 28 lines | 3. | 14 lines (4 lines dropped) |
| | | 4. | 14 lines |
| 4. | 22 lines | 5. | 12 lines (4 ll. added) |
| | | 6. | 14 lines (4 ll. added; largely rewritten) |
| 5. | 24 lines | 7. | 12 lines (2 ll. dropped) |
| | | 8. | 14 lines (4 ll. added; largely rewritten) |
| 6. | 20 lines ⟶ | 9. | 22 lines (2 ll. added) |

Finally, the chart of changes reveals his effort to subordinate the "natural" strophic divisions to a scheme based more or less upon the same number of lines. In short, the theory of tonal modulation enables us to understand that Hölderlin is subordinating his poem to a pattern quite different from the pattern of the elegy. The result of this accommodation of the poem to the theory of tonal modulation is a shift away from the articulation of parts that we noted in the case of earlier elegies, where the parts are set off not by numbered sections of rigorously equal length but by internal shifts of rhetoric.

Clearly we are dealing here—in "Elegie" as well as "Menons Klagen"—with an elegy that closely fits the pattern of the generic norm. And everything that we know about Hölderlin—his inherently elegiac disposition, his reverence for (and struggle against) Schiller, his meditative temperament that requires meditative poetic forms, the original generic title of the poem—suggests that we are dealing with a case of conscious emulation. Above all, the classical German elegy provided the poetic form that corresponded perfectly to Hölderlin's conception of humanization: it is the ideal expression for the individual in the "eccentric course," looking back to the lost past of highest simplicity and forward to the future of highest culture and consciousness. At the same time, we are also dealing with a major poet who, not content merely to appropriate the model, modifies it to meet the needs of his own temperament and ideas—in this case, the demands of the theory of tonal modulations. We can see another more radical transformation of the generic norm if we consider Hölderlin's other great elegy, "Brot und Wein."

If "Menons Klagen" represents Hölderlin's attempt to compete with Goethe's "Euphrosyne," then "Brot und Wein" constitutes his effort to rewrite "Der Spaziergang." The triadic rhythm of humanization—from naive harmony through heroic alienation to ideal unity—that in the earlier poem was still entirely personal and psychological is intensified, in "Brot und Wein," to the national and historical level.[41] As in all Hölderlin's elegies we find the typical situation of a wanderer who goes to a high place from which he has an open vista: but here the vista that he contemplates is neither Swabia nor the vision of his youth but the past of Western civilization.

The strophe opening "Brot und Wein" contains a portrayal of nightfall so hauntingly lovely that these eighteen lines, which were separately printed in 1807, entered nineteenth-century anthologies as a poem entitled "Die Nacht," regarded by writers ranging from Clemens Brentano to Hermann Hesse as the most beautiful poem in the German language.[42] The strophe opens with the hush that falls over the city at dusk as the torches are lit and the carriages depart:

> Rings um ruhet die Stadt; still wird die erleuchtete Gasse,
> Und, mit Fackeln geschmückt, rauschen die Wagen
> hinweg.

As the people go home to rest from their labors, the market place stands silent, enabling the listener to hear the sounds of a distant violin and the rushing waters of a fountain. The watchman calls the hours, and an evening breeze begins to stir the treetops in the groves. Finally night rises over the mountains, a stranger among men:

> Voll mit Sternen und wohl wenig bekümmert um uns,
> Glänzt die Erstaunende dort, die Fremdlingin unter den
> Menschen,
> Über Gebirgeshöhn traurig und prächtig herauf.

At this point it is not clear what this strophe has to do with the potential elegiac content of the poem. But the second strophe, through one of those astonishing explosions of meaning so typical of Hölderlin, prepares us to understand this specific night as an image of the cultural darkness that has fallen over humanity as a whole in its "eccentric course" between the naive harmony of classical antiquity and the higher unity of some unspecified future. At this point the poet simply outlines various attitudes toward the mystery of night. In what seems to be a response to the romantic reverence of night and, more specifically, to Novalis' recently published

"Hymnen an die Nacht" (1800), the poet points out that some people revere the night and devote songs to it:

> Oder es blickt auch gern ein treuer Mann in die Nacht hin,
> Ja, es ziemet sich, ihr Kränze zu weihn und Gesang,
> Weil den Irrenden sie geheiliget ist und den Toten, . . .

More importantly, however, night provides two kinds of succor for our despair in this darkness of history: the vatic intoxication that enables us to lose ourselves in poetic ecstasy, and the atavistic memory that enables mankind to remain "awake" and to recall an earlier "day" of humanity:

> Aber sie muß uns auch, daß in der zaudernden Weile,
> Daß im Finstern für uns einiges Haltbare sei,
> Uns die Vergessenheit und das Heiligtrunkene gönnen,
> Gönnen das strömende Wort, das, wie die Liebenden, sei,
> Schlummerlos, und vollern Pokal und kühneres Leben,
> Heilig Gedächtnis auch, wachend zu bleiben bei Nacht.

It is this power of sacred memory that inspires the poet, in the third strophe, to invite his friend Heinse—the author of the novel *Ardinghello*, to whom the elegy is dedicated—to join him in his search for "the Open" (a code word for "divinity" in Hölderlin's vocabulary):

> So komm! daß wir das Offene schauen,
> Daß ein Eigenes wir suchen, so weit es auch ist.

Intoxicated by the night, the poet undertakes a journey of the imagination to Greece, where he situates himself on a height—perhaps one of the three mountains he mentions—that affords a view of the entire isthmus:

> Drum an den Isthmos komm! dorthin, wo das offene Meer
>                                                    rauscht
> Am Parnaß und der Schnee delphische Felsen umglänzt,
> Dort ins Land des Olymps, dort auf die Höhe Cithärons,
> Unter die Fichten dort, unter die Trauben, von wo
> Thebe drunten und Ismenos rauscht im Lande des Kadmos,
> Dorther kommt und zurück deutet der kommende Gott.

The following three strophes, which begin with an apostrophe to "Blessed Greece, thou home of all deities" ("Seliges Griechenland! du Haus der Himmlischen alle"), amount to a grand survey of Greek culture, whose history is traced in analogy to organic growth. First, from his lofty vantage point, the poet describes the landscape of Greece, as yet devoid of deities. But in a moment of ecstasy the people spontaneously cry out "Father Aether," and this invocation summons the deities who come to earth among men. At first, in the stage of naive harmony with nature, men simply accept the gods; but as they become consciously aware of their presence, they invent names for them. The first poetic expression is created as a religious response:

So ist der Mensch; wenn da ist das Gut, und es sorget mit Gaben
   Selber ein Gott für ihn, kennet und sieht er es nicht.
Tragen muß er, zuvor; nun aber nennt er sein Liebstes,
   Nun, nun müssen dafür Worte, wie Blumen entstehn.

When the veneration of the gods becomes conscious, culture can finally begin: a code of ethics determines right and wrong according to divine standards; people organize themselves into societies so that they may be worthy to appear before the deities; and they create great temples and cities in honor of the gods. It is a panorama reminiscent of "Der Spaziergang":

Und nun denkt er zu ehren in Ernst die seligen Götter,
   Wirklich und wahrhaft muß alles verkünden ihr Lob.

Yet according to the inevitable dialectic—Hölderlin is, after all, Schiller's spiritual protégé—the decline sets in. The great cities wither away, the sacred theaters fall silent, the dance is stilled, the gods disappear. For according to Hölderlin's mythic theology, Christ was not the initiator of a new aeon but the last fulfiller of classical mythology:

Oder er kam auch selbst und nahm des Menschen Gestalt an
   Und vollendet' und schloß tröstend das himmlische Fest.

In strophe 7 the poet returns from his imaginary journey to Greece, announcing to Heinse that they arrived too late, for the gods have already departed:

> Aber Freund! wir kommen zu spät. Zwar leben die Götter,
> Aber über dem Haupt droben in anderer Welt.

During the dark years men are unable to endure the radiant presence of deities. The *dei absconditi* will not return to earth until a stronger generation of heroes has been born. At this point the poet's meditations cause him despondently to question the usefulness of poets in such a time of deprivation ("und wozu Dichter in dürftiger Zeit"). But his elegiac interlocutor points out that poets have the important function of preparing mankind for the return of the gods, much like the priests of Bacchus, who roamed from land to land before the arrival of culture in Greece:

> Aber sie sind, sagst du, wie des Weingotts heilige Priester,
> Welche von Lande zu Land zogen in heiliger Nacht.

In the meantime, the departed gods have left behind gifts for mankind: bread and wine as a sign of their former presence and as a token of their return "at the proper time" when mankind is again deserving of their glory:

> Brot ist der Erde Frucht, doch ists vom Lichte gesegnet,
> Und vom donnernden Gott kommet die Freude des
> Weins.
> Darum denken wir auch dabei der Himmlischen, die sonst
> Da gewesen und die kehren in richtiger Zeit.

The ninth strophe attains a rapture of hymnic euphoria, for the poet now realizes that through the symbols of bread and wine the god of the Greek "day"—who is spiritually evergreen, like the fir tree and the ivy—continues to remain among men and to bring evidence of the departed gods down among the "god-remote" peoples of the dark present. In his final vision the poet exults that the ancient prophecy concerning the return of the gods shall be fulfilled in the Hesperian occident, and not in ancient Greece:

Was der Alten Gesang von Kindern Gottes geweissagt,
  Siehe! wir sind es, wir; Frucht von Hesperien ists!

Mankind will follow its "eccentric course" forward to a new
and higher consciousness, not back to a naive harmony lying
in the unrecoverable past. But until Father Aether has again
returned to earth, as once he did during the day of Greek antiquity, man is consoled by the presence of the god of communion, the son of the Almighty, the "Syrian," a strange
amalgam of Christ and Dionysos:

Aber indessen kommt als Fackelschwinger des Höchsten
  Sohn, der Syrier, unter die Schatten herab.
Selige Weise sehns; ein Lächeln aus der gefangnen
  Seele leuchtet, dem Licht tauet ihr Auge noch auf.

Since "Brot und Wein" has been exhaustively interpreted
by various scholars, we can restrict ourselves to this brief recapitulation, which should make it clear that all the elements
of the generic norm are present. The poem consists of a personal framework embracing a meditative core. In the opening
half of the framework the poetic persona is driven by his
elegiac despair at living in an age of deprivation, a nocturnal
period of god-remoteness, to seek out in his imagination a
lofty vantage point from which he can console himself by reviewing the coming of the gods to classical antiquity. This
central meditation brings him to the realization that he has
come too late: Greek antiquity has irrevocably disappeared.
But the moment of anagnorisis enables him to see that the
gods themselves have not died; they have merely moved to
another world where they await their return to a new and
reinvigorated humanity. In the course of the poem and its
movement from darkness to light, the poet's own crisis is resolved: he sees the justification of his own "Hesperian" society as the new site to which the gods will return when mankind has proved itself to be ready. Schiller standing on his
mountaintop realized that the sun of Homer still shines upon
the present; Hölderlin, in his reworking of "Der Spaziergang," has the insight that Bread and Wine afford a communion with deity even in a godless age.

Yet it is even more striking here than in "Menons Klagen" how much Hölderlin strains against the generic norm even as he is exploiting it. This is evident, first of all, in his treatment of the landscape. In "Der Spaziergang" and "Euphrosyne" we accompany the poet step by step in his mountainclimb, and the landscape is clearly laid out before our inner eye. The mountain setting may be used for symbolic purposes—as the image of nature's permanence—yet the mountains have an undeniable reality within the poems themselves. In "Brot und Wein," in contrast, the entire landscape is internalized—even more than in Hölderlin's earlier elegies. In "Der Wanderer" Hölderlin imagines the African deserts and the arctic wastes, but his vision of Swabia is intense and experienced, as it is in the other Swabian elegies. Even in "Menons Klagen," at least until the last visionary strophe, the landscape is experienced: the wounded animal driven through the forests by the cruel arrow, the affectionate swans gently rocked by the waves in which silvery clouds are reflected—these are scenes that we visualize vividly and unforgettably. In "Brot und Wein," in contrast, after the incomparable depiction of nightfall in the first strophe, the entire landscape is so totally interiorized that it almost takes on the quality of a surreal vision. Thus, even though the poet mentions three different mountains, it is never clear on which of them his shifting locus is supposed to be found. When the poet looks down at Greece in strophe 4, what he sees is not a landscape but a festive hall for the gods, in which the ocean represents the floor and the mountains the tables:

> Festlicher Saal! der Boden ist Meer! und Tische die Berge,
> Wahrlich zu einzigem Brauche vor alters gebaut!

And later all natural categories are confused as words arise like flowers (strophe 5) and cities wither like plants (strophe 6). The reader sometimes has the weird sensation that he is looking at a painting by Salvador Dali.

The breakdown of the elegiac norm stands out even more sharply when we consider the structure of the poem. Like "Menons Klagen," "Brot and Wein" has nine strophes of roughly equal length. But there are two principal differences. We have noted that Hölderlin believed in a "calculable law" of poetic effects, and we have seen how the theory of tonal modulation worked in the earlier poem to produce the revisions in the second version. Here, however, the organization of the strophes follows according to a much stricter triadic principle: every strophe except strophe 7 has precisely 18 lines—that is, nine distichs. And in almost every strophe the nine distichs fall neatly into three groups of three distichs. In addition, the strophes themselves are organized into three clusters of three each: strophes 1-3 portray the present world as night; strophes 4-6 depict Greek antiquity as day; and strophes 7-9 describe the resolution of night and day in the Hesperian future.

Now we have observed, to be sure, that both "Der Spaziergang" and "Euphrosyne"—and indeed even "Menons Klagen"—can be described according to rather precise mathematical divisions. But the extreme regularity of "Brot und Wein" is countergeneric for at least two reasons. First, the triadic structure within and among the strophes is the culmination of a tendency that is evident in Hölderlin's other elegies as well.[43] In other words, the poem is subordinated to an extrinsic pattern that overshadows the pattern of the generic norm. Second, the triadic structure of the elegy as a whole reduces the meditative core to a third of the poem, producing a significant reduction in the elegiac portrayal of the past. (In "Menons Klagen," in contrast, it still amounted to five of the nine strophes.) In return, we find a corresponding inflation of the framework, with the result that the end of the poem does not simply anticipate the resolution of the elegiac conflict developed in a large meditative core; rather, it emerges as a fullscale depiction of the state of resolution. What we witness, in short, is a movement away from elegiac lament toward the jubilation of the hymn—the genre that dominated Hölderlin's last great period of productivity.

This loosening of form on the structural level is paralleled by a relaxation of the metrical form—a process that begins in the earliest elegies.[44] First, the hexameters are reduced often

to five-beat lines by the frequent use of initial phrases that can
more easily be read as anapests (xxx́) than as dactyls (x́xx) or
trochees (x́x): "aber nimmer," "wenn ihr Bösen," "über
sterblichem Haupt," "von den Ästen," "unter trautem Gespräche," and so forth. Second, Hölderlin is capable of lines
that look like very poor pentameters indeed since the third ac-
cent would normally fall on otherwise unaccented syllables:

Jámmernd und schlúmmerlós // tréibt es der Stáchel umhér
Séndet die zártlichén // Wiegengesánge dir zú
Rúft es von sílbernén // Bérgen Apóllons vorán.

It is more likely that Hölderlin did not read such lines as bad
pentameters but simply as five-beat dactylic lines. In any case,
the effect would be to play down the distinctive balance of the
elegiac pentameter. The tendency to level down the pentameter and to reduce the dactylic rhythm at the beginning of the
hexameter is intensified by the frequent enjambement—rare
in Goethe and Schiller—from pentameter to hexameter:

Bin ich allein denn nicht? aber ein Freundliches muß
Fernher nahe mir sein, und lächeln muß ich und staunen,

. . .

Generally speaking, Hölderlin does not so much exploit the
potentialities of the distich as write straight through it.[45] The
author does not strive to subordinate the logic of the sentence
to the logic of the distich. Finally, Hölderlin's hexameters display a conspicuous rhythmic leitmotif—one so extended and
emphatic that it tends to dominate the lines in which it occurs:
x x́x x́xx x́x.

| | |
|---|---|
| und such ein Anderes immer | (l. 1) |
| die Schatten alle besuch ich | (l. 3) |
| und nicht die Kühle der Nacht hilft | (l. 9) |
| ihr abendrötlichen Berge | (l. 31) |
| ihr schönen Kinder des Maitags | (l. 35) |
| ein Jahr verdränget das andre. | (l. 37) |

As this rhythmic leitmotif emerges more strongly, the
hexameter disappears. In fact, in Hölderlin's later hymns this

rhythmic leitmotif has become the basic metrical unit of poems that are sometimes loosely and incorrectly designated as "free rhythms." In "Der Rhein," for example, many entire lines consist wholly of what was once a rhythmic leitmotif in a longer hexameter:

| | |
|---|---|
| Das mir die göttlichgebaute | (l. 5) |
| Nach alter Meinung, wo aber | (l. 7) |
| Geheim noch manches entschieden | (l. 8) |
| Vernahm ich ohne Vermuten | (l. 10) |

And many other lines correspond to the same rhythmic leitmotif without the final syllable.

All these factors—the breakdown of the hexameter, the reduction of the pentameter to a five-beat line, the loosening of the distich through frequent enjambement, and the growing dominance of the rhythmic leitmotif—accompanied the more general shift that we have observed away from the simple elegiac encapsulation of "Elegie" through the triadic pattern of "Brot und Wein" toward the late hymnic form with its greater emphasis on ecstatic praise.

Hölderlin's refashioning of the classical German elegy is important for at least two reasons. It affords additional evidence for the fact that the generic norm we have detected in "Euphrosyne" and "Der Spaziergang" was recognized and acknowledged by contemporaries of Goethe and Schiller and not simply imposed retrospectively by critical oversophistication. At the same time, Hölderlin's poems provide an exemplary model for the manner in which genres change and grow. For only poetasters are content to appropriate a poetic model and, polishing it to a high gloss, to fill it with any content at hand. Great poets use the model merely as a stepping stone, a starting-point for their own innovations. In Hölderlin's deformations of the elegy we see a specific but absolutely valid example of his anomalous position in literary history, outside of and beyond the prevailing German classicism and romanticism. Without Goethe and Schiller, Hölderlin would not have been able to write his elegies; he would have had only such lesser models as the sentimental elegies of Kosegarten, Voss, or Salis-Seewis. For poetry is not created from a vacuum: even the greatest poets are dependent upon the literary tradition and existing models. But the fact that he was able to take the form and shape it into something new—to interiorize it, so to speak—reveals the creative power that sets Hölderlin, along with such contemporaries as Heinrich von Kleist in the drama and Jean Paul in the novel, outside the literary movements of his day.

Hölderlin's brilliant innovations—at least in the elegy—had little immediate influence outside his immediate circle of friends. The effect of "Menons Klagen" was diluted by the circumstances of its publication: Bernhard Vermehren published the first four strophes as a self-contained poem in his *Musen-Almanach für das Jahr 1802* and the remaining five strophes, without indicating that they were a continuation, a year later. "Brot und Wein" was not published in full until 1894; only its first strophe achieved a fame of its own. Several of the shorter elegies appeared in almanacs and anthologies of the period. But in general we must wait for the twentieth century and, specifically, for Rilke and Trakl before we can see the continuation of the trend that Hölderlin initiated. During the nineteenth century, however, the development of the classical German elegy proceeds as though Hölderlin had never existed.

# 5 · The Transmission: The Romantic Decades

It must not be imagined, of course, that the classical German elegy as established by the powerful example of Schiller and Goethe immediately replaced the older literary kinds known traditionally as "elegies." In fact, the elegiac distich was so widely used in the first decade of the nineteenth century—no issue of an almanac was complete without several examples—that the situation resembled what had obtained at the end of the Middle Ages. Because so many varieties of poetry were being composed in distichs, the genre threatened to lose its distinctive outline. Initially the generic norm we have isolated represented only one possibility among many for poems called "elegies" merely because they were written in distichs. The model, moreover, was at first imperfectly perceived and faultily realized. To understand its gradual emergence in the course of the century we must distinguish it from at least five other categories commonly labeled as "elegies" during the age of romanticism: 1) the traditional "elegy" of mixed sensations; 2) imitations of the "Römische Elegien"; 3) poems after the fashion of Hölderlin's hymns; 4) didactic poems; and 5) epigrams in imitation of the "Xenien."

Karl Philipp Conz, Hölderlin's Greek tutor at Tübingen, composed the kind of conventional elegy we might expect of a translator of Greek and Latin poetry who was to become, in 1804, the professor of classical literature at Tübingen. His short "Gruß an die Gegend zu ★ ★," for instance, invokes "mixed sensations" to characterize his affection for his native Swabian countryside:

> Meinen Gefühlen verwandt bist du; des Leides, der Freude,
>   Doch der Freude noch mehr hab' ich geschöpfet auf dir.[1]

In his elegy in commemoration of his deceased son ("Dem Andenken meines Eduard") the mixed sensations manifest themselves in the repeated juxtaposition of former happiness and present grief:

> Alles theilt' ich mit Dir, und jegliche Freude genoß ich
> Froher und doppelt in Dir, seeliges freundliches Kind!
> Nun im Lande der Schatten Du ruhst, ist öde mein Daseyn;
> Aller Freude verschloß sich mein erstarrtes Herz.[2]

Mixed sensations are similarly evident in the elegiac poems of Conz's school friend, Karl Friedrich Reinhard, a professional diplomat who in his youth anonymously published the first translation of Tibullus into German distichs (1783). In a poem written to celebrate his engagement ("Am Tage meiner Trauung," 1796) he begins by saying that he is "fanned" by elegiac feelings ("Angefächelt vom Wahn elegischer schöner Gefühle") because this day bridges past and future:

> Dieser Tag, der die Gattinn mir gibt, ist die schicksalvolle
> Brücke, die künftiges Glück an die Vergangenheit
> knüpft.[3]

This symbolic link provides the occasion for a rapid autobiographical survey of his experiences in England, Italy, and France, and for his reflections on the French Revolution. After congratulating himself on the previous stages of his education, which have inculcated in him a respect for truth and duty and aroused a reverence for transcendent laws, he now anticipates a third stage: education to virtue and love with his wife-to-be. The poem ends with that archetypal gesture of the elegy of mixed sensations—the smile moistened by tears:

> Komm, vom Segen der Ältern geleitet, vom Jubel der
> Freunde,
> Thränen im lachenden Blick, drücke dein Herz an mein
> Herz.

Precisely the same image reappears in the elegy he wrote a year and a half later ("Meiner Christine," 1798) to console his wife when she was about to leave her parents to accompany him on a diplomatic assignment abroad:

Komm', und weine mit mir, sanftes, entsagendes Weib!
Komm und lächle mit mir in die Thränen! . . .[4]

Although the representative "elegies" by Conz and Reinhard could have been written before Goethe's example and Schiller's essay, going back as they do to earlier eighteenth-century theories of the genre, Goethe's "Römische Elegien" provided the model for a second group of poets. But because other writers lacked Goethe's ability to maintain a balance between Amor and Roma, the imitations tend to fall into two distinct categories: erotic autobiography and historical meditations on Rome. The first imitations appeared quite early. On October 2, 1797, Schiller sent Goethe a copy of his latest *Musen-Almanach*, expressing his expectation that Goethe would be pleased with the elegies by a Swiss artist named Heinrich Keller.[5] Goethe may have been flattered by the imitation, but he could hardly have been gratified by the quality of the poems. Schiller's friend, Körner, observed immediately that the elegies, though not without talent, displayed all too clearly the imprint of Goethe's elegies, which the author appeared to have understood only imperfectly.[6] In Goethe's poems, Körner astutely noted, the revelry was nothing but the sensuous garment in which Goethe chose to cloak his genius; but for Keller it has become the central matter of the poems. The four poems suggest that Keller was attempting to reenact with his Italian mistress, Nina, all Goethe's adventures with Faustine.[7] The couple flirts behind the back of Nina's uncle (Elegy I); they rendezvous in the vineyards and watch the Bacchic festivals of the vintners (Elegy III); he bids adieu to the groves that have witnessed their embraces and gives thanks to the beneficent deities, especially Amor (Elegy IV). But the entire imitation remains quite superficial—as indeed it must, given the fundamental difference between the two girls. For Keller's sophisticated Nina is incapable of the modest devotion that characterizes Faustine and determines the relationship. In fact, Keller's cycle is self-consciously literary and artistic. The lovers work up to an embrace, for instance, by reading Dante's account of Paolo and Francesca:

Da umwand ich das Mädchen, und wagte was Paolo
gewaget,
Drückte den feurigsten Kuß ihr auf den seufzenden
Mund. . . .
(Elegy I)

Nina entertains her German lover with songs on the zither and mandolin. Yet at no point, though the scenes take place in and around Rome, do Keller's imitations transcend their erotic nature to become *Roman* elegies in a broader cultural sense.

In the "Elegieen" that Ludwig Robert published in 1804, the setting has shifted from Rome to Vienna, but the model is still clearly Goethe's cycle.[8] Ludwig manages to tell a little story in his three elegies. The first poem, a brief anecdote, depicts the poet as a shy youth, so confused that he misses an opportunity to meet the girl he has long admired from afar. In the long middle elegy the poet is walking in the hills near the Danube when he comes upon a lovely young woman. Mistaking him for her lover who has deserted her, she faints, whereupon the poet revives and assists her. Afterwards she tells him the story of her treacherous lover, and for a time the poet visits her daily at home. The third poem, finally, amounts to a gnomic epigram to love and its pleasures. Each night the poet slips away to the house of his mistress, a dancer, pleased that he is about to enjoy the favors of a woman whose merits he hears acclaimed all day long:

Ich aber höre des Tages die Liebste von Jeglichem loben:
Wie Sie die Göttergestalt glücklich Terpsichoren weiht,
Und in traulicher Nacht erfahr' ich das schöne Geheimniß:
Keine von Allen vermag Liebe zu geben wie Sie.

If there were any uncertainty concerning the inspiration for these poems, Ludwig's paean "An Göthe" at the end of the same volume would quickly resolve the question.[9] In his poem Ludwig—who was introduced to the German literary establishment by his sister, the future Rahel Varnhagen von Ense—says that his friends have finally persuaded him to publish some of his works; he intends to step onto the literary scene with the proud acknowledgment that Goethe is his model:

Ich trete in die Welt—und aller Welt
Bekenn' ich es mit stolzer, froher Stimme,
Daß Du mein Vorbild, Du mein Meister bist
Und laut und kühn nenn' ich mich Deinen Schüler.—

Yet the differences are conspicuous. Faustine is no longer a young Roman widow but a Wiener Mäderl, heroine of poems that read like sketches for tales by Arthur Schnitzler. Above all, as in Keller's elegies, the autobiographical eroticism displays no cultural aspects at all.

Equally dependent upon the "Römische Elegien," though in a totally different way, are the thirty-three "Elegieen" by the popular writer, Ernst Schulze.[10] Although the poems were written in 1812 to commemorate his brief romance with Cäcilie Tychsen, who had died earlier that year, Schulze's conception of the genre is anything but threnetic. At the beginning (Elegy II) he apostrophizes Elegy as the lithely skipping daughter of the Graces who is no longer covered by the gloomy veil that opinion had once attributed to her:

Nahe dich mir, Elegie, leichthüpfende Grazientochter,
    Freundin zarten Gefühls, nahe dich mir, Elegie!
Nicht vom düsteren Schleier verhüllt, den herrisch der
                                    Volkswahn
    Einst um die Stirn dir wob, nicht mit geröthetem Blick.

And the cycle closes (Elegy XXXIII) with an appeal to his elegies to go forth and bring back their father, Amor, so that their mother will once again be able to smile:

Geht, Elegien, des beweglichen Leichtsinns süße Gespielen,
    Geht Elegien, des Gefühls süße Gespielen auch ihr.
Amor hat euch gezeugt, und die Grazie wiegte die

Und mit Blüthengedüft zog sie die Freundlichen auf.

Schulze is inspired not only by the "Römische Elegien" but, for some of his episodes, by other distich poems of Goethe as well. Elegy IV, for instance, imitates "Alexis und Dora," in which the lover is maddened by jealousy at the thought that another man might be entering his beloved's garden. Elegy XVII consists of a dialogue after the fashion of "Der neue Pausias." And Elegy XXII begins very much like "Euphrosyne" as the poet ascends a mountain path and experiences a vision:

> Einsam stieg ich empor auf des Harzwalds steilerem
> Bergpfad,
> Nahete dir mich schon, ewiger, alter Granit,
> Wo hochlodernd einst durch die Nacht vom felsigen Altar
> Hell in's ferne Gefild flammte das Opfer des Mays.
> Träumend schritt ich dahin, und es dämmerte leise der
> Vorzeit
> Riesengebild mit des Wahns Wundergestalten umher.

But it quickly develops into simply another episode in Schulze's love affair with his coy mistress, in the course of which they go to dances, attend a rural festival, and pick flowers in the woods. Schulze's professor's daughter is no more like Faustine than is the Harz region like Goethe's Rome. A real tease, she never permits her lover to go one step beyond chaste kisses, which he apostrophizes interminably in almost every one of the thirty-three poems. Once while they are picking wild flowers in the grove, he is so overcome by passion that he tries to put his arm around her waist; she reproaches him gently, and, like the German youth of Romantic story and legend, he is eternally grateful to her for rescuing him from his own crude passions (Elegy XXIV):

> Lieber, flüstertest du, o bleib mein Freund und zerstöre
> Nicht muthwillig in mir, welche dir traute, dein Bild!
> Züchtiges Kind der Natur, du rettetest mild den
> Verlohrnen;
> Ewiger Dank sey dir freundlich im Herzen bewahrt!

Small wonder that poor Schulze is finally reduced, by all this display of virtue, to talking to the bed in which his beloved Cäcilie is soon to rest (Elegy XXVII):

> Seidenes Bett, bald hegst du den reizenden Leib der
> Geliebten,
> Ach, schon harret dein Schooß auf die beglückende Last,
> Ueppiger schwillst du empor, in den Flaum sank friedliche
> Ruhe,
> Still durchs dämmernde Zelt schlüpfen die Träume
> dahin.

For all their obviously genuine feeling, the tediously earnest poems remain strangely disembodied: we never sense the physical presence of Schulze and his professor's prim daughter. And because Schulze is utterly unselective, including in his cycle apparently every poem and every distich he could write, we detect no plot or development. The poet obviously set out to write a cycle of elegies after the fashion of Goethe— that is, he set himself a literary task instead of attempting to find the most appropriate form in which to record an auto- biographical episode that provided the focal point of his short life and brief literary career.

Keller, Robert, and Schulze appropriated from the "Römische Elegien" nothing more than the cyclic form in which to clad autobiographical erotic experience; other poets were inspired by Goethe's poems to write cultural elegies about Rome. Ludwig I, the king of Bavaria who subsequently abdicated for the love of the Spanish dancer Lola Montez, was long fascinated by the "Römische Elegien," and on one of his visits to Weimar he pestered the aged poet for details about the autobiographical circumstances underlying his Roman poems.[11] Even if we did not have this information, it would be obvious from the text itself where Ludwig got the model for the twelve elegies that he wrote during his travels in Italy in 1805 ("Erinnerungen aus Italien im Jahr 1805").[12] This is not to suggest that there is any real comparison between Goethe's cycle and Ludwig's short elegies. Ludwig's poems amount to snapshots, picture postcards of his travels in Italy: from Rome, Tivoli, the Campagna, the Via Appia, Molo di Gaeta, Pompeii, Salerno, and Paestum.[13] But Italy in general and Rome more specifically represented for the young crown prince nothing but a cultural experience. Future rulers should go to Rome, he opines (Elegy VII), in order to discover a fundamental law: that everything is transitory:

> Nach Rom gehe die künftig zu herrschen berufene Jugend,
> Damit frühe bereits werde von solcher erkannt:
> Daß wie das Kleinste, das Größte, daß alles auf Erden
> vergehet;
> Trost wird leichter in Rom für den verlorenen Thron.

The elegiac theme that unifies all twelve poems is the not particularly profound conclusion that the glory of Rome has passed:

> Innigste, namlose Wehmuth fasset mich bei dem Gedanken
> Immer an dich, o Rom, nie zu vergleichende Stadt!
> Die Jahrtausende, wie die Geschlechter entstanden und
> schwanden,
> Denkmal der Größe bist du und der Vergänglichkeit
> auch.
> (Elegy V)

Ludwig is able to maintain this gloomy and fatalistic conviction since, unlike Goethe, he is interested solely in the decline of ancient Rome and not in its living present.

> Neues erscheinet, das Alte vergeht, ist nicht zu erhalten;
> Roma's Zeit ist vorbei, herrschen wird Roma nicht
> mehr,
> Mumie aus der Vergangenheit; unbedeutend erscheinet
> Uns darum nunmehr, was sich ereignet in ihr.
> (Elegy VII)

Small wonder that he was so depressed and that he could think of nothing but grandeur in decline. After all, an eighteen-year-old crown prince traveling in Italy in 1805 was permitted to have little private life, few personal friends, and certainly no girls. As a result, his individuality emerges only on a few rare occasions. He confides to his distichs that he would rather be a citizen of Hellas than heir to the throne (Elegy XII). Only once does he mention another living human being, a young patriot from Hanover (Elegy VI). And, most pathetic of all, in the absence of any mistress he calls to mind his German bride—whom he has never even met:

> Liebte, doch hatt' ich keine Geliebte, da dachte ich meine
> Nie noch gesehene Braut mir aus dem Norden hierher,
> Uns zufällig begegnend, nicht aber einander uns kennend,
> Beide ergriffen zugleich flammender südlicher Glut. . . .
>
> (Elegy III)

While young Ludwig was wandering around Rome, sublimating his lust into lofty thoughts, the Prussian resident (later minister) in the Vatican was none other than Wilhelm von Humboldt. Appropriately, we find a much more mature attitude in the five short poems in distichs that Humboldt wrote in the course of his morning or evening strolls around the city.[14] Again we find snapshots of familiar Roman scenes: the marble statue of the Dioscuri ("Die Rossebändiger"), a street on the Aventine hill ("Der Publicische Weg"), the *balnea Surae* ("Das Haus des Sura"), the Protestant cemetery near Cestius' pyramid ("Der Lorbeer"), and a general tribute to Rome ("Rom"). But Humboldt was not afflicted by the cultural pessimism that depressed young Ludwig. Like Goethe, he appreciated the interplay of past and present in the Eternal City. He pays tribute to the power of sculpture to preserve the best of antiquity and to lead us back into a more beautiful age:

> Tempel stürzen in Schutt; hinwelken der Menschen
> Geschlechter;
> Doch der gerettete Stein führet die Gottheit zurück.
> Gottheit ja stralet aus Euch, Quirinalische Heldenkolosse,
> Und in schönere Zeit führt ihr den staunenden Blick!

He senses the presence of faith in contemporary Rome even though the deity has changed. He smiles ironically at the races of the *circus maximus*, in which he detects an image of life itself, going around in an eternal circle without reaching a goal. The greening laurel reminds him of his son, who also thrived for a time and then died at a tender age. Yet despite the collapse of ancient glory and the ironies that qualify the present, Humboldt sees in Rome a symbol of grandeur, not of despair:

> Nichts geht über die Einsamkeit, Freund, die im Busen
> genießet,
> Wer in der heiligen Rom steht auf den Gipfeln Quirins.
> Nichts vermisset sein Herz, auch die Nähe nicht der
> Geliebten;
> Alles was schön ist und gross, stehet lebendig vor ihm.

It is commonly agreed that these five poems represent the nucleus of a cycle that Humboldt intended to write in imitation of the "Römische Elegien."[15] However, when he accomplished his magnificent tribute to the Eternal City two years later, it was inspired by Schiller, not Goethe. And even though Humboldt wrote a variety of brief poems in elegiac distichs throughout his lifetime, he chose a different metrical form for his major elegy. Humboldt's great meditative poem "Rom" (1806) is totally elegiac in Schiller's sense of the word—a rumination on Rome that acknowledges the decline of ancient glory while recognizing its meaning for the present.[16] Humboldt was fully aware of his debt to his friend Schiller. He wrote to a common acquaintance that the thought of Schiller, whose recent death constituted an irreplaceable loss for him, had inspired him during the work on his poem—indeed, that Schiller had first drawn his attention to the classical text (Camillus' speech reported by Livy) that occupies the center of his poem.[17] The poem is dedicated to Caroline von Wolzogen, Humboldt's boyhood friend and Schiller's sister-in-law. And the ottava rima in which the poem is composed resembles the eight-line stanzaic form of Schiller's early elegiac poem, "Die Götter Griechenlands." In fact, it is not unlikely that Humboldt's tribute to Rome was consciously conceived as a poetic counterpart to Schiller's tribute to Hellas.[18] At the same time, for all its explicitly elegiac qualities, the poem is certainly no classical German elegy in form: it is not written in distichs, and it has no framework surrounding the meditative core. In fact, the speaker is totally disembodied, with neither a definable persona nor an identifiable locus.

> Tibris, der du rollst die stolzen Wogen,
> Denkst du wohl noch jener grauen Zeit,
> Wo noch nicht, gewägt auf luftgen Bogen,
> Stand des Capitoles Herrlichkeit;
> Roma's Name, noch von Nacht umzogen,
> Nicht des Nachruhms Stimme war geweiht?—
> Kehrt einst Nacht, die wieder ihn verschlinget?
> Strahlt ein Tag, wo keinem Ohr er klinget?—
>
> (ll. 1-8)

For all its power and value as a document of German classicism, Humboldt's poem constitutes an anomaly in the history of German poetry.

While traditional elegies of "mixed sensations" were being turned out by older poets with a classical background and while admirers of Goethe were imitating aspects of the "Römische Elegien," still another contemporary group of poets—those close to Hölderlin—was writing distich poems of an entirely different sort: poems in which the elegiac mode, even if it is present, is entirely subordinated to the note of hymnic praise. Hölderlin's school friend Christian Ludwig Neuffer, for instance, used distichs for a hymn to friendship on the birthday of a friend ("Meinem Freunde Christian Landauer" 1798).[19] Hölderlin's young admirer, Siegfried Schmid, employed his idol's distichs in several hymnic poems: to celebrate nature in springtime ("Frühlingsspatziergang," 1797):

> Drängt nicht alle so mächtig auf einmal, gewaltige Götter,
> Aus der verjüngten Natur, auf das verjüngte Gemüth![20]

or to characterize various figures in his cycle, "Die Verwandten" (1803), e.g., his portrait of "Der Exzentrische":

> Taumelt! Taumelt, ihr Brüder, nur durch das Leben im
> Rausch hin.
> Sinnend werden euch nie klarer die Zwecke des Zeus.[21]

The talented but undisciplined Casimir Ulrich Boehlendorff, who entered literary history principally as the recipient of one of Hölderlin's most significant letters, apostrophizes a consoling nature in his hymn "Nepenthe":

> Nicht verhüllt mir die Sterne der Sorge ängstliches Bild
> mehr,
> Mit den Düften des Hains schöpf' ich Elysiums Luft—
> Und ein Nepenthe dringt aus seinem ewigen Frieden,
> Wie mit geistiger Hand hebt es die Seele empor.[22]

But it was not only in the Hölderlin circle that such hymns in elegiac distichs were composed. Chamisso's early "Elegie" deserves its title only because of the execrable distichs of which it consists. Otherwise the poem is clearly a hymn to the beloved:

> Schön entschlossen und trauend, sie eilet dem Freund in die
> Arme,
> Schmieget sich ihm an die Brust, pressend das Herz an
> das Herz;
> Reicht ihm die wonnigen Lippen zum Kusse des ewigen
> Bundes
> Ueberhimmlisches Glück, seelenberauschender Kuss![23]

The fact that the last six lines reveal the preceding idyll to have been only a dream hardly suffices to transform the poem into an elegy in mode.

Finally, most of the longer poems in elegiac distichs contained in the widely read volume of *Gedichte* by August Mahlmann amount to hymns in praise of one thing or another: faith and love ("Die Götter"), God as manifested in a storm ("Die Sturm-Nacht"), sun-beams ("Die Sonnen-Strahlen"), or the enlightened mind ("Freisinn").[24]

The early romantic critics seized eagerly upon the elegiac distich as a congenial form for didactic poetry. August Wilhelm Schlegel's "Die Kunst der Griechen" (1799), though labeled an "Elegie," is actually purely didactic—a 216-line survey of the sculpture, painting, architecture, and literature of Greek antiquity.[23] The personal element we expect in elegies is evident only in a few lines tacked on at the beginning and end, where Schlegel apostrophizes Goethe, to whom the tedious work is dedicated. Although the Greek genius has disappeared, he says, it is up to modern poets, led by Goethe, to create a new world of art upon the ruins of the past:

> Dir vertraut' er, o Goethe, der Künstlerweihe Geheimniß
> Daß du im Heiligthum hütest das Dichtergesetz.
> Lehre denn dichtend, und führe den Weg zum alten
> Parnassus!
> Wie? du schwindest dem Blick höher empor zum
> Olymp?

The single major poem in distichs written by Friedrich Schlegel is also didactic—an extension, as it were, of his brother's effort. "Herkules Musagetes" (1801) amounts to a survey of modern German literature followed by a theory of criticism in which Schlegel expresses the typical romantic view of an absolute art:

> Nicht nach dem Zweck und der Wirkung frag' und dem
> äußern Verhältnis,
> Sondern von innen heraus bilde für sich nur das Werk.[26]

Schelling emulates Goethe's "Metamorphose der Pflanze" as well as Schiller's "Die Geschlechter" in his poem "Tier und Pflanze" (1802), in which he attributes plant-like characteristics to woman—tenderness, affection, calmness—in contrast to the freer and more animal nature of man:

> Pflanzennatur auch gab sie dem Weib: ich nenn es die
> Pflanze
> unter den Tieren, den Mann unter den Tieren das Tier.[27]

The romantic generation, finally, was fond of the elegiac distich as a vehicle for the epigram. Novalis, for instance, wrote a number of two-line epigrams that are often cited as a distillate of his belief:

> Einem gelang es—er hob den Schleier der Göttin zu Sais—
> Aber was sah er? Er sah—Wunder des Wunders—Sich
> Selbst.[28]

One of his best-known poems, which goes under the title of "Kenne dich selbst," is actually a gnomic epigram in distichs. But almost every writer of the period—including younger romantics like Kleist and Uhland—used the distich for frequent epigrams. And most journals of the decade are punctuated with epigrams in elegiac distichs.[29]

Occasionally, of course, the now-fashionable form of the elegiac distich was preempted for unconventional purposes. Achim von Arnim's "Elegie aus einem Reisetagebuche in Schottland," which first appeared in the *Zeitung für Einsiedler* (April 30, 1808), looks at first glance almost like an elegy after the pattern of the classical German elegy.[30] As the poem opens, the poet is lying on a cliff in Scotland, writing in his travel journal and thinking fondly of Genoa, which he had visited earlier (1802) in the course of his Grand Tour.

> Genua seh ich im Geist, so oft die unendlichen Wellen
> Halten den Himmel im Arm, halten die taumelnde Welt;
> Seh ich die klingenden Höhlen des nordischen
> Mohren-Basaltes,
> Seh ich die Erde gestützt auf den Armen der Höll'; . . .

As the poet gazes down at the harsh Scottish landscape, elegiac contrasts thrust themselves upon him: between south and north, Petrarch and Ossian, the bright Carrara marble and the gloomy basalt of Scotland, the teeming Mediterranean crowds in the market-places of Genoa and the Highlands solitude. Yet following this introductory framework what we get is nothing like the anticipated elegiac meditation. Rather, the central core of the poem amounts to a ballad in distichs—almost as though Arnim had set a text from *Des Knaben Wun-*

*derhorn* in classical meter. The poet describes his approach to Genoa, coming down the mountains from Switzerland. Taking an apple from a seductive girl he meets on the mountain path, he resolves to throw it away because of its associations with evil and temptation. (He thinks of Proserpina, Helen of Troy, and Eve.) But he keeps it until he boards the boat that is to take him to the port of Genoa, and there he gives it to a young mother, who cuts it up and distributes the pieces to her children. A sudden storm proclaims the devil's wrath that the poet got his fruit of temptation away from him; but the boat is kept safe by protective angels. Soon the boat arrives in the harbor and the poet steps ashore. At this point, unexpectedly, the narrative ends and the framework is reintroduced, almost as though it were being tacked on artificially to an unfinished poem. The poet simply laments the fate that has caused him to wake up again in Scotland, which he has come to detest. In the concluding distich he calls upon the northern moon to witness his misery and the filthy food he must eat and the absence of all joy:

> Siehe mein Leiden o Mond durch deine gerundete Scheibe,
> Schmutzig ist Speise und Trank, was ich mir wünsche
> das fehlt.

In Arnim's poem only the framework is potentially elegiac—in contrast, say, to Humboldt's "Rom," which displayed an elegiac tension in the meditative core with no corresponding personal framework.

Paradoxically, none of the categories we have so far observed fulfills the prescriptive definition of the elegy provided by the early romantic theorists, who were quite rapturous in their praise of the "Römische Elegien." We have seen how enthusiastically A. W. Schlegel greeted Goethe's elegies in his review of 1796, and the tone is no less effusive in his Berlin lectures of 1802-1803 on the history of classical literature, which include a section on the elegy.[31] Yet the elegies that Schlegel actually describes come closer to the generic norm of the classical German elegy than to Goethe's cycle. Even in the

oldest elegies, he observes, the meditative tendency is pre-
dominant. As a result, the true elegy transcends lament to arrive at detached contemplation. "The elegy as an indissoluble
mixture of passion and contemplative calm, of desire and
melancholy, created solely to express the vacillating mood
pendulating back and forth between memory and premoni-
tion, between gaiety and sadness, affords in its light-hearted
freedom the loveliest area for all those sweet contradictions,
those enchanting disharmonies that constitute the pain and
the charm of life, and for this reason the elegy will be the delight of all feeling souls wherever it appears in its genuine
form."[32] For Schlegel, the metrical arbiter of the age, the
"genuine form" of the elegy is linked closely to the distich.
Like Gottsched, he ridicules the efforts of modern poets to
write elegies in other verse forms. "According to the view of
the ancients this is wholly impossible: for among them the
generic label was attached to the metrical form, and rightly
so, because the form, properly employed, determined in turn
the inner form of the treatment."[33] Attempts to compose
elegies in alexandrines and other forms, Schlegel asserts con-
temptuously, justify a literal translation of Horace's expression, *miserabiles elegi*: for most modern elegies are indeed
wretched. The fact that Gray's "Elegy" could achieve such
fame, he reasons, merely proves the impoverishment of the
genre in modern times. Fortunately for Germany, he concludes, Goethe has succeeded in creating true elegies, thereby
reviving the true form of the ancient genre.

Friedrich Schlegel shared his brother's admiration for the
"Römische Elegien," which prompted him to his study of the
Greek elegists. His translations of Phanocles, Hermesianax,
and Callimachus, which he published in the *Athenäum* (1798),
were prefaced by a short essay sketching the history of the
genre and stressing the same combination of the personal and
the contemplative.[34] Apart from the epic, Schlegel maintains,
no other form of poetry has displayed the same vitality as the
elegy. A history of the Greek elegy would be able to omit
very few of the great poetic initiators; and the Romans came
closer to Greek excellence in this genre than in any other.

Without mentioning any names, Schlegel says that the Germans of the present have begun imitating the meter of the classical elegy. "One poet—whose greatness is matched only by his charm—has added to his earlier laurels the title of restorer of the ancient elegy."[35] The elegy embraces the present, but it prefers to look back into the past rather than forward into the future. Given the example of Goethe and Propertius, it ought to be superfluous to warn against the conventional definitions of the genre, which seek to restrict the elegy to "lamenting sentimentality."[36]

Schelling's discussion of the elegy in his *Philosophie der Kunst* (1802-1803) reiterates essentially the same ideas.[37] Schelling begins by attacking the prevailing notion that the elegy must be a song of lament: that is only one aspect of a genre so flexible that it is capable of embracing all of life. In fact, its capacity for grief stems only from the fact that it enables us to look into the past. Schelling believes that the elegy is not limited to the individual and his specific condition; rather, it moves outward from the individual "into the epic circle." We can most easily become acquainted with the elegy in the works of the ancients, but in modern times Goethe, through his "Römische Elegien," has restored the genuine genre. In all three Romantic theorists, then, we ascertain precisely the same criteria: the rejection of the conventional definition of the elegy as nothing but a lament; the insistence on the meditative aspect of the genre, which generalizes individual experience; and the citation of the "Römische Elegien" as a model. In other words, the romantics conceived of the elegy in a new way that remarkably resembles the generic norm of the classical German elegy, with its personal framework embracing a contemplative core. It is all the more surprising, therefore, that the "elegies" of August Wilhelm and Friedrich Schlegel as well as Schelling tend not to fulfill their own definitions, being—as we have noted—rather traditional didactic poems.

Yet one major poem of the period is clearly based on the romantic definition and, hence, comes close to the generic norm of the classical German elegy: A. W. Schlegel's "Rom"

(1805). It is a curious—indeed, flabbergasting—thought that in the same year, 1805, at least three German poets were wandering around Rome composing elegies about their impressions: the crown prince of Bavaria, the Prussian minister to the Vatican, and the traveling companion of Mme de Staël. But though Ludwig was inspired solely by the "Römische Elegien" and Humboldt almost entirely by Schiller's theory of the elegy, Schlegel had a full-fledged theory as well as many possible models before him when he sat down in the spring of 1805 to compose an elegy on Rome. To be sure, no German poet writing about Rome only ten years after the publication of the "Römische Elegien" could say that he was totally free of their influence. Yet Schlegel was also familiar with an older tradition of Roman elegies, extending back by way of Jacob Balde and Joachim du Bellay to Hildebert of Lavardin's two great early-twelfth-century elegies "De Roma."[38] In addition, Schlegel admired "Der Spaziergang": shortly after its publication he wrote to Schiller—at that time still a close friend—to express the great pleasure the poem had provided him.[39] And as a result of his close collaboration with Goethe on the metrical revisions of "Elegien II," in March of 1800, he was intimately familiar with "Euphrosyne."

In one sense, of course, Schlegel's "Rom," which is designated as an "Elegie" in the subheading, is another of those versified survey courses that he regarded as poetry. But if we examine the organization of the material, we recognize, at least in outline, the familiar pattern of the generic norm.[40] As the framework opens (ll. 1-10) the poet, following his return from the lively city of Naples, resolves now to familiarize himself with death in Rome, that "grave of the world":

> Hast du das Leben geschlürft an Parthenope's üppigem
> Busen,
> Lerne den Tod nun auch über dem Grabe der Welt.

Having established in the first distich the elegiac tension between life and death, present and past, the poet makes his way through the "labyrinth of the ruins" to a proper locus for his meditations: not a mountain, to be sure, but Cestius' pyramid, where he enjoys a broad view of the horizon stretching from the Sabine hills to the sea.

The meditative core, which amounts to some two hundred fifty lines, is little more than a compendium of Roman history. The poet goes back in his imagination to "the beginning of things" and to the mythic pre-history of Latium from the Golden Age of Saturn down to the founding of Rome (ll. 11-28). He then outlines the emergence of law, culture, and religion under the seven princes, from Romulus to the Tarquins (ll. 29-50). The following section depicts the glory of the Republic (ll. 51-64). Then, in a long apostrophe (ll. 65-88), the poet warns the ancient Romans against discarding their virtue; Rome will never be destroyed by outside enemies, only by inner decay:

> Nicht der Samnite, des Galliers Wuth, nicht Hannibal
> dämpft euch.
> So will's eurer Geschick: selbst nur erlieget sich Rom.

This passage, clearly reminiscent of "Der Spaziergang," ends with a distich in which law has deteriorated to a false shell, religion to a mask, and freedom to unbridled license:

> Alles ja folget dem Strudel; das Recht wird falsches
> Gewebe,
> Freyheit wildes Gelüst, Larve die Religion.
>
> (ll. 89-90)

The poet goes on to describe the period of enervating civil war and the ensuing despotism, when the old virtues have given way to increasingly depraved sensationalism:

> Dieß Zeitalter, entwöhnt der Bewunderung, buhlt um
> Erstaunen.
>
> (l. 103)

Finally Rome has become so weakened by excesses within that it easily succumbs to the onslaught of Germanic hordes sweeping down from the Alps (ll. 163-90). At this point, in a passage punctuated by the word "Sieh," the poet introduces a series of elegiac contrasts between past glory and present degradation (ll. 191-258). The triumphal ways have become mule-paths along which peasants cart their wares to market. The Palatine hill is now a vine-covered ruin where the vintners' children cavort. Flocks graze in the Velabrum while, in the Forum, the lowing of cows can be heard. The race of noble warriors has degenerated into a pale and sickly people. In an image reminiscent of Goethe's "Amyntas" the poet compares contemporary Rome to an oak tree in which the strangling vines prevent the invigorating sap from reaching the crown:

> Aber umsonst. So sah ich verdorrt Appenninische Eichen,
>   Welchen sich Epheu rings, Bacchus geselliges Laub,
> Schlang um die Aeste zu lockigem Schmuck; wohl lügt es
>                                         die Krone,
>   Doch nie dringet die Kraft mehr von der Wurzel ins
>                                         Haupt.
>                                   (ll. 233-236)

The only redeeming grace Schlegel can detect in Roman history between the Fall and the present is Renaissance art:

> Einzig die Bildnerin Kunst wetteiferte noch mit der
>                                         Vorwelt.
>                                   (l. 239)

Otherwise, Rome's motto is *Gewesen* (l. 245)—an expression that explicitly recalls the topos familiar from earlier Rome-elegies: *Roma fuit*. At this point Schlegel once again invokes Janus, who was mentioned in the early lines of the poem: now his forward-looking face has lost its earlier youthful hopes, and the backward-looking visage is wrinkled with grief.

When the meditation ends, we find the poet again at the foot of Cestius' pyramid. The twilight world has become so quiet that he wonders, for a moment, if perhaps he has not himself joined those shades of the past who have just flitted in review before his imagination. In this twilight state between day and night, existence seems ephemeral, and life comes to a pause:

Alles, gedämpft und erblaßt, mahnt unser entschwindendes
Daseyn,
Und kein Hoffen erhebt über den irdischen Staub.
Noch nicht funkeln die Sterne, und gleichsam zwischen das
Leben
Dränget ein Stillstand sich, und die Unsterblichkeit, ein.

Then, amazingly, just when the poem has come to its apparent conclusion (l. 274), Schlegel tacks on twenty-two more lines as an apostrophe to Mme de Staël. In the descending night the stars remind him of his noble companion's gaze, which contains both truth and inspiration. In fact, the phrase Schlegel employs smacks of the old elegiac topos of smiling amidst the tears:

Tröstend begegnete so dein Blick mir, edle Gefährtin,
Jener entzückende Strahl göttlichen Doppelgestirns.
Wahrheit wohnet in ihm, und die liebende hohe
Begeistrung,
Welche, zur Wonne dem Schmerz, selber in Thränen
erglänzt.
(ll. 276-79)

Mixing tenderness with profundity, the good with the beautiful, she surrounds the poet with an enchantment that consoles him in his depression. In one sense, clearly, she represents that light of anagnorisis toward which the poet aspires at the end of every classical German elegy: Homer's sun, the rising sun at the end of "Euphrosyne," the radiance of Diotima. But Schlegel destroys the effect by going too far and reducing Mme de Staël from a star of inspiration to a radiant salon hostess. In their brilliant conversations, Schlegel continues, they will summon up the noble men of the past and, as an example of nobility in the present, she will tell him from time to time about her father, the banker Necker, whom Schlegel never had the honor of meeting:

Und wann unter den Weisen, die rein für das Ganze
gestrebet,

Wir aufsuchen ein Bild mildester Väterlichkeit,
Streng' in der eigenen Brust, langmüthig dem Wahn und
dem Undank,

Gleichwie ein Schutzgeist schwebt über dem
Menschengeschlecht:
Dann sey dessen Gedächtniß geheiliget, welchen zu kennen
Nicht mir gegönnt war, ach! welchen du ewig beweinst.

On this note the poem ends.

Schlegel was proud of his poem, on which he worked at least as hard, he wrote to various friends, as on many of his longer works. Quite possibly it is the best poem of a man whose real strength lay in criticism, not poetry. Yet despite its control of the generic norm the failings of the poem are conspicuous. The meditative center is a pedantic compendium with no real tension: Schlegel neglects to develop, for instance, the obvious dialectical contrast between freedom and virtue or imperialism and morality among the Romans. The center, moreover, has no real focus or articulation of parts to lend shape to its encyclopedic content: the arrangement of the historical material is strictly chronological, but there is no aesthetic balance between the various sections. The framework, in turn, is much too short in proportion to the meditative core: as a result, the locus and persona are not sufficiently defined to provide a satisfactory setting for the elegiac meditations. We simply have no way of knowling what it is, beyond a general cultural pessimism, that sends this particular poet to this particular place on this particular occasion to rehearse his gloomy vision. Finally, the unmotivated apostrophe to Mme de Staël, with its inclusion of Necker in a succession of great men reaching back to Roman antiquity, is so incongruous as to be grotesque.

Yet for all its shortcomings Schlegel's "Rom" clearly is based on the generic norm of the classical German elegy as it was recognized by one of the most perceptive critics of the age. We have already seen that the exploitation of the form is not particularly successful, but it is necessary to specify the nature of the flaw. A genre is preserved by gifted writers who manage to imitate the form perfectly without filling it with a new content. And a genre is changed by writers who strain at the limits of the form in order to accommodate it to their new insights. In Schlegel's case, however, we are dealing with neither maintenance nor change but simply with a poor poem—a failing that can be attributed to Schlegel's weakness as a poet. He was simply not capable, as a poet, of handling the genre whose characteristics he was fully capable of identifying as a critic. So Schlegel's "Rom" contributes nothing to the history of the genre. At the same time, we can single out several reasons why this form appealed to a poet-critic with Schlegel's characteristics. First, the meditative core represents a large attraction to a *poeta doctus* whose poetry tends toward the didactic. Second, the relegation of the poetic persona to a relatively brief framework offered a welcome escape for a writer with no real lyric gift. Third, the dialogic nature of the elegy provided him with an opportunity to apostrophize his benefactor, Mme de Staël, in a lofty context. Finally, the elegy as one of the most venerable forms of Greek and Roman literature appealed to a critic with Schlegel's strong classical background.

Yet despite Schlegel's "Rom" and the many distichs of the decade the elegy cannot properly be called a romantic genre. We can ascertain at least two reasons, both formal and thematic. First, the elegiac distich enjoyed its greatest popularity among such early romantic writers as the Schlegels and Novalis, who were still quite close to German classicism and its reverence for classical antiquity. This situation changed as subsequent generations of romantic writers shifted their attention away from pagan antiquity to the Christian Middle Ages. Although virtually every writer of the age experimented at one time or another with elegiac distichs, few of them used the form extensively. Often, as in the case of Brentano, the poet tried the form once, early in his career, and then never attempted it again. In general, the distich along with all classical strophic forms was soon driven out of romantic poetry by those forms that became identified with the romantic infatuation with the medieval past and the Romanic tradition: e.g., the *Lied*, the ballad, and the sonnet. The principal exception to this neglect of the distich was of course the epigram.[41] Many writers who neglected the distich otherwise—like the dramatists Grillparzer and Hebbel—used it frequently for their epigrams.

Second, the fundamental romantic belief in the unity of all knowledge and being precluded, thematically, the dualistic tension that is the necessary precondition for the elegy. A generation that believed with Schelling that "nature aspires to be visible spirit while spirit aspires to be invisible nature"[42] or with Novalis that "death is life's loftiest goal"[43] would find it difficult to generate the kind of tension between freedom and nature that underlies "Der Spaziergang" or between life and death that informs "Euphrosyne." The representative poem of German romanticism, formally as well as thematically, is Eichendorff's lovely "Mondnacht," a simple twelve-line *Lied* that culminates in an expression of faith in the identity of the human soul and nature:

> Und meine Seele spannte
> Weit ihre Flügel aus,
> Flog durch die stillen Lande
> Als flöge sie nach Haus.

Even when the theme is potentially elegiac—such as the death of the beloved—the treatment manages to convert it quickly into a resolution. Novalis' "Hymnen an die Nacht" move rapidly from the initially stated opposition between life and death, light and dark, to a harmony of all being that dominates the remainder of the poem, which symptomatically labels as a "hymn" precisely the same situation that Hölderlin called an "elegy" when he wrote "Menons Klagen."

During the first decade of the nineteenth century, then, the poetic energies that had inspired the classical German elegy expired both formally and thematically. It is important to stress this fact because we can appreciate the subsequent development of the genre only if we remember that we are dealing with a break in its continuity. For "elegies" continued to be written after, say, 1810. But the form of the elegiac distich was no longer automatically associated with the mode. Even writers who had earlier used distichs for their elegies now sometimes turned to other forms. Goethe, for instance, adopted a simple stanzaic form, possibly influenced by Humboldt's elegy "Rom," when he wrote his great Marienbad "Elegie" in 1823. And Grillparzer, one of whose earliest extant works is the fragment of an elegy in distichs from the year 1804, also employed a simple stanza consisting of four-beat trochees for his Roman elegy, "Campo Vaccino," in 1819. Meanwhile, for younger writers the elegiac distich became simply another form—along with other classical, romantic, and newly popular oriental forms—with no specific thematic associations. At the same time, certain thematic changes were taking place. Some writers who handled the elegiac distich with great virtuosity were too content with life as it was to be capable of experiencing life elegiacally. Others, paradoxically, gradually converted this very inability to feel elegiacally—that is, their sense of being an epigonal generation—into the theme of their elegies. We can observe these various processes at work if we examine three poets of the immediate post-romantic period.

Ernst Moritz Arndt was moved to his finest poetry not by vague romantic ideals but by the War of Liberation, and he subverted for the purposes of his fanatical patriotism and ardent Francophobia every available poetic genre, including the elegy. His three major poems in elegiac distichs display at least rudimentarily a framework embracing an inner core. But as a result of his single-minded obsession with the war, the form gets curiously inverted. In the classical German elegy the framework is personal, and the meditative core is general—indeed, usually historical, cultural, and even political. But in Arndt's elegies we find precisely the opposite relationship: the framework is general and political whereas the meditative core is personal. In two of his poems—"An Antonia Amalia, Herzogin von Württemberg" (1812) and "Lug ins Leben" (1813)—the core is autobiographical.[44] The earlier poem begins as though it were going to be an elegy on his childhood:

Knabe war ich, es drang kein Klang von gewaltigen Dingen
Unter das strohene Dach, welches die Kindheit
geschirmt,
Einfalt wohnte mit mir und stille freundliche Sitte,
Frömmigkeit lullte mich ein, Frömmigkeit weckte mich
auf, . . .

Soon a certain pensiveness began to trouble his parents, who urged him to mend his ways lest his moodiness become an annoyance to others:

Denn sie meinten, es werde der Sohn, ein finsterer
Träumer,
Sich und andern die Lust töten in künftiger Zeit.

Years later Arndt realizes that the gloom of his youth, which he attributes to an early awareness of destiny, has been justified by political events:

Doch die Ahnung hat auch ihr dunkles Verhängnis erfüllet,
Bis auf den heutigen Tag alles mit Strenge erfüllt.

He now offers his prophetic voice to the princess to commemorate the inevitable victory that God shall vouchsafe the "holy people of the Germans":

Gott wird richten und hat gerichtet, der mächtige Walter,
Klinge prophetischer Klang! Halle, verfliegendes Wort!

We might say uncharitably that Arndt is using the elegiac form to justify retrospectively the sulking of a moody child. There is no real elegiac contrast since he is not looking back at a happy past from a melancholy present. The meditative sadness of the conventional elegy is obviated by Arndt's thundering rage at Napoleon. And though the framework is at least implicit in the poem, it does not actually appear until the end.

The same situation prevails in the second poem, which was written while Arndt was working as a nightwatchman in the Silesian town of Reichenbach during the ceasefire of 1813. The poem, which consists of fifty-one sets of double distichs, begins with a statement of the temporary tranquillity:

Still steht das Leben, es steht der Zorn der Männer
gefesselt,
Durch der Könige Wort ruhet das Eisen der Schlacht.
Ich auch sitz' hier in Engen, an Reichenbachs bröcklichte
Mauer
Lehnt sich das Häuschen, wo Streit kaum mir ein
Stübchen gewann.

The unwonted peace and quiet causes him to think about his
life, which he surveys from childhood and youth through
marriage and the death of his first wife. Then he speaks of the
Napoleonic war, which gave his life a new meaning:

Denn nach traurigem Schlaf, der trübliche Jahre
verdämmert,
Weckte in Wetter und Sturm Gott der Gewaltige uns;
Daß wir wieder gedächten der glorreichen Ehren der Väter,
Hob sich ein wilder Tyrann, Geißel des Himmels,
empor.

Then in a series of powerful rhetorical questions—"Bin ich
nicht glücklich?"—Arndt reaches the astonishing, yet for him
quite characteristic, conclusion that the war has given his life a
meaning it previously lacked. Again: the sensations of wrath
and patriotism annul any possible elegiac feeling—either for
his youth or for his deceased wife:

Rollt denn, ihr Räder, die weiter mich tragt, und flattert, ihr
Segel!
Glaube und Liebe sind mit, Zorn fliegt fröhlich voran,
*Vaterland* klinget der Ruf, die Freiheit schwebt wie ein
Engel,
Schwingend den leuchtenden Kranz, über der staubigen
Bahn.

Toward the beginning of "Lug ins Leben" he makes the
point that such moments of tranquillity are more conducive
to visions of the past than of the future:

Zukunft, dich fraget nicht gern in solchen Zeiten die Seele;
Darum, Vergangenheit, komm! Sei mir Erinn'rung,
gegrüßt!

Yet that same year he coopted the elegiac form for a poem that specifically looks into the future. For the first hundred and fifty lines of "Lebenstraum" the poet outlines for his new bride-to-be the various places where they might live after their marriage—in Reichenbach, the North Sea islands, or the Rhine region.[45] Suddenly, toward the end, he interrupts this vision to state that the dream is premature because the war against the French is still going on:

> O der zu glückliche Traum! Schon hör' ich's trommeln und
> blasen:
> Das klingt Reise und Krieg, selige Stille, fahr wohl!

The Rhine, "the sacred river of the Germans," is under foreign control, and the rest of his country is also unfree. Nothing is certain any longer—least of all material possessions. And yet with that twist so characteristic of Arndt's thinking the poem finds in these deprivations cause for rejoicing. He implores his beloved to forgo all earthly claims and to join him in celebrating a spiritual space that transcends mere reality:

> Erde vergeht, und Irdisches flieht, o laß uns den Busen
> Dehnen zum himmlischen Raum, welcher es alles
> umfaßt.

Again, Arndt's passionate hatred of Napoleon and his almost masochistic enjoyment of the war dispels the mood of elegiac contemplation as the elegiac distich is inverted into a patriotic hymn.

Arndt had a single message that he repeated over and over in a variety of forms; Friedrich Rückert had a variety of forms that he polished incessantly even though he had no real statement to make. Rückert was a virtuoso of metrical forms, capable of versifying anything and everything with virtually no selectivity. In fact, the ease with which he packed almost any topic into almost any pre-selected metrical form is symptomatic of the approaching age of literary epigones who found themselves cursed with enormous technical facility and nothing to say. The section of his poetic works entitled "Distichen" is typical of this dilemma.[46] Written around 1818, it contains a variety of thirteen poems, ranging from such occasional topics as wedding poems ("Hochzeits- und Abschiedsgeschenke an eine fürstliche Braut") to translations of Martial's epigrams and adaptations of grave inscriptions of Greek poetesses. We find a humorous anecdote in dialogue ("Wiederhergestellter Haushalt"), gently erotic poems ("Galatea," "Asteria," "Narzissus"), and a lyrical nature poem ("Abendgespräche im Walde"). One poem—"An die Nacht"—looks like a précis in distichs of Novalis' "Hymnen an die Nacht"—an analogy wholly in keeping with Rückert's tendency to appropriate familiar motifs (in the absence of original ones of his own) from the existing poetic corpus.

Rückert was familiar with the elegiac tradition: in 1805, while still a schoolboy, he translated Schiller's "Nänie" into Greek verse. In fact, his unselective command of the corpus of world literature, including the newly fashionable Oriental languages and literatures, prevented him from developing a characteristic tone of his own. Above all, his solid bourgeois ideals, his spiritual assurance, and a retiring disposition that entirely lacked the grand pathos of preceding generations precluded the elegiac mood in his own work. His longest and most familiar poem in distichs, "Rodach," reflects this characterization. The Biedermeier idyll portraying the life of Rückert's elderly friend, Christian Hohnbaum, the senior district minister in Rodach near Coburg, was written as a thank-you note following a visit at Hohnbaum's, probably in 1814.[47]

Laß mich die einzige Nacht noch ruhn im gastlichen Dache,
    Morgen im leeren Nest findest du dieses Gedicht.

Rückert's praise of Hohnbaum's modest life with its modest goals and modest achievements embodies an utterly unelegiac attitude corresponding to Rückert's own ideal:

Dreimal seliger Mann! im verworrenen Lotto des Lebens,
    Wo der Nieten so viel, hast du mit glücklicher Hand,
Wenn nicht das große Loos, doch gewiß ein großes
                                    gezogen;

Welch ein großes, das hast selbst du am schönsten
bekannt,
Als du freudiges Rühmens und dankbar sprachest, daß
weiter
Nichts, als zweierlei dir fehle: ein Wunsch und ein Feind.

The same epigonal quality is evident in the works of the writer whose novel, *Die Epigonen* (1836), bestowed a name on his entire generation. Karl Immermann's "Elegien I–IX" (1823) were originally published as a cycle with subtitles based on the names of the Muses[48]—a device borrowed, no doubt, from Goethe's epic, "Hermann und Dorothea." The lack of any inherent cyclical unity, however, is displayed by the fact that Immermann subsequently gave the poems new titles and published them separately in later editions of his works.[49] Once again we are dealing with highly derivative poems—the flaw of a writer who is stronger and more original in almost every other area of literature.[50] "Der Tanz" (originally "Elegien III. Terpsichore") is clearly inspired by Schiller's elegy of the same title: an observer standing apart from the activity compares the movements of the dance to the order of the world. But instead of contenting himself with that simple analogy, Immermann exaggerates his comparison in true epigonal fashion to take in the very heavenly spheres in their courses:

Also schauet der Vater der Welt, der erhab' ne Kronide
Ernst auf dem himmlischen Thron, schaut in den Reigen
des Alls.
Stumm hin wandeln vor ihm die Gestirn' in den goldenen
Kreisen,
Aber sein göttliches Ohr höret der Sphären Gesang.[51]

"Reizende Wahrheit" (originally "Elegien II. Erato") is an erotic fancy after the fashion of the "Römische Elegien"; "Die Freunde" (originally "Elegien IV. Euterpe") is a gnomic poem on friendship; and "Thalia" (originally "Elegien VII. Thalia") is a satirical epigram on the literary life.

In view of Immermann's imitative ability combined with

his lack of selectivity it is hardly surprising that one of the nine poems fulfills—by chance, as it were—the generic norm of the classical German elegy. "Der Dom zu Köln" (originally "Elegien I: Clio"), unlike the other poems of the cycle, has a personal framework embracing a meditative core.[52] A traveler, having eagerly awaited this moment all his life, has just paid his first visit to the cathedral of Cologne (whose restoration was finally being undertaken in 1823). In a state of intense excitement he steps out onto the porch of the "miraculous building" ("Wundergebäude"), where he catches sight of the flying buttresses, so slender and at the same time so mighty. This sight catalyzes in his excited imagination a vision of the great men of the past, who were so much larger than present life:

Also dünken die Menschen der Zeit, der auf ewig vergangnen,
Dich von gewöhnlichem Maß, denkst du des ganzen Geschlechts;
Rissest du einen jedoch aus der Gruppe der Freunde und Feinde,
Schreckt' er als Riese, o glaub! deinen verzagenden Blick.

His recollection of the magical illumination within the cathedral and the mighty resonance of the organ arouses in his mind an elegiac contrast between past and present:

Selige, dunkele Zeit, da der Stein dem Ewigen diente,
Während die heutige Kunst nur die Kaserne begreift!

Depressed at the thought of the present "disinherited" ("enterbt") generation, the traveler steps over to the tower of the cathedral, whose delicate lacing reminds him that the past was so rich that it could afford to be lavish. The sight of the building crane makes him wonder how long the cathedral will have to wait for its completion. Then closing his eyes in a vision, he sees a panorama of human achievement, from Greek and Roman antiquity through the Middle Ages to the present. (The vision is stated, not described.) When he opens his eyes in wonder, he sees the completed cathedral. The vision lasts only for an instant and then disappears, but the poet is consoled by his epiphany of humanity and its accomplishments:

> Plötzlich schlug die Augen ich auf: o erhabenes Wunder!
> Fertig sah ich den Dom, Türme und Kirche und Chor!
> Nur den Moment. Es verschwand, wie ein Traum, das
> > hohe Gesichte,
> Aber ich hatt' es erblickt, da ich der Menschheit gedacht.

Described in this way, the poem seems to fit the generic norm almost perfectly: the poetic persona is located near a great height (not a mountain, to be sure), where he has a vision in which past greatness and the present state of humanity are elegiacally contrasted. The moment of anagnorisis in the concluding framework enables the poet to reconcile through the power of imagination the problem posed by the meditative core: humanity will again be capable of greatness and of completing the cathedral, which is itself a symbol of humanity. Clearly, Immermann has grasped the structure and implications of such models as "Der Spaziergang." Yet certain symptomatic flaws in the realization of the generic norm stamp this poem as imperfect and derivative.

First, the poet plays a self-conscious game with the poetic persona. In the opening lines he writes in the third person about the visitor to the cathedral:

> Aus dem Dome zu Köln mit erglüheten Wangen und
> > Augen
> Trat ein reisiger Mann, der ihn zum erstenmal sah.

It is only toward the end that he coyly concedes the traveler is none other than himself:

> Zu dem Turm hin zog es mich jetzt. (Ich war's, ich gesteh'
> > es!)

This transformation, forcing us to rethink what we have read, distracts our attention needlessly. A similar imprecision characterizes other aspects. For instance, the poem dallies with the sense of height and distance. At the beginning the speaker gazes up at the soaring buttresses:

Siehe, dort steigen die Pfeiler empor des herrlichen Chores,

. . .

The grand epiphany is projected onto the perspective of the building crane high above:

Jetzo hatt' ich gefunden den Kran, der ernst von dem Dache
Fragt: wie lang', o wie lang' werd' ich der Steine noch
harr'n?

And the concluding vision of the completed cathedral demands a vantage point at some distance from the edifice. Yet during his entire monologue the poet is located at ground level near the cathedral. By the same token, the description of the illuminated windows and the organ music suggests a standpoint within the cathedral although the poet has already stepped outside. Finally, the vision itself is not a single sustained whole: it is interrupted by a fragment of framework when the traveler steps across from the portal to the base of the tower. As a result, the power of the vision is fragmented.

All this fuzziness—our uncertainty about the identity of the speaker, the location of the point of view, the integrity of the vision—prevents the poem from achieving its full effect. Yet for all its flaws we are clearly dealing here with an imitation, no matter how imprecise, of the classical German elegy. Of interest in our context, however, is the fact that this imitation is flawed in a manner entirely different from that of Schlegel's "Rom." In the romantic imitation we noted, above all, an absence of dialectical tension in the meditative core. Here, in contrast, the elegiac tension between past and present is well represented. The weakness of epigonal poetry is the fragmentation of experience, as though the epigone were unable to sustain, as an integral whole, the vision that was still whole in the classical German elegy. Or to put it another way: Schlegel had the form intact but not the power of meaning; Immermann has the power of meaning but he cannot hold together the form. A decade later an elegy appeared that exemplified still another facet of the epigonal dilemma.

On May 7, 1787, Goethe climbed up to the ancient theater on the mountainside overlooking the Sicilian town of Taormina. "If one takes a seat in the very top row, one must concede that probably never did a theater audience enjoy such a view."[53] Above the theater rugged citadels jut up from cliffs that fall, in a sheer precipice, to the town nestled against their base. A mountain ridge leads the eye from the theater across to the smoking mouth of Mount Etna, which shuts off the inland view, while on the horizon, across the Strait of Messina, the observer can make out the coasts of Calabria. Goethe found the prospect so overwhelming that on the following day he let his traveling companion, the painter Kniep, go back alone to sketch the scenes they had viewed. He himself retreated to the confines of a neglected garden and thought about his projected drama "Nausikaa."

It is possible, even likely, that August von Platen had this passage in mind, almost fifty years later, when he spent a week in Taormina. He had studied the *Italienische Reise* with great attention, and his decision to go to Italy, where he lived from 1826 until his death in 1835, seems to have been a conscious *imitatio* of Goethe.[54] In any case, when he recorded his visit in his diary he noted: "Nature here equals the loveliest sections of the Gulf of Naples: one rediscovers Sorrento and Amalfi, and perhaps even more. Also," the entry continues, "I wrote an elegy here and two hymns, . . . All this, for the most part, while strolling around in the ancient theater."[55] Platen's elegy, "Im Theater von Taormina," begins with a scenic description that incorporates precisely the same features of the landscape that had impressed Goethe: Mount Etna and the sea, the town rising abruptly from below and, in the distance, "the blessed coasts of Italy":

Zarte vergängliche Wölkchen umfliegen den schneeigen
Ätna,
Während des Meers Abgrund klar wie ein Spiegel
erscheint;
Steil auftürmt sich die Stadt, hoch über die Gärten der
Klöster,
Über den blühenden Wein ragen Cypressen empor.

> Fern in der Sonne verglühn die gesegneten Küsten Italiens,
> Schöner und üppiger noch, als die sikulischen Au'n.[56]

Whether Platen was thinking specifically of Goethe on that day, or only of his benefactor Ludwig I, who had also written an elegy in the theater some years earlier,[57] in a more general sense his presence in Taormina had a distinctly literary motivation. He was blessed with an immense formal virtuosity that was not matched by any corresponding creative originality. Unable to generate original topics for his poems, he pored over books in the twelve languages that he read with ease, diligently casting about for suitable subjects. And he restlessly roamed Europe, seeking inspiration in museums and palaces and sites with cultural associations: some of his most beautiful poems can be found in the cycle of sonnets he wrote about Venice. It was almost, on these occasions, as though he hoped that the *genius loci* would stir him. As he walked around the theater above Taormina, contemplating the landscape, he invoked the spirits of the Middle High German poets who flourished in the courts of the Sicilian Hohenstaufens (Walter von der Vogelweide and Wolfram von Eschenbach). And he reminded himself of seven Greek poets associated with Sicily: the elegist Simonides of Ceos, who spent his last ten years there; Aeschylus, who died there; Pindar and Theocritus, who lived there for several years; Epicharmus, Stersichorus, and Ibycus.

The harried self-consciousness that sent Platen to literary and artistic sources for much of his inspiration also caused him constantly to measure himself against the poets he admired—in his youth somewhat abjectly, but later with an increasing confidence in his own poetic merits. Quite a few of his poems turn out to be little more than literary scoresheets. Thus in his sonnet about sonneteers ("Sonette dichtete mit edlem Feuer," 1820) he alludes to Petrarch, Camoëns, and Rückert: the final tercet states that he follows these three masters as a gleaner follows the reaper, for he does not presume to join them as an equal.[58] In the poetic epitaph that he composed for himself ("Grabschrift," 1826-1829) he boasts that he has written comedies in a style as yet unexcelled and that he has won "the second prize for odes."[59] (Oddly, he neglects to tell us who won the first prize—presumably he had either Pindar or Klopstock in mind.) The sense of insecurity evident in this constant need to rank himself shows up in his elegy as well, where he lists himself as the possible ninth in a succession of German poets beginning with Ewald von Kleist, Gottfried August Bürger, and Friedrich Leopold von Stolberg and continuing through Schiller, Klopstock, and Goethe right down to his contemporaries, Rückert and Uhland.

Platen was agonizingly aware of his own deficiencies, which he tended to blame on the epigonal age in which he was condemned to live. In an epigram to "Horaz und Klopstock" (1829) he points out that the German poet, who tried to imitate the Latin hymns and odes, was not always able to achieve sublimity because he lacked the grandiose subject matter provided by Caesar's Rome. The modern poet, he concludes, should strive through wit and style to compensate for the lack of an adequate subject matter and the shortcomings of the age:

> Such', o moderner Poet, durch Geist zu ergänzen des Stoffs
>
> Fehl,
> Durch vielseitigen Stil decke die Mängel der Zeit.[60]

As a result of this belief, he trained himself to become a highly conscious virtuoso in every form that he touched. Among the various forms he mastered as a young man we find ballads, romances, and the classical meters. After his meeting with Rückert in 1820 Platen dedicated himself for a time to oriental ghazels and the sonnet. Later, during his Italian years, he returned almost exclusively to such classical forms as odes, eclogues, epigrams, hymns and—almost at the end of his life— the elegy.

Unaware of Hölderlin and contemptuous of German romanticism, which he ridiculed in such dramatic parodies as *Die verhängnisvolle Gabel* (1826) and *Der romantische Ödipus* (1829), Platen turned to the German classical tradition for his models. His proclivity for rhetorical pathos led him, as a young man, to Schiller, under whose direct inspiration he wrote his earliest poems.[61] In 1817 we find Platen in Switzerland where, inspired by the scenery, he studied Schiller's aesthetics and read "Der Spaziergang" aloud to a lady.[62] Goethe was important to Platen's development from the formal point of view. It was the "Römische Elegien," he noted in his diary, that first attracted him to the elegiac distich,[63] which he employed in a number of elegies that he wrote during his youth (1812-1820).[64] These early elegies are quite conventional in their form: resembling eighteenth-century erotic and threnetic elegies, they anticipate in no way the generic norm of the classical German elegy that Platen was to use in his one late poem.[65] But they reveal quite clearly his inherent elegiac temperament, in sharp contrast to Rückert, with whom he is sometimes rather casually coupled. In these poems we can detect at least three of the elegiac themes that inform Platen's mature poetry. First, many of the poems—"Anteros," "Rückblick," or "Gedanken der Liebe"—are erotic elegies, whose poignancy is sharpened by the sexual confusions that caused Platen to adapt this form to celebrate homosexual love. Second, in the poem "Amerika" there is a fleeting anticipation of the theme of freedom that Platen in later poems was to posit so elegiacally, in contrast to the prevailing despotism of contemporary governments. Finally, in "Der Abschied" and "An die neue Schule" we hear the theme that is to emerge in the late elegy—the alienation of the poetic youth who feels himself to be out of step with the goals and ideals of his own literary generation, notably the sonnets and religiosity of late romanticism:

> Tadelt ihr mich, daß ich noch die homerischen Götter
> beschwöre?
> Daß ich zu griechischer Form flüchtete, tadelt ihr mich?
> Leider gelang mir's nie, euch selbst zu verstehn und das
> Eure,
> Nicht den andächtigen Sinn, nicht das Geklingel des
> Schalls.

But all too often a scolding tone turns these youthful poems into satires against the present rather than elegies for the vanished ideal, as in the short "Elegie" of 1813:

> O wie bin ich der törichten Welt und des törichten Treibens
> Aller der Menge so satt, welche mich täglich umgibt!
> Das ist der Städte Fluch, und der weitumfassenden Mauer,
> Daß sie der Toren so viel, viele der Bösen verschließt.
> Überall herrscht nur ein einziger Gott, der leidige Vorteil,
> Tugend und Kunst und Verstand opfert ihm dieses
> Geschlecht.

For a variety of reasons Platen neglected the form of the elegy during the next decade, even though the mode of his poems remained conspicuously elegiac according to the definition of his cherished Schiller. But shortly before the end of his life he returned one final time to the form of the elegy, and this time the organization of the poem shows quite clearly that he had assimilated the lesson of the masters, Goethe and Schiller, whose works he had studied with such critical attentiveness. Platen's last elegy was written as the dedicatory poem for a group of nine Pindaric hymns that he intended to publish under the title *Festgesänge*. The plan was frustrated by his death, but because Platen regarded these late poems as his "literary heritage" and as the best poems that he had hitherto written,[66] the elegy deserves our particular attention.

"Im Theater von Taormina" is considerably shorter than the elegies that define the generic norm (for a reason that remains to be discussed). But formally and structually its forty-two lines display all the subtleties we would expect from a poet as perceptive and talented as Platen. Like many of his poems, the elegy is a discourse on poetry. More specifically, it is a lament that modern times have been unable to match the great poetry of the Greek and Germanic past. The poem begins rather well. The opening lines, quoted above, establish a mood of tension by means of a series of contrasts reminiscent of Schiller: images of height and depth, nearness and distance, light and dark, gradually give way to a transitional contrast between past and present as the poet looks down at the bay and thinks of the nymphs who formerly bathed there:

> Vor mir seh' ich die kleine, die felsenumschattete Seebucht,
> Welche zum Bad vormals seligen Nymphen gedient,

Die sich der ewigen Jugend erfreut in der tiefen Krystallflut
Oder der Brandungen auch rauschende Welle behorcht.

Once the scene has been set, the poet shifts to a more reflective mood (ll. 11-19) in the form of an extended apostrophe to
the muse of poetry who has led him here to Greek soil—
Taormina was founded by Greeks—where formerly medieval
German poetry flourished. But then the German muse fell silent for six centuries. It occurs to Platen that centuries also
elapsed in Greece between the works of Homer and the "Aeo-
lian lyre" of Sappho. This historical observation leads to the
generalization, precisely in the middle of the elegy (ll. 20-24),
that "storms of rebirth" surround "nobler peoples" from
which they emerge "in doubled beauty." He apostrophizes
the Art that has newly awakened in Germany: still "drunken
with sleep and shy," it will be "steeled" by the times:

Selig der Morgen, an dem wieder, o Kunst, du erwachst!
Freudvoll seist du begrüßt, wiewohl schlaftrunken und
                                                    scheu noch,
    Dich wird stählen jedoch bald die geschäftige Zeit.

This crucial passage merely suggests the possible resolution:
the tender blossom of German poetry, which—this, thirty
years after the major poems of Goethe, Schiller, and
Hölderlin—has not yet come to maturity, may still flourish.
But Platen does not become specific at this point. The poem
continues (ll. 25-32) with a list of eight poets in whom "the
rich vein of lyric art" has manifested itself: Goethe, for instance, is "the flower of grace" ("die Blume der Anmut").
Platen finishes his list by suggesting that certain "prudent
men" have agreed that he himself might be included as the
ninth in that group:

Darf ich der neunte zu sein mich rühmen? Bedächtige
                                                    Männer
Leugnen es nicht, mir ward lieblicher Äste Gewind.

At this point (ll. 33-42) the poet awakens from his meditations
to find himself once again on the island where formerly so
many Greek poets sang, and he intones still another catalogue.

Then, with an apostrophe to "Germania," Platen advances solemnly across the "immortal ruins" to pluck the laurels that she has bestowed upon him. He will not entwine them around his own melancholy head, he says, but lays them on her altar:

> Hier, Germania, laß auf diesen unsterblichen Trümmern
>    Brechen die Lorbeern mich, die du bewilligetest!
> Doch nicht sei'n um mein schwermütiges Haupt sie
>                                        gewunden,
>    Nein, auf deinen Altar seien sie niedergelegt!

Formally, the poem is impressive—in contrast to the attempts by Schlegel and Immermann. The distichs are metrically quite acceptable, and the structure reveals a calculated concinnity of parts. We find the conventional framework embracing a meditative core that, in turn, encloses central lines that anticipate a final resolution:

| | | |
|---|---|---|
| | 1-10 | Scenic description |
| | 11-19 | Meditation: poetry of the past |
| | 20-24 | Turning point: rejuvenation of poetry |
| | 25-32 | Meditation: modern German poetry |
| | 33-42 | Resolution of past and present in Taormina |

As in other elegies, the poet is put into a contemplative mood by the vista revealed to him from the mountainside. He is thus spiritually prepared by the landscape for the apparition of the muse who suggests to his mind the thematic tension between past and present. When he emerges from his meditations, his new awareness enables him to achieve the resolution of the elegiac tension.

This elegy is not one of Platen's best poems. Despite his own estimation of it, his true achievement should probably be sought in those symbolic poems describing objects of art, which stand in a direct line leading to the *Dinggedichte* of Conrad Ferdinand Meyer, Stefan George, and Rilke.[67] But the elegy illustrates Platen's predicament. For in its final effect, it is almost a travesty: a brilliantly wrought formal shell with no adequate substance. In the classical German elegy the poetic self was led by its meditations to a moment of anagnorisis, an awareness of supra-individual meaning, and this is the expectation that we have come to associate with the form. We await revelations that may resolve the personal plight of the poetic persona, but that also transcend the individual to assume universal implications. We want to be assured that nature is eternal behind the apparent transitoriness of human society; that temporality can be eternalized by art; that the timeless realm of being is omnipresent for those whose eyes have been opened through the power of love—even that the Cologne cathedral can be completed. This is the great mission of the classical German elegy that even Immermann grasped despite the insufficiency of form in his poem: for his poetic persona grows through a vision of a humanity that transcends his own epigonal self. Now Platen takes this powerful rhetorical tool, whose effect he fully comprehends, and with the utmost skill arouses our expectations: he poses a grand problem—the disparity between the mighty poetry of the past and the "shy" muse of the present—and suggests, through the elegiac form, that he has discovered the answer. But after stirring our emotions and our curiosity with all the rhetorical devices at his command, what does he offer us as a grand anagnorisis? No sweeping generalization, no bold combination, no transcendent vision—but only himself. Unable to sustain by power of original thought the mood of meditation in the isolated splendor of the mountain theater, he falls back quickly—note the relatively short length of the poem—to the only certainty he knows: his own tormented personality. Platen's elegy, then, fails for reasons quite different from those in the case of Schlegel and Immermann. There is no lack of elegiac tension or of aesthetic control. But Platen was driven into introspective isolation by so many factors: personally through his homosexuality, politically through his disenchantment with the prevailing oppressive regimes, and culturally by his epigonal love for a vanished literary past. Accustomed to look to himself, he was incapable in his elegy of looking beyond himself for the grand resolution.

If we take a more critical look at Platen's poem, we find that even the mountain has been included because of convention, not necessity. In "Der Spaziergang" the poet's vision arises from the landscape itself, and so the mountain is fully justified as the locus of the poem. In "Euphrosyne" the mountain symbolizes the forces of nature set in opposition to human frailty: again, the setting is inherent in the poem. In the interiorized world of "Menons Klagen" the mountain presents itself, at the end, as the logical correlative of the heights toward which the poet's course leads him. But in Platen's elegy there is absolutely no compelling reason why the resolution should take place in the theater above Taormina: it could just as well have been written in his hotel room at sea level. Platen forces both history and logic in order to make the locus seem plausible. Platen himself had no profound feeling for nature or for mountains. His finest poems are those written about things and places created by man: Venice, great works of art, and the like. His favorite flower was the tulip, which must be cultivated by man.[68] And when he went to Switzerland, he reacted in the spirit more of the eighteenth century than of the post-Goethean age: he indulged his sensations indirectly by reading a poem ("Der Spaziergang") and he analyzed his reaction by studying Delille's rationalist poem on gardening.[69]

Platen was clever enough to know that the mountain is supposed to produce elegiac thoughts, but when he got up to the theater at Taormina nothing new occurred to him, so he resorted to the same old theme that informs many of his poems: an anguished analysis of his own position in the history of German literature. Several years before Platen wrote his elegy, Goethe made an uncannily prophetic remark to Eckermann: it is unpardonable of such a lofty talent, he said with reference to Platen, "that in the great surroundings of Naples and Rome he can think of nothing but the wretchedness of German literature."[70] This exclusively literary orientation dominated Platen to the end of his life: it was both the source of his personal misery and, at least in part, the reason for his failure to achieve a more impressive stature. For even when he was confronted with the magnificent view from the theater at Taormina, he could find nothing better to do than to count on his fingers the major lyric poets of Germany.

Goethe, of course, had found a better use for his fingers: he stroked the back of his lover in gentle accompaniment to the distichs in which he celebrated his love.

Platen was an exception in his own time, for the age in general was not elegiac. This is evident if we consider two of Platen's younger contemporaries, who also wrote a number of poems about Italy in elegiac distichs: Wilhelm Waiblinger and Friedrich Hebbel.[71] In both cases the poets specifically used the term "Bilder" to designate these poems: they are attempts to capture, in distich form, scenes from Italian life with no elegiac content, for both writers are obsessed with the present. In his "Bilder aus Neapel and Sicilien," for instance, Waiblinger writes:

> Immer schlendr' ich umher, und keiner Arbeit gedenk' ich,
> Unter dem wilden Gewühl irr' ich betrachtend herum.
> Meer und Hafen und Stadt, und der rauchende Berg und
> die Inseln,
> Und dies tobende Volk fesselt mein Auge, mein Herz.
> Gegenwärtiges freuet mich nur, dem Glücklichen lächelt
> Nur der goldne Moment, lächelt die Wirklichkeit nur.
> (III)[72]

The one hundred poems of the cycle contain contrasts, to be sure; but they are contrasts of the two cities that Waiblinger loves:

> Wohnst du auf Roma's Hügeln, der Welt uralte
> Geschichte:
> Hast in Parthenope du, Mythe, dein Reich dir erwählt.
> (XXXVI)

> Wenn in Rom das Schicksal dir nur und die Parze begegnet,
> Mahnt dich der Schmetterling hier nur an das Glück des
> Moments.
> (XXXVIII)

Waiblinger's distichs are poems of celebration, with no nostalgia for the past:

Rühm' ich die freundlichen Plätze, wo oft die Sehnsucht
mich hintreibt,
Sei auch ein Distichon dir, Santa Lucia, geweiht.
(XXVIII)

Hebbel was quite conscious of writing in a specific tradition
tied quite closely to the form of the elegy. One of his "Bilder"
from Italy, for instance, playfully alludes to the motif of the
vine-choked tree as used by Goethe in "Amyntas" and A. W.
Schlegel in his "Rom"-elegy:

Efeu, man hat dich verklagt, du sollst die Bäume entseelen,
Aber ich spreche dich los, da du die Steine belebst!
Jenen Frevel erblickt' ich noch nie; dies reizende Wunder
Sah ich noch heute vollbracht: grünt doch das traurige
Grab.[73]

Yet at no point do we hear an elegiac note in Hebbel's "Bilder"; he is too keenly aware of presentday Rome:

Rom, schon bist du Ruine und wirst noch weniger werden,
Aber dein Himmel verbürgt dennoch die ewige Stadt.
Wo die Myrte gedeiht, und wo der Lorbeer nicht mangelt,
Siedeln zu Liebe und Krieg immer auch Menschen sich
an.[74]

The only major poet of the period who wrote many of his
finest poems in elegiac distichs was perhaps the least elegiac of
men: the Swabian pastor Eduard Mörike. Almost all of
Mörike's works exemplify his constant attempt to maintain a
Golden Mean, a balance and harmony between reality and the
ideal in his own life and work. He rejected as a matter of principle the heroic posturing of elegiac longing that characterizes
the poems of Platen.

With the friend of his student days, Waiblinger, Mörike
frequently visited Hölderlin in Tübingen; he admired his fellow Swabian, Schiller, and devoted one of his most poignant
distich poems to Schiller's mother ("Auf das Grab von Schillers Mutter," 1835); and he revered Goethe. Yet the model for
the many poems in elegiac distichs that he wrote in the thirties

and forties was none of these modern German writers but rather the Latin and Greek elegists whose works he translated and edited in his *Classische Blumenlese* (1840): notably Callinus, Tyrtaeus, Theognis, and Tibullus, whom he characterized as "certainly the most lovable elegist among the Romans."[75] Scattered among Mörike's collected poems are dozens of poems in the most elegant and graceful elegiac distichs of the period. Yet few of these poems are even vaguely elegiac in mood: e.g., the poem to his boyhood friend Hermann Hardegg ("An Hermann"), in which the poet is reminded by a dream of the closest friend of his youth, from whom he parted in anger as the result of a childish misunderstanding. Otherwise the poems contain a number of erotic elegies, at least one of which ("Lose Ware") is reminiscent in part of Goethe's "Römische Elegien": Amor slips into the poet's room disguised as a boy selling ink ("Amor, verkleideter Schelm!"), and the poet uses the ink to compose a love poem which he designates, using Goethe's term, as an "eroticon":

> Angeführt hat er mich doch: denn will ich was Nützliches
> schreiben:
> Gleich wird ein Liebesbrief, gleich ein Erotikon draus.[76]

Another poem—the delightful "Häusliche Szene"—consists of a bedtime dialogue between a schoolmaster and his wife on the subject of—pickles! To the extent that there are reminiscences of Goethe's elegies, they are parodistic:

> "Unsinn! Brechen wir ab. Mit Weibern sich streiten ist
> fruchtlos."—
> "Fruchtlos nenn ich, im Schlot Essig bereiten, mein
> Schatz."—
> "Daß noch zum Schlusse mir dein Pentameter tritt auf die
> Ferse!"—
> "Dein Hexameter zieht unwiderstehlich ihn nach."—[77]

In addition there are dedications as well as brief characterizations (e.g., of Theocritus and Tibullus), many epigrams, a few anecdotes (e.g., "Hermippus," which amounts to the elaboration of a Latin epigraph), and several idylls (e.g., "Wald-Idylle"). "Bilder aus Bebenhausen" resembles the "Bilder" of Waiblinger and Hebbel: it is a cycle of eleven brief scenes that constitute a portrayal of the old Cistercian abbey. Two of Mörike's most famous "elegies" are the two poems devoted to beech trees: one dealing with a tree in whose trunk he carved the initials of the poet Hölty ("An eine Lieblingsbuche meines Gartens") and the other describing the magical atmosphere created within the perimeter of a lovely specimen in the woods ("Die schöne Buche"). In both cases, however, the mood is clearly idyllic,[78] consecrated as all these poems are to a moment of utter fulfillment in the present:

> Eingeschlossen mit dir in diesem sonnigen Zauber-
> Gürtel, o Einsamkeit, fühlt ich und dachte nur dich![79]

In short, Mörike's "elegies" exemplify the frequently noted tendency of the Biedermeier to "idyllicize" all genres, thereby reducing all literary forms to the common denominator of its principal mode, the idyll.[80] But no "elegy" that is "idyllic" in mode can be called a classical German elegy in the sense we have defined. A change is necessary before the genre can be restored.

# 6 · THE TRANSMISSION: THE EPIGONAL DECADES

The decades following the Revolution of 1848 were no time for elegies. The prevailing tendencies of the age—materialism in philosophy, positivism in science, liberalism in politics, and realism in art—turned people toward present reality rather than toward ideals thought to be lost in the past or not yet achieved in the future. These tendencies, in turn, favored a literature that produced its best results in prose rather than poetry: it is no accident that Germany's major contribution to European literature in the mid-nineteenth century was the narrative genre of the *Novelle*. Even the writers who are today considered to be the finest poets of the period did not regard themselves primarily as poets. Friedrich Hebbel, Theodor Storm, and Gottfried Keller all began with poetry, but soon turned to drama or prose, the genres in which they accomplished their greatest work. Conrad Ferdinand Meyer, though he wrote poetry all his life, viewed his poems as offshoots of his novellas, through which he hoped to make his true contribution to literature. Moreover, the poems these writers did produce were anything but elegiac in genre or mode. Apart from occasional epigrams they used almost no distichs, preferring such simple strophic forms as the *Lied*. And through a poetry that depended heavily on symbols and images drawn from nature to deal with present reality they resisted any urge they might have felt, as Hebbel did, toward conspicuous reflectiveness.

At the time, however, the literary situation looked completely different. Among their contemporaries the most popular poets were not Hebbel, Storm, Keller, and Meyer, but such highly acclaimed figures as Emanuel Geibel and Paul Heyse, who achieved their greatest distinction not in prose but in a poetry that depended explicitly on an elegiac turn away from a materialistic present toward the Greco-Roman past that had become the basis of nineteenth-century German bourgeois culture. Let us not be misled by the fact that Geibel and Heyse are scarely known today outside specialized histories of German literature.[1] At the time of his death in 1884 Geibel was hailed all over Germany as the prince of poets, the heir apparent to Goethe; his collected poems had just reached their hundredth edition; a crowd of thousands followed his funeral cortège through the streets of Lübeck; Bismarck and Crown Prince Friedrich of Prussia sent wreaths. At the beginning of the twentieth century his biographers—hagiographers would probably be the more appropriate designation —were able to list over 3,600 settings of his poems, far more than for any other poet in German literature, including Goethe. Although Heyse had the misfortune to outlive the huge popular success he enjoyed in the nineteenth century, nevertheless in 1910 he was awarded the Nobel Prize in recognition of his literary accomplishments over a career spanning some sixty years.

Munich was the center from which Geibel, Heyse, and their friends dominated the literary life of Germany for almost two decades. Following his accession to the Bavarian throne in 1848, Maximilian II sought to elevate Munich to the same level of distinction in literature that it had attained in art and architecture through the efforts of his father, Ludwig I (whom we have already encountered as the author of Italian elegies). To achieve this goal Max invited a number of promising young writers to Munich, beginning in 1852 with Geibel, and supported them with various sinecures. (Geibel was appointed to an Honorary Professorship of German Literature and Metrics at the university.) The epigonal tendency of the so-called Munich school (*Münchner Dichterschule*) is exemplified from the start by a conspicuous imitative impulse: Max modeled his cultural sponsorship on Karl August at Weimar; the frequent "symposia" at the palace, at which matters of science and the arts were discussed, were inspired by no lesser model than Plato; and the informal gathering of writers, known as "Das Krokodil," was patterned after a well-known Berlin literary club, "Der Tunnel über der Spree."

The whole undertaking was colored from the outset, moreover, by the fact that Max, who had attended the universities of Göttingen and Berlin, ignored the local talent and looked outside Bavaria for his protégés, gradually importing a group of North German writers whom local cultural leaders ironically termed the "Northern Lights" (*Nordlichter*): Geibel from Lübeck, Heyse from Berlin, Friedrich Bodenstedt from Peine (near Hanover), and Adolf Friedrich von Schack from Schwerin (in Mecklenburg), to mention only the most prominent. The inevitable tensions produced by this situation—the political tension between Prussians and Bavarians, the religious tension between Protestants and Catholics, the social tension between northerners and southerners—made more acute the sense of alienation that already cut off these writers from the prevailing values of industrialized mid-nineteenth-century Germany and intensified their inherent cultural elitism.

The poets were unified in their cultural strivings by their reverence for Goethe and Weimar culture—a reverence suggested, of course, by the analogy between Weimar and Munich that Max was intent upon establishing. If they felt ill at ease in a German present that was becoming increasingly democratic and technological, they could always renew their cultural vitality in Italy and Greece: in all their biographies the *Bildungsreise* to the south represents the cultural high point whose memory sustains each one for the remainder of his life. But it is also evident that they encountered in Italy and Greece not a living present, as Goethe did, but the classical antiquity they knew from history and literature. The sense of loss of a glorious past—both Weimar and Greco-Roman antiquity—aggravated by their contempt for a present they considered sordid created the vaguely elegiac melancholy that informs most of their poetry. As they sifted through recent German literature in search of kindred spirits, they discovered their immediate spiritual predecessor—the single poet of the post-romantic era who seemed to share their ideals and their rejection of a tawdry present—in Platen. It is no accident that almost all of them pay explicit homage to Platen in their writings.

The varied poetic forms through which they shaped their elegiac longings these poets found in world literature, which, like Platen, they read in many languages. Not content merely to imitate the forms, they translated steadily—often in collaboration—and added to the wealth of first-rate translations that distinguish German literature. Geibel's activities are representative for the group. He began his career with a volume of translations from the Greek produced in collaboration with his university friend, the historian Ernst Curtius, while the two of them were residing in Greece: *Klassische Studien* (1840). In the following years Geibel collaborated on poetic translations with several writers of the Munich school: with Paul Heyse he brought out a *Spanisches Liederbuch* (1852); with Schack a volume of *Romanzero der Spanier und Portugiesen* (1860); and with Heinrich Leuthold *Fünf Bücher französischer Lyrik* (1862). These three collaborators also happen to be the Munich poets who, along with Geibel, wrote poems in elegiac distichs.

The Munich school, which got its start in 1852 with Geibel's arrival, began to disintegrate following Max's death in 1864, when his son, Ludwig II, shifted his interest from literature to music and his sponsorship from the poets to Richard Wagner. It ended abruptly in 1868, when Ludwig suspended Geibel's pension as a result of some laudatory verses Geibel had addressed to the King of Prussia ("An König Wilhelm"). Geibel returned to his home town, where he was celebrated as the "Swan of Lübeck"; in a gesture of solidarity with his friend, Heyse renounced his own pension. Most of the distichs written by the poets were produced, in fact, either before or after the period of their closest association in Munich. But in all their work we detect evidence of the characteristics that identify them as a spiritual brotherhood united against what they perceived as the attacks of a pernicious and valueless present on the treasured cultural ideals of a glorious heritage. Their *Bildungspoesie* degenerated often enough into versified history lessons; but at its best it gives poignant expression to a tragic human situation: the realization by writers of genuine sensibility that they have come too late upon the cultural scene to match or approach even remotely the achievements of their predecessors.

It has been fashionable ever since the gleeful attacks on Geibel and Heyse by the young theoreticians of naturalism (notably in the early issues of the journal *Die Gesellschaft* from 1885 on) to see in the Munich poets nothing more than living examples of Nietzsche's cultural philistines—men whose mindless clinging to outmoded forms and ideals incapacitated them for life in the present. It is true enough that often in their writing reflection substitutes for emotion, and literary reminiscence replaces experience. But this criticism fails to do justice to their genuine accomplishments. Even though their reverence for the dignity of art and their respect for lofty forms easily deteriorates into self-parody, it often seems that their writing is motivated more strongly by pedagogical ambitions—to provide material for the *Bildung* of the German middle class—than by genuine poetic impulses. Yet their attitude can be properly appreciated only if we recall the deplorable state to which poetry had sunk around 1850 in Germany as a result of two factors. On the one hand, the spokesmen of late romanticism and Biedermeier culture contributed to the trivialization of literature by encouraging people indiscriminately to write poetry, which they published uncritically in their journals and almanacs. On the other hand, the hotspurs of the *Vormärz*, with their politicizing tendencies, often enough reduced poetry to political sloganeering of the most prosaic sort. The Munich cult of form becomes comprehensible as a reaction against Biedermeier *Kitsch* just as their insistence on the value of pure art should be seen as a response to the often crude *littérature engagée* of the political bards. Without the civilizing accomplishments of Geibel and his cohorts it would have been difficult for poets like Stefan George to emerge at the end of the century.

Adolf Friedrich von Schack (1815-1894) is paradigmatic for the Munich poets with their reverence for Platen and their lofty ideals. Early in his memoirs he informs us that "Platen was among all living poets the one who made the greatest impression on me."[2] When he undertook his *Bildungsreise* through Italy, "Platen, who should serve as a companion for every traveler in Italy, was constantly in my hands."[3] It comes as no surprise, therefore, to determine that Platen supplied the unacknowledged model for Schack's early elegy, "Im Theater des Dionysos," which amounts to a translation into Greek terms of Platen's Sicilian elegy.

Schack's poem is based, to be sure, on first-hand experience. An enthusiastic Hellenist like his university friends, Geibel and Curtius, he reports of his first trip to Athens in 1839 that he wandered ecstatically beneath the columns of the Parthenon, watching the sun set over Salamis. It was also one of his delights, he confides, "to rest on the steps of the theater of Dionysos while my spirit enlivened the scene once more with characters from Aeschylus and Sophocles walking on cothurns and the choral singers in their flowing white gowns surrounding the altar."[4] Schack's "Im Theater des Dionysos" reshapes this experience poetically. Consisting of ninety-four lines of elegiac distichs, the poem begins with the poet in the theater watching the sun set over Salamis:[5]

> Mählich erblaßte das Licht um Salamis' zackige Klippen,
>     Während die Sonne versank in das Aegäische Meer . . . .

Sitting among the ruins, the poet summons up in his imagination the dramatic figures that once stirred Athenian audiences in this very theater, especially Prometheus and Oedipus:

> Während ich saß und das Auge bethränt auf den Trümmern
>                                                 mir ruhte,
>     Schweifte die Seele zurück in Perikleische Zeit.
> Wechselnd schwebten vor mir die erhabnen Gestalten der
>                                                 Dichter,
>     Welche zu Thränen wie Lust hier die Athener bewegt. . . .

Suddenly, before his eyes, the scene is transformed: the ruins are restored; statues of Parian marble stand in the niches; thousands of spectators in Hellenic garb throng the seats; incense rises from the altar; and the choral ode rings sweetly to the sounds of flutes. Then silence spreads across the great theater as the bloodless shade of Clytemnaestra appears, urging the Erinyes to their frightful revenge upon her matricidal son. As the entranced poet looks on, the grim maenadic chorus swarms toward Orestes, who approaches the city in the hope of redemption. But as the fearful pack dances its ever-narrowing circles around the half-crazed youth, Pallas Athene appears and summons in judgment the citizens of Athens. Before the assembled populace the debate takes place between the implacable Furies and the mercy-seeking youth. Following lengthy deliberations the judges are equally divided; but the goddess casts her ballot for mercy, thus banishing the curse from the unhappy Orestes. As the joyous refrains of the chorus recede into the distance, the poet ponders the great drama he has witnessed. Then, aroused by cool breezes, he finds himself once again among the ruins of the theater while the sky brightens with signs of approaching dawn:

> Kühl da fühlt' ich ein Wehn mir die Schläfe berühren; ich fand mich,
> Als ich die Augen erschloß, wieder auf nacktem Gestein.
> Trümmer, wohin ich nur sah; im Frührot glühte der Himmel,
> Her von Ioniens Strand morgendlich hauchte der Ost,
> Und mir über dem Haupte, den Marmorspalten entsprossen,
> Rauschte, vom Winde bewegt, wildes Olivengesträuch.

Schack's poem fulfills all the requirements of the classical German elegy, which the young admirer effectively learned from his model, Platen. A long poem in elegiac distichs, it consists of the familiar framework embracing a central core. In the framework, which lasts from dusk to dawn, the poetic persona is put into a properly elegiac mood by the long view upon distant mountains and the sea. At this point, however—when the Muse of Poetry reveals herself to Platen in the theater at Taormina—nothing occurs to this twenty-four-year-old imitator of an epigone. Literary recollection intrudes before personal experience, and instead of a revelation or an epiphany we get a felicitous recapitulation of Aeschylus' *Eumenides* along with a running commentary. As though he wanted to supply examples for Nietzsche's ridicule of the *Bildungsphilister* and his trivialization of Greek antiquity, Schack's interpretation reduces the mighty drama to a simple triumph of tenderness over necessity, lacking all ambiguity:

> So denn sind sie bezwungen, die düsteren Mächte der
> Vorwelt;
> So hat Milde gesiegt über das starre Gesetz.

For all the reverence he felt, Schack disagreed with Platen's efforts to introduce classical meters into German poetry and the rigorous metrics of the ancients.[6] So his early elegy represents one of the few efforts in distichs among the hundreds of poems that Schack included in the ten volumes of his collected works.

In contrast, the slim volume of *Gedichte* by Heinrich Leuthold (1827-1879) contains poems in a variety of classical meters, ranging from Sapphic and Asclepiadean odes to epigrams and elegies in distichs. It is no wonder that one of his first missions, when he arrived in Sicily in 1855, was to visit Platen's grave and pay homage to the poet who, though neglected in his own time, wrote words to which the future would pay heed.[7] Elegiac by disposition, Leuthold was temperamentally akin to the poets surrounding King Max whom he met when he came to Munich as a journalist following his return from Italy. In the elegies that he wrote around 1870 and that recapture his experiences in Italy, we constantly encounter the contrast between past and present and, especially, between the Greece that Leuthold never saw and modern Europe. Thus in one of his elegies he attends a village festival in the Sabine hills and notes that the Christian celebration actually goes back to a pre-Christian ritual:

> Mythische Deutung gibt dem Feste das Volk; es entstamme
> Uralt heidnischem Dienst eines vergessenen Gotts.

Denn es wechseln die Götter; dem Kultus der Freude nur
bleibst du,
Mühsalduldend Geschlecht sterblicher Menschen,
getreu.[8]

The procession, led by his mistress, reminds him of a bacchantic chorus. If the analogy between the modern procession
and the ancient ritual is reminiscent of the *Römische Elegien*,
the concluding paean to "Eros, den Schalk" leaves us in no
doubt concerning Leuthold's debt to Goethe.

Leuthold, perhaps the most genuine lyric talent among the
poets associated with the Munich circle, was not reflective by
nature. He excelled at the short lyric utterance, and as a result
few of his "elegies" grew into major meditative poems, remaining "Bilder" of the sort we encountered with Hebbel
and Waiblinger. Only his "Elegie aus dem Süden" displays a
form approaching that of the classical German elegy.[9]

Again the situation involves the celebration of a saint's day
in rural Italy. Standing high on the citadel outside the town,
the poet watches the procession as it winds from the mar-
ketplace through the town gates and up the hill (ll. 1-14). Here
in Italy, he observes, a church procession, stirring memories
of Greek cults, is quite different from ecclesiastical occasions
in the North:

Aber es mutete nicht wie im Norden die kirchliche Feier,
Nein, wie des griechischen Volks heiterer Kultus mich
an.

As the procession, in which his girl Annina is also walking,
approaches, the poet is reminded of Athenian processions in
which the daughters of ancient races bore honey and fruit,
barley and oil, as offerings while myrtle-wreathed youths followed the image of the goddess until they reached the temple
of Pallas high on the Acropolis (ll. 15-30). At this point the
vision is interrupted by the gloomy thought that the Greek
gods have disappeared, dethroned by the crucified deity of
Christianity (ll. 31-44):

> Doch längst sind sie entthront, die erhabenen Uranionen;
> Über den Göttern Homers herrscht der gekreuzigte
> Gott.

The Parthenon having fallen into disrepair, the Muses and Graces have departed. No Phidias sculpts the eternal shapes of the gods; no Plato teaches virtue; and no Pindar proclaims Olympian victories. The glory of Greece has given way to a degenerate posterity:

> Hellas' Größe erlag dem herben Gesetz der Vernichtung;
> Über den Gräbern des Ruhms haust ein entartet
> Geschlecht.

Yet the poet is consoled (ll. 45-66) by the thought that the reality of present-day Italy—notably the charm and appearance of the girls—retains at least a trace of Greek beauty, worthy of a Praxiteles. Indeed, as he catches a young priest eyeing Annina the poet is reminded that even the clergy might not be so remote from classical antiquity as might be assumed:

> Stechenden Blickes verschlang—ein lüsterner
> Cybelepriester—
> Dich der Prete, der jüngst Bilder im Dom uns erklärt.

Leuthold's poem demonstrates clearly that he had recognized and mastered the form of the classical German elegy. Again the conventional framework embraces a meditative core. The poet's lofty vantage point—a mountain citadel—enables him to make the associations between past and present that produce his cry of despair, in the middle, when it occurs to him that Greece has vanished irretrievably. And in the conclusion the poet accomplishes the expected thematic resolution through his insight that human reality preserves Greek qualities even when external reality has fallen into ruin. Yet for all the Schillerian pathos that informs the elegiac core—the image of the Greek deities replaced by a pallid Christ is an elegiac topos that goes back to "Die Götter Griechenlands" (1788)—the tone of the poem reminds us far more of Goethe and the sense of life that motivates the "Römische Elegien."

Certainly Leuthold's eye for a pretty girl is not an adequate substitute for meditative profundity. It was his irrepressible delight in the present that prevented Leuthold, for all his elegiac inclinations, from exploiting more extensively the form of the classical German elegy.

Like all the Munich poets, Paul Heyse (1830-1914) also paid his respects to Platen, whom he called "the Moses of our prosody, who inscribed on stone tablets the ten commandments of euphony."[10] Though he shared the elegiac longings of his fellows for the lost glory of classical antiquity, like them he lacked the intellectual power to sustain genuine meditation. As a result, the twenty-one poems in distichs that constitute Section XI of his collected poems ("Kunst und Künstler") never rise to the level of elegies.[11] Instead, like the "Bilder" of Hebbel and Waiblinger, they present "snapshots" of Rome from the winter of 1877-1878. Yet characteristically the snapshots do not depict present-day Rome. Instead, Heyse describes cultural monuments in a manner that might well serve as a Baedeker for the culture-hungry German traveler: an eager cicerone, he points out various reliefs, the Farnesi Hercules, Bernini's fountain in the Piazza Navona, the Dying Medusa, and so forth. Heyse comes closest to an elegy in the lines entitled "Naturtrieb," which begin with the lament of an epigone who, arriving in Rome to practice his art, finds himself so dwarfed by the might of classical antiquity that he lays aside his brush, chisel, and pencil:

> Wer als strebender Künstler nach Rom wallfahrtet voll
> Andacht,
> Mitleidswürdig zuerst scheint er den Andern und sich.
> Denn hier ist so Großes geschehn, so gewaltige Fußspur
> Ließen die Alten zurück in dem empfänglichen Staub:
> Ach, wie klein, wie verspätet und kümmerlich scheint sich
> der Enkel!
> Pinsel und Meißel und Stift legt er mit Seufzen beiseit.[12]

But no sooner has the poet stated this theme, which might serve nicely as the basis for an elegiac reflection, than he resolves it with a cynical twist. For the "natural impulse" awakens to save the artist, who stakes out a tiny area of specialization—gay *vedute* for wealthy travelers—through which he is able to earn enough money to support himself. It is the twofold irony of this poem that Heyse is unaware of the fact that he is unwittingly characterizing himself and his entire generation.

Unlike Schack and Heyse, who wrote their distichs respectively early and late in their poetic careers, Emanuel Geibel (1815-1884) composed hundreds of distichs throughout his life. In 1839, when Schack visited Geibel and Curtius in Athens, he found the two friends busily engaged in translating Greek poetry under the explicit inspiration of Platen. As Curtius described their routine to his parents: "In the evening we read our verses to each other. Our master, whom we read daily and study in the finest detail, is Count Platen."[13] At this time Geibel was already writing poems in elegiac distichs. But his thirteen "Distichs from Greece,"[14] which amount simply to brief autobiographical sketches and "Bilder" (e.g., "The Plains of Marathon" or "Themistocles' Grave"), are noteworthy only as an early expression of Geibel's epigonal consciousness. He leafs industriously through the ancients, we read in the second poem, and then thinks of a poem of his own, leafs some more, and thus the hours pass:

> Fleißig blättr' ich die Alten mir durch, dann sinn' ich auf Lieder,
> Blättre wieder, und so fliehn mir die Stunden dahin.
> Glücklicher Doppelgenuß! Kaum weiß ich, ist das Empfangen
> Süßer, ist's das Gefühl, selber ein Dichter zu sein.

(Only many years later, in one of his most powerful poems, "Der Bildhauer des Hadrian," would Geibel come to realize that his dependence on the ancients was a curse rather than a blessing.) Likewise, the "Elegie" he wrote in Athens, though a sustained poem in distichs, is not an elegy at all:[15] in fact, the normal sequence is reversed. The poet sits blissfully in Greece and tells us that he has at last found the joy that escaped him so often while he was still living at home in the north. The poem ends with the plea that joy, "the loveliest of all the daughters of heaven," will remain with him and guide him through life.

In the late collection *Spätherbstblätter* (1877) Geibel published another poem explicitly designated as an elegy ("Charmion").[16] This poem, which looks like an inversion of his earlier "Elegie," begins as though it were going to be truly elegiac. Beneath the snowy skies of his northern home the poet sits before the twilight fire and muses over the manuscripts he filled as a young man in Greece. As he meditates, memory bears his soul as though on swans' wings back to the sun, seas, and mountains of Greece:

> Und im belebenden Hauch der Erinnerung schwebt die
> befreite
> Wie von Flügeln des Schwans leise getragen hinaus.
> Sieh, schon sinkt das Gewölk, durch die flatternden Schleier
> ergießt sich
> Goldener Glanz, weithin dehnt sich im Grunde die Flut,
> Und im Kreise verstreut, umspült von schmeichelnder
> Woge,
> Tauchen ins leuchtende Blau sonnige Gipfel empor.
> Seid mir gegrüßt! . . .

The poet's reflections lead smoothly to recollections of a journey through the Aegean isles, whereupon he recalls his encounter with Charmion, the sixteen-year-old sister of his boatman. So we find all the requisites for an elegy: contrast of north and south, gloomy present and joyful past, a dreamy transition to the recollection of things past. But just at this point literature intrudes upon reality: for the little anecdote that Geibel recounts in the remaining lines of his poem is so patently modeled after Goethe's "Alexis und Dora" that any residue of genuine personal experience is lost. At the moment of his departure, Charmion invites the poet into her "fragrant garden," where she offers him half an orange. After they have eaten their fruit, she loosens her "agate" locks and gives him a tearful kiss as her brother summons the tardy voyager. Unlike Alexis, who is tormented by jealousy as his ship bears him away, Geibel's poet sits contentedly in his hyperborean study and thinks of Charmion, who remains eternally young in his heart, a sort of spiritual heating-pad:

> Bei den Rosen Athens will dein ich denken, und wenn mich
>     Kalt und düster dereinst wieder der Norden umgraut,
> Soll dein reizendes Bild im hyperboreischen Dunkel
>     Mir wie die Sonn' aufgehn, Charmion, liebliches Kind.

In the last years of his life Geibel returned repeatedly to the elegiac distich, which he liked to use for epigrammatic cycles. His fondness for the form was enhanced, no doubt, by the Greek and Roman elegies that he translated for his *Classisches Liederbuch* (1875): Callinus, Tyrtaeus, Solon, Theognis, Simonides, Tibullus, Propertius, and Ovid, among others.[17] Geibel's "Distichen aus dem Wintertagebuche" amounts to a series of diary jottings—scenes, aphorisms, portraits—from a winter in Lübeck.[18] Similarly, "Distichen vom Strande der See" comprises seventy-one brief autobiographical reflections over a period of three stormy autumn days on the Baltic coast.[19] Two other collections, each containing sixty epigrams in distichs, range over a variety of topics: "Ethisches und Aesthetisches in Distichen" deals principally with literary matters,[20] and "Kleinigkeiten" covers an assortment of opinions on art and life.[21]

Fittingly enough, Geibel's last completed work was a group of poems in distichs entitled "Ein Buch Elegien" (1883).[22] The ten poems do not constitute a unified cycle: written during the last seven or eight years of his life, they are poetic album-leaves depicting significant moments from his biography. But by assembling them into "Ein Buch Elegien" Geibel tries to suggest that his poems possess the kind of cyclical unity that characterizes, say, Goethe's "Römische Elegien." In fact, they are largely epigrammatic, like the collections mentioned above, and have little in common but the basic autobiographical thread.

The first "elegy" of eight lines recaptures the moment of Geibel's birth in Lübeck as the bell in the tower of Saint Mary's greeted the new day with twelve resounding peals.

The next poem characterizes the poet's parents: his father the minister, studious, serious, and remote; his mother, who loved dancing and the theater, sang at the piano, and played gaily with her children. The third poem shows young Geibel in an attic room of his house, reading the Grimms' fairy tales, Fouqué's poems, and Schiller's tragedies, and beginning to write verses of his own, which came with almost suspicious ease although he did not yet know the rules of poetry. The album-leaves from Lübeck conclude with a poem celebrating the sixth of November: on that day, several years before his birth, the French had captured Lübeck, but the day stands in Geibel's memory as the one on which, at eighteen, he met his first love, Cäcilie Wattenbach (to whom Geibel dedicated this poem in 1878).

The next four poems resemble picture postcards from Geibel's *Bildungsreise*, depicting stages in his journey to Athens, where from 1838 to 1840 he was tutor in the home of Prince Katazakis. We see him leave Verona, tour Venice, and cross the Adriatic eating the inevitable oranges and tossing the peelings into the sea. The eighth poem, in Athens, is worth a closer look. First Geibel smuggles in an allusion to the last line of "Der Spaziergang." While still a youth, he says, he looked at Homer's sun on Hellenic soil: ". . . noch ein Jüngling, / Auf hellenischem Grund schaut' ich die Sonne Homers." We can almost hear the complacency in his voice: he achieved as a youth what poor Schiller never attained. This ecstatic insight leads to an epiphany in which Apollo nods favorably upon Geibel, whereupon he vows to serve art courageously, to strive for beauty, and to keep the "sacred mean" piously in his songs. This bourgeois travesty of romantic inspiration is concluded by a line in which "the first thunder of the year" solemnifies his vow and "the grove rained blossoms." We can almost see the matinee idol in a poor movie peering off into a Hollywood sunset:

Aber es drängte mich auch mein Herz, des erlesenen
                             Glückes
Würdig zu sein und bewegt that ich ein ernstes Gelübd,

Muthig im Dienste der Kunst nach dem einfach Schönen zu
ringen,
   Wahr zu bleiben und klar, wie's mich die Griechen
gelehrt,
Und, was immer verwirrend die Brust und die Sinne
bestürme,
   Stets das geheiligte Maß fromm zu bewahren im Lied.
Also schwur ich mir selbst. Und es rollt' in den Lüften der
erste
   Donner des Jahrs und der Hain regnete Blüten herab.

It is the thunder that I find unforgivable. Platen also conferred
with the Muse about his poetry in a similar situation, reducing a general theme to a personal problem. But Platen had
impeccable taste: he could never have descended to the cheap
effect of the thunder that seals Geibel's vow to Apollo. The
ninth poem offers a sentimental description of Geibel's return
to Lübeck on the Saturday before Pentecost in 1840, where, as
the church bells toll, he sinks into his mother's arms—and at
this point, no doubt, every literate bourgeois *Hausfrau* in
nineteenth-century Germany burst into tears. Again we note
Geibel's melodramatic tendency to link the events of his life
with high points of the ecclesiastical and political calendar.

    After all this, it is with some surprise that we come to the
tenth and final poem, which constitutes both formally and
thematically a classical German elegy in the narrower generic
sense. This poem, which was written in 1879, depicts a situation in his life almost forty years earlier. When Geibel arrived
back in Germany, his poetic career did not at first proceed as
smoothly as his vision in Athens had led him to hope. In fact,
for almost a year he sat at home without employment or any
specific plans for the future. The strictly classical forms he had
cultivated in Greece under the influence of Platen's poetry
were as much out of fashion in *Vormärz* Germany as was
Geibel's political conservatism. Overcome by doubts, he retreated in 1841 to the estate of Karl Freiherr von der Malsburg
at Escheberg, near Cassel.[23] Von der Malsburg, who had met
Geibel in Lübeck and been impressed by his abilities, invited

the young poet to catalogue the extensive library of Spanish
literature he had inherited from his brother, Ernst Otto, a
noted translator of Calderón. (This archival activity resulted,
ten years later, in the excellent translations of the *Spanisches
Liederbuch*, which Geibel and Paul Heyse published in 1852.)
The elegy, which consists of ninety-four lines, traces the
course of a typical day at the estate and, at the same time, the
resolution of the conflict that forced the poet to seek this
romantic and convenient isolation.

The elegy begins with an eight-line description of the estate, which lay (and still lies in the possession of the family
von der Malsburg) "near the precipice of the mountain," half
hidden by hundred-year-old ash trees; the garden that
stretches away into the distance is bounded by the forest on
either side and by a pond at its end. The next section (ll. 9-30)
describes his work on the manuscripts. Sitting comfortably in
the bright cheerful library, the poet is carried back to Granada
and the Cid and to King Rodrigo, who lost scepter and life for
a woman. This activity lasts until noon. Then (ll. 31-44) he
rushes out into the shady forest, where he finds the "still reflection" ("stilles Besinnen") that he has long desired. He fled
his home, he tells us, tormented by doubts concerning his poetic powers. But his work and the mountain breezes dripped
balm into his convalescing breast. As his courage returned, he
"obeyed the mighty impulse" to render his sensations in
poetry—at first gently, then ever more boldly until "the full-
ness that moves [his] soul surges forth in a stream from his
lips." Then his depression vanishes "like a mist" and he even
begins to savor his own pain in its poetic expression:

> Sieh da zerging wie ein Nebel der Druck allmählich, der
> Schmerz selbst
> Sanft im Liede gelöst wurde bescheid' ner Genuß.

This poetic catharsis enables him, consoled, to return to the
"cheerful circle" for the social activities of the afternoon and
evening (ll. 45-84). First Geibel introduces the family of the
widowed baron: two daughters, a "cloverleaf" of fine sons,
and the dignified but lively grandmother. Then there are

stories: the baron tells of his journeys to Spain and Russia in the reluctant service of Napoleon. After dinner, they move out onto the terrace for conversation or various games with balls, swings, and hoops. When the cool breezes from the mountains drive them back into the cozy room, they read aloud: Goethe's *Iphigenie* and *Tasso* or Schiller's *Wallenstein* and *Wilhelm Tell*. These readings inspire the grandmother to reminisce about her youth and the days when she "caroused" ("geschwärmt") with Schiller and admired Goethe's "Olympian head" from afar. These anecdotes are followed by music: Beethoven's "sublime melancholy," Weber's "forest melodies," and "seductive" waltzes by Strauss. But long after the others have retired the poet sits dreamily at his window (l. 85-94), contemplating the moon above the tree-covered heights and listening—of course—to the nightingale. Full of "consoling hope" he thinks of the grief that he has overcome and dreams of the future. He thanks the "heavenly powers" ("himmlische Mächte"—a phrase reminiscent of Goethe's "Gesänge des Harfners") that vouchsafed him this refuge. The elegy ends with his prayer for the power to create:

> Tröstlicher Hoffnung voll dann sann ich hinaus in die
> Zukunft,
> An das bezwungene Leid dacht' ich, das herbe, zurück;
> Doch es versank schon fern; und ich dankte den
> himmlischen Mächten,
> Die mir die Freistatt hier treu mich behütend gewährt,
> Als ich zu scheitern gemeint, und ich bat: Vollendet das
> Werk nun,
> Und dem Geretteten gebt gnädig zum Wollen die Kraft!

The two explicit references to Schiller as well as the hidden quotation are hardly an accident, for the rhetorical pathos of Geibel's language is clearly indebted to Schiller, whose rhythms he also seems to imitate. In addition to the elegiac distich, we find most of the other characteristics of the generic norm. Like "Der Spaziergang" Geibel's elegy traces the course of a day to accompany the reflections of the poetic Self. The meditative core is embraced by a framework in which the landscape is described. There is a temporal tension between present and past that is resolved in anticipation by a look into the future. But upon closer examination nothing turns out to be precise. This is evident when we consider the structure of the elegy:

| 8 ll. | 1–8 | Scenic description |
| 22 ll. | 9–30 | Morning activity: literary past |
| 14 ll. | 31–44 | Meditation |
| 40 ll. | 45–84 | Evening activity: present society |
| 10 ll. | 85–94 | Scenic description: resolution |

Nothing here is precisely balanced: the parallel sections are uneven in length, and the turning-point comes well before the middle of the poem. If we examine the text more closely, we see that there are many breakdowns of the norm. First, the meditations on the literary past are not prompted by the landscape or a vision but are purely bookish, resulting from Geibel's activities in the baronial library. Second, Geibel does not attempt to render the resolution, the overcoming of the elegiac tension: he merely tells us about it. And this is all connected, third, with the fact that Geibel never really goes out into nature: he hears the birds and scents the fragrance from his seat in the library; he contemplates the nocturnal scenery from his third-floor window in the country house; and when he does go out for a short while at noon, it is not into the isolation of the mountains but merely into the cultivated park surrounding the estate. (This alienation from open nature exemplifies a general tendency of the Munich poets.) But in our present connection it is worth noting that Geibel attempted to imitate the generic norm with no feeling whatsoever for the needs that originally produced it. He realized that the elegy requires mountains, which he mentions three times in the course of the poem. But he did not know that in the classical German elegy the resolution arises directly from the mountain landscape itself. As a result, we find here the separate elements of the generic norm—reflective self, tension between past and present, encapsulated form, mountains—

but the parts are as poorly integrated as the overall structure. Geibel's insufficient comprehension of the form and its loosening to the point of meaninglessness attest the trivialization and epigonalism of which he was Germany's leading representative.[24]

In sum, among the Munich poets all the conditions for the renewal of the classical German elegy were present except one. Their reverence for the cultural past—notably Weimar culture and Greco-Roman antiquity—and their disenchantment with the European present provided them with the basis for lament and meditation. Their respect for Platen and the purity of aesthetic form led them to a new appreciation of the classical meters, and notably the elegiac distich. And in Platen's "Im Theater von Taormina" as well as "Euphrosyne" and "Der Spaziergang" they found models they endeavored to imitate. What they lacked, however, was the power of intellect that is the necessary precondition for any fruitful meditation. In the absence of original ideas they reverted to autobiography and to materials drawn from the cultural heritage that they explored indefatigably. The first-person framework, which in the elegies of Goethe, Schiller, and Hölderlin functioned as a mediator between the general and the particular, becomes for Schack, Leuthold, Heyse and Geibel an excuse for autobiographical reminiscence. And the elegiac vision, potentially capable of encompassing the mightiest themes, is narrowed in focus until it recognizes nothing but the predicament of the poet in a prosaic age. The great possibilities of the classical German elegy have deteriorated into nothing more than an epigone's lament.

In the representative aesthetic theory of this period—Friedrich Theodor Vischer's *Aesthetik oder Wissenschaft des Schönen*—we can see these developments anticipated. Vischer discusses the elegy in a section entitled "Poetry of Meditation" ("Lyrik der Betrachtung"), and his model for theory and practice alike is Schiller, who has displaced Goethe from the central position he occupied in romantic theory. "The elegy, then, does not stand within the ideal fantasy, but strains away from the standpoint of the real toward the ideal"[25]—a definition based explicitly on Schiller's essay "Über naive und sentimentalische Dichtung." And he compares "Der Spaziergang" as "a more objectively epic" poem ("eine mehr objektiv epische") quite favorably to the "Römische Elegien," which are too "subjectively lyrical" ("eine mehr subjektiv lyrische") to be truly elegiac. The meditative poetry exemplified by Schiller is produced, he argues, by the initial dissolution of the pure state of feeling, whereby feeling separates into an examining and an examined aspect ("eine beschauende und beschaute Seite"). It is this dissociation of consciousness, and not sadness or melancholy, that properly constitutes the essence of the elegy. "The lyric poet feels," Vischer concludes; "the elegiac poet discusses what he feels." ("Der Liederdichter fühlt; der elegische bespricht, was er fühlt.") This definition of the elegy looks perfectly acceptable as long as we think of Schiller's great poem as the model; as soon as we substitute Geibel's little efforts for "Der Spaziergang," we see to what blandness the elegy can be trivialized in the hands of a poet who lacks intellectual power: to a poetic pablum of *Bildung* or biography produced by formula for a bourgeois public that, having lost sight of the great intellectual and ethical demands of Weimar culture, longs only for rhythmic readings in cultural history and versified literary gossip. As one critic has wittily observed of Geibel, his poems resemble arrangements of old familiar melodies for a salon orchestra.[26]

Although the poets of the Munich school may not have been gratified by cultural developments in Germany, their published dissatisfaction provided them generally with financial security, public esteem, and—notably in the case of Geibel—with a considerable degree of authority as the reigning prince of poets. Their somewhat younger Austrian contemporaries had greater cause for discontent and fewer rewards for their pains. To take the most radical contrast, Ferdinand von Saar (1833-1906)—as a poet probably more gifted than any member of the Munich group—grew up in penury and, after he resigned his military commission at twenty-six, never again had a steady income.[27] Hounded by creditors who put him in debtors' jail on several occasions, eking out a hand-to-mouth existence with the help of a few friends, noble patronesses, and occasional paltry stipends from the government, unable to marry until he was close to forty and then losing his wife through suicide after three years, Saar managed to create a literary opus that includes some of the finest poetry of his age, several masterpieces in the psychological novella, and an impressive group of dramas. Despite his accomplishments, recognition came to Saar only toward the end of his life, a few years before he took his own life to escape the agony of an inoperable cancer.

Saar also lacked the solidarity and authority of a "school" of like-minded writers. Even if there had been a "Viennese school," Saar was far too prickly a man to have gotten along with its members. In any case, the only two important elegists of the period were Saar and his friend Stephan von Millenkovich (1836–1915), who published plays, stories, and poems under the pen-name Stephan Milow. There are remarkable similarities, produced by temperament rather than by cultural aspirations, in the lives and works of the two friends, who met in 1854 while both were junior officers in the Austrian army. In a poem written for Milow's seventieth birthday Saar speaks of the linked course of their youth ("vereinte Jugendbahnen").[28] Bonded by their common interest in theater and opera, the two lieutenants studied Schopenhauer together and discovered in him a philosophical justification for their inherent melancholy and for their escape into art from a military present that neither enjoyed.[29] In time, Schopenhauer provided a source also for the compassion that partly mitigated the bitterness that increasingly marked their poetry. Though not wealthy, Milow was able to help Saar financially from time to time and, following his own resignation from the army, sheltered his friend for months on end at the small estate in Styria where he lived happily with his wife and two sons. (Eventually Saar's irascibility and suspicious nature cut him off from even this devoted and loyal friend for almost a quarter of a century.)

From the start, both writers felt alienated from society. In a poem entitled "Sündflut" Milow complains that the world is overrun by a "a breed of curse-laden sin" ("vom Gezücht / Der fluchbeladenen Sünde"). Since there is no unblemished spot to which virtue might flee, he longs for a deluge that will wash away the sin of the world.[30] The image for modern society that Saar chooses, in a poem of that title, is "Chaos." Initially the world, recognizing clearly what was right and wrong, sanctified the differences by law. But such ethical distinctions have been undermined. Neither the Nietzschean "superman" on his spiritual heights nor the degenerate grunting in his filth knows the meaning of these terms any longer:

> Was Recht! Was Unrecht! Schwelgend in Größenwahn,
> Auf Höh'n des Geistes ruft es der Übermensch—
> Was Recht! Was Unrecht! Droh' nden Blickes
> Grunzt es im Schlamme der Untermensch nach.[31]

In an ode to "Austria" Saar laments the sad decline of his beloved country, the last remnant of the proud realm of Charles V, which now threatens to fall apart:

> Trauernd senk' ich das Haupt, o du mein Österreich,
> Seh' ich, wie du gemach jetzt zu zerfallen drohst,
> Vom unendlichen Reiche
> Karls des Fünften der letzte Rest.[32]

It is a time, both poets complain, that cares little for poetry. Milow wrote many poems bemoaning the lack of recognition his work had enjoyed.[33] Elsewhere he replies rhetorically to the accusation that the great writers have disappeared. They have vanished, he argues, because a prosaic age refuses to acknowledge them or to enable them to develop:

> Mich dünkt, ihr könnt sie nur nicht sehen,
> Weil ihr die großen Dichter haßt;
> Ihr laßt sie nicht mehr auferstehen,
> Weil's eurer Prosa paßt.[34]

Similarly, Saar's ode "Der Dichter" makes the point that poets are venerated when they eulogize their times; but if they

do not share the mood of their contemporaries, they are rejected and rewarded with a crown of thorns rather than laurel:

> Nicht bloß, daß dann ihm nimmer die Mitwelt lauscht,
> Daß sie statt Lorbeers Dornen zum Kranz ihm reicht:
> Ihn martert, so wie selbstverschuldet,
> Auch in der eigenen Brust der Zwiespalt.[35]

This was the fate that Grillparzer suffered, already forgotten
and ignored by his countrymen.[36] A similar change has also
destroyed the great tradition of the Austrian theater, pushing
out lofty poetic drama for the sake of halting prose.[37]

These two writers, who shared neither the political aspirations nor the moral values nor the literary standards of their
day, looked away from the naturalism and impressionism of
the eighties and nineties to the literature of the past. Although
Saar studied the works of Geibel during the seventies, when
Geibel was at the height of his career and Saar himself still an
aspiring failure,[38] he and Milow turned principally to Goethe
and Schiller as their models. The point is worth stressing because here, for the first time, we are dealing with elegists who
had no direct access to the poetry of classical antiquity. Hence
their "elegies" often betray a clear and direct influence—
notably, of Geibel on Milow and of Schiller on Saar. Characteristically, although the two friends made a brief *Bildungsreise*
to Italy in 1875, the occasion left virtually no mark on their
poetry. Saar, who left school at sixteen to enter the cadet
corps, never completed his formal education, and his record
in Latin was poor while he was still in school. In both cases
the classical forms that Saar and Milow used were learned indirectly, from German models, rather than from the Greek
and Roman poets. Saar has given ample poetic evidence of his
indebtedness. In "Nänie" he asks the Muse why she has never
since Goethe and Schiller embraced a poet completely rather
than merely touching him lightly with her pinion:

> Muse!
> Die du einst Goethes,
> Die du einst Schillers Stirn geküßt:

Warum nicht wieder,
Nachdem ein Jahrhundert verflossen,
Umfängst du—
Statt nur hier und dort mit leisem Fittich zu streifen—
Ganz und voll einen Auserwählten. . . .[39]

In a dedicatory poem to Grand Duke Karl Alexander of
Sachsen-Weimar-Eisenach, Saar concedes that the glorious
days of Goethe and Schiller are gone; modern poets can aspire
to no more than the pale reflection of that great past.[40] Toward the end of his life Saar composed celebratory poems
both to Goethe (for the unveiling of his monument in Vienna
in 1900) and to Schiller (on the occasion of the Schiller cente-
nary in 1905).[41] Indeed, one of Saar's last poetic works was an
"Idyll in Five Cantos" entitled "Hermann und Dorothea" and
written in explicit emulation of Goethe's epic.[42]

In view of the melancholy that dominates almost all their
work and the explicit choice of Goethe and Schiller as their
models, it is small wonder that both writers experimented
with the elegiac distich. One of Milow's earliest volumes was
a cycle of elegies originally entitled *Auf der Scholle* (1867) and
subsequently reissued in a revised and augmented edition
under the title *Deutsche Elegieen* (1885). The sixty poems in
elegiac distichs do not constitute a true cycle in any precise
sense of the word. Basically a celebration of Milow's young
marriage, they reiterate in tedious variation the happy configuration of father, mother, and baby son:

Wahrlich, die reichlichste Fülle gewährte mir gütig der
Himmel,
Mehr als im stolzesten Traum ich zu ersehnen gewagt.
Weib und Kind als teuern Besitz im Innersten fühlend,
Ruh' ich im Schatten, umrauscht von der erblühten
Natur,
Während das sinnende Haupt mir süße Gedanken
durchgleiten,
Schwärmend von Bild zu Bild, das mich zu fesseln
vermag.
(Elegy XXI)[43]

The poems on familial bliss are interspersed with observations on life and art. Clearly, Milow is imitating the erotic elegy as fashioned by Goethe; but apart from the fact that the situation itself displays none of the erotic tension of the "Römische Elegien"—in fact, it is more reminiscent of Ernst Schulze's tepid "Elegieen," right down to the spelling of the title—the poems are so vague, so colorless, so lacking in vivid and well-defined scenes that they blur into vacuous affection.

Most of Milow's poetic volumes contain poems in distichs. For instance, the 1882 "Gesammtausgabe" of *Gedichte* includes a section of "Sprüche und Distichen." But the "elegies" amount simply to flaccid love poems after the fashion of the *Deutsche Elegieen* and the "distichs" feature Milow's bittersweet reflections on art and artists, with their inevitable complaints about lack of appreciation. His attempt to imitate the *Xenien* lacks the sharp wit that characterized and distinguished the originals. Not until late in his life did Milow's melancholy mature into a feeling approaching elegiac reflectiveness, a mood evident in the title poem of the volume *Fallende Blätter* (1903), in which the poet looks back in tears and searches for a vanished happiness:

> Ich suche voll Sehnen
> Entschwundenes Glück;
> Ich schaue in Thränen
> Tiefbang zurück.[44]

Appropriately, in this volume we find two poems that approach, if they do not reach, the form of the classical German elegy. The poem "Norden und Süden"[45] begins with the poet's greeting of a rural landscape—forest and meadows—that he is seeing again after many years:

> Ja, so prangte die Flur, so baute empor sich die Landschaft,
>   Drin ich als Werdender einst Stunden um Stunden
>                                   geschweift.

In this northern landscape the poet recalls the south, where he spent many years, intoxicated by its colors and light and its sea. Returning to the present, the poet gazes up at the moun-

tains and the dark forests that blanket their sides; and he is
touched by a momentary shiver, even though he is warmed,
in the valley, by the sun. He is struck by the difference, here in
the northern forests, from the south: here even the people are
deliberate and ponderous, in contrast to the breeziness of the
southerners. Suddenly the resolution of these contrasts occurs
to the poet:

> Dies auch ergreift mich mit Macht, und ich weiß es nun so
> mir zu deuten:
> Trinkt der Süden das Licht, wurzelt der Norden im
> Grund.

Even though he may not be transfigured and is slow to mature, the northerner does not waste his energies frivolously.
And for all its dreaminess, the northern soul is always prepared for action:

> Und wie gerne sie träumt und genießt, was hold ihr
> geworden,
> Fühlt sie doch stets sich dabei stark und zu Thaten bereit.

We find here all the elements of the classical German elegy,
from the elegiac distichs and the mountains to the tension between north and south (including mountain and sea, cold and
warmth), and its resolution. Yet Milow's use of the generic
norm is just as fuzzy as his colorless use of the erotic elegy.
The poetic persona has no more identity than the unspecified
"north" and "south" of the title; the poet never ascends the
mountains that mean so much to him, and his reflections
never achieve the distance and lucidity of the mountain view.
Finally, the conclusion is not so much a resolution of "north"
and "south" as, rather a justification of northern man with his
ponderous, graceless ways.

"Tusculanische Tage"[46] resembles nothing so much as a retake of Geibel's tenth (Escheberg) elegy. Presented in the fall
of 1890 to the Countess Selma Coronini-Cronberg as a token
of gratitude for her hospitality during Milow's stay at her
country estate, the poem begins as the poet looks back to the
preceding May when he arrived at the rural refuge, which,

situated on the precipice of the mountain, affords a magnificent view over the countryside:

> Ach, wie eilen die Tage! Im lebendurchfluteten Mai war's,
>     Als ich geflüchtet hieher nach dem ersehnten Asyl,
> Welches, am Hange des Berges, umrauscht von Palmen
>                                    und Lorbeer,
>     Herrliche Blicke gewährt in das gesegnete Land.

The poet describes the transformations of the landscape from the fragrant blossoms of spring through the lush, heavy summer to the ripe grapes that proclaim the fall. As the season cools and the land becomes desolate, the poet's thoughts turn to death:

> Kühler und trüber schon wird's; bald geht es ans Sterben
>                                    im Kreise,
>     Eins nach dem Anderen sinkt, mählich verödet das Land.

Yet in the midst of natural change the human element remains constant. Looking down from his window, the poet points out the members of the household: the lady of the manor, walking through the meadows with her snow-white spitz and her light-footed daughter, and followed by her devoted husband. In the evening the grandmother in her wheelchair and the son with his "Apollonian head" join the others on the graveled area before the gate, where the poet passes an hour of cheerful chatter with them. For all the pleasure nature vouchsafes us, he concludes, it is man alone who brings the greatest happiness and consolation into our lives:

> Ja, wie viel die Natur uns beut als Labe des Innern,
>     Höchste Beglückung und Trost spendet allein nur der
>                                    Mensch.—

Thinking ahead to the cold fogs of winter, the poet knows that he will longingly recall these happy days.

The poem contains almost every element of Geibel's elegy: the estate "am Hange des Berges," a strikingly similar constellation of characters, the reflections on nature by the poet from his lofty room, the gratitude for the refuge from the turmoil of everyday existence. Yet the parts are not given meaning by the organization of the poem, which moves rather limply from section to section—from the poet in his room to the sequence of seasons to the members of the household to the conclusion that is taken straight out of "Der Spaziergang." In fact, the conclusion is again not a true resolution, for instead of ending with the anagnorisis, however trivial it may be, Milow goes on for four more lines to anticipate his misery in the months to come. Moreover, the seasons are not so much experienced immediately as recollected; their move from spring to fall is characteristic of Milow's melancholy, but a far cry from the *sacre du printemps* we encountered in such seasonal elegies as "Menons Klagen um Diotima." Finally, the characters lack the liveliness and definition of the von der Malsburg clan as portrayed by Geibel. In short, in Milow's hands the classical German elegy looks as though it had spent its last energies and become wholly and irreparably trivialized.

It is with considerable astonishment, therefore, that, turning to Milow's bosom companion, we encounter one of the most splendidly realized elegiac cycles of the nineteenth century. Though Saar's career, as we noted, displays remarkable parallels to Milow's, his poetry is as much finer as his life was more tragic. Although Saar, poor Latinist that he was, wrote no poems in classical meters during his youth, he did compose some of his most powerful odes during the eighties in a variety of strophic forms: Alcaic, Asclepiadean, and Sapphic. Before he undertook his great cycle, however, he had published only one brief epigrammatic poem in distichs.[47] And his posthumous works contain only about a dozen short poems in distichs, written during the last decade of his life: occasional poems (e.g., "Bei Empfang einer Ananas"), "epistles" to friends, commemorative epigrams for other poets (Goethe, Schiller, Stifter), and a couple of ambivalent "Xenien" about women.[48] All the more impressive, therefore, are the suppleness and expressiveness of the distichs that he accommodated to the exigencies of modern urban reality in his "Wiener Elegien" (1893)—the best-known of his works, praised upon publication by such discerning young critics as Hugo von Hofmannsthal, Arthur Schnitzler, and Hermann Bahr.

The "Wiener Elegien," consisting of 426 lines, are over twice as long as "Der Spaziergang" or "Euphrosyne."[49] The poem is divided into fifteen sections or strophes, of which the shortest and longest are respectively sixteen and fifty-eight lines. However, unlike Geibel's "Ein Buch Elegien," Saar's poem amounts to more than loosely linked album leaves; like "Menons Klagen," it constitutes a tightly interconnected cycle of poems that must be considered as a whole rather than as a series of discrete parts. The first and last stophes form a general framework embracing the central thirteen strophes: having returned to Vienna after an absence of many years, Saar goes about the city comparing the Vienna of the nineties with the town he knew as a young man. This generally elegiac theme is shaped and unified by two devices. First, the separate sections present the city from the center outward as in a series of concentric circles. (In fact, the word "Kreis" occurs with the frequency of a leitmotif throughout the poem.) In the last poem, gazing down upon the city from the Kahlengebirg, the poet traces once again with his eyes the "circles" of the city he has explored; then, expanding the focus, he visualizes ever broader circles that finally encompass the entire Austro-Hungarian empire. Second, the strophes also parallel the seasonal movement: beginning in the late spring, they move through the year until the week before Easter of the following year, when the poet climbs up to the Kahlengebirg for his moment of anagnorisis. The cycle of annual regeneration is closely linked to the resolution of the poems, which attains a vision of eternal Vienna underlying the great changes that have taken place in its external development.

Strophe I is an address to Vienna, which the poet now—"in the evening of life"—is visiting again for the first time in years, driven back to the scenes of his youth, he tells us, by memory and longing. The city is no longer as he knew it before, and he himself has become a stranger to the new generation. The repeated contrasts between past and present in these opening lines anticipates the elegiac tension that dominates the entire cycle:

Jetzt, am Abend des Lebens, nach fast vollendetem
Tagwerk,
Treibt Erinnrung mich, treibt mich die Sehnsucht
zurück.
Freilich bist du nicht mehr, die du warst! Es gingen die
Zeiten
Mit veränderndem Lauf über dein Weichbild dahin.
Altes, Gewohntes versank, daran mir die Seele gehangen,
Und ein Fremdling längst bin ich dem neuen Geschlecht.

First (Strophe II) the poet strolls along the Ringstrasse, which glitters in the spring air, admiring the great buildings—especially the city hall and the two museums—which have remained unchanged. But as he peers into the faces of the people (Strophe III) he notices differences that are brought out in a series of statements punctuated by temporal expressions: "today," "formerly," and "no longer." The crowds are no longer carefree; the men look worried, the youths keener and coolly reserved. The splendid mansions and plazas no longer reverberate with joy. Vienna may be lovelier and grander, but it is no longer the poet's Vienna:

Ja, du hast dich verändert, ich fühl' es. Bist du auch schöner,
Bist du auch größer, als einst—bist du doch nicht mehr
mein Wien!

It is only when he penetrates the inner part of the city around St. Stephan's cathedral (Strophe IV) that he encounters the soul of the people that has remained immortal even in the shifting times. Here the old asserts itself along with the new, and the past dreams quietly into the future:

Aber noch immer behauptet sich Altes inmitten des Neuen,
Und Vergangenheit träumt still in die Zukunft hinein.

There in the heart of the city he also finds the school (the famous old Schottengymnasium) that he attended as a boy, and the sight inspires the longest of the strophes (V), which anticipates the seasonal movement of the whole by recalling the pleasures of the schoolboy's year. Did that blissful age really disappear, he muses. No, for the chestnuts of autumn and the joys of Christmas are still there, and life renews itself in its eternal cycle:

Und im Kreislauf erhält ewig das Leben sich jung!

These reflections suggest to the poet (Strophe VI) the glories of that familiar old Vienna, no matter how small it was: he recalls its great political and military figures as well as its cultural heroes. Other people, he continues (Strophe VII), may be inclined to leave the city in the summer, but he finds many oases against the heat and dust: a café in the Stadtpark, the terraces of Belvedere or Schönbrunn, the Prater or the shady reaches of the Wienerwald. In the summer evenings longer walks sometimes lead him out into the suburbs (Strophe VIII), where the differences strike him most sharply. In the overcrowded proletarian apartment buildings "misery makes itself at home" in the crowded damp rooms. He peers into the wretched houses and factories, whose inhabitants are plagued by hunger and addicted to drink. But instead of shying away and escaping into an idyllic past, Saar realizes that here, and not in the grand palaces, the destiny of the modern world is shaping itself:

Schaudernd empfind' ich es jetzt: in stolzen Palästen
                    nicht—*hier* nur
Webt sich dein Schicksal, o Wien—webt sich das
                    Schicksal der Welt.

Not since Goethe have elegiac distichs been used with such natural ease to describe the reality of the contemporary world.

A fall day sees the poet strolling out to Döbling (Strophe IX), the neighborhood where he lived when it was still a village with quiet streets. Now it can scarcely be distinguished from any other suburb: the linden trees have been cut down to make room for widened roads and streetcar tracks, and the fields have been taken over by apartment houses and expensive villas. But in the midst of the urban development the poet discovers the house where, as a young man, he once occupied a lonely room and suffered the torments of creativity and love. He reflects that he has achieved many of the goals of which he once dreamed and he no longer must break his bread in tears, as once he did; but his spring has lost its blossom and his summer its warmth. The autumn of the poet's life coincides with the fall of the year (Strophe X), when he wanders farther out to taste the new wine in the villages of Grinzing, Nussdorf, and Sievering. Here, amidst the people with their music and jokes, it occurs to him again that there is constancy in the midst of change: even though the people may be less prosperous than before, eating sausages rather than roast chicken, they manage to preserve their Viennese character:

> Wahrlich, ihr geht nicht unter, ihr Wiener! Dreht sich auch
> nicht mehr
> An dem Spieße das Huhn—brätelt noch immer die
> Wurst.

As the mists of fall become denser and the season more melancholy (Strophe XI), the poet makes his way to the cemetery situated far out of town, where the tombstones and crosses remind him of past generations. But when the snow falls (Strophe XII), the poet recounts the winter amusements of the Viennese: theater, concerts, social affairs, and—above all—ice-skating. Then *Fasching* is suddenly at hand (Strophe XIII), the gayest time of year, which lends wings to aging feet and intoxicates even the aging heart. When the poet seeks out the quiet street where formerly he lived (Strophe XIV), he finds a new school in neo-Gothic style whose students are emphatically "modern." He sees a slender youth who looks as though he might be writing a "veristic" drama that begins in a clinic and ends on the autopsy table. An attractive girl with lively eyes may be dreaming of stories racier than Boccaccio's while her companion with the boyish haircut seems to be plotting the emancipation of women. It occurs to the poet that he is previewing the stages of the future, and he contemplates the future makers of the world with ironic compassion:

> Ja, hier bereitet sich vor in allen Phasen die Zukunft,[50]
> Achtlos trippeln an mir ihre Vertreter vorbei:
> Wahrer des ewigen Friedens, Begründer der gleichesten
> Gleichheit,
> Weltbefreier vom Gift schnöden Mikrobengezüchts. . . .

The year having now come full circle, spring has arrived again (Strophe XV). Under a warm blue sky the girls are wearing their spring hats; the people vie eagerly to buy the new violets and primroses; in this week before Easter the streets are filled with people visiting the churches and cemeteries; the city is resplendent with the ornaments of the festive season. But the poet, leaving the city, follows the paths that lead up to the Kahlengebirg, which he has already saluted in the first strophe. As he walks up the mountain, he can see the landscape open around him in ever wider circles: the Danube, meadows, forests, isolated farms. (It is almost the landscape of "Der Spaziergang" in reverse.)

> Ich doch wandle hinaus ins Freie und suche die Pfade,
> Die zum Kahlengebirg führen allmählich hinan.
> Weiter und weiter erschließt sich im Kreise die liebliche
> Landschaft;
> Dort schon schimmert der Strom, schimmern die
> knospenden Aun.

Finally reaching a spot that offers a broad prospect, he sits on a bench to enjoy the view familiar to him from his childhood:

> Endlich ist sie erreicht die Fernen eröffnende Stelle,
> Wo ich als Knabe bereits schwelgenden Auges geweilt.
> Dort eine Bank auch—vielleicht noch dieselbe! Nun ruh'
> ich im Anblick. . . .

From the mountain top his prospect takes on new dimensions: he suddenly sees Vienna, which he has hitherto experienced in ever-expanding concentric circles but always from within, in a broader context. He feels a surge of love for home ("wonniges Heimatgefühl") as he realizes that he is "in the heart of the old, the splendid Eastern March, whose banner once fluttered proudly above the realm." But now Austria is virtually a stranger within the realm: the word "Fremdling," used in the first strophe to characterize the poet's alienation from contemporary Vienna, is now applied to Vienna herself in her relationship to the rest of the monarchy. The poet is not dismayed because Austria is cut off from the other lands and dependent upon herself alone; but it grieves him to see her rent asunder and divided within herself. And yet, as he recognizes in his final epiphany, Vienna will endure, no matter what the future may bring. The poet sees the evening approach—an analogy to his own "evening of life" in the first strophe—yet he knows that morning also returns. He concludes by offering his blessing to his city:

> Sieh, es dämmert der Abend, doch morgen flammt wieder
> das Frührot—
> Und bei fernem Geläut' segnet dich jetzt dein Poet.

Since Saar makes no attempt to achieve any precise symmetry of lines in his elegy, it would be pointless to set up a diagram of the poem. Yet even our quick survey should have disclosed the basic elegiac structure underlying the whole— a structure that betrays especially the influence of "Der Spaziergang." The first and last strophes constitute a framework embracing the central strophes, which revolve in turn around a middle section (Strophe VIII) that contains the bleakest juxtaposition of the old and the new. There are further balanced sections in the first and second half: the school years in Strophe V act as a counterweight to the modern school in Strophe XIV; and the poet manages by skillful juxtaposition of historical past and present as well as his own youth and age to maintain a steady elegiac tension throughout the poem.

The resolution anticipated at several points within the meditative core is not fully achieved until the poet, ascending the Kahlengebirg, escapes his immediate involvement with the city and gazes down upon Vienna in the broader perspec-

tive exposed by the view from the mountain. At that point he
realizes that the conflict between past and present is resolved
by the constancy of human generations just as the continuity
in nature is assured by the cyclical regeneration of the year
from spring to spring, as well as the day itself, where each
dusk is followed by a new dawn. In the "Wiener Elegien" the
resolution is once again—as in the classical German elegies—
directly dependent upon the mountain locus, which is anticipated in the first strophe by the reference to the Kahlengebirg
and then achieved in the final strophe. Saar, in other words,
succeeds where both Platen and Geibel failed: he achieves a
genuine elegiac anagnorisis that transcends the narrowly personal resolution in which "Im Theater zu Taormina" and
"Ein Buch Elegien" culminate. He succeeds in expanding an
initially purely subjective reaction to youth and age, old Vienna and the modern city, into a suprapersonal vision that
amounts to a new level of awareness. This authentic renewal
of the classical generic norm is achieved in a language that is at
once faithful to the finest tradition of the elegiac distich and
uncompromisingly modern.

It can be argued that the "Wiener Elegien" represent the
finest embodiment of the classical elegy since Goethe and
Schiller. For in Hölderlin, as we noted, the vision was so
powerful that it strained against the form; in Platen the mastery of the form was vastly superior to the vision it accommodated; and in Geibel the shoddiness of the form reflected
the triteness of the poet's egocentric obsessions. In the
"Wiener Elegien" there is no sense that the form has been artificially imposed upon a reluctant subject matter; the balance
of the parts reflects the integrity of the poet's vision. Though
Saar clearly foresaw the great social and political upheavals
that were about to transform Europe, his faith in the enduring
qualities of nature and humanity justified the classical form
that he practiced with such a brilliant adaptation to the
exigencies of modern speech. In fact, the inherent demands of
the form itself may have helped him to suppress the under-
tone of bitterness that characterizes and often ruins many of
his late poems.

In two successive waves and with varying degrees of mastery the classical German elegy maintained itself through the second half of the nineteenth century. From a critical point of view, as we have seen, the Munich school and the Viennese Dioscuri produced few memorable elegies. But artistic success, though it is the only proper criterion by which the poetic merits of a text may be judged, is not the only standard by which the historical significance of the elegies should be measured. Only the efforts devoted to the form by Geibel, Saar, and their colleagues kept the classical German elegy alive as a genre that remained accessible to poets. Equally important: the influence of Geibel and the popularity of Saar's "Wiener Elegien" kept the reading public accustomed to the genre: elegies were not simply antiquated poems practiced a century earlier by Goethe, Schiller, and Hölderlin; they constituted a viable genre in which contemporary poets could talk of modern concerns in a manner comprehensible to their readers. This factor is important. For without this maintenance twentieth-century audiences would have responded with a degree of perplexity and even consternation to the final brilliant revival of the classical German elegy.

# 7 · THE RENEWAL: TWENTIETH-CENTURY FORMS AND DEFORMATIONS

The Peace of Prague, which in 1866 excluded Austria from the German Confederation, and the re-orientation of the North German states toward Prussia, which followed the foundation of the Empire in 1871, produced in Ferdinand von Saar and many of his fellow Austrians a sense of alienation coupled with the awareness of lost power and prestige. These same events, acclaimed with a pride that amounted to chauvinism by many Prussians of the so-called *Gründerjahre*, signified in the eyes of other Germans something far less gratifying: the deprivation of their historical past and the collapse of the bourgeois cultural tradition that had constituted Germany's pride—in short, the beginning of the modern crisis of values. Perhaps the most articulate and passionate spokesman for this viewpoint was Rudolf Borchardt (1877-1945), poet, scholar, essayist, translator, and—above all—captivating orator. In 1900, in one of his first major essays, Borchardt announced that Germany, following "the indescribable decades" of the immediate past that marked "for all times the lowest cultural state of the nation," was entering a new cultural era.[1] A quarter of a century later he no longer believed that the cultural renewal was imminent, but he still regarded the nineteenth century as the rent in the fabric of German history. It was scarcely possible to write the intellectual history of the second half of the nineteenth century, he said, because the new empire, created by the violent exclusion of Austria from the former confederation of German states, "had no history and wrote itself a false one. It had nothing but an immediate past. Its birthdate was the war and the proclamation in Versailles. . . ."[2] Paradoxically, while the Austrians suffered their isolation, Borchardt proclaimed Hugo von Hofmannsthal as "the organic cultural expression of the last

German universal monarchy of Europe"—the figure who most directly continued and transfigured the heritage of German culture.[3] Germany, in contrast, "during the decades in which it seized the political and economic hegemony of Europe, allowed the intellectual hegemony of Europe to slip away from it."[4] As a result, Borchardt concluded, Germans were living in what he chose to call an "interregnum" during which the memory of their great past was extinguished. It was Germany's most urgent need, he argued, to heal "the rip through the middle of our people" by reaching back to an earlier tradition—back past the epigonal imitations of classicism to the true classicism of Weimar and its invocation of a cultural continuity extending through the Middle Ages into Greco-Roman antiquity.[5] Consistently enough, in his idiosyncratic and autocratic anthology of German poetry Borchardt omitted the nineteenth century almost altogether, on the ground that first-rate poets cannot exist in a spiritual vacuum.[6]

Borchardt devoted his life and energy to this *restitutio in integrum*, to what in the title of a speech at the University of Munich in 1927 he was to call "creative restoration."[7] In part he attempted to fulfill this need by restoring to the German people cultural possessions of which he felt they had been dispossessed by a German scholarship that had become increasingly pedantic and specialized. He did this in a series of masterful essays and monographs—e.g., his classic studies on the interaction of landscape and history in "Villa" (1907), "Volterra" (1935), and "Pisa" (1938)—as well as in his translations from the many languages he mastered with prodigious facility: Homeric hymns, Platonic dialogues, Pindaric odes, Tacitus' *Germania*, lays of the troubadours, Middle High German epics, nineteenth-century English poetry, and—above all—Dante's *Divine Comedy*, which he translated into a curious pseudo-medieval German that he created expressly for that purpose by combining modern Alemannic dialects with Middle High German. In addition, he propagandized tirelessly for cultural renewal in the eloquent public addresses for which he was widely acclaimed.

As we might expect, this elegiac disposition, which looks back longingly at a tradition of wholeness from the standpoint of a fragmented present, shows up in Borchardt's own poetry—notably in the three elegies that, privately printed in 1901-1902, belong to his earliest poems.[8] It seems surprising at first glance that a *poeta doctus* so deeply committed to the cultural tradition should have written only one of his "elegies" in elegiac distichs. But there is an easy explanation. First, Borchardt admitted while still a young man that he entertained the ambition of producing a contemporary model of every literary genre.[9] His literary oeuvre exemplifies that ambition: he wrote one of every type but few repetitions. Second, a linguistic genius who composed poems in classical Greek[10] and who was capable of tossing off impromptu distichs in Doric dialect[11] had no need to demonstrate his command of the meter in German.

Borchardt's elegies, then, are elegiac in mode but not in genre. The common mode bestows upon them, however, an appreciable degree of similarity, for in all three elegies we find not only the same complex of images but also essentially the same situation. The poet is located in an unhappy present, from which he looks back at a happy past characterized in each case by the same group of images: a lovely garden shut off from the world by thorny paths and guarded by watchful angels. Within the garden is located a house, the residence of the beloved, whom the poet attempts to rescue or recapture. The lost beloved is characterized in various ways, but it is clear that she represents not only or even principally a real person but also the poet's own childhood and innocence. There is another dimension, however, that is even more important in our context. In order to recapture the past, Borchardt wrote in one of his late essays, we need "to go into the underworld, like Herakles, in order to bring back the dead."[12] This metaphor suggests that in Borchardt's elegies, in which the poet actually does go into the past and the underworld in order to reclaim his beloved, the attempt to be re-united with the beloved is not just psychological but also symbolic for the "creative re-experiencing of the past" that is necessary to heal the spiritual rent in Germany's history. This conclusion is wholly consistent with Borchardt's assertion that German poetry distinguishes itself from other European literatures by its tendency, from its origins to the present, to focus on the relationship of man to what is immortal.[13] Borchardt's elegies are important, in short, because they address a major problem of contemporary German culture.

If the noun "Elegie" denotes for Borchardt the mode of the poem, the qualifying adjectives of the titles have a certain generic force. The "Saturnische Elegie,"which is written in terza rima, amounts to a portrayal of the Golden Age— Vergil's *Saturnia regna*—when the poet still resided within the magic garden with his beloved, protected from threatening demons by watchmen with spears and trumpets. Now that he lives "in the iron land far from sanctuaries" ("Im Eisen-Lande, fern von Heiligtumen"), that enchanted Saturnian past exists only in his dreams. The "Heroische Elegie," which uses the ottava rima of Renaissance romances, brings action into the situation: here the poet actually enters the lofty mansion of the past within the enchanted garden. Content at first to look on while the dead dance their intricate patterns, he eventually yields to the attractions of the beloved and, escaping the present, joins her in an idyllic realm between past and present, death and life.

In the "Pathetische Elegie" we encounter essentially the same situation and images again. But in this elegy, the only one in distichs, the familiar motifs are presented in a manner reminiscent of the classical German elegy. There is no mountain view, to be sure, and the disposition of the parts is not geometrically precise. But we recognize the familiar pattern underlying the whole. As the poem begins, the poetic persona is standing at sunset on a seacoast, watching the shadows thicken:

Also schwimmt der Tag in das Rot verführender Länder
  Wieder hinunter, es sinkt Schatten an Schatten gedrängt,
Schauernd der Zug der Stunden hinab. . . .

(p. 106)

The flowers of autumn, sinking into darkness, no longer bring life and joy into the garden or into the desolate house ("das verödete Haus") the poet sees in his imagination. He recalls the days when the garden was animated, when laughter and speech and poetry were at home there:

> Ihnen war mit Lachen und Kuß das wilde Geflüster
> Lange, das herzliche Wort, ihnen der scherzende Zorn
> Und die Stimme vertraut der Leidenschaft. . . .
>
> (p. 107)

But now all is silent, and the poet walks through the dusk until he comes upon the beloved, Memory, sleeping in the garden:

> Und es geziemt sich wohl, daß der Dichter durch die
>                                     betrübte
> Dämmrung gehe, der Nacht feuchterer Wölbungen zu,
> Wo ins schwellende Bett unsicher schwankender Beete
> Eingesunken, von Tau triefend die Locken und schwer
> Atmend, tief im Traum, Erinnerung schläft. . . .
>
> (p. 107)

When Memory awakens and speaks, the garden and house seem to come to life. But Memory soon falls asleep again, and mist covers up the image she had aroused:

> . . . Aber es schweigt halb die Entschlafende schon,
> Und der Gesang schwimmt hin in den Lärm irrplaudernder
>                                     Bäche,
> Duftender Nebel verhüllt schwach das erstarrende Bild.
>
> (p. 108)

Standing alone once more on the beach, the poet sees nothing but empty shades. The last cloud of evening stirs in him the image of his own lost soul and a past that he addresses "with fruitless tear and vain word":

> Bild der verlorenen Seele, erhaben trauerndes, dunkle
> Wolke, auf Händen der Luft ruhende über der Flut,
> Führst du mit Nacht und steigendem Mond und
>                         rauschendem Winde

Wieder das Gestern herauf vor den erschütterten Blick,
Daß ich das ferne Herz anrede mit fruchtloser Träne
Und mit vergeblichem Wort. . . .

(p. 109)

But the past—both the poet's youth and the receding season—
is unrecoverable because man in his despair is chained to the
present, and the path to the past is impenetrable. Night covers
the earth, ordering the poet and his beloved to seek out their
cold lair. And now Dream arrives, showing a way into the
future and consoling the poet with visions of his youth until
once more dawn rises over the extinguished sea:

Traum, nun tanze den schwankenden Weg vor unseren
Schritten
Führe mit Masken den Chor, stygische Bilder heran,
Zeige die Liebe zerrütteten Haars und ewiger Fessel
Eingezwungen, der Tod steige in Schleiern herauf,
Zeige mit starrenden Augen und starrender Wimper das
Schicksal,
Unbekümmert und schön schreite das Ewige hin,
. . . . . . . . . . . . zeige mit wankendem Fuß
Jugend, ein schuldlos Kind, bis über den fliehenden
Dingen
Auf dem erloschenen Meer neu sich entzünde der Tag.

(pp. 109-110)

For all its perfumed obscurity the poem reveals many features of the classical German elegy. The elegy, amounting to
120 lines, consists of a personal framework embracing a
meditative core. In the framework, which lasts from sunset to
sunrise, the poet is standing on the seacoast, where nature
vanishing in the dusk reminds him of the house and garden of
his childhood which, formerly alive, now lies dead and deserted as winter approaches. Within the central meditation,
which leads him on a walk through the gardens of the past,
the poet summons up Memory in the form of the beloved;
but Memory is able to animate the past only as long as she is
awake. The poet realizes that Memory alone will not suffice
to bring life back into the garden—that is, into his personal

past and into Germany's national culture. More is required, a more active attitude than epigonal memory—*dream*, which keeps images alive before the poet's eye until, once again, a new day dawns. In Borchardt's "Pathetische Elegie," in short, the classical German elegy is once again being exercised for the purpose for which it was originally created: not the egotistical complaints of nineteenth-century epigones but a profound meditation on the destiny of an entire culture. It is worth noting at this point, however, that Borchardt's poem goes back to a model for the generic norm different from that of almost all the earlier elegies. Despite his great, and rather untimely, admiration for Schiller's philosphical poems, Borchardt got the guiding female spirit of his elegies not from "Der Spaziergang" but from "Euphrosyne," by the poet he considered unique in German literature.[14] Much of Borchardt's poetry—and quite conspicuously these early elegies—is so difficult and demanding that it is inaccessible to any but the most tenacious reader. Borchardt's elegiac concerns regarding German culture had their broad public effect through his essays and lectures rather than his poetry. Yet it perhaps required this profound seriousness of purpose to rescue the elegy from the trivial uses to which it had so often been put during most of the nineteenth century.

Borchardt's elegies provided the basis for his acquaintance with Rudolf Alexander Schröder (1878-1962), co-founder of the literary journal *Die Insel*. In 1900 Borchardt began sending manuscripts and private printings of his poems to Schröder, the only contemporary poet he later considered worthy of including (along with Hugo von Hofmannsthal) in his anthology of German poetry. Schröder was so deeply impressed by Borchardt's elegies that he reprinted them in *Die Insel*;[15] and half a century later he was still able to quote from memory the opening stanzas of the "Heroische Elegie."[16] It was in particular the haunting melodiousness of Borchardt's early poetry that enchanted Schröder, who saw there the first adequate response in German to the great lyric poetry of English romanticism from Wordsworth and Shelley to Rossetti and Swinburne. But beyond their poetry another common concern bound the two young contemporaries, who soon met personally and founded a lifelong friendship. "It was the feeling that already in those days—despite resounding watchwords and despite undeniably great talents—our age was caught up in a steady intellectual decline."[17] Regarding it as their mission to combat that decline, Schröder and Borchardt became the leading German representatives of the movement that eventually entered cultural history, in the phrase of their friend Hugo von Hofmannsthal, as the Conservative Revolution. Finding, like Borchardt, little to praise in contemporary culture, Schröder early turned back to the same humanist tradition that inspired his friend. "At that time I had escaped, beyond the self-evident orientation by way of Goethe, into a well-nigh idolizing veneration of classical antiquity."[18] Also like Borchardt, Schröder assumed the responsibility of mediating between modern Germany and the humanist tradition by means of essays and translations. A scholar neither by temperament nor by training—he never attended a university—Schröder wrote essays that are more personal and accessible than Borchardt's. Although he was not a linguistic prodigy like Borchardt—in fact, he modestly asserted that his achievements in Latin and Greek in school were barely adequate—Schröder provided his generation with a steady stream of excellent translations: the complete Homer, Vergil, and Horace as well as many individual titles from Racine to Valéry, from Shakespeare to T. S. Eliot, and from recent Dutch literature. And in his poetry, which was inspired by a genuine poetic temperament and not produced by sheer force of will like Borchardt's. Schröder reached a wide and enthusiastic audience.

As a poet he regarded himself explicitly and consciously as the heir and continuator of the Western literary tradition—not as an innovator. "Early awareness and subsequent recognition of the continuity of all genuine happening taught me that the genres and themes of poetry have remained identical since their first appearance."[19] Their number remains constant, he continues, and all development takes place by way of variation and permutation—not invention. In accordance with this principle, Schröder was always more deeply concerned with the mode ("das 'Was' ") than with the manner ("das 'Wie' ") of his poetic utterances. "If thoughts or emotions seemed important enough to be stated, I appropriated from the wealth of forms standing at the disposal of the late-born the one that seemed suitable and that I felt confident of mastering."[20]

As a writer with a reverence for tradition, he organized his collected poems by genre. As we would expect, his "elegies" are related, unlike Borchardt's, not by their mode but by their distichs. In fact, the section entitled "Die Elegien" displays a pronounced resemblance to the elegies in Goethe's collected poems, consisting as they do of six individual elegies followed by a cycle of "Römische Elegien."[21] If we look first at the "Römische Elegien," which were undertaken in 1913 but not completed until 1940, we see immediately that they were written, as the title suggests, in explicit imitation of Goethe's cycle. The introductory poem ("Vorwort") justifies the undertaking by arguing that any poem, no matter how modest, is pleasing to the *genius loci* of Rome; therefore his own offering, merely an ephemeral wreath, may take its place beside the marble wall on which Goethe engraved his works:

> Jeglich Lied ist Spende dem Genius: auch das geringste,
>   Aus unschuldiger Hand nimmt er's. So hange getrost
> Neben der Wand, da leuchtend im Marmor *Goethe* sich
>                                               einschrieb,
>   Nelken und Rosen und Mohn, euer vergänglicher Kranz!
>                                                 (p. 119)

The seven poems of the cycle are mainly erotic elegies, interspersed with distichs of a more epigrammatic kind. Returning from an excursion, the poet watches Rome approach in the distance and thinks of his beloved, who waits for him impatiently in the city ("Die Ausfahrt"). He recalls a carefree friend, now dead, with whom he first explored Rome ("Harald"). He reveals anecdotally how his acquaintance with the beloved was facilitated by her aunt, who lives in the same house as he ("Die Muhme"). Awaking alone, he recalls the previous night spent with the beloved and their various entertainments ("Serafina"). He enumerates in mock despair the delays that make him late for a rendezvous with his girl ("Die Vesper"). He remembers humorously how the street sounds of Rome drove away his muse ("Die Muse"). And crossing the Alps on his homeward journey, the poet consoles himself for the departure from Rome by thinking of the friends and the glass of wine awaiting him in his northern home ("Die Heimkehr").

Schröder's "Römische Elegien" amount to little more than a felicitous attempt to pay homage to Goethe by adapting his Roman cycle to the early twentieth century. But we are clearly dealing with the imitation of a literary work, not an *imitatio* of Goethe. Repeatedly the reader feels that the adventures are not Schröder's but Goethe's at second hand. (Thus "Serafina" is really a retake of the fifth of Goethe's "Römische Elegien"; we have no confidence that Schröder experienced the events being narrated.) The other six elegies, however, are both more personal and explore a wider variety of subjects. Schröder is conscious of a threnetic tendency that manifested itself early in his poetry:

> Frühe schon galt mein Lied Verstorbenen. Immer von
> Kindheit
> Flog mir ein Tönen ums Ohr, innig wie Klagegesang.
> Und ein Gefühl war mein: Lebendiges wandelt vorüber;
> Aber das Bleibende wohnt hinter den Pforten der Nacht.
> (p. 114)

Accordingly, two of the elegies are funereal: "In memoriam G. W." (1911) recalls the long illness and courageous suffering of an older friend; "Der Jahrestag" (1912) commemorates the anniversary of his mother's death. In both poems the death of the individual exemplifies the transitoriness of human existence in general, which Schröder contemplates elegiacally, but in neither case does the meditative quality dominate the entire composition. The latest of the elegies, "Mnemosyne" (1918), is dedicated to "misery's sole friend"—the goddess who, after World War I, is able to console the defeated Germans with memories of the past:

Ihr, die alleine getreu, des Elends einzige Freundin,
  Noch das verfallene Haupt tröstlich mit Träumen
                                          besucht,
Da der gewährenden Götter Geleit dich, Deutscher,
                                          verlassen,
Opfre der Letzten zuletzt, stumm und gedenkend wie sie.
                                          (p. 118)

Two of the elegies are occasional poems in the largest sense
of the word. The briefer of the two, "Abschied von der Villa
dell' Orologio" (1907; 1940) describes Schröder's feelings on
leaving one of the villas in Italy where from 1907 on he visited
Borchardt and his family almost annually. "Der Landbau"
(1907) is an "elegy as epistle to Hugo von Hofmannsthal,"
which commemorates a visit to Hofmannsthal's villa at Rodaun outside Vienna. This long (270 lines) poem employs a
number of contrasts—notably between north and south, city
(Berlin) and country (Rodaun), flatland and mountains, modern urban and ancient rural, dark and light, cold and warm.
But Schröder is not primarily intent upon elaborating the la-
tent elegiac tensions of the material. Rather, he wishes to celebrate friendship and the civilized existence exemplified by life
at Rodaun, which he, like Borchardt, regarded as the humanistic ideal lost to modern industrial Germany. He does
this by describing the estate—the house and its gardens—with
an accuracy that can be measured against the essay he wrote
some twenty years later about his first and final visits in Rodaun.[22] But the framework in which he chooses to locate this
celebration is not elegiac but pastoral. This formal tendency is
suggested by the title, which is nearly identical with the title
Schröder subsequently used for his translation of Vergil's
*Georgics*—"Gedicht vom Landbau" (1924). And the poem
contains an explicit reference to Vergil, whom Schröder cites
as a witness for the Romans' wisdom in praising rustic life:

Weise:—die Alten waren's gewiß; doch weiser in keinem
  Als in dem Ruhm, den sie bäurischem Leben gezollt.
Sang doch Vergils zartstimmig Rohr die Mühen des Ackers

Und die Freuden zumal, heilige Feste der Flur,
Sang einfältiges Leid und Glück ausonischer Hirten, . . . .

(p. 82)

He could pay no higher tribute to his friend than to laud him
in a poem based on the *Georgics*, which he regarded as "the
most enchanting product of Latin literature."[23] But in the
course of this pastoral portrayal of life at Rodaun any initial
elegiac tension gets lost, and the elegy turns rapidly into an
idyll.[24]

In short, five of the six poems are elegies in the ancient
sense of the word—poems in elegiac distichs on topics ranging from the threnetic and political-gnomic to the pastoral.
This generic focus is perfectly consistent with Schröder's conception of the elegy, which is based not on modern theory but
on ancient practice—upon the Latin elegists themselves,
whose work Schröder knew and loved as well as he knew
Goethe's "Römische Elegien." In an essay on Schiller's poetry
Schröder observed that Schiller is not an elegiac poet—at least
as far as we can judge by the only examples of the genre that
have been wholly preserved, the Latin ones.[25] In that sense of
the word, he argues, the true elegist was Goethe, who could
cite Propertius as the model for his "Römische Elegien" and
Tibullus for "Amyntas." Schiller's poems, he continues, lack
what is properly speaking the true "elegiac" quality—"the
sometimes consuming sweetness of tone, the loving dwelling
in a sensuous present."[26] "Der Spaziergang" is the only one
of Schiller's poems in distichs Schröder considered a proper
elegy; even it, he felt, had a tendency to fall into a string of
epigrams.

Nevertheless, one of Schröder's elegies bears a closer resemblance to the classical German elegy than to the Roman
elegies. In fact, "Tivoli" (1911), composed in the form of an
epistle to his sister Clara, looks like a weird amalgam of two
poems Schröder admired—"Euphrosyne" and "Der Spaziergang." It resembles "Euphrosyne" to the extent that the poet,
throughout much of the poem, imagines that he is accompanied by the shade of his sister, who once visited Rome with

him but who is now at home in Germany, taking care of her house and children. But the landscape through which they wander—out of the city and up the mountain to Tivoli, from where they look down upon Rome and the river making its way to the sea—is analogous to the landscape of Schiller's poem, which begins, as Schröder points out in his study of Schiller's poetry, "with a portrayal of landscape that is more warmly experienced and depicted than almost anything similar in Schiller's works."[27]

The poem opens with a six-line apostrophe to his sister, which anticipates the theme of constancy amidst turmoil:

> Eins, o Schwester, sag ich dir gern: daß einzig die Treue
> Das erschütterte Herz über dem Strudel erhält.
>
> (p. 87)

The next sixty lines offer a vivid portrayal of Rome and the course of a typical day in the city—from the cock's crowing in the misty dawn to the lively street life at night. As he savors these sensuous impressions of the immediate present, the poet recalls an earlier visit to Rome he made with his sister while she was hardly more than a child; and he remembers her tears when, overwhelmed by the majesty of the ancient city, she felt incapable of coming to grips with her experiences:

> Und ich besinne mich wohl, du sprachst: Wie soll ich ertragen
> Solches Gesicht, und wie berg ich die Gaben, ein Kind,
> Nicht zu behalten geschickt und nicht zu lernen verständig?
>
> (p. 90)

Returning to the present, the poet imagines that he is taking his sister, to escape the noise and heat and dust of the city, on a trip up into the Sabine hills. The carriage bears them through the poppy-covered fields outside Rome and up the hills, past the thermal baths and villas, until they reach the ancient Sabine settlement of Tibur. Their journey carries them on through space and time past the Roman gardens of Lucullus and the Renaissance Villa d'Este, where the laurel and ivy are the only sign of life among the desolate marble decorations.

After this journey through the historical landscape—an insight no doubt enhanced by Schröder's contact with Borchardt—the poet reaches the ruins at the top of the mountain, which he chooses to identify as the Temple of Venus. To his consternation, an innkeeper has set up tables around the sacred scene, where he offers wine and food to the traveling mob ("dem reisenden Pöbel"). In his dismay the poet invokes the gods to witness the defamation of their ruins. Thereupon the muse appears and, with a smile, consoles him, saying that the gods are calm because they know that time changes all things, just as each tide brings in flotsam that the next one washes away. The poet ought to be able, like the gods, to recognize what is merely transitory:

> Und du solltest doch auch mit Dichterblicken
> Vergänglichs
> Als Vergängliches schaun: denn vor dem übrigen Volk
> Ist's euch einzig gegönnt, mit uns die Kunde zu teilen.
>
> (p. 94)

Accompanied by his muse, the poet now descends into the grottoes and galleries of Tivoli, where he marvels at the beauties within the mountain. At length, terrified by the dizzying abysses, he ascends to the light and, taking his sister's image by the hand, climbs through the heat of the afternoon to a peak where they can admire the waterfall thundering down the side of the mountain. As they contemplate the incessant cascade, the poet ponders its meaning, for it symbolizes constancy and change simultaneously:

> Lausche dem unaufhaltsamen Sturz! Das Toben und
> Streiten
> Dünkt dem bezwungenen Sinn immer die gleiche Musik,
> Ruhe- und Wandergesang, nicht Deutung heischend noch
> Frage;
> Denn das Geheimnis ist: Ruhen und Wandeln zugleich.
>
> (p. 96)

This insight provokes a meditation on the river itself, the Anio, and its course from the highest mountains toward the goal of its longing, the "blessed surfaces of the sea":

Wo aber steht des Fremdlings Haus? Da steilsten Gebirges
    Schnee in Schründen versiegt, wardst du empfangen, o
                Fluß,
Sprangest aus Schlüften zutag; und da du dich droben
                erkanntest,
    Sahst du gen Untergang ferne die ruhenden schon,
Selige Flächen des Meers; und wilder und unmutsvoller
    Warf dich die Sehnsucht hin, trümmernd das straubichte
                Bett.
                (p. 96)

As evening falls, the ghostly image of his sister disappears and the impressions of the day produce a mood of meditative tranquillity in the poet, who compares his own inconstant destiny to that of the river; while his sister is at home with her responsibilities, life washes him irresistibly along so that he can never take root:

Daß sich so wie rinnende Flut das Leben der Menschen
    Weiter spielt, und nicht Herz sich an Herzen erhält,
Nichts Ergriffenes bleibt, und nie die heftige Seele
    Wurzeln gewinnt und eins über dem andern vergißt!
                (p. 98)

And yet man feels a deep need to find a place of rest above the center of things, just as the river pauses in its timeless cascade in the course of its rush toward the sea. The poet points out to his distant sister that the meaning of these metaphors is clear: within each person as within nature itself there is a principle of loyalty at work that produces constancy in the midst of change:

Treue! Wie Tag und Tag die gleichen, treuen Geschenke
    Beut, und die Sonne den Weg jeglichen Morgen beginnt,
Immer von neuem der Grund das Grün und die Früchte
                heraufschickt,
    Halte dein weidlich Herz sich und das Seinige fest.
                (p. 99)

At this point the poet gazes down upon Rome, which still blossoms like a queen even though the residences of the Caesars lie devastated:

> . . . keinerlei Alter beschwert
> Dir die erhabene Stirn, mit hundert rauschenden Bronnen
> Kündest du Nacht und Tag selber den eigenen Ruhm, . . .
>
> (p. 100)

Even if Rome should be totally destroyed and forgotten in song, some other wayfarer would arrive on her shores, like Aeneas, and Rome would arise again in full glory.

The poet concludes his poem with a final word of consolation to his sister. Those who are patient and who do not disdain the responsibilities of daily life, he says, heap up treasures within, like the clear crystal he saw in the grottoes of Tivoli:

> Was die verrauschende Frist rauschend entführe, dir
> wächst
> Heimlich, aber gewiß, als unterm Herzen der Berge
> Klarer Kristall, ein Schatz, welchen dir keiner versehrt.
>
> (p. 102)

He and his sister were privileged to experience spring in Rome during their youth; they will yet return, in age, to witness its bacchantic autumn.

As a poem, Schröder's "Tivoli" has several conspicuous flaws. First, it is too obviously a pastiche of motifs from classic works of German literature. We have already noted that "Der Spaziergang" provided the framework for the landscape—the trip through space that becomes a journey through time, coupled with the view from the mountaintop—while "Euphrosyne" supplied the situation: the poet who talks to the shade of a distant loved one. But there are other familiar motifs as well. The motif of constancy in the midst of change, as symbolized by the waterfall, received its classic formulation in Conrad Ferdinand Meyer's poem "Der Römische Brunnen"; the rushing torrent as an image of headstrong man is tied unmistakably to Goethe's "Mahomets-Gesang." Moreover, like much of Schröder's poetry, this poem is simply too long: it takes Schröder hundreds of lines to make the point that C. F. Meyer states more effectively in the eight lines of "Der Römische Brunnen." In addition, the poem tries to do too much: the man as the rushing river, the woman as the fertile mountain, the eternity of Rome as opposed to its shifting image from pre-Roman antiquity down to its noisy modernity, in addition to other secondary motifs. At times the poem resembles a page from Baedeker's *Italy* and, at others, a daily column of Advice to the Weary Housewife. Yet somehow it works. Largely because of Schröder's command of the meter and the energy of the style, the poem passes the test of repeated reading. And if we ignore the fact that it is packed so full that it constantly strains at the seams of the genre, we can see that the poem fulfills all the criteria of the classical German elegy. The personal concern that bothers the poet in the opening framework—how to console his sister for the differences in their lives—and that sends him out of the city into the mountains is gradually generalized through the meditations prompted by the landscape—grotto, river, Rome—and then resolved in the closing framework, in which the poet achieves his anagnorisis. "Tivoli" comes as close as is imaginable to a re-writing of "Euphrosyne" in the twentieth century. As such, it does not constitute any advance in the genre—simply an updating of the existing form. In theme and form, however, it vividly exemplifies the cultural restoration toward which Schröder and Borchardt were both beginning to strive during the first decade of the century.

Borchardt and Schröder, as we have noted, regarded Hugo von Hofmannsthal as the enviable heir of the great and unbroken humanist tradition, as the model for their conservative revolution, as the embodiment of wholeness and integrity. By a curious paradox, it was two of Hofmannsthal's fellow Austrians, Rainer Maria Rilke and Georg Trakl, who pressed the classical German elegy to the limits of its potentialities, and indeed beyond, in an effort to accommodate their sense of collapse in the modern world.

Admirers of Rilke (1875-1926) were long scandalized by

the low esteem in which he was held by Hofmannsthal, Borchardt, and Schröder. Borchardt, who allegedly encouraged Hofmannsthal's disregard of Rilke,[28] did not include a single poem by Rilke in his anthology of German poetry, which appeared in the year of Rilke's death. Schröder, in an appreciation written two years later, called Rilke, George, and Hofmannsthal the three most important poets of contemporary German literature.[29] But even Schröder, who published a few of Rilke's early works in *Die Insel* and who was personally acquainted with him around the turn of the century, was honest enough to admit that he did not properly appreciate Rilke during his lifetime, being put off by what he regarded as his weakness and ignoring him because his work seemed irrelevant to the grand goals toward which Schröder was singlemindedly striving at the time.[30] Even in his late evaluation Schröder felt that Rilke was not truly representative because of the peculiar combination of traits, both personal and literary, that made him an outsider in his own time.[31] Ironically, it is precisely these qualities that characterize the cycle of poems marking the culmination of the classical German elegy in the twentieth century.

At first glance the *Duineser Elegien* seem to have, formally, little in common with the elegies we have considered up to this point. Two of the ten elegies (the fourth and the eighth) are written in blank verse, whereas the other eight feature a loosely dactylic *parlando* that is so flexible as to defy precise categorization. The opening lines of the First Elegy are typical:

Wer, wenn ich schriee, hörte mich denn aus der Engel
Ordnungen? und gesetzt selbst, es nähme
einer mich plötzlich ans Herz: ich verginge von seinem
stärkeren Dasein. Denn das Schöne ist nichts
als des Schrecklichen Anfang, den wir noch grade ertragen,
und wir bewundern es so, weil es gelassen verschmäht,
uns zu zerstören. Ein jeder Engel ist schrecklich.[32]

What we hear is a clearly dactylic line with, for the most part, a five-beat rhythm. But out of this rhythm there emerges in

lines 5 and 6, so inconspicuously as to be almost impercepti-
ble, a perfect elegiac distich. As we examine the poem more
closely, we find that these distichs appear rather insistently in
all the dactylic elegies but the Fifth; and even the Fifth begins
with a couplet consisting of a perfect hexameter followed by
the first half of a pentameter:

Wér aber *sínd* sie, ság mir, die Fáhrenden, díese ein wénig
Flúchtigern nóch als wir sélbst, [die dringend von früh an]

In other words, even when the meter is not perfect, the elegiac
rhythm is unmistakable. Sometimes the lines can be read as
perfect distichs consisting of a dactylic hexameter plus a pentameter:

[Wirf aus den Armen die Leere]
zú den Ráumen hinzú, die wir átmen; vielléicht daß die
Vögel
díe erwéiterte Lúft fühlen mit ínnigerm Flúg.
(First Elegy)

The tendency to reduce—after the fashion of Hölderlin—the
initial dactyl to an anapest leads to frequent cases in which the
hexameter has lost an entire foot. But the effect is still clearly
that of an elegiac distich, and probably no one but an inveter-
ate syllable-counter would notice that a foot is missing:

Séhnt es dich áber, so sínge die Líebenden: lánge
nóch nicht unstérblich genúg íst ihr berúhmtes Gefúhl.
Jéne, du néidest sie fást, Verlássenen, díe du
só viel líebender fándst áls die Gestíllten. Begínn. . . .
(First Elegy)

Occasionally a distich of this sort has been playfully obscured
even further by being broken down into four lines:

Zwíschen den Hámmern bestéht
unser Hérz, wie die Zúnge
zwíschen den Záhnen, die dóch,
dénnoch, die préisende bléibt.
(Ninth Elegy)

But it is important to remain alert to these metrical tricks; otherwise we might fail to note that the entire cycle ends with a perfect pentameter:

Und wir, die an *steigendes* Glück
denken, empfänden die Rührung,
die uns béinah bestürzt,
wénn ein Glückliches *fällt*.

(Tenth Elegy)

The elegiac distich is precipitated by the free rhythms of the elegies, then, within six lines of the beginning; it is clearly present in all but two of the poems as the underlying pattern from which the poet departs; and the primacy of the elegiac rhythm is reasserted once again by the perfect pentameter with which the cycle closes. It seems clear that, though in most of his lines he used the distich merely as a metrical *terminus ab quo*, Rilke returned to it often enough in the course of the ten Elegies to ensure that the reader—even better, the listener—would be reminded rhythmically of the elegiac tradition within which he wanted his cycle to be located.[33] Through his sophisticated use of the distich, in fact, Rilke achieves the same kind of tantalizing effect that certain contemporary composers were achieving by postponing, almost to the point of frustration, the inevitable resolution of a chord: our expectations are aroused, teased, played with, until the rhythmic suspense becomes almost unbearable, and is then finally relieved. But we are talking about something that goes well beyond word-play. In the *Duineser Elegien* the elegiac tensions of the theme are reflected in the rhythms: the disparity between our expectation and the actual line exemplifies the disparity between the ideal and reality. As in life itself, it is only through occasional glimpses of perfection that our otherwise unbearable tensions are relaxed for a moment, only to be intensified even more sharply than before.

The poems that Rilke wrote before the period of the *Duineser Elegien* (1912-1922) fall, generally speaking, into one of two formal categories. Either they are simple strophic poems: sonnets, four-line song strophes, occasionally a *Lied* of five or six strophes. Or they are longer discursive poems in iambic pentameter: either blank verse, as, for instance, in the two "Requiems" of 1908; or rhymed, as in the third book of *Stunden-Buch* (1905) or various longer poems in *Buch der Bilder* (1902; 1906). There is very little experimentation with classical, oriental, or other more exotic forms. The poems are metrically simple and traditional; the poetic interest is aroused by what goes on within the formal structure—by Rilke's subtle play with rhyme, rhythm, enjambement, and so forth. Against this metrically stark background the dactylic rhythms of the *Duineser Elegien* stand out sharply as a totally new beginning—a fact suggesting that we should pause to consider the reasons more carefully.

The year 1910 marked a major turning point in Rilke's life. After the great wave of productivity that produced his *Neue Gedichte* (1907; 1908) and *Die Aufzeichnungen des Malte Laurids Brigge* (1910), Rilke suffered what he considered a radical abatement of his creative energies. His despair of ever being able to write again was coupled with anguished doubts regarding the legitimacy of poetry altogether—particularly the kind of poetry he professed in the *Neue Gedichte*: the so-called *Dinggedichte* in which he had sought to portray objects of the external world—especially *objets d'art* and animals—in such a manner as to enter imaginatively into their existence. It is this doubt that the poet expresses in the First Elegy, when he realizes that he has failed to carry out the "commission" imposed on him from time to time by reality. Instead of responding with directness to the world—to spring, to the stars, to the sound of a violin from an open window—he had searched behind the phenomena for some signal concerning his own hopes and feelings:

> Das alles war Auftrag.
> Aber bewältigtest du's? Warst du nicht immer
> noch von Erwartung zerstreut, als kündigte alles
> eine Geliebte dir an?

Rilke's spiritual crisis is reflected in the physical restlessness that caused him to give up his residence in Paris and to roam the Mediterranean world—North Africa, Spain, the coasts of the Adriatic—in search of a new mission.

The departure from Paris is significant in another respect. Rilke's works until 1910 were inspired largely by foreign models—notably Russian, Scandinavian, and French. With the exception of works by occasional contemporaries such as Gerhart Hauptmann and Detlev von Liliencron, the traditions of German literature meant far less to Rilke than did the writings of Herman Bang, Jens Peter Jacobsen, Dostoevsky, Tolstoy, Baudelaire, and Mallarmé. Rilke's search for spiritual renewal in the years following 1910 produced his first real encounter with the major writers of German literature. He had of course the average schoolboy's acquaintance with German literature. But the erratic course of his education—military academy followed by business school and a few unfocused semesters at the University of Prague—left him with a knowledge less extensive than that of the average well-educated German. These shortcomings were not alleviated by the fact that after his twenty-seventh year he spent most of his life outside German-speaking lands. His attitude toward Goethe is representative in this connection.[34] As a young poet he rejected Goethe completely, seeing in him the stiff old Poet Laureate that he portrays so disparagingly in *Malte Laurids Brigge*, where Goethe fails to pass the test of love imposed upon him by Bettina von Arnim.

But in 1911 a great change is evident. On August 25, only five months before he began composing the First Elegy, he wrote to the Princess of Thurn and Taxis about his activities during a visit to Weimar. After her departure, he reports, he went to the Goethe House, where he was absorbed by the collection of small objects in an upstairs room that give such eloquent testimony about Goethe's life—for instance, the lovely portrait of Ulrike von Levetzow as a young girl. "Then I was seized more and more by the figure of the scarcely twenty-year-old Christiane Neumann, upon whose passing away Goethe wrote the great poem 'Euphrosyne.' Do you remember?"[35] When he got back to Leipzig, Rilke continues, he immediately read the elegy. It is quite obvious that he came to Goethe's poem indirectly, as a result of his initial interest in the figure of the girl about whom Goethe wrote his elegy. But once he reached the text, he was profoundly moved. His reading of it sounds almost as though he were talking about certain passages in his own *Duineser Elegien.* "There is truly a resplendence surrounding those who have died so young; through them, death takes on a certain quality of boldness, wealth, even fame."[36]

In 1910 Rilke met Norbert von Hellingrath, the brilliant young scholar from the circle around Stefan George, whose dissertation on Hölderlin's Pindar translation and whose edition of the works contributed immeasurably to the rediscovery of the Swabian poet in the early twentieth century.[37] But the full influence of Hölderlin did not make itself felt until Rilke needed it—that is, when he was already at work on his own elegies. By 1914 Rilke was totally absorbed in Hölderlin: in February he sent his friend André Gide "une bonne édition de Hölderlin";[38] in March he heard Hellingrath lecture on Hölderlin's madness;[39] in July he wrote to Hellingrath that he had been reading in the two published volumes of his edition "with particular emotion and devotion" and that Hölderlin's influence upon him was "profound and generous";[40] in September, finally, he wrote his great ode "An Hölderlin."

It is unnecessary for our purposes to trace in detail the story of Rilke's discovery of the German classics. His letters from this period contain a running commentary on his reading, and various studies have illuminated the specific influence upon Rilke of Goethe, Hölderlin, and other German poets.[41] What matters is simply that Rilke began his first intensive study of classical German literature shortly before he undertook the *Duineser Elegien.* We can safely assume—given the absence of the elegiac tradition in other modern literatures and Rilke's ignorance of Greek and Latin literature in the original—that he was introduced to the elegiac distich, for him a totally new form, by his reading of Goethe, Klopstock, and Hölderlin. And this conscious location of his elegies in the tradition of the classical German elegy suggests that we might do well to look for parallels beyond the metrical ones.

Rilke's study of German literature seems to have filled him

with no particular enthusiasm for Schiller. Certainly there is no evidence that he ever studied Schiller's philosophical and aesthetic essays. Yet Rilke might have walked straight out of the pages of the essay "Über naive und sentimentalische Dichtung." Like Hölderlin, Rilke was obsessed with the "eccentric course" that had led him away from the world of creatural things and yet not all the way to the level of higher beings. The *Duineser Elegien* constitute an anguished testimony to the tragedy of the modern consciousness, which has alienated itself from the security of wholeness and unity. Rilke is a "sentimental" poet par excellence, and his sentimental awareness produces the elegiac tensions that inform the *Duineser Elegien*.

In the world of the Elegies, the characteristic tension is created by the extremes of total self-awareness and absolute lack of self-awareness. Translated into spatial terms, these poles are presented as pure interiority and pure externality. The symbol of total inwardness, of total self-awareness, that emerges in the *Duineser Elegien* is the angel, which has absolutely nothing in common with the angels of the Judeo-Christian tradition. "The angel of the Elegies," Rilke wrote in 1925 to his Polish translator, "is that creature in whom the transformation of the visible into the invisible—which we are still carrying out—already appears as completed."[42] The angel makes no distinctions between inner and outer, between past and future, between life and death: for him all being coexists in an undifferentiated continuum, on what Rilke in that same letter calls "a higher level of reality" ("einem höheren Rang der Realität"). At the other extreme stands the marionette, the symbol of pure externality, lacking any self-awareness whatsoever. Its face, as Rilke puts it in the First Elegy, is nothing but surface or appearance. These two beings, angel and marionette, represent absolute security of being, for they experience no conflict or tension. The marionette, lacking any interior life and any sense of self-awareness, is absolutely at home in the external world of things. The angel, on the other hand, has succeeded in converting all being into a vision of pure inwardness.

Now, every creature can be rated as to its "security"

("Sicherheit") according to its position on an imaginary scale between these two extremes. Creatural life is generally quite close to the pole of total exteriority and lack of self-awareness because no element of reflection interferes with its view of reality:

> Mit allen Augen sieht die Kreatur
> das Offene.
>
> (Eighth Elegy)

But Rilke's scale has calibrations subtle enough to grade the shifting degree of security in the various animals. Thus he speaks of the sheer bliss of the gnat, which knows no distinction of inner and outer, of womb and world:

> O Seligkeit der *kleinen* Kreatur,
> die immer *bleibt* im Schooße, der sie austrug;
> o Glück der Mücke, die noch innen hüpft,
> selbst wenn sie Hochzeit hat: denn Schooß ist alles.

According to this same weird zoology[43] birds are somewhat less secure and at one with the world because they are born from eggs that require the protection of the nest. The bat has some of the security of birds and insects, for like them it is at home in the air, the element through which it freely flies. But because the bat is born not from an egg but from the womb, it shares in the "burden and care of a great melancholy" that afflicts all mammals which are cast out of the womb into an alien world and which recall their former security with a sense of longing:

> Und doch ist in dem wachsam warmen Tier
> Gewicht und Sorge einer großen Schwermut.
> Denn ihm auch haftet immer an, was uns
> oft überwältigt,—die Erinnerung. . . .
>
> (Eighth Elegy)

Men, in contrast, are situated close to the middle—and nadir—of this parabola, the "eccentric course" leading from the security of pure exteriority to the supreme security of total self-awareness. Cursed by a certain degree of consciousness, they are alienated from the unity with being that characterizes creatural life; instead, men stand apart from the world like "observers" and try to impose order on the world instead of accepting it as it is:

Und wir: Zuschauer, immer, überall,
dem allen zugewandt und nie hinaus!
Uns überfüllts. Wir ordnens. Es zerfällt.
Wir ordnens wieder und zerfallen selbst.
(Eighth Elegy)

But mere mortals are limited by consciousness because they do not pursue consciousness to its end: the angels have advanced so far in self-awareness that they have converted all being into inner vision, making no distinctions between past and future, between the living and the dead:

—Aber Lebendige machen
alle den Fehler, daß sie zu stark unterscheiden.
Engel (sagt man) wüßten oft nicht, ob sie unter
Lebenden gehn oder Toten.
(First Elegy)

Only three types of mortals are exempt from the general anguish of the human condition. In children, consciousness has not yet developed to a degree that alienates them from the world: they still look directly at reality without thinking constantly of the past or future that lies behind it. Lovers whose love is unreciprocated and thus not absorbed by a single object have, according to Rilke, an immense capacity for feeling that makes them responsive to reality. And great heroic figures tend to make no distinction between life and death since an early death belongs, by definition, to the destiny of the hero.

The poet's position is quite precarious. As a human being, he is afflicted by all the anguish of his fellow men, but even more keenly since his high degree of consciousness makes him acutely aware of the transitoriness of man's creatural part. At the same time, his vocation as poet requires of him a detached attitude toward life: he is supposed to portray objectively the reality he sees. Yet his instincts cause him repeatedly to forsake the "commission" of reality by falling out of his role of detachment and seeking the thrill of a simple human emotion.

This, then, is the general background from which the specific theme of the *Duineser Elegien* emerges: the quandary of the modern poet. The angel, as total consciousness, represents in one sense the ideal critic. But how can a mortal poet possibly create art that will have any validity in the eyes of a consciousness so much larger than his own? The solution that Rilke works out in the course of the Elegies is paradoxical. The angel, being timeless, is at home in the realm of eternal feelings and thoughts. Here the mortal poet cannot possibly tell him anything new. Man, in contrast, is fleeting. The very transitoriness of his human condition provides him with the single experience the angel does not possess: the angel has never been earthly and mortal:

> Aber dieses
> *ein* Mal gewesen zu sein, wenn auch nur *ein* Mal:
> *irdisch* gewesen zu sein, scheint nicht widerrufbar.
> (Ninth Elegy)

The solution Rilke reaches is this: not to compete with the angel in his own realm, the kingdom of great thoughts, but to praise this world of humanity:

> Preise dem Engel die Welt, nicht die unsägliche, *ihm*
> kannst du nicht großtun mit herrlich Erfühltem; im
> Weltall,
> wo er fühlender fühlt, bist du ein Neuling. . . .
> (Ninth Elegy)

The sole justification for the poet is to render what is typically human in such a way that it can be comprehended by the angel. Since the angel dwells wholly in the interior consciousness, the poet must seek to "transform" external reality by rendering it "invisible," to give it permanence and validity by reshaping it in the eternal images of art.

> Erde, ist es nicht dies, was du willst: *unsichtbar*
> in uns erstehn?—Ist es dein Traum nicht,

einmal unsichtbar zu sein?—Erde! unsichtbar!
Was, wenn Verwandlung nicht, ist dein drängender
Auftrag?
(Ninth Elegy)

Instead of seeking, as he had done in his earlier poetry, to deal with the world of things, the poet now resolves to come to grips with the world of human emotion: to seek images that will render permanent the transitory reality in which human existence takes place. In comparison with Rilke's earlier poetry, what we see here is a shift from symbol to myth— from the attempt to find in external reality human dimensions of meaning, to the endeavor to render human emotion through mythic action.

In the *Duineser Elegien*, of course, this theory is not set forth in such a systematic way as I have attempted in the preceding exposition. It was a theory and solution that he evolved only gradually over the course of some ten years.[44] The Elegies were first published in 1923, but they had been composed at intervals ever since 1912. The first two were written at Duino Castle near Trieste in January and February of 1912. The Third Elegy, begun at the same time, was expanded and completed a year and a half later in Paris; the Sixth was written largely in 1913 in Spain and France; and the Fourth was completed in Munich in November of 1915. The remaining five Elegies, though certain lines go back to 1912, were for the most part the product of one week of inspired activity in February, 1922, when Rilke was living in the Château de Muzot in Switzerland. But despite the extended genesis of the separate poems, we are justified in regarding the ten elegies as an organized cycle arising out of a single motivating impulse, as Rilke repeatedly emphasized in his letters. The First Elegy anticipates the major themes of all the following elegies as well as the resolution ultimately achieved. In addition, the elegy Rilke wrote last (on February 14, 1922) was inserted, for thematic reasons, into the cycle in the fifth position. If we consider the *Duineser Elegien* not in thematic abstraction but in their actual poetic sequence, we can see clearly how the elegiac mode is enhanced by the elegiac structure of the cycle.

The First Elegy functions as an introduction and table of contents for the entire cycle. It begins with the poet's plight: how is he to write lines that are justifiable before the absolute consciousness represented by the angels? He is so little at home in the world he has dissected with his consciousness that even the animals notice it:

> und die findigen Tiere merken es schon,
> daß wir nicht sehr verläßlich zu Haus sind
> in der gedeuteten Welt.

The poet's past failures crowd in upon him. He recalls instances when reality made demands upon him, but instead of responding immediately he limited his perception by looking beyond present reality for memories of the past or prophecies of the future. These failures suggest to him the examples of mortals who have a different attitude toward life: forlorn lovers and heroes who died at an early age. If only he might learn a lesson from them, his own response to reality would be unclouded by the expectations that hitherto have interfered with his perceptions: he too would hear the "uninterrupted news that forms itself out of stillness" ("die ununterbrochene Nachricht, die aus Stille sich bildet"). But this, he realizes, would be tantamount to viewing life from the standpoint of the angels, from the standpoint of death, where things no longer have "the significance of human future" ("die Bedeutung menschlicher Zukunft"). From that vantage point beyond human temporality all things that were formerly bound in a causal nexus seem to flutter freely in space:

> Seltsam,
> alles, was sich bezog, so lose im Raume
> flattern zu sehen.

But the ultimate resolution anticipated here at the end of the First Elegy is too difficult to sustain at this point. So the poet indulges himself, during the next three Elegies, in an elegiac contemplation of those beings who, by their nature, have more security than he: angels (Second Elegy), lovers (Second and Third Elegy), marionettes and children (Fourth Elegy).

The Fifth Elegy constitutes the nadir of despair. Coming from the example of the marionette and the child, in whom consciousness is still undeveloped, Rilke returns metaphorically to the dilemma of the poet. On the level of description Rilke portrays a family of acrobats performing their feats. As he watches their skillful acts, whose virtuosity is so superb that it has become pure routine, he longs to see them at a stage at which their facility was not yet fully developed: where the weights were still too heavy, where the plates still fell from the balancing poles—where, in other words, the artist had not yet progressed beyond his naive, childlike being into a state of consciousness. But the moment of equilibrium between awareness and lack of awareness—like the Golden Age with its balance of freedom and necessity in "Der Spaziergang"—is never attained: for the "pure insufficiency" of non-consciousness gives way directly to the "empty surfeit" of consciousness, of virtuosity. And the moment of ideal balance remains inexpressible:

Und plötzlich in diesem mühsamen Nirgends, plötzlich
die unsägliche Stelle, wo sich das reine Zuwenig
unbegreiflich verwandelt—, umspringt
in jenes leere Zuviel.

This is precisely the dilemma of the poet, who moves directly from the poignancy of the human condition into the empty virtuosity of his craft without maintaining the delicate balance that would enable him to remain equally at home in both worlds and to "render invisible" through poetic prowess the experiences of a human condition from which he has not yet become alienated. The example of the artist, who "blossoms" into meaningless facility at the expense of substance, suggests the contrasting theme of the Sixth Elegy: the hero. For the hero who dies at an early age, Rilke suggests, is not like the artificial flowers created in the Fifth Elegy by Madame Lamort, which represent sterile artistry: rather, he is like the fig tree, whose growth into substance, to fruit, is so rapid that the stage of blossoming is almost totally overleaped.

These reflections lead to the Seventh Elegy, in which for

the first time the poet tentatively achieves the attitude of affirmation in this world: "Hiersein ist herrlich." Forsaking his earlier attempts to compete with the angel by praising those things the angel knows better than mere mortals, he resolves to praise human endeavor. This feeling of affirmation is interrupted by the Eighth Elegy, where the poet once more contrasts the uneasy consciousness of man with the security of creatural life. But in the Ninth Elegy, after the preceding retardation, the note of affirmation resounds even more strongly than before. It is the very transitoriness of human existence that cries out for the poet's art: all being is unique and present only once in its inevitable form. Since the poet, as a mortal, is present in this transitory reality, only he can capture evanescent life and preserve it for the eternal contemplation of the angel:

> Aber weil Hiersein viel ist, und weil uns scheinbar
> alles das Hiesige braucht, dieses Schwindende, das
> seltsam uns angeht. Uns, die Schwindendsten. . . .

The tension between consciousness and unconsciousness, between death and life, between interior vision and external appearance, is finally resolved here in the Ninth Elegy when the poet recognizes and accepts his modest function as mediator. For human life acts itself out in that border area where the various sets of contrasts overlap. Only the poet, as a representative of that human condition, can perform the necessary function of transmuting the visible into the invisible.

When we turn to the Tenth Elegy, we are confronted with an entirely different type of poem: instead of the meditation that characterizes the earlier elegies, we find pure narrative. In the Tenth Elegy, in other words, the poet puts into practice the insights achieved through the meditation of the earlier poems, especially the Ninth. Here he attempts to perform that translation of human reality into mythic vision. As a result, the Tenth Elegy is the only one that renders actions in a landscape: a walk from the city through the valley up to the mountain. But it is a strangely interiorized landscape that is portrayed here, and the principal technique that Rilke uses to achieve his effect is the genitive metaphor. In order to render an inner state as exterior action, he combines in each case a specific concrete noun with a noun of human sensibility. Thus the landscape has trees, fields, and animals; but they are "trees of tears" ("Tränenbäume"), "fields of blossoming melancholy" ("Felder blühender Wehmut"), and "animals of grief" ("Tiere der Trauer").

We can approach the technique through a poem Rilke wrote in 1914, "Ausgesetzt auf den Bergen des Herzens."[45] Looking down from his precarious perch on the mountainside, the poet sees "the last village of words" ("die letzte Ortschaft der Worte") and, somewhat above it, "a final farm of feeling" ("ein letztes Gehöft von Gefühl"). Contrasted with the poet, who is imperiled by his consciousness, we see an occasional mountain animal with intact consciousness ("heiles Bewußtsein") and, circling the peaks above, "the great secure bird" ("der große geborgene Vogel"). But in this fifteen-line fragment the metaphor of the first line, which is repeated three times in the course of the poem, constantly reminds us that the landscape being so precisely described within the poem is, in fact, an image for the human heart or sensibility: "die Berge des Herzens."

The Tenth Elegy employs landscape in precisely the same way: it depicts a wholly exteriorized landscape that acts as a metaphor for the human condition. But despite the frequent genitive metaphors in the descriptive phrases, the narrative passage is not introduced as a metaphor. It is a "landscape of the heart," but the second half of the metaphor is suppressed. First the poet angrily portrays the tawdry life of everyday modern reality as a cheap fairground—a "reality" that has no validity in the eyes of the angel:

O, wie spurlos zerträte ein Engel ihnen den Trostmarkt,

. . .

But directly behind this superficial world lies true "reality," and here Rilke lists once again all the images of secure existence: children play, lovers embrace, dogs "have nature," and those who died at an early age continue to live. It is the realm of death, timelessness, inwardness, rendered as objective land-scape. It is the "land of suffering" ("Leidland") mortals nor-mally try to deny or to avoid. But the poet, whose vision now embraces all poles of being, renders that aspect of inner reality as though it had external form as well.

He does this by introducing the figure of a youth who takes a walk from the city of appearances through "the landscape of the Laments" ("Landschaft der Klagen") to the "mountains of primal suffering" ("Berge des Ur-Leids"). As the youth ventures from the city, he is met by "a young Lament," dressed in "pearls of suffering and the delicate veils of pa-tience" ("Perlen des Leids und die feinen Schleier der Duld-ung"), whom he follows into the neighboring fields. There, in the valley, one of the elder Laments greets the youth and relates the saga of her family. They were once, she says, a great race, whose forefathers were responsible for mining in the great mountains. Leading him through the vast landscape of the Laments, she points out the ruins of temples and castles from which the Laments had formerly ruled the land. He sees the trees and crops and animals as well as the graves of the ancient prophets of the noble race. And at night the Lament points out to the youth various stars in the heavens above the land of suffering ("die Sterne des Leidlands")—nine constella-tions that recapitulate many of the main themes of the cycle (e.g., the Staff, the Marionette, the Wreath of Fruit). But the youth must continue on his journey, and so the elder Lament leads him to the source of the waters of joy: among men, she says, it has grown to be a great river. Standing at the foot of the mountains, where joy has its source in grief, she embraces him, and the youth departs, alone, "into the mountains of primal suffering." The couplet with which this narrative sec-tion ends is emphatically a distich:

Einsam steigt er dahin, in die Berge des Ur-Leids,
Und nicht einmal sein Schritt klingt aus dem tonlosen Los.

The entire narrative of the Tenth Elegy is based on a pat-tern of reversal: what is ostensibly real is treated as false; what we customarily relegate to the realm of the imagination is rendered with the most vivid realism. Suffering, normally avoided by people, is exposed as the uniquely human experience and depicted, as such, in a manner accessible to the angel. It is fitting, therefore, that the Elegy concludes with a distich in which this reversal is formulated almost epigrammatically. From the standpoint of this life men tend to believe that happiness rises, and we are touched by sympathy when we see something happy fall. But from the vantage point of the angels up and down have as little meaning as the other polarities. So if we succeed in adopting their view, we are stirred by emotion to see something happy fall:

Und wir, die an *steigendes* Glück
denken, empfänden die Rührung,
die uns beinah bestürzt,
wenn ein Glückliches *fällt*.

Summarizing our findings, we see that the *Duineser Elegien* correspond surprisingly closely to the generic norm of the classical German elegy as we have become acquainted with it in more traditional works. It is a long meditative poem based rhythmically on the elegiac distich. The meditative core is embraced by a personal framework consisting of the First Elegy and the Tenth: the First announces the quandary of the poetic persona and states the principal themes treated more fully in the reflective core (especially the tension between consciousness and innocence). In the course of his meditations the reflective self is led from his initial despair—"Wer, wenn ich schriee, hörte mich denn . . ."—to a level of higher awareness, a moment of anagnorisis, at which he is enabled to see life as a new unity and to appreciate the meaning of human suffering. In the middle of the reflective core—the Fifth Elegy—there is a turning point at which the moment of ideal balance to be achieved at the end of the cycle is anticipated in the play of the acrobats, but not yet attained. The Tenth Elegy completes the framework, for there the poet is no longer dwelling elegiacally upon the conflict between the real and the ideal but rendering human reality and suffering with a new sense of fulfillment: for "Hiersein ist herrlich." Here, in the only nar-

rative section of the cycle, the symbolic figure representing
the poetic persona—the youth—is conducted to his moment
of spiritual illumination by a female guide strongly reminiscent, in her function, of Euphrosyne and Diotima in the
elegies by the two poets from whom Rilke learned the art of
the elegy. The symbolic reenactment of the movement from
despair to higher awareness is rendered in the metaphor we
have found to be so frequent as to be virtually constitutive for
the classical German elegy: the walk leading from the turmoil
of the city below to the meditative isolation of the mountain
above, the symbolic locus from which all apparent contradictions are resolved in a great concluding vision.

Our brief consideration of Rilke's use of the distich indicated how far he has moved away from the classical generic norm: and this straining against the strictures of the
genre is evident in the structure of the cycle as a whole, which
has been adapted to the exigencies of a new age and its fragmented vision. Yet the rhythms, the organization, the thematic tension, the development of the reflective self, the
female guide, and the locus of the action suggest that Rilke
was consciously exploiting expectations that cultivated
readers might well pose to any poem that announced itself, in
German at least, as an "elegy."[46] Obviously, any detailed interpretation of Rilke's cycle must go far beyond these brief
suggestions. Yet it does not seem unreasonable to propose
that the *Duineser Elegien* are "elegies" in a far more specific
sense than has commonly been assumed by those critics who
consider them in isolation from the literary tradition in which
they belong.[47] It might be argued that any interpretation that
neglects the tradition within which Rilke consciously located
his cycle is missing important dimensions of this monument
of modern German poetry.

Borchardt and Schröder considered Rilke "weak" because
he succumbed to and portrayed the plight of modern man
rather than heroically resisting it. Clearly, it was his sense of
the collapse of traditional beliefs in our age that encouraged
him to collapse the poetic forms that he appropriated—the
sonnets of *Sonette an Orpheus* as well as the elegy—so that they

would reflect through their form a reality that he perceived as just barely holding together. Borchardt and Schröder, as we have seen, confronted the same spiritual situation by heroic resistance: to a contemporary reality they disdained they opposed ancient humanistic values and conventional forms that they had mastered to a mind-dazzling degree. The difference is strikingly clear if we contrast Schröder's use of landscape with Rilke's: Schröder portrayed the actual mountains of Tivoli and then interpreted them as symbols of human qualities; Rilke created an imaginary landscape in which "the mountains of primal suffering" provide the background for a myth of human action. The fact that the *Duineser Elegien* are cherished today by readers in many languages, whereas Borchardt's poetry is unknown and Schröder's still familiar only to a small group of readers in German, suggests that Rilke's vision has proved to be a more adequate response to the twentieth century.

It is no accident that the epoch-making anthology of expressionist poetry, Kurt Pinthus' *Menschheitsdämmerung* (1920), contains neither a single line in distichs nor a single poem that calls itself an elegy. The elegy as a form and the elegiac as a mode were utterly inconsistent with the ideals of the young poets of the generation following Borchardt, Schröder, and Rilke. Regarding form as "voluptuousness" (according to the title of Ernst Stadler's programmatic poem "Form ist Wollust"), they rejected traditional genres and reduced their poems to elemental forms: the single ejaculative phrase, the long prose-like line, the simple four-line strophe. Concerned as they were with man's future rather than his past, they favored odes, psalms, and hymns. Ecstatic rather than meditative by disposition, they did not cultivate a genre created to enable the poetic persona to transcend his individualism and to contemplate man's fate in the light of human history. It is not surprising, then, that Georg Trakl (1887-1914), the only expressionist poet with a conspicuously elegiac temperament, turned to the elegy almost *malgré lui* and, in doing so, deformed it to such an extent that only bits and pieces of the genre are still evident in his poems. And yet, as I shall argue, some of his poems can be most fully understood if we see them in relation to the very tradition they undermine.

An urgent consciousness of the radical disintegration of accepted reality was one of Trakl's earliest and most fundamental experiences—an experience that was no doubt related to his experimentation with narcotics while he was still an adolescent and that finally led to his death by an overdose of drugs—a probable suicide—shortly after the outbreak of World War I. "It is such a nameless misfortune," he wrote to his friend Ludwig von Ficker in late November of 1913, "when the world breaks in two before your very eyes."[48] The misery produced by the decline of human society was symbolized for Trakl by the modern city and its denizens—figures without innocence or grace. For Trakl, Vienna was "this city of ordure"[49] and Innsbruck "the most brutal and most common city."[50] Yet when his friends asked him why he did not absent himself from places where he felt so forlorn, he replied: "I don't have the right to withdraw from Hell."[51] The religious overtones inherent in the image of Hell—secularized though they may be —are characteristic of Trakl's view of the world. To modern decay he opposed visions of a lost paradise, inhabited by such representatives of unspoiled human innocence as Kaspar Hauser or the youth Elis. It is this experience of loss together with the ensuing tension between reality and ideal, city and country, present and past, that informs the "play of opposites"[52] in Trakl's poetry and that justifies the general characterization of his poetry as "elegiac."[53]

But if the elegiac mode conspicuously dominates Trakl's poetry from the beginning, the same cannot be said of the form. As students of Trakl have long been aware, his poetry exploits an uncommonly small number of motifs, images, and rhetorical figures, which recur in constantly varying configurations.[54] A poem by Trakl is almost instantly recognizable by its language, long before the reader has begun to comprehend its meaning. But these characteristic elements occur in a variety of forms, ranging from the sonnets and simple four-line strophes that he favored in his early poetry to the free rhythms, unrhymed tercets, and poetic prose that he used in his later works. Trakl's poems also tend to reflect the formal characteristics of the poets whose writing impressed him at various stages of his growth. In his early work the influence of various writers is frankly evident—from the hymnic rhythms of Goethe and Schiller and the erotic images of Novalis to the dithyrambs of Nietzsche and the autumnal tones of Hofmannsthal.[55] His first mature poems—e.g., "Psalm" and "Helian"—are clearly indebted to Rimbaud (more specifically: to the German translation of Rimbaud).[56] Much of the late poetry stands under the aegis of Hölderlin: some of the poems display borrowings of phrases and lines;[57] others reveal an underlying dactylic rhythm that is based upon Hölderlin. For Trakl had no access to the classics: he failed in his studies at the gymnasium mainly because he was unable to master Latin and Greek; the French models he imitated—in addition to Rimbaud, principally Verlaine and Baudelaire—used no distichs; and among the few German writers that he read as a mature poet, only Hölderlin used elegiac distichs. Some poems, finally, seem to be more generally indebted to Hölderlin. It has been demonstrated, for instance, that "An den Knaben Elis" extensively parallels Hölderlin's fragment "Hälfte des Lebens."[58]

Among these late poems with dactylic rhythms, at least two display still other characteristics that tie them specifically to the tradition of the classical German elegy as Trakl knew it in the works of Hölderlin—poems written, moreover, just after Trakl confessed that his life had "been unutterably destroyed in a few days, and there remains only a wordless pain to which even bitterness is denied."[59] His elegies represent a response to that despair.

In "Abendländisches Lied" (December, 1913), as the title suggests, the generally elegiac mode that characterizes all Trakl's poetry intensifies into a vision that goes beyond the personal to embrace Western civilization as a whole. The twenty-two-line poem consists of a series of compact images that move abruptly from line to line and from strophe to strophe. The poem begins with six lines that establish a basically dactylic rhythm:[60]

> O der Seele nächtlicher Flügelschlag:
> Hirten gingen wir einst an dämmernden Wäldern hin
> Und es folgte das rote Wild, die grüne Blume und der
> lallende Quell
> Demutsvoll. O, der uralte Ton des Heimchens,
> Blut blühend am Opferstein
> Und der Schrei des einsamen Vogels über der grünen Stille
> des Teichs.

In Trakl's highly condensed language the colon following the first line signals that everything following that line is a dream or vision of the soul while the poet sleeps at night. In the liberation of the dream, the individual re-experiences the history of mankind as a whole. The vision itself falls into four stages corresponding roughly to the four strophes of the poem. In each stage, moreover, the innocent soul is brought one step closer to consciousness, and ultimately guilt, by religious activity. At the beginning of its voyage through time the soul recalls that primal state during which man lived in innocence in forests, at one with the animals and flowers of nature—an age of tranquillity interrupted by the act of violence represented by blood sacrifices. The second strophe moves on to that stage when the soul walked in gardens as a pious youth, until later his innocence was replaced by crusades and tortures and war in the name of faith.

> O, ihr Kreuzzüge und glühenden Martern
> Des Fleisches, Fallen purpurner Früchte
> Im Abendgarten, wo vor Zeiten die frommen Jünger
> gegangen,
> Kriegsleute nun, erwachend aus Wunden und
> Sternenträumen,
> O, das sanfte Zyanenbündel der Nacht.

In the third strophe the pious youths have developed into peaceful monks enjoying the gold autumn of life. But the image of men meditating in their still chambers contains the disturbing hint of a degree of consciousness that has produced alienation—from man (hence the need for law) and from God (hence the need for theology).

> O, ihr Zeiten der Stille und goldener Herbste,
> Da wir friedliche Mönche die purpurne Traube gekeltert;
> Und rings erglänzten Hügel und Wald.[61]
> O, ihr Jagden und Schlösser; Ruh des Abends,
> Da in seiner Kammer der Mensch Gerechtes sann,
> In stummem Gebet um Gottes lebendiges Haupt rang.

This development from a childlike innocence through pious youth to reflective manhood is followed by the moment of solipsistic alienation when man, cut off by his self-reflection from the rest of the world, peers into dark waters only to see his own stony countenance mirrored there:

> O, die bittere Stunde des Untergangs,
> Da wir ein steinernes Antlitz in schwarzen Wassern
>                                                   beschaun.

At this point in the last strophe, when the historical vision has reached the present again (a movement indicated by the tenses of the verbs), the moment of anagnorisis arrives in a blaze of radiance announcing harmony and unity:

> Aber strahlend heben die silbernen Lider die Liebenden:
> E i n Geschlecht. Weihrauch strömt von rosigen Kissen
> Und der süße Gesang der Auferstandenen.

We cannot presume here to deal with all the problematic details of interpretation—notably the ambivalent associations with incest bound up in Trakl's private vocabulary with the notion of "lovers" and "Geschlecht." What concerns us is the structure of the poem—the manner in which, in this specific instance, the familiar poetic materials are organized. What we recognize, in starkest outline, is again the traditional elegiac pattern: a meditative poem written in a generally dactylic rhythm consisting of the familiar framework and core. The rudimentary framework, comprising the first line and the last three lines, depicts the moment of falling asleep and the awakening. Within the core the soul recapitulates the course of Western man, in a series of strophes dialectically balanced within, from primal innocence through various stages to the "bitter hour of decline." But in the concluding part of the framework the moment of awakening is not merely physical: it is also a metaphorical awakening, an anagnorisis accompanied not only by song but also by the familiar images of illumination ("strahlend"). Though there is no mountain in the poem, the allusion to resurrection contains a suggestion of the spiritual and physical elevation required if modern man is to achieve the resolution of the elegy.

It would be a mistake to press our conclusions any further. I want to suggest only that the organization of "Abendländisches Lied" can be most satisfactorily explained if we regard it as a variation on the pattern of the classical German elegy, reshaped with a poetic license that amounts to a radical deformation. It is not the point to force Trakl's poem into the mold of the generic norm. But the poem displays a movement that is wholly different from that of others in which precisely the same images, themes, and rhythms are found— "Stundenlied," "Jahr," "Abendlied," "An den Frühverstorbenen," and several others. They may be "elegies" in the loosest sense of the term,[62] but only "Abendländisches Lied" belongs within the tradition of the classical German elegy. We can observe much the same structure in another late poem.

While "Abendländisches Lied" is framed by a movement from dark to dawn, the temporal movement of "Frühling der Seele" (early 1914) leads from dawn to dusk.[63] The poem opens with two lines of iambic trimeter describing a springtime morning in the city. Suddenly in lines 3 and 4, with the kind of unmotivated rhythmic shift typical of Trakl, a perfect elegiac distich emerges and establishes a new rhythmic pattern for most of the rest of the poem:

Aufschrei im Schlaf; durch schwarze Gassen stürzt der
                                                    Wind,
Das Blau des Frühlings winkt durch brechendes Geäst,
Púrpurner Náchttau únd es erlöschen ríngs die Stérne.

Grünlich dämmert der Fluß, silbern die alten Alléen
Und die Türme der Stadt.

As the poem continues, its images are unified by two principal motifs: the progress of the day from rosy dawn through
silent noon to the darkness of late afternoon parallels the
growth of the soul from childhood innocence through sexual
maturity to impotent age; the movement of a boat as it drifts
down the stream from the city past meadows and villages of
the tamed countryside to the wilderness recapitulates an in-
verse movement from civilization back through the stages of
growth to the garden of innocence. This poem plays with
many of the same images we encountered in "Abendländisches Lied." In the last strophe of each, for instance, the images of dark waters, rosy colors, and sweet song predominate.
In both, moreover, vague allusions to sin and incest interrupt
the course of human development. Given the associations of
Trakl's images (notably "thorn" and "dying") the fourth
strophe is explicitly sexual:

Schwester, da ich dich fand an einsamer Lichtung
Des Waldes und Mittag war und groß das Schweigen des
Tiers;
Weiße unter wilder Eiche, und es blühte silbern der Dorn.
Gewaltiges Sterben und die singende Flamme im Herzen.

Again, nevertheless, we note the characteristic elegiac structure, to which we have been alerted by the perfect distich
shortly after the beginning: notably the movement from
dawn to dusk that stands in dialectical contrast to the progress
from city to country. The apparition of the sister at mid-
course, no matter how perverse the associations may be,
exemplifies the female guide—an incestuous Diotima. In this
case, moreover, there is a specific reference to a hill from
which one hears the gentle and redeeming song of the brother
in the evening ("Der sanfte Gesang des Bruders am Abend-
hügel"). The poem can be seen as a modern deformation of
"Menons Klagen um Diotima"—an association that is not
farfetched if we keep in mind Trakl's indebtedness to Hölder-

lin and his tendency to pattern his poems after existing models.

In at least two of Trakl's late poems, then, we can make out the generic norm of the classical German elegy, even though it has been pushed to its extreme: the underlying dactyls, the encapsulated form, the guiding female spirit, the meditation on a grand elegiac theme finally resolved in a moment of anagnorisis characterized by elevation and illumination. But in Trakl's poetry the generic norm has been shattered as radically as the world that it is supposed to express. Hence its importance in our context. With Trakl the classical German elegy has reached and indeed passed the limits of the generic norm. Rilke, though he pushed the elegy up to the limits of recognizability, still acknowledged the tradition to the extent that he exploited the expectations of his readers by calling his poems "elegies." Trakl, in contrast, never uses the generic label—even though in his earlier poems generic labels for various forms are quite common. Rilke represents, we might say, the last poet within the tradition of the classical German elegy; Trakl is the first poet who used that tradition as a point from which to step beyond the genre.

We are coming to the end of our story. Poets of course continued to write "elegies" even after the dissolution of the classical German elegy, just as they had done before its creation by Schiller, Goethe, and Hölderlin. But few post-expressionist elegies belong to the category whose history we have been tracing. Poets who attempted to extend the tradition were unable to go beyond the vanishing point to which Trakl had brought the genre. As a result, they tended to turn back to Rilke or to earlier models, either in imitation or in parody. Let us consider an example of each reaction.

In an unusually frank and perceptive letter to a literary scholar, the Austrian poet Josef Weinheber (1892-1945) provided an extensive analysis of his ambivalent relationship to Rilke.[64] Exposed to what he called the "bel canto" of *Stunden-Buch* early in his career, Weinheber wrote some hundred or so poems in explicit imitation of the young Rilke before, at about the end of World War I, his introduction to Trakl's poetry showed him, by exposing him to an entirely different poetic imagination, how "servile" ("hörig") he had become to Rilke. Gradually Weinheber came to realize that Trakl could not serve him as a model, for Trakl was "too far along, spoke too much from a demonic world of the beyond, which remained veiled in mystery."[65] It was only after Rilke's death that Weinheber began to find his way slowly back to him—this time to the mature poet of the *Duineser Elegien* and *Sonette an Orpheus*. At first it was Rilke's extraordinary formal achievement—"his well-nigh uncanny ability to undertake and carry out anything by means of language"[66]—that impressed him. Later, becoming more secure in the validity of his own style, Weinheber felt confident enough to take up the tone of Rilke's Elegies when it seemed suitable for his purposes. "Indeed, I even appropriated there for the first time the figure of the angel."[67] During the thirties, when he was at the height of his classical phase and, as a humanist skilled in classical languages, writing dozens of poems in a wide variety of Greek and Latin meters, he "did not hesitate to sound the tone of the Rilkean elegy whenever it seemed suitable for encompassing my poetic contents."[68] Summing up his relationship to the two great "fraternal existences" ("Bruderexistenzen"), Hölderlin and Rilke, Weinheber explains that he made use of the language of his great predecessors whenever he needed to transcend "the level of what is temporally contingent" ("die Ebene des Zeitgebundenen") in a poem of large scale—in hymns, odes, and elegies. For he had at his disposal no other poetic language for treating lofty themes, and his artistic instinct prevented him from attempting, out of sheer vanity, to be original.

After this confession, we are hardly surprised to hear echoes of Rilke's elegies in the section entitled "Elegien und Hymnen" that Weinheber included in the volume *Späte Krone* (1936).[69] In particular, "Auf das Vergängliche" amounts to a reworking in a Rilkean dactylic *parlando* of the principal theme of the *Duineser Elegien*. But though Weinheber catches Rilke's tone, we are reminded of a boast he made: that he felt capable of surpassing Rilke at least in substance if not in form. "After all, I am actually a thinker by avocation."[70] For his elegy amounts to a critique of Rilke's theme: according to Weinheber, our reverence for lofty visionary poetry causes us to stand, admiringly, on the periphery of life while the simple things pass us by. Divided precisely into two halves, the elegy begins with the lament that poets prefer to look beyond the present and do not deign to praise everyday reality:

> Gern gehen die Sänger voraus. Ihnen genügt nicht,
> was vergeht auf der Erde, zu preisen: Die nahen
> wirklichen Dinge, die Herzen, leidend
> das Vergängliche. . . .
>
> (p. 222)

Instead, they proclaim great heroes and saints and the eternal order. But, he continues in the second half, do not the simple things suffice? These things get ignored in the midst of great songs, and their rewards are modest:

> Ein geringes
> "Du" ist der Preis. Kein Sang.
> Aber dort ist die Liebe.
> (p. 223)

We do not find any fully developed examples of the classical German elegy. If we discount "Den Gefallenen"—the hymn in free verses to the war dead, which introduced the figure of Rilke's angel—only two more of the poems are elegiac in some sense. The second poem, "Die Taten," amounts to a fatalistic reflection in five-beat dactyls on the inevitable violence attached to any kind of activity: "Wir aber, wir Täter verliern uns / immer hinab in den Töter . . ." (p. 224).

In the last elegy, "Auf das Unabwendbare," Weinheber is still obsessed by the theme of fatalism, and although the meter has developed into full elegiac distichs, the language is still clearly Rilkean. The poem begins with the image of a carousel in which we are led round and round by higher powers, which destroy anyone who attempts to escape the inevitable cycle:

Aber blind sind wir alle. Sehn nicht, wie uns das Höhere
Ringelbahn führt und es kommt jeder im Kreise vorbei
an dem starrenden Antlitz, und jeder noch einmal und
wieder,
und mit jedem Mal reift größer, gewisser die Angst.
(p. 224)

The poet cites further examples of destructive destiny: a plant-
ing is consumed by drought; a house destroyed by fire; a son
goes to the dogs. "Immer schlägt uns zutiefst, was wir am
tiefsten geliebt." Yet we are reluctant to escape even when a
way out is offered, just as the addict continues to take his
poisonous drugs. If the door is unlocked, we even refuse to
leave our cell:

Draußen ist vieles: das Recht, die Würde, der Mensch. Aber
*kann* denn,
wem das Herz längst schwand, so zu den Seinen zurück?
(p. 226)

Despite Weinheber's pretensions to thought, his elegy
amounts to little more than the advice to accept one's lot in
life.

He wrote a few more poems in elegiac distichs, including
one entitled simply "Das elegische Distichon," which turns
out to be an elegy on the responsibility of poetry to preserve
meaning in times of war:

Wer behütet den Sinn und wagt das Unzeitgemäße,
haben die Dichter nicht Mut: Klage und Trauer und
Traum?[71]

But what he borrowed from Rilke was the lofty tone of the
*Duineser Elegien*, not the specific characteristics of the classical
German elegy. Rilke's reshaping of the elegy was simply one
more form among the dozens that Weinheber mastered with
impressive facility in his increasingly desperate attempts to
offset the chaos of the world, and its meaningless fatalism, by
aesthetic organization. It was his tragedy that, failing to find
absolute security in art, he turned instead to the political "or-

der" promised by National Socialism. Something of the ambivalence that he felt about that decision, I believe, contributes
to the tone of his elegies.

It would be difficult to find a writer who differed more
sharply with Weinheber in matters of art as well as politics
than Bertolt Brecht (1898-1956). Unlike Weinheber, Brecht
had nothing but contempt for Rilke. Observing in his early
notebooks that God appears in some of Rilke's poems, Brecht
remarks that "Rilke's expression, whenever he is concerned
with God, is absolutely that of a fag."[72] No one who has
noticed this, he continues, can ever again read a line of Rilke's
verses without grinning. Brecht is talking here about God and
not about angels—a fact that suggests Rilke's early poems
rather than the *Duineser Elegien.* Yet it is impossible to read his
"Hollywood-Elegien"—a collection of six short poems
Brecht wrote in 1942 during his reluctant American exile—
without hearing parodistic allusions to Rilke's Elegies.[73]
Brecht makes much of the circumstance that Hollywood—
actually Los Angeles—is named for the angels. But these
angels are utterly un-Rilkean, for they reek of perfume, carry
gold pessaries, shade their eyes, and feed the writers each
morning in the swimming pools:

> Die Stadt ist nach den Engeln genannt
> Und man begegnet allenthalben Engeln.
> Sie riechen nach Öl und tragen goldene Pessare
> Und mit blauen Ringen um die Augen
> Füttern sie allmorgenlich die Schreiber in ihren
> > Schwimmpfühlen.

After this blatant and scornful Rilke-parody Brecht used the
term "elegies" once again, to characterize a cycle of poems
written in 1950 shortly after his return to Berlin. The "Buc-
kower Elegien" have even less to do with the tradition of the
classical German elegy than the "Hollywood-Elegien," which
were related to it at least through parody. Most of these
twenty-one brief epigrams are based formally on the Japanese
haiku, a form that fascinated Brecht and one whose brevity
offered him a good opportunity for the kind of parodox he

loved to pose. But the last poem, "Bei der Lektüre eines spät-griechischen Dichters," not only introduces the term for lament into the poem; it also manages to establish a genuinely elegiac mood within its six lines. Brecht is making the point that the Trojans, even at the moment when their destruction was certain, went about their daily business as though nothing were wrong, ignoring the reality of the situation:

In den Tagen, als ihr Fall gewiß war—
Auf den Mauern begann schon die Totenklage
Richteten die Troer Stückchen grade, Stückchen
In den dreifachen Holztoren, Stückchen.
Und begannen Mut zu haben und gute Hoffnung.

Auch die Troer also.[74]

In general, however, Brecht is neither by temperament nor by formal preference an elegist: his "elegies" achieve their effect principally by means of contrast with the concept of elegy as it had been made familiar by the *Duineser Elegien*.

Weinheber's imitations and Brecht's parodies exemplify the problem of any genre that has been pushed to the limits of its potentialities. At the beginning of its history the classical German elegy emerged in response to the specific modal need for a reflective poem that could deal with problems presented by the new German notion of *Bildung*. By the end of World War I the values and indeed the mode of thought that produced the elegy had vanished, leaving intact only the form, in the idiosyncratic extreme to which it was carried by Rilke. It is this form to which Weinheber and Brecht are responding, not to any meditative impulse of their own or to any perception of the tradition of the genre as a whole. In general, post-Rilkean writers who were moved by a genuinely elegiac emotion tended not to adapt the form of the classical German elegy, which had become so stylized that it obscured its own content. Although the expressionist generation was not noticeably elegiac by disposition, many writers of the thirties had a good deal to be meditative about—especially if they remained in Germany as opponents of the Nazis. It is no accident that two of the most widely circulated resistance poems—Friedrich Georg Jünger's "Der Mohn" and Hans Carossa's "Abendländische Elegie"—take the form of elegies. It is also typical that the most representative anthology of resistance poetry—Gunter Groll's *De Profundis* (1946)—contains, in addition to a number of poems that are elegiac in mode, at least two that are also elegies in name: Carossa's "Abendländische Elegie" and a selection from a volume of elegies by Rüdiger Syberberg.

In general, resistance poetry of the period 1933 to 1945, in contrast to the dissolution of form advocated by the expressionists, returned to traditional forms—notably the sonnet.[75] In part this turn to fixed and clearly identifiable forms represented an attempt to oppose aesthetic form to the chaos the writers perceived in the world surrounding them. In part the use of traditional forms was an act of symbolic protest by which writers expressed their allegiance to the humanist ideals of Western civilization in opposition to the pseudo-Nordic ideals of the Nazis. Finally, of course, the return to familiar forms resulted from the urgent need to place meaning above formal experimentation. All these factors are evident in the poetry of Friedrich Georg Jünger (born 1898). "Der Mohn" was first published in Jünger's *Gedichte* in 1934, where it appears in the middle of a section containing a number of poems in elegiac distichs that deal with gardening, with mythological subjects, and with his brother Ernst.[76] Most of the poems are straightforward apostrophes to flowers ("Iris," "Die Rose") or hymns to the seasons ("Der Sommer," "Der Herbst"). But occasionally tones arise that suggest political implications. "Der Garten," for instance, is ostensibly about the struggle of the gardener to keep his garden free of weeds, but many of the distichs apply equally well to the writer who seeks to preserve traditional cultural values in the face of the growing barbarism in Germany:

> Was der Gärtner gezogen,
> Fällt, wenn er fortgeht, sogleich wieder dem Anfang
> anheim.

Was mich durch Formen ergötzt, was lieb mir durch Farbe
und Duft ist,
Ist durch des Stärkeren Recht mühsam und künstlich
gepflanzt.
Drum bekämpft mit Wut mich das Volk, es ruft nach dem
Lande,
Das der Ahne bewohnt, ficht unermüdlich mich an.
(p. 22)

Doch ich will dich, Gesindel, als Herr nicht, will dich nicht
nähren,
Kann dich nicht brauchen als Knecht, ob du auch Dienste
gewährst.
(pp. 22-23)

Similarly, "Der Gesang des Prometheus" leaves little to the
imagination: every word the Titan utters can be read as a
speech of resistance to the Nazis and a prophecy of their even-
tual fall, even if Prometheus himself is struck down by Zeus'
bolt in the last line of the poem. Of all these poems, the one so
generally regarded as a poem of resistance that it was circulated widely in typewritten copies and that invited for its author the attentions of the Gestapo was "Der Mohn." The
poem begins, like many of the other garden poems, with a
characterization of the poppy, which often grows on grave-
sites and which also supplies the bitter white juice that brings
sleep, dreams, and relief from pain. The associations with
death and pain aroused in the first strophe provide a transition
to the second strophe, which points out that the poppy can
alleviate pain. But what can help us to forget baseness, which
is less tolerable and which drives out the muses?

Mohnsaft, du stillst uns den Schmerz. Wer lehrt uns das
Niedre vergessen?
Schärfer als Feuer und Stahl kränkt uns das Niedere doch.
Wirft es zur Herrschaft sich auf, befiehlt es, so fliehen die
Musen.
(p. 34)

Clio and the others muses have departed, along with the noble citizens. Only the loud-mouthed boaster remains behind, adulated by the mobs:

> Prahlend blieb der Schwätzer zurück, umjauchzt von der
> Menge.
> (p. 34)

The demagogue and his spokesmen cheapen all values and deceive the people:

> Gaukler treiben mit Worten ihr Wesen, Lügner sie deuteln,
> Retter, sie retten den Trug, Ärzte, sie scheuen den Tod.
> Wollt ihr betrügen das Volk, so schmeichelt ihm schamlos
> und lobt es,
> Dient ihm mit Worten zuerst, eh ihr es redend beherrscht.
> (p. 35)

Carried along by deceptive rhetoric, the mob ignores the honest men who point out the useless sacrifices and deaths. Instead, they celebrate festivals and march more proudly than the ancient Germanic tribes that defeated Roman legions:

> Feste seh ich und Feiern, ich höre Märsche, Gesänge,
> Bunt ist von Fahnen die Stadt, immengleich summet der
> Schwarm,
> Lauter als der Cherusker, der Romas stolze Legionen
> Weihte der Nacht und dem Tod, stimmen den Siegruf sie
> an.
> (pp. 35-36)

But these mobs are not celebrating victories over hostile armies or oppressive dictators; they have been battling their own brothers. The noise that calls itself "rapture" deafens the poet's ears, but amidst it all the dead sleep on, unaffected by the infamous intoxication:

> Wehe! Begeisterung! Silberner Brunnen der Stille, du
> klarer,
> Du kristallener Born, nennt es Begeisterung nicht.

Tiefer schweigen die Toten, sie trauern, sie hören das
Lärmen,
Hören das kindische Lied ruhmloser Trunkenheit nicht.
(p. 36)

Jünger's poems are inspired by a genuinely elegiac mood—the
recollection of a noble past during a base present from which
the finest spirits have been exiled by demagogues and the un-
ruly mob. And the poems are written in graceful distichs that
betray the classically trained poet who wrote essays on Greek
antiquity (*Griechische Mythen*, 1947; *Orient und Okzident*, 1948)
as well as a handbook of metrics (*Rhythmus und Sprache im
deutschen Gedicht*, 1952). But the poems have nothing to do
with the form of the classical German elegy as we have seen it
emerge from Schiller and Goethe through Rilke and Trakl
down to the imitations and parodies of Weinheber and
Brecht. Rather, they are satires formally based on the classical
models, including specifically Martial, whose work Jünger
knew and appreciated.

The case of the other well-known resistance poem,
"Abendländische Elegie" (1943) by Hans Carossa (1878-
1956), is somewhat different. Here the generic qualification of
the title is necessary since the poem itself is written not in distichs but in free blank verse—a fact that is rather surprising in
the light of Carossa's confession only a few years earlier, in a
talk on Goethe's influence in the present, that "Euphrosyne"
was the work through which he, as a sixteen-year-old, had
first been drawn to Goethe. "The splendid elegy on the death
of the young actress Christiane Neumann probably did not
often encounter a more devout heart."[77] In fact, Carossa expresses the belief that it is primarily the rhythm that first at-
tracts a young person to a work of poetry. However, even if
Carossa's own elegy lacks the metrical form that originally attracted him to Goethe—indeed, with minor exceptions the
classical forms are wholly absent from his poetry—it displays
conspicuously the humanism for which he is justly celebrated
and which he expressed in the concluding sentence of his
essay on Goethe when he proclaimed his allegiance to "the

order of those who would not be satisfied by all the lands and seas of the world if the realm of the spirit and heart remained unconquered."[78]

In 1942, while visiting wartime Florence, Carossa went to see one of his favorite works of art, Michelangelo's statue of Night in the Medici Chapel. Finding the sculpture completely encased in heavy concrete protective walls, Carossa was stirred to thoughts on the state of Western civilization. "Every journey in the West today is a great leave-taking; never again will it show us that countenance that was familiar to us. We are excluding ourselves from the chorus of the lovely images, and when they once again move up into the light, we old people shall be lying in our coffins; but to coming generations they will perhaps reveal a Medusa face."[79] These melancholy reflections provided the impulse for the "Abendländische Elegie."

The poem begins with a word-play in which the poet asks rhetorically if Western civilization is entering the period of its decline: "Wird Abend über uns, o Abendland?"[80] The opening strophes are filled with a sense of doubt. Although he has learned all that the schools had to offer—the Western humanist tradition—he has been brought back to that fundamental fact known even by the sunflower at his window: that the earth is nothing but another star in the universe. Man himself has summoned up the Furies that race through the skies destroying the cities:

> Selbst riefen wir die grauen Furienchöre,
> Die nun durch unsern Heimathimmel jagen,
> Entsetzen streuend: Stadt um Stadt erliegt.
>
> (p. 84)

Though the cathedral is still standing, it too may collapse at any minute in a heap of ruins. The libraries have been destroyed by fire. Human discourse has ceased to be a source of consolation:

> Ein jeder hört den andern irre reden,
> Und wer noch Strahlen in sich hegt, verbirgt sie.
>
> (p. 85)

Now that the present has lost its religious faith, its secular knowledge, and its human community, the poet turns to the past in search of his earliest productive consciousness. In memory he seeks out Florence, the loveliest city of Western civilization ("deine schönste Stadt"). Encountering no human acquaintances, he is drawn to the chapel—"the cool temple"—where he finds the statue of Night, who is represented as the timeless Mother of the "Abendland":

> Doch zieht mich leis in ihren kühlen Tempel
> Die große nackte Schlummernde, die Nacht,
> Zeitlose Mutter aller unsrer Tage,
> An ihr gehn die Jahrhunderte vorüber.
>
> (p. 85)

Describing Michelangelo's statue in precise detail, Carossa praises Night as the goal of our longing and the source of our creative powers:

> Heimweh nach ihr ist unser holdes Erbteil,
> Und jede Liebe sucht in ihr den Himmel.
>
> (p. 86)

If we attempt to boast to Night of our accomplishments, we become aware of our impoverishment, for we have nothing but mechanical prowess to cite—weapons of destruction, conduits through which we send falsehoods through the ether. To find a gift worthy of Night, the poet turns back to the humble sunflower mentioned at the beginning—a flower once cast over the fence as a weed by passers-by. He has come to regard the sunflower as an image, a tiny mirror of the sun and the light ("diese kleine Gegensonne"), which loses its leaves and blossoms and yet constantly bears anew: "Die Blüte stirbt, jedoch ihr Sinn ist ewig" (p. 87). At this point the poet turns back to his grand theme, exhorting Western civilization to let transitory reality pass, for on the spiritual level the ancient values persist.

> O Abendland, so reich in der Verarmung,
> Blick auf! Laß das Vergängliche vergehn!

Du weißt es doch, daß in der obern Sphäre
Nicht alles mitstürzt, was im Irdischen fällt.

(p. 87)

Let us preserve some child that will grow whole in a sick world. For out of the present ruins there will emerge a new day:

Aus Trümmern steigt einmal ein Segentag,
Wo wir das Licht nicht mehr verhehlen müssen
Und wieder frei mit Urgewalten spielen.

(p. 88)

For that hour, he concludes, it would be worth enduring years of darkness.

Surveying Carossa's "Abendländische Elegie," we find that it displays various elements of the classical German elegy—enough, in any case, to justify the generic title. Within the familiar encapsulated form the poet looks back from a blighted present to the past, from which renewal is possible. The female guide in this elegy is not, to be sure, a young woman like the Euphrosyne in Carossa's favorite Goethe poem. But his meditation on the symbols of eternal nature leads the poet to the conclusion that what has been destroyed by war is nothing but superficial technological achievement: man's spirit remains intact and, as he predicts in the last strophe, will emerge once again in the customary blaze of light. Like much resistance writing, "Abendländische Elegie" is not a great poem; but it is a moving human document and, as such, revealing in our context. For—in a sense similar to Brecht's parody—it shows that the form of the classical German elegy has become so familiar and, indeed, so accessible that it can be used for what is essentially a poem of consolation. But in order to use it in this way, Carossa had to skip back not only over Trakl but also over Rilke to Goethe to find a model of sufficient simplicity and familiarity for his purpose. We learn something further about the nature of the classical German elegy from the fact that Carossa was able to employ its organization, if not its metrical form, for a poem celebrating the values of the humanistic tradition. Jünger, in a poem that involved not so much praise of the past as an excoriation of the present, was able to use the rhythms of the elegiac distich; but for his model he had to reach back—perhaps by way of Goethe's and Schiller's *Xenien*—to the satiric epigrams of Martial.

If the two resistance elegies, for all their differences in tone, are related by their common faith in eternal humanistic values underlying the pretensions of contemporary wartime reality, two representative elegies of the immediate postwar period also display remarkable parallels of a different sort. In Rudolf Hagelstange's *Meersburger Elegie* and Werner Bergengruen's *Lombardische Elegie* we are dealing with leisurely autobiographical reminiscences written by poets living in the south, who think about their childhoods in northern homes in an effort to assess what heritage remains to them following the physical and spiritual exhaustion of the war.

Rudolf Hagelstange (born 1912) emerged into prominence immediately after the war as the author of one of the finest works of resistance poetry, the cycle of thirty-five sonnets entitled *Venezianisches Credo* (written and circulated in 1944; published 1945). Since in his resistance poems Hagelstange was concerned not with juxtaposing past and present in a judicious assessment but with exposing in a series of epigrammatic statements characteristic moments in the present and expressing his unshaken faith in a new day, the sonnet (the most popular form during the resistance period) lent itself admirably to his purposes. But after the war his concern was different. Living in Meersburg, a small medieval town on the shores of Lake Constance, Hagelstange thinks back to his childhood in the central German town of Nordhausen and reassesses his experiences of those years in an effort to determine what is left to him, now that Nordhausen has been totally destroyed by bombing raids. It is autumn, and in dactylic rhythms borrowed directly from Rilke—the principal influence on his poetry—the poet celebrates the season:

Herbst ist geworden. Aus schrägeren Bahnen
rollen die Reste des glühenden Jahres. Der Vögel

trunkenes Lied ist verstummt. Die Säge
frißt sich kreischend ins Holz, und die Fische
bergen das silberne Leben
tiefer am Grunde.[81]

His reflections on the cycle of time—"the narrow spiral of
hurtling years" ("die schmale Spirale / jagender Jahre")—stop
him in astonishment as he realizes how easy it is to forget that
secure peaceful time before the war:

Kann mans vergessen, kann man
wirklich vergessen, daß einmal
—eben erst, gestern—alle die Stühle und Betten
im Lande standen gerückt und bereitet,
blankgescheuertes Holz und weißes gewaschenes Linnen,
für jeden?

In appreciation the poet invites us to contemplate Meersburg—"die runde und glänzende Perle, / die uns das Wasser
gebildet und redlicher Sinn / sauber gefaßt hat"—as a token
and witness of a time that has vanished. He thinks of Annette
von Droste-Hülshoff, the nineteenth-century poetess who
spent her last years here—"die zarte Sibylle am steinernen
Turme"—consumed by a hopeless love. This memory provokes in the poet the thought that man himself is a creature
torn apart by divine longing and human infirmity:

Ach, wo ist Heimat für diesen schrecklichen Zwitter,
der wir doch sind: eine silberne Ader göttlicher Sehnsucht
in diesem düsteren Bergwerk von Fleisch und Gebrechen?

The thought of Droste's childhood in her northern German
home leads the poet to remember his own home town, so
much like Meersburg as a medieval town, where he had first
been exposed to the great myths of man and where he had
first begun to find his voice as a poet, in imitation of Orpheus:

Oh diese Stunde: da ich, ihm lauschend, versuchte
die eigene Stimme! Wie sie noch dünn klang und kindlich,
nur von Gespielen erwidert; und wie sie noch Spiel war.

In those days, he continues, all Germany was like Nordhausen and Meersburg—a variegated and rich tapestry of stone, woven by time. Was she dissatisfied? Why did she permit violence to join her, tearing apart the fabric and weaving incompatible strands together and snarling the yarn? For now that past is destroyed—the town along with the gods and heroes and friends who populated his childhood. Everything has grown silent, including his poetic voice. Returning to the present from his memories of Nordhausen, which was demolished in the war, the poet meditates on the meaning of home:

> Ach, wo ist Heimat . . . Nur wo die Dächer gedeckt,
> die Schüsseln gefüllt sind? Geschwister und Freunde
> wie eh dich umgeben?

Now he realizes that home is not what he was taught as a child, when he was expected to accept all the lies he was told and to close his eyes to guilt:

> Wie Fleisch von den Beinen
> mußt du es lassen, so man dir nahlegt,
> die Zunge zu spalten und über die Lider
> Blindheit zu senken, wenn Zeugnis zur Schuld wird.

In a world still in turmoil, the poet turns back to Meersburg and asks what gives this town any advantage over other places:

> Wie plagt sich die Zeit, ein Fädchen der Hoffnung
> heimlich zu mischen ins graue Gewebe
> entgötterten Tags!

But here among the peasants who follow the ancient rules of nature and still worship devoutly in their simple chapels, he hopes to learn "the pious mystery" of life again:

> Hier lern ich es wieder, das fromme Geheimnis
> der unermüdlichen Erde, des Wassers
> entsühnende Kraft und die Stillung des Äthers.

It is only earth and freedom that man requires in order to prosper:

Gebt ihnen Erde und Freiheit,
den zahllos Vertriebenen, wieder zurück,
Ihr Großen der Erde!
So stiftet ihr Frieden.

The fish of the sea and the birds of the sky exemplify a nature that survives without law and domination. The thought of nature brings him back again to Droste, the great poetess of nature, standing on her tower overlooking the lake. And he wishes for himself the release that will enable him to sing again—a poetry of earth, water, and light:

Denn mich verlangt es, vor allem,
des süßen mitreißenden Dreiklangs
aus Erde, Wasser und Licht, auf daß mir
dieser in meiner Brust so ruhelos flatternde Vogel,
diese aus lauter Purpur und Wollust gewirkte
Nachtigall, singe und singe. . . .

Hagelstange's poem betrays a profound indebtedness to Rilke—not just in its rhythms and the ecstatic language, but also in the motif of the poetess of unrequited love; the motif of the tower, which links Meersburg to Duino; the vivid image of the weaver time, which is close to that of the modiste Madame Lamort in Rilke's Fifth Elegy; and in various other details. At the same time, the general structure of the classical German elegy is more clearly evident than in Weinheber's imitations. Apart from the typical encapsulated form, we can cite the elegiac contrast between past and present, the tutelary female spirit, and the moment of anagnorisis accompanied by visions of light as the poet gazes out over the landscape from the elevation of the tower. Again, as in the classical German elegy, the resolution of problems produced by the decline of human civilization—specifically the destruction of the past by the war—emerges from the vision of nature and the experienced landscape, which assures the poet that his spiritual heritage has remained intact despite all destruction.

Werner Bergengruen's *Lombardische Elegie* also begins with

the urgent question of inheritance: "Was erbte ich? Was bleibt
mir zu vererben?"[82] But for Bergengruen (1892-1962) the
problem is stated in more tangible terms. As he sits in Italy,
the poet thinks about his home in Riga, at the other end of
Europe, which was completely sacked and destroyed during
the war, and remembers the various totems of his childhood.
In leisurely blank verse he describes his great-grandfather's
desk, which had been destined for his own son; an Empire
mirror decorated with Delft tiles; the etchings and paintings
on the walls of his father's house. Who cares for all these trivial things from the past, he now wonders. Yet the past deserves our recognition, for it is now past change, living in a
state of eternal authenticity in our memories:

> Und dennoch bleibe seine Ehre auch
> dem Abgelebten. Denn das Langvergangne
> steht unverletzbar und in Gültigkeit,
> und keinem Wandel ist es zu erreichen.
>
> (p. 20)

At this point the poet returns to the present with the thought
that Lombardy—a place so deeply saturated with history—is
the proper place to think of the past, for nothing has died
here; indeed, the war exposed things that had lain buried for
centuries:

> Nichts starb hier ab. Der Krieg
> hat mancherlei Verborgenes blossgelegt.
>
> (p. 23)

As they rebuild their houses, the inhabitants set into their new
masonry stones from walls the Langobards destroyed centuries earlier. Yet those ancient conquerors also passed, leaving no trace behind except an occasional unusually tall man,
an exceptionally blond woman, or a dialect word that only
scholars recognize. These changes suggest to the poet the
analogy of a tree, which remains constant even though the
leaves come and go with the seasons: "Wie Blätter wachsen
wohl die Völker auf / am weitverzweigten Baum" (p. 25).
And all this change takes place so that men can experience the

power of the world and destiny, although the meaning of history remains obscure. His reflections on the antiquity of Lombardy lead the poet to recall that he had always learned best by hearing stories told about treasured objects, and he recounts the anecdotes of his parents connected with various household possessions: goblets, weapons, jewelry boxes filled with commemorative coins. The memory of the coins leads into an extended meditation on metals, which serves as the connecting link for a survey of civilization:

> Seit fünf Jahrtausenden ist der Metalle,
> seit drei Jahrtausenden des Eisens Zeit.
>
> (p. 38)

The survey of precious objects from the jewelry case concludes with the miraculous rose-branch his grandfather brought back from the Holy Land—a symbol of life that he opposes to death and the symbols of iron:

> Schwermütiges Geschäft, das Angedenken
> der Dinge zu erneun, die nicht mehr sind!
>
> (p. 51)

Sitting in Lombardy, the poet again poses the melancholy question with which he began: "Was erbte ich? was bleibt mir zu vererben?" (p. 52). Everything destined for him and his sons has been destroyed or looted by plunderers. His father, driven like a beggar from his own home, lost even his wedding ring. Nothing remained except a gold pin given to him by a friend, whose story is briefly recounted. This pin, which constitutes the poet's sole inheritance, is described with its carnelian head and faded motto from 1 Corinthians 13:13: "Die Liebe ist die größte unter ihnen" (p. 53). With this message the poet perceives that the meaning of life lies not in its objects but in the love that we bring to life:

> Doch alle Stunde ist der Liebe Zeit,
> es sei in jungen, sei in alten Jahren,
> und jeden Tag wird neu der Ring gereicht.
>
> (p. 59)

Looking up, the poet sees the bright skies of Lombardy and feels the cool breezes rushing down from the Alps. He realizes that he is an heir everywhere on earth: even without possessions he shares in the heritage of the past and in all future accomplishments:

> Dein Los ist schön. Auch unbegütert hast,
> auch schweifend du an Allem deinen frommen,
> bemessenen Anteil: an der grau entfernten
> Vergangenheit und allen künftigen Ernten.
>
> (p. 62)

For it is love that assures our participation in the human heritage. A few drops of love will cause the rose of Jericho to bloom again.

In the very general sense that it is a meditation on the past which finally arrives at the consoling resolution that commitment and love will compensate us for all losses, Bergengruen's poem is elegiac. When Bergengruen wrote his elegy, he had recently (1947) received the Wilhelm Raabe Prize for his life's work, which specifically commended his concern for eternal order and his attempt to integrate his love of country with his Christian faith. His poem is representative of those values and concerns. But with its loose organization, its rambling reminiscences, and its chatty tone it hardly qualifies as an elegy in any stricter sense—either classical or German classical. In fact, the comparison with Hagelstange's poem, which treats essentially the same theme from the same point of view, highlights the difference between a poem that is simply elegiac and one that is also formally an elegy.

In conclusion, let us examine another poem of cultural stocktaking, the "Pruzzische Elegie" (written 1952) by the East German poet Johannes Bobrowski (1917-1965). Unlike Hagelstange and Bergengruen, Bobrowski is concerned not with his personal heritage following the war but rather with the heritage of the Borussi, a Baltic people destroyed in the thirteenth century by the knights of the Teutonic Order, from whom Prussia got its name. Bobrowski remarked frequently that it was his principal theme and literary mission to deal with the guilt and responsibility of the Germans toward their Eastern neighbors of past and present.[83] To stress that he did not conceive his theme according to contemporary political boundaries and that he was concerned with history as much as with the immediate past, Bobrowski borrowed from Roman geographers the name Sarmatia to adumbrate that vast cultural realm, entitling his first volume of poems *Sarmatische Zeit* (1961).

"Pruzzische Elegie" was the first major poem Bobrowski composed after the war.[84] A devoted disciple of Klopstock, during the war he began writing poems in Alcaic strophes dealing with his experiences as a soldier on the Russian front.[85] It was not until 1952—several years after his return to Germany from a Russian prisoner-of-war camp—that Bobrowski began writing again, "now in an externally freer form—which to be sure for those who understand anything about metrics betrays rather clearly the Greek odic and verse patterns."[86] This new direction is evident in "Pruzzische Elegie," whose title explicitly uses the archaic word for the ancient Baltic Borussians in order to distinguish them emphatically from modern Prussians. The elegy begins with an apostrophe to the Borussians, in which the dactylic rhythm emerges strongly—an apostrophe expressing the poet's urge to sing a song both bright with love and bitter dark with lament, combining the mixed emotions of the traditional elegy:

> Dir
> ein Lied zu singen,
> hell von zorniger Liebe—
> dunkel aber, von Klage
> bitter. . . .

Following this introduction the poet looks back to the past immediately preceding the Borussians' decline ("Untergang"), to the time when they still lived in childlike, dreamy peacefulness in their Baltic forests—a life we now know only from the songs preserved as one of the few legacies from that ancient past:

So in der Greisinnen Lieder
tönt noch,
kaum mehr zu deuten,
Anruf der Vorzeit—

At this point the poet apostrophizes the still happy people of the forests, the rivers, the sea, of the hunt, of the herds and summer meadows:

Volk
der schwarzen Wälder,
schwer andringender Flüsse,
kahler Haffe, des Meers!
Volk
der nächtigen Jagd. . . .

It is only when we read these lines aloud or recast them linearly that we realize that out of the general dactylic rhythm of the poem a perfect elegiac distich has emerged:

Vólk der schwárzen Wälder, schwér àndríngender Flüsse,
Káhler Háffe, des Méers! Vólk der nächtigen Jágd. . . .

This single distich, coming almost precisely in the middle of the seventy-six-line poem, marks the turning point. The following strophes shift from idyllic peace to the slaughter of the Borussians by the knights of the Teutonic Order in the service of "the alien God's mother":

Volk
der schwelenden Haine,
der brennenden Hütten, zerstampfter
Saaten, geröteter Ströme—
Volk,
geopfert dem sengenden
Blitzschlag; dein Schreien verhängt vom
Flammengewölke—
Volk,
vor des fremden Gottes
Mutter im röchelnden Springtanz
stürzend—

The last strophe points out that nothing more remains of that crushed people than a few place names, isolated words, songs, and sagas. To these pathetic remnants the poet now adds his own lament, which is as poor, he says, as an ancient fisherman's catch at eveningtime:

> Namen reden von dir,
> zertretenes Volk, Berghänge,
> Flüsse, glanzlos noch oft,
> Steine und Wege—
> Lieder abends und Sagen,
> das Rascheln der Eidechsen nennt dich
> und, wie Wasser im Moor,
> heut ein Gesang, vor Klage
> arm—
> arm wie des Fischers Netzzug,
> jenes weißhaarigen, ewgen
> am Haff, wenn die Sonne
> herabkommt.

For all its differences, then, Bobrowski's elegy resembles the two other "heritage" elegies written shortly after the war to the extent that it is concerned with the heritage of the destroyed people of Borussians for contemporary inhabitants of Prussia—a questioning no less anguished, for its historical remoteness, than Bobrowski's concern for German responsibility to the Poles and Russians of the immediate past. But more than that: the poem also displays several constituents of the classical German elegy, a fact to which we are alerted by the dactylic rhythms of the whole and the elegiac distich that functions as its pivot. The traditional personal framework is evident in the poet's concern, at the beginning and end, with his own lament. (The word "Klage" occurs in line 4 and again six lines from the end.) Within this framework the meditative core deals with the tension between then and now, Borussia and Prussia, innocence and guilt. And the meditation is constructed tightly around the central axis of the one perfect distich of the poem.

Bobrowski, not only an heir of Klopstock but also an admirer of Hölderlin and Trakl, was a highly conscious craftsman, a *poeta doctus* who recognized the potentialities of the genre whose generic label he wittingly used in his poem. But like Hagelstange, who reached back to Rilke for his model, Bobrowski exemplifies the central conclusion of this chapter. Trakl, carrying the classical German elegy to its vanishing point, marks the end of the development of the genre. Subsequent poets who sought to use the genre had to reach back to earlier models from a stage at which the genre had not yet lost its recognizable form. It is for this reason that poets like Paul Celan (1920-1970) and Nelly Sachs (1891-1970), though sometimes cited as elegists, do not properly belong within our discussion. Thematically, to be sure, their obsession with the destruction of the Jews during the Holocaust provides the potential material for elegiac meditation. But formally their poems betray little awareness of, and less influence by, the classical German elegy. The lamentations of Nelly Sachs, who drew heavily upon the Bible for her rhythms and images, are closer to Job than to Rilke. And Celan, while he began with an appreciation of Hölderlin and German poetry, moved so rapidly beyond these traditions that even his earliest major poems—e.g., the justly celebrated "Todesfuge"—have already passed the point at which they could still be plausibly tied to the tradition we have been tracing.[87]

# 8 · Conclusion

In the preceding chapters we have examined major poems by some twenty poets that display a strikingly similar set of characteristics. From Schiller to Schröder, from Goethe to Rilke, from Hölderlin to Hagelstange, in every case we were dealing with extended poems in elegiac distichs (or in rhythms based unmistakably upon the elegiac distich) consisting of a meditative core embraced by a first-person framework. Although the meditative core naturally reflects the concerns of the poet and his age, it is distinguished *mutatis mutandis* by that tension between the real and the ideal that we have become accustomed ever since Schiller to call "elegiac." Within the framework, in turn, the poetic persona moves from an initial entanglement in the exigencies of the present, by way of a walk that involves the ascent of a mountain (or some similar elevation), to a moment of anagnorisis characterized by great radiance during which he experiences, or at least anticipates, the resolution of his dilemma.

Because the creators of this form explicitly designated their poems as "Elegien," I have chosen to refer to the type as "the classical German elegy" and its characteristics as the "generic norm." But is it in fact a genre we have been discussing? The notion of genre is a controversial one that extends from those formalists who believe that genre should be described solely in terms of external characteristics (e.g., metrical form or type of narrative) to the philosophers who insist that genre should designate fundamental human attitudes—the lyric, the epic, the dramatic, etc.—underlying literary forms of various sorts.[1] The normative attitude, which goes back to such classical authorities as Aristotle and Horace, dominated European poetics until the middle of the eighteenth century. The anthropological approach, an essentially romantic and post-romantic development, finds its justification in such sources as Schiller's discussion of "modes of sensation" in "Über naive und sentimentalische Dichtung" and in the triad of "Naturformen der Dichtung" that Goethe outlined in the Notes to his *Westöstlicher Divan*. My own understanding of genre, a compromise between those two extreme positions, is close to the definition proposed by Wellek and Warren in their *Theory of Literature*: "Genre should be conceived, we think, as a grouping of literary works based, theoretically, upon both outer form (specific meter or structure) and also upon inner form (attitude, tone, purpose—more crudely, subject and audience)."[2] Accordingly, the proposed generic norm of the classical German elegy contains specifications of meter (elegiac distich) and structure (encapsulation) as well as inner form (an "elegiac" attitude produced by tension and culminating in a resolution). In addition, we found that the setting of the poem—the mountain or other elevation—is so conventional as to be constitutive.[3] Clearly, not every mountain poem is an elegy; but we have seen few elegies that were not mountain poems. By the same token, not every poem in distichs is an elegy. During the nineteenth century, for instance, the distich was frequently used for epigrams and travel snapshots ("Bilder") as well as idyllic poems. Yet we encountered few classical German elegies that did not employ distichs or some variation based on that form. It is the configuration, and no single element, that characterizes the genre.

It needs to be stressed again that the genre we have defined as the classical German elegy is by no means the only category of poem, even during the same period, entitled to the label "elegy." Goethe's "Römische Elegien" provided the model for an entire minor genre of elegies with characteristics quite distinct from those of the classical German elegy: Heinrich Keller's "Elegien," Ludwig Robert's "Elegieen," Ernst Schulze's "Elegieen," Ludwig I's "Erinnerungen aus Italien," Wilhelm von Humboldt's Roman distichs, Heinrich Leuthold's "Elegie aus dem Süden," Stephan Milow's "Deutsche Elegieen," and Rudolf Alexander Schröder's "Römische Elegien." Moreover, no sensible critic would deny the label of elegy to such non-distich poems as Goethe's Marienbad "Elegie" or Grillparzer's cycle "Tristia ex Ponto." But Goethe's "Römische Elegien," as we saw, did not add to the possible forms of the elegy but merely brought up to date an existing one, resetting the classical Roman elegy of Propertius in the Rome of the 1780's. And such works as the Marienbad "Elegie" or "Tristia ex Ponto," though elegiac in mode, neither exploit the traditional forms of the elegy nor establish a new genre in themselves. The classical German elegy, in contrast, amounts to a wholly new form created during and in response to the needs of German classicism. It has a history of its own. And it was practiced by many of the finest German poets between 1795 and 1950—poets who were fully aware of the literary tradition in which they were working.

The classical German elegy is essentially the poetic form created in response to the concept of *Bildung* as defined by bourgeois humanism. To accommodate the new notion of *Bildung*—that process of self-reflection whereby the individual assesses the fruits of his learning and experience in an effort to determine his place in history and his role in society—a large form was needed that could encompass the central moment of meditation. Yet in distinction to the conventional philosophical poem of the eighteenth century the new form also required a personal framework to accommodate the poetic self undergoing the process of *Bildung*. And it demanded, finally, a poetic locus that offered both solitude and a grand overview. It was the coming together, in 1795, of all three factors—the new notion of *Bildung*, the elegiac poem, and the newly discovered suitability of the mountain as a philosophical locus—that produced "Der Spaziergang" as the first example of the genre. As the genre devoted to *Bildung*, the elegy can be seen as the poetic counterpart to the fictional form of the *Bildungsroman*, which was being created almost simultaneously by Goethe in *Wilhelm Meisters Lehrjahre* (1795-1796) and whose history—with its imitations and adaptations, its modern parodies and deformations—displays remarkable parallels.[4] As the genre dedicated essentially to self-reflection, the elegy constitutes the poetic counterpart to the idealism that dominated German philosophy from Kant through most of the nineteenth century.[5]

The suitability of the new form was appreciated almost immediately. Within five years Goethe had produced a brilliant example, while Knebel and Hölderlin initiated the history of the genre by emulating both "Der Spaziergang" and "Euphrosyne" in separate poems. Throughout the rest of its history, as we have seen, the classical German elegy thrived during periods when writers were obsessed with the notion of *Bildung*—including quite specifically the elegiac sense of its loss: during early romanticism (A. W. Schlegel), during the age of epigones (Immermann, Platen), among the poets of the Munich circle (Geibel, Schack, Leuthold), among the Austrian melancholists (Saar and Milow), during the Conservative Revolution (Borchardt and Schröder), in response to National Socialism (Weinheber, Jünger, Carossa), and during the period of cultural reassessment following World War II (Hagelstange, Bergengruen, and Bobrowski). Rilke, individualist that he was, does not fit neatly into any of these groups, but his cultural aspirations were not far from those of Borchardt's creative restoration. Among the great German elegists, Trakl alone displays little or no concern for *Bildung*; yet even in his case the profoundly elegiac disposition stemmed from the poet's keen awareness of cultural decline in modern civilization.

It is a characteristic of such *Bildung*-oriented poetry that it requires grand historical or philosophical themes for its meditations. In the finest examples of the genre the themes are developed to a point at which they can be creatively integrated into the poet's vision. Its less successful examples degenerate into tedious lectures on history (A. W. Schlegel), solipsistic reflections on literature (Platen), or personal reminiscences on family heirlooms (Bergengruen). If the classical German elegy emerged in response to the Weimar notion of *Bildung*, as defined by Goethe in his novel and by Schiller in his theoretical writings, it disappeared—appropriately enough—at a time when a new generation of writers, analyzing the downfall to which Germany had been brought by leaders educated according to the principles of Weimar classicism, scornfully rejected the entire notion of bourgeois humanism. The classical German elegy, then, constitutes a closed genre, beginning as it does quite suddenly in 1795 and ending almost as abruptly around 1950. It is of course not inconceivable that the genre may be resurrected someday. But that is hardly likely to be the case so long as the hostility toward the notion of classical *Bildung*, evident in the German educational system since the sixties, continues to prevail.

Between its inception and its termination, the elegy displays a clearly defined history—a history remarkable, moreover, for its almost unbroken continuity. Our study, which has sought to be representative if not exhaustive, includes examples from every decade between 1795 and 1950, with the exception of the period from 1840 to 1870. It is not necessary to accept the Darwinian notions underlying Ferdinand Brunetière's *L'Evolution des genres* (1890) to recognize that genres undergo certain processes of development and alteration.[6] Our study of the classical German elegy has encountered two basic forms of generic change: imitation and adaptation. Through imitation the genre is preserved and transmitted; through adaptation it grows and changes. In fact, the generic norm might almost be defined as those constitutive elements that can be singled out by other poets for imitation or adaptation. In the history of the classical German elegy the process begins within the first decade of the genre's existence. Knebel's two poems amount to little more than slavish imitations of, respectively, "Der Spaziergang" and "Euphrosyne," while Hölderlin's two elegies exemplify creative adaptations of those same two definitive models—adaptations so radical that they threaten to shatter the contours of the genre before it even becomes established. As a result of various accidents of literary history, however, Hölderlin's adaptations had little immediate effect. During the first century of its existence, the process of imitation was far more important for the transmission of the classical German elegy. In the absence of a compelling personal theme or grand vision, epigonal poets relied on the generic norm itself for inspiration and effect. The form became a shell constructed with great formal virtuosity and surface brilliance but containing no original impulse that might require it to be reshaped or altered. It is in such elegies that we found poets who climbed up mountains simply because the genre requires that effort—not because there is any inherent relationship between the landscape and their subject. In the absence of genuine *Bildung* these poets groped with pathetic eagerness for poetic forms associated with that revered notion, in the hope that the form might produce *Bildung*—not realizing that they were reversing cause and effect. Yet these poets perform an essential function in the history of any literary genre. Although they do not contribute to its growth, or its glory, they assure its continuity, keeping the genre alive until a poet appears who suddenly revitalizes and reshapes it for a new age. In the history of the classical German elegy this was the function of a host of respectable poets from A. W. Schlegel to Ferdinand von Saar and Rudolf Alexander Schröder.

Other poets are moved by such a powerful vision that they feel constrained by any generic norm, and yet—because no artist creates out of a vacuum—they must use, or at least build upon, existing forms. As a result, they adapt the genre by more or less violent deformations to fit their needs. They strain against the meter (Rilke's and Trakl's distichs), they adjust the balance of the parts (Hölderlin's reduction of the meditative core, Trakl's reduction of the personal framework), they tamper with the locus (Hagelstange's substitution of Droste's tower for the conventional mountain), and so forth. Yet they never deform the constitutive parts so radically that the visibility of the generic norm itself is effaced. These poets, as we repeatedly saw, were eager to exploit the expectations of a genre whose characteristics they recognized and appreciated. In this way—in the tension between preservation and creative adaptation—the genre changes and grows. Indeed, the history of any genre can be written from the standpoint of this struggle, waged on the battleground of individual poetic texts, between continuity and change in poets' response to the generic norm as exemplified in a few authoritative works.[7]

In addition to the general principle of generic transmission by imitation and adaptation, another more specifically historical factor emerged in the course of our study. During the entire nineteenth century the model for the classical German elegy was "Der Spaziergang": Schiller's elegy provided the paradigm underlying poems from Knebel's "Die Wälder," Hölderlin's "Brot und Wein," and Schlegel's "Rom" through Immermann's "Der Dom zu Köln" and Platen's "Im Theater zu Taormina" down to Geibel's "Ein Buch Elegien" and Saar's "Wiener Elegien." Although in almost every case we were able to establish a specific indebtedness to Schiller, his pervasive influence is generally evident in the theoretical writings of the period. In Vischer's *Aesthetik*, as we saw, the discussion of the elegy is based almost wholly on Schiller's theory and on the model of "Der Spaziergang." And Schiller enjoys the same authority in other standard reference works of the period: e.g., Philipp Mayer's *Theorie und Literatur der deutschen Dichtungsarten* (1824), in which the elegy is defined in strict accordance with Schiller's theory as a "sentimental" genre.[8]

At the beginning of the twentieth century, however, a striking change made itself felt. We became aware, first of all, of a new element in the elegies under discussion—an element so pervasive that it seemed to be genre-constitutive: the tutelary female spirit. Yet this figure—which shows up in Borchardt's "Pathetische Elegie," in Schröder's "Tivoli," in Rilke's *Duineser Elegien*, in Trakl's two elegies, in Carossa's "Abendländische Elegie," in Hagelstange's *Meersburger Elegie* —and, through parodistic imitation, in Brecht's "Hollywood-Elegien"—does not occur in "Der Spaziergang." It appeared originally in Goethe's "Euphrosyne." And in almost every case we were able to establish lines of continuity, either direct or indirect, from the modern poets back to Goethe— notably in the cases of Borchardt, Rilke, and Carossa. (Trakl received the tutelary female spirit from Hölderlin, who got it in turn from Goethe.) It is worth noting that this shift from one model to another, which modified the generic norm by adding a new element, parallels the reassessment of Goethe that took place around the beginning of the twentieth century.[9] During the decades following his death in 1832 Goethe was largely ignored, or actually often attacked, by the new wave of "democratic" writers impatient with the ideals of Weimar classicism. In the last third of the century that contempt gave way to a sterile adulation of the "Olympian" Goethe, the unproblematical Prince of Poets emulated by the poets of the Munich circle. But not until the turn of the century did Goethe, as the result of biographical discoveries and a thoughtful reassessment of his works, become interesting to writers and thinkers who had learned to appreciate the essentially modern consciousness underlying the seemingly tranquil surface of Goethean *Bildung*. This reassessment of Goethe, in turn, produced a certain disenchantment with Schiller, who had been reduced through mindless quotation to little more than a source for commonplaces.[10]

It was important for our purposes to establish lines of continuity and influence whenever possible, for our working definition of genre, as suggested in the Preface, involves the influence of specific works among writers historically associated, rather than the imitation of an abstract model or timeless pattern. Yet despite the general trend just mentioned— Schiller's dominance giving way around the turn of the century to that of Goethe—our study does not justify us in reducing the history of the classical German elegy to a simple unilinear pattern. In fact, the lines of development have various offshoots. We have already noted that Hölderlin's adaptations of the genre anticipated in their radicality certain twentieth-century deformations. Appropriately, the adaptations of Rilke and the deformations of Trakl were inspired in large measure by Hölderlin's elegies, which had been rediscovered and popularized shortly before the two modern poets wrote their elegies. In another variation, we observed that the elegies of Schack and Milow were influenced not directly by Schiller, but indirectly by way of Platen and Geibel. In the twentieth century we encountered what amounts to a subgenre of the classical German elegy in the various responses to Rilke's *Duineser Elegien*: Weinheber imitated them, Brecht parodied them, and Hagelstange adapted them creatively. But the essential fact is this: all these poems, whether imitations or adaptations, parodies or deformations, must be read within the context of the genre if they are to be fully understood and if all their implications are to be appreciated.

In sum, the poems we have examined are related in at least three ways: they share a clearly definable set of constitutive elements; they occur within a closed historical period in a sequence that displays development by means of imitation and adaptation of prior models; and the poets themselves are fully conscious of their indebtedness to these models. In the light of these circumstances it seems appropriate to assume that we have indeed been dealing with a genre and its history.

In the Afterword to his *Ewiger Vorrat deutscher Poesie* Rudolf Borchardt asserted, "To write the history of genres from the standpoint of the genres contributes nothing to human thought and wastes time."[11] Borchardt's statement is perfectly comprehensible in the light of his great admiration for that arch-enemy of all genres, Benedetto Croce, and his antipathy toward the academic establishment. When he wrote that sentence in 1926, academic genre histories had reached their high tide in Germany. But how valid is the criticism? Does it challenge the legitimacy of this study?

As a poet, Borchardt was attacking what he took to be a tendency inherent in all genre history: the subordination of individual poems to the abstract genre. That regrettable subordination may indeed prevail in some histories of genre. But the kind of genre history I have attempted to practice here resists abstraction by focusing on the influence of one or two specific generic examples. Indeed, genre history can provide significant benefits for our understanding of the poem itself. In the first place, recent studies in the aesthetics of poetic reception ("Rezeptionsästhetik") have increased our appreciation of the extent to which our understanding is dependent upon categories and, in literature, upon genre.[12] We would be incapable of grasping many of the important elements in our reading—from detective stories and Gothic romances to the most esoteric literary forms—were we not guided by certain conventions that help us to organize our responses. Our recognition of the generic norm, explicit or tacit, provides us in each case with expectations concerning works that display its characteristics. An experienced reader beginning a poem in distichs that is pronounced by a wanderer who ascends an elevation of some sort and then begins to meditate is conditioned to expect certain things: an encapsulated form, a thematic contrast of some sort, and a resolution of the tensions in a luminous moment of anagnorisis. We more quickly grasp the purpose and the organization of the poem if we recognize the generic norm, which becomes a useful tool of analysis and interpretation.

Moreover, our enjoyment of the poem is greatly enhanced by our awareness of the skill with which the poet fulfills the generic expectations or delights us by his creative and surprising adaptations. By the same token, if we recognize what is conventional in the poem, we do not run such a great risk of attributing originality to aspects that are quite traditional—a danger endemic in much Rilke criticism, which fails to take into account the generic elements of the *Duineser Elegien*. In contrast, the reader who acknowledges the generic norm is in a position to render a more informed judgment of the poem by measuring the achievement against the most appropriate standard. Many of the poets of the classical German elegy, *Bildung*-oriented as they were, were extraordinarily learned writers. These *poetae docti* knew a great deal about literature and worked with a high degree of consciousness. It is a methodological error to assume that they knew less than they actually did—or that they were limited by the ignorance of conventions produced in our own age by an often undisciplined search for "uniqueness" and "originality." Thus, for instance, the generic critic can measure precisely how far Platen falls short of the model that he was explicitly imitating. Conversely, he appreciates how extensively Rilke or Trakl needed to reshape, by adaption or deformation, the genre they wittingly appropriated from Goethe and Hölderlin in order to accommodate their private visions. If we locate a poem within its proper generic context, we automatically measure it against the highest standards—against the best poems composed in that genre. At the same time, a respect for generic continuity impels us to give due credit to poems that fulfill a worthy historical function by simply transmitting the genre even if they do not alter or enhance it. In short, although genre criticism does not exhaust the meaning of any good literary work, it is the assumption underlying this book that it provides the necesssary framework within which to understand and evaluate any poem.

Finally, the generic approach enables the historian of literature to put the emphasis where it properly belongs. For genre history, as long as it does in fact focus on individual texts and not on any abstract theory of genre, provides a logical way of writing the history of literary works—not of their authors, not of the times that produced them, not of literary theory. Genre study, making use of biography, history, theory, and other extrinsic sources in order to understand each work, actually comes to grips with the work in its principal capacity as poetry. By analogy, genre history enables us to see literary works in context with other works of the same literary kind—not with works that happen to be written by the same author or by authors of the same generation or with works related in any other extrinsic manner. The lines of continuity between Hölderlin's "Menons Klagen um Diotima" and Trakl's "Abendländisches Lied," between Goethe's "Euphrosyne" and Schröder's "Tivoli," are purely literary. In fact, the elements that relate "Der Spaziergang" and the *Duineser Elegien* might almost be defined as their essentially poetic elements in contrast to their more contingent aspects.

To the extent that this study has been concerned with poems of *Bildung*, a commodity that currently does not enjoy the highest esteem, it shares the elegiac mode with the genre it has been scrutinizing. And as the table of contents suggests, it endeavors through its encapsulated organization to emulate the elegy in the balance it achieves between the specific and the general. Whether this procedure has resulted in imitation or adaptation, in parody or deformation, others must decide. Yet the act of writing the history of this genre has fulfilled for its author much the same function that the classical German elegy traditionally performed for its poets—the integration of a segment of cultural history into the writer's own consciousness. I hope that it will enable other readers to share that elegiac experience of the poetic mountainclimbers.

# NOTES

*Chapter 1*

1. *Gedichte von Friederich Schiller* (Leipzig: Crusius, 1800–1803), I, 49–65. I cite the text with the modernized orthography and punctuation of Schiller's *Sämtliche Werke*, ed. Gerhard Fricke and Herbert G. Göpfert, 4th ed. (München: Hanser, 1965–67), I, 228–34. The edition is cited henceforth as *SW*.

2. See Eduard Castle, "Das Formgesetz der Elegie," *Zeitschrift für Ästhetik und allgemeine Kunstwissenschaft*, 37 (1943), 42–54. My disposition of the parts, based on the rhetoric of the poem, differs slightly from that of Castle, who distributes the distichs as follows: 13 + 16 + 21 : 20 + 16 + 14. Castle provides no explanation for his diagram of Schiller's elegy, but he seems in general to divide the poems solely according to content. I am indebted to Castle's essay for drawing my attention to the principle of encapsulation in elegies. Numerical composition was of course a common principle in classical and medieval literature. See Ernst Robert Curtius, *Europäische Literatur und Lateinisches Mittelalter*, 2nd ed. (Bern: Francke, 1954), pp. 491–98 ("Zahlenkomposition").

3. See Wilhelm Vosskamp, "Emblematisches Zitat und emblematische Struktur in Schillers Gedichten," in *Jahrbuch der deutschen Schillergesellschaft*, 18 (1974), 397–98.

4. *Briefwechsel zwischen Schiller und Wilhelm von Humboldt*, ed. Albert Leitzmann, 3rd ed. (Stuttgart: Cotta, 1900), pp. 220–21: "Ich will Ihnen nicht läugnen, daß ich mir auf dieses Stück auch am meisten zu gut thue. . . . Mein eigenes Dichtertalent hat sich, wie Sie gewiß gefunden haben werden, in diesem Gedichte erweitert: noch in keinem ist der *Gedanke* selbst so poetisch gewesen und geblieben, in keinem hat das Gemüth so sehr als *Eine* Kraft gewirkt."

5. I cite Schiller's essay according to the excellent translation by Elizabeth M. Wilkinson and L. A. Willoughby in their edition: Friedrich Schiller, *On the Aesthetic Education of Man* (Oxford: Clarendon, 1967). For the convenience of readers consulting German editions I refer to the passages by letter rather than by page.

6. Schiller's morphological view of history, his dating of the shift from "culture" to "civilization," and the images he uses to characterize declining civilizations constitute a remarkable anticipation of Oswald Spengler's view, notably as set forth in section 12 of the introduction to *Der Untergang des Abendlandes*.

7. In his emphasis on the sense of sight as the most important mode of perception Schiller exemplifies a tendency typical of rationalism and the Enlightenment. See August Langen, *Anschauungsformen in der deutschen Dichtung des 18. Jahrhunderts: Rahmenschau und Rationalismus* (Jena: Eugen Diederichs, 1934), esp. pp. 11-19; and Marjorie Hope Nicolson, *Newton Demands the Muse: Newton's Opticks and the Eighteenth Century Poets* (Princeton: Princeton Univ. Press, 1946), esp. chap. 4.

8. *SW*, V, 792-808, esp. pp. 795-99. See Jürgen Stenzel, " ' 'Zum Erhabenen tauglich': Spaziergang durch Schillers 'Elegie,' " in *Jahrbuch der deutschen Schillergesellschaft*, 19 (1975), 167-91.

9. The revised passages can be found in the notes to *SW*, I, 882-84. The full text of "Elegie," as it appeared in Schiller's *Die Horen* (1795, no. 10), has been reprinted in vol. I of the Nationalausgabe of Schiller's *Werke*, ed. Julius Petersen and Friedrich Beissner (Weimar: Böhlau, 1943), pp. 260-66. See H. B. Garland, "Schiller the Revisionist—the poet's second thoughts," in *Reality and Creative Vision in German Lyrical Poetry*, ed. August Closs (London: Butterworths, 1963), pp. 136-49. Garland counts 42 changes, including the title.

10. *Briefwechsel*, pp. 172-73 (23 October 1795).

11. *Briefwechsel*, pp. 221-22: "Ihr Einwurf gegen zu frühe Einführung der Landstraße in das Gemälde ist nicht ungegründet; hier hat die Wirklichkeit der Idee vorgegriffen, die Landstraße war einmal in der Szene, die meine Phantasie sich empirisch eingedrückt hatte. Es wird mir Mühe kosten, die Landstraße nachher einzuführen, und doch muß ich die sinnlichen Gegenstände, an denen der Gedanke fortläuft, so sehr als möglich zu Rath zu halten suchen. Sie werden bemerkt haben, daß ich biß da, wo die Betrachtungen über die Corruption angehen, beynahe immer von einem äusern Objekt ausgehe." In his revision, by the way, Schiller did not remove the road.

12. *SW*, V, 884-91.

13. *SW*, V, 889: "Ländliche Simplizität und versunkene städtische Herrlichkeit, die zwei äußersten Zustände der Gesellschaft, grenzen auf eine rührende Art aneinander, und das ernste Gefühl der Vergänglichkeit verliert sich wunderbar schön in dem Gefühl des siegenden Lebens. Diese glückliche Mischung gießt durch die ganze Landschaft einen tiefen elegischen Ton aus, der den empfindenden Betrachter zwischen Ruhe und Bewegung, Nachdenken und Genuß schwankend erhält und noch lange nachhallet, wenn schon alles verschwunden ist."

14. "Über Matthissons Gedichte," *SW*, V, 1001: "Seine Sache ist nicht sowohl, uns zu repräsentieren, was *ist*, als was *geschieht*; und versteht er seinen Vorteil, so wird er sich immer nur an denjenigen Teil seines Gegenstandes halten, der einer *genetischen* Darstellung fähig ist."

15. *SW*, V, 1009-10: "Will uns also der Dichter aus dem Gedränge der Welt in seine Einsamkeit nachziehen, so muß es nicht Bedürfnis der Abspannung, sondern der Anspannung, nicht Verlangen nach Ruhe, sondern nach Harmonie sein, was ihm die Kunst verleidet und die Natur liebenswürdig macht."

16. Schiller was familiar with the topographical tradition both in Germany and England. See John A. Walz, "Schiller's *Spaziergang* and Thomson's *Seasons*," *Modern Language Notes*, 21 (1906), 117-20.

17. The walk has been a topos in the essay, as an image of its train of thought, ever since Montaigne. See Gerhard Haas, *Essay* (Stuttgart: Metzler, 1969), pp. 47-48.

18. *SW*, V, 801.

19. *SW*, V, 694: "Jeder feinere Mensch, dem es nicht ganz und gar an Empfindung fehlt, erfährt dieses, wenn er im Freien wandelt, wenn er auf dem Lande lebt oder sich bei den Denkmälern der alten Zeiten verweilet, kurz, wenn er in künstlichen Verhältnissen und Situationen mit dem Anblick der einfältigen Natur überrascht wird."

20. *Briefwechsel*, p. 173: "Auch bei mir haben sich von jeher an eine Landstraße soviele Ideen gereiht, und Sie erinnern sich vielleicht, daß wir einmal auf einem Spatziergang weitläufig davon redeten."

21. *Schillers Briefe*, ed. Fritz Jonas (Stuttgart: Deutsche Verlagsanstalt, n.d.), II, 330: "Ich komme von einem Spaziergang zurück. In dem grossen freien Raume der Natur, wie in meinem einsamen Zimmer—es ist immer derselbe Ether in dem ich mich bewege, und die schönste Landschaft ist nur ein schönerer Spiegel der immer bleibenden Gestalt. Nie hab ich es noch so sehr empfunden, wie frey unsre Seele mit der ganzen Schöpfung schaltet—wie wenig sie doch für sich selbst zu geben im Stande ist, und alles alles von der Seele empfängt."

22. Ibid., pp. 330-31: "Und wie wohlthätig ist uns doch wieder diese Identität, dieses gleichförmige Beharren der Natur. Wenn uns Leidenschaft, innrer und äussrer Tumult lang genug hin und her geworfen, wenn wir uns selbst verloren haben, so finden wir s i e immer als die nehmliche wieder, und u n s in ihr. Auf unserer Flucht durch das Leben legen wir jede genossene Lust, jede Gestalt unsers

wandelbaren Wesens in ihre treue Hand nieder, und wohlbehalten gibt sie uns die anvertrauten Güter zurück, wenn wir kommen und sie wieder fodern. . . . Unsre ganze Persönlichkeit haben wir ihr zu danken, denn würde sie morgen umgeschaffen vor uns stehn, so würden wir umsonst unser gestriges Selbst wieder suchen."

23. For a survey of the concept *Erlebnis* and its often debilitating effect on German critical theory see René Wellek, "Genre Theory, the Lyric, and *Erlebnis*," in his *Discriminations: Further Concepts of Criticism* (New Haven: Yale Univ. Press, 1970), pp. 225-52.

24. See Friedrich Meinecke's study of Schiller's theory of history, "Schillers 'Spaziergang,' " in his *Werke* (Stuttgart: Köhler, 1959), IV, 323-40; rpt. in *Interpretationen: Deutsche Lyrik von Weckherlin bis Benn*, ed. Jost Schillemeit (Frankfurt-am-Main: Fischer Bücherei, 1965), I, 99-112. Meinecke makes the important point that the view embodied in "Der Spaziergang" represents only one aspect of Schiller's constantly evolving theory of history.

25. See Hans Mayer, "Schillers Gedichte und die Traditionen deutscher Lyrik," in *Jahrbuch der deutschen Schillergesellschaft*, 4 (1960), 72-89; Gerhard Storz, "Gesichtspunkte für die Betrachtung von Schillers Lyrik," in *Jahrbuch der deutschen Schillergesellschaft*, 12 (1968), 259-74; and Johannes M. Anderegg, *Friedrich Schiller: Der Spaziergang. Eine Interpretation* (St. Gallen: Zollikofer, 1964), p. 8. Anderegg's useful dissertation is concerned mainly with the thematic development of the poem—which, in contrast to my analysis, is presented as tripartite—rather than with its poetic form and organization.

26. M. H. Abrams, *Natural Supernaturalism: Tradition and Revolution in Romantic Literature* (1971; rpt. New York: Norton Library, 1973), p. 453.

*Chapter 2*

1. Familiarum Rerum, IV, 1; in Francesco Petrarca, *Le Familiari*, ed. Vittorio Rossi (Florence: Sansoni, 1933), I, 153-61.

2. See J. A. MacCulloch, "Mountains, Mountain-gods," in *Encyclopedia of Religion and Ethics*, ed. James Hastings, VIII (New York: Scribner, 1916), 863-68; and "Berg," in *Handwörterbuch des deutschen Aberglaubens*, ed. Hanns Bächtold-Stäubli, I (Berlin: De Gruyter, 1927), 1043-56.

3. Gertrud Stockmayer, *Über Naturgefühl in Deutschland im 10. und 11. Jahrhundert* (Leipzig: Teubner, 1910), esp. pp. 38-47.

4. Marjorie Hope Nicolson, *Mountain Gloom and Mountain Glory: The Development of the Aesthetics of the Infinite* (1959; rpt. New York: Norton Library, 1963), chap. 2 ("The Theological Dilemma"). At this point I would like to express my admiration for Nicolson's brilliant study. Although it does not take up German or continental examples, its discussion of English works provides a model for the understanding of mountains in eighteenth-century literature and thought.

5. *Luther's Works*, vol. I (Lectures on Genesis 1-5), ed. Jaroslav Pelikan (St. Louis: Concordia, 1958), esp. verses 3: 17-19 and 4:16.

6. The following passages are cited by Nicolson, *Mountain Gloom*, p. 76, p. 61, and p. 116.

7. Klaus Garber, *Der Locus Amoenus und der Locus Terribilis: Bild und Funktion der Natur in der deutschen Schäfer- und Landlebendichtung des 17. Jahrhunderts* (Köln: Böhlau, 1974).

8. Andrew Dickson White, *A History of the Warfare of Science with Theology in Christendom* (New York: Appleton, 1922), I, 89-98.

9. I quote from the second edition (London, 1691), which has been reprinted with an Introduction by Basil Willey (London: Centaur, 1965); here p. 42 (chap. IV). Concerning Burnet see Katharine Brownwell Collier, *Cosmogonies of Our Fathers: Some Theories of the Seventeenth and the Eighteenth Century* (New York: Columbia Univ. Press, 1934), pp. 68-80; and Nicolson, *Mountain Gloom*, pp. 186-224.

10. Burnet, *Sacred Theory*, p. 53 (chap. V).

11. Burnet, *Sacred Theory*, p. 63 (chap. V).

12. Burnet, *Sacred Theory*, p. 64 (chap. VI).

13. Burnet, *Sacred Theory*, pp. 65-66 (chap. VI).

14. See Collier, *Cosmogonies*, pp. 81-91; and Nicolson, *Mountain Gloom*, pp. 225-70.

15. Nicolson, *Mountain Gloom*, p. 194.

16. Collier, *Cosmogonies*, pp. 100-104.

17. *Großes Vollständiges Universal Lexikon Aller Wissenschafften und Künste*, III (Halle and Leipzig: Johann Heinrich Zedler, 1733), 1229-30: ". . . daß man also von dem Ursprunge derer Berge so viel sagen kan, daß derselbige theils von dem Anfange der Welt, theils von der Noachischen Sündfluth, theils aber von andern verschiedenen Ueberschwemmungen herzuleiten sey."

18. Collier, *Cosmogonies*, pp. 190-92.

19. 2nd ed. (Leipzig, 1735), I, 320-34 (esp. paragraphs 607 and 618); here p. 328: "eine entsetzliche Veränderung."

20. *Erste Gründe*, I, 334: "Zum wenigsten ist die Absicht des Ver-

fassers nicht zu tadeln, die er in dem ganzen Buche gehabt, nemlich den Religionsspöttern zu zeigen, daß die Lehre der Schrift vom Ursprunge der Welt, der Sündfluth und der letzten Verbrennung der Erdkugel, der Vernunft, Weltweisheit und neuern Astronomie, ganz gemäß sey."

21. Nicolson, *Mountain Gloom*, pp. 220-21.

22. Nicolson, *Mountain Gloom*, p. 323.

23. *Universal Lexikon*, III, 1229: ". . . daß die Berge was herrliches und prächtiges an sich haben, und in uns hohe Gedancken und Gemüts Bewegungen erwecken, daß wir dabey natürlicher Weise an GOtt, an dessen Grösse und Hoheit gedencken müssen."

24. Richard Weiss, *Das Alpenerlebnis in der deutschen Literatur des 18. Jahrhunderts* (Zürich: Münster-Presse, 1933), pp. 51-52.

25. George Sarton, "The Quest for Truth: Scientific Progress during the Renaissance," in *The Renaissance: Six Essays* (New York: Harper and Row, 1962), pp. 55-76.

26. Willi Flemming, *Der Wandel des deutschen Naturgefühls vom 15. zum 18. Jahrhundert* (Halle: Niemeyer, 1931), pp. 52-57 and pp. 64-65.

27. Barthold Heinrich Brockes, *Auszug der vornehmsten Gedichte aus dem Irdischen Vergnügen in Gott* (Hamburg: Christian Herold, 1738); facsimile edition, ed. Dietrich Bode (Stuttgart: Metzler, 1965), pp. 124-31.

28. Albrecht von Haller, *Versuch Schweizerischer Gedichte*, 9th ed. (Göttingen, 1762; rpt. Bern: Herbert Lang, 1969), pp. 24-56.

29. See Karl S. Guthke, "Albrecht von Haller," in *Deutsche Dichter des 18. Jahrhunderts*, ed. Benno von Wiese (Berlin: Erich Schmidt, 1977), p. 89.

30. "An den Herrn Reichsgrafen von Gotter . . . als eine Zuschrift vor Benjamin Neukirchs Gedichten," in J. C. Gottsched, *Gedichte*, ed. Johann Joachim Schwaben (Leipzig: Breitkopf, 1751), II, 526.

31. Alfred Anger, *Literarisches Rokoko*, 2nd ed. (Stuttgart: Metzler, 1968), pp. 54-55.

32. Weiss, *Das Alpenerlebnis*, p. 85.

33. *Klopstocks gesammelte Werke in vier Bänden*, ed. Franz Muncker (Stuttgart: Cotta, n.d.), III, 46-48.

34. *Klopstocks gesammelte Werke*, III, 116-20.

35. Flemming, *Der Wandel des deutschen Naturgefühls*, pp. 97-99.

36. *Les Confessions* (Paris: Livre de Poche, 1963), I, 271: "Au reste, on sait déjà ce que j'entends par un beau pays. Jamais pays de plaine,

quelque beau qu'il fût, ne parut tel à mes yeux. Il me faut des torrents, des rochers, des sapins, des bois noirs, des montagnes, des
chemins raboteux à monter et à descendre, des précipices à mes côtés
qui me fassent bien peur."

37. *Les Confessions*, I, 272: "... cela faisait que je pouvais contem-
pler au fond et gagner des vertiges tout à mon aise, car ce qu'il y a de
plaisant dans mon goût pour les lieux escarpés, est qu'ils me font
tourner la tête, et j'aime beaucoup ce tournoiement, pourvu que je
sois en sûreté."

38. *Julie ou La nouvelle Héloïse* (Paris: Garnier 1960), p. 52 (part I,
letter xxiii): "En effet, c'est une impression générale qu'éprouvent
tous les hommes, quoiqu'ils ne l'observent pas tous, que sur les
hautes montagnes, où l'air est pur et subtil, on se sent plus de facilité
dans la respiration, plus de légèreté dans le corps, plus de sérénité
dans l'esprit; les plaisirs y sont moins ardents, les passions plus modé
rées. Les méditations y prennent je ne sais quel caractère grand et
sublime, proportionné aux objets qui nous frappent, je ne sais quelle
volupté tranquille qui n'a rien d'âcre et de sensuel. Il semble qu'en
s'élevant au-dessus du séjour des hommes, on y laisse tous les sentiments bas et terrestres, et qu'à mesure qu'on approche des régions
éthérées, l'âme contracte quelque chose de leur inaltérable pureté."

39. *Julie*, p. 53: "... enfin le spectacle a je ne sais quoi de magique,
de surnaturel, qui ravit l'esprit et les sens; on oublie tout, on s'oublie
soi-même, on ne sait plus où l'on est."

40. I have taken the references in this paragraph from Weiss, *Das
Alpenerlebnis*, pp. 47-80.

41. Cited by Weiss, *Das Alpenerlebnis*, p. 76.

42. Letter of 2 March 1780 to Dalberg; in Gedenkausgabe, ed.
Ernst Beutler (Zürich: Artemis, 1951), XVIII, 486-87: "eine kleine
Operette, worin die Akteurs Schweizerkleider anhaben und von Käs
und Milch sprechen werden."

43. Karl von Zittel, *History of Geology and Paleontology*, trans.
Maria M. Ogilvie-Gordon (London, 1901), p. 46; cited by Charles C.
Gillispie, *Genesis and Geology* (1951; rpt. New York: Harper
Torchbooks, 1959), p. 41.

44. Collier, *Cosmogonies*, pp. 401-402.

45. *J. Gaudenz von Salis-Seewis*, ed. Eduard Korrodi (Zürich: Fretz
& Wasmuth, 1937), pp. 91-95.

46. Friedrich Matthisson, *Gedichte* (Zürich: Orell, Füßli, 1808), pp.
81-85. In an epigram entitled "Die Alpenhirten" Matthisson qualifies

ironically this idealizing view of the Alpine shepherds. On the mountain meadows, he observes, the peasants are driven by the same ambitions and anxieties as everyone else:

Wißt! Auf den Triften der Alpen treibt herdengesegnet ein
Völkchen,
Wünschend und fürchtend wie wir, nimmer befriedigt, sein Werk.
(p. 211)

47. *Gedichte*, p. 90.

48. Goethe, *Werke*, ed. Erich Trunz (Hamburger Ausgabe), X, 152 (part IV, chap. 19): "jene unbedingte Richtung nach einer verwirklichten Naturfreiheit"; "ihre frische Jünglingsnatur zu idyllisieren."

49. *Werke*, X, 138 (part IV, chap. 18): "die Sehnsucht nach jenen blauen Gebirgshöhen."

50. *Werke*, X, 146 (part IV, chap. 18).

51. *Werke*, XIII, 255: "Auf einem hohen nackten Gipfel sitzend und eine weite Gegend überschauend, kann ich mir sagen: Hier ruhst du unmittelbar auf einem Grunde, der bis zu den tiefsten Orten der Erde hinreicht."

52. *Werke*, XIII, 255: ". . . werde ich zu höheren Betrachtungen der Natur hinaufgestimmt, und wie der Menschengeist alles belebt, so wird auch ein Gleichnis in mir rege, dessen Erhabenheit ich nicht widerstehen kann."

53. *Werke*, XIII, 256: "Ich fühle die ersten, festesten Anfänge unsers Daseins, ich überschaue die Welt, ihre schrofferen und gelinderen Täler und ihre fernen fruchtbaren Weiden, meine Seele wird über sich selbst und über alles erhaben und sehnt sich nach dem nähern Himmel."

54. *Werke*, XIII, 257: "Hier ist nichts in seiner ersten, alten Lage, hier ist alles Trümmer, Unordnung und Zerstörung."

55. *SW*, V, 489: "*Erhaben* nennen wir ein Objekt, bei dessen Vorstellung unsre sinnliche Natur ihre Schranken, unsre vernünftige Natur aber ihre Überlegenheit, ihre Freiheit von Schranken fühlt; gegen das wir also *physisch* den kürzern ziehen, über welches wir uns aber *moralisch*, d.i. durch Ideen erheben."

56. *SW*, V, 491: "Ein ungeheuer hoher Turm oder Berg kann ein Erhabenes der Erkenntnis abgeben."

57. *SW*, V, 568: "Höhen erscheinen durchaus erhabener als gleich große Längen."

58. *SW*, V, 1005.

59. *SW*, V, 801: ". . . und das relativ Große außer ihm ist der

Spiegel, worin er das absolut Große in ihm selbst erblickt. . . . Der Anblick unbegrenzter Fernen und unabsehbarer Höhen, der weite Ozean zu seinen Füßen und der größere Ozean über ihm entreißen seinen Geist der engen Sphäre des Wirklichen und der drückenden Gefangenschaft des physischen Lebens."

60. Christian Garve, *Vermischte Aufsätze*, II (Breslau, 1800), 143-88.

61. *Vermischte Aufsätze*, II, 150: "So ist es also der auf Bergen gleichsam zur Schau ausgestellte Reichtum der Natur. . . ."

62. *Vermischte Aufsätze*, II, 157-58: "Alle Gegenstände erscheinen in denselben verkleinert, und doch deutlich. Dadurch bekommen sie das Ansehn von Feinheit und Kunst und werden Gemählden ähnlicher. . . . Dieß macht das Ganze, welches zugleich auf einmal übersehn wird, einer gemahlten Landschaft, oder einer Abbildung in der *Camera obscura* ähnlich."

63. *Vermischte Aufsätze*, II, 160.

64. *Vermischte Aufsätze*, III, 161: ". . . mehr ein Vergnügen, das aus *Ideen*, als eines, das durch den sinnlichen Anblick der Gegenstände entsteht."

65. *Vermischte Aufsätze*, II, 169: "Überhaupt sind die hohen Gebirge die Region für die Empfindungen des Erhabenen; die Mittel- und Vorgebirge sind die Region für die Empfindungen des Schönen."

66. *Vermischte Aufsätze*, II, 170: "Nirgends sehe ich deutlicher, als im Gebirge, daß nicht immer alles auf der Erde so gewesen ist, als es gegenwärtig ist; daß die größten und dauerhaftesten Gegenstände doch entstanden, und nach gewissen Gesetzen erzeugt und gebildet worden sind."

67. *Vermischte Aufsätze*, II, 171: ". . . weit mehr durch die Betrachtungen, zu welchen sie Anlaß geben, als durch die Empfindungen, die sie unmittelbar erregen."

68. For instance, in 1803 Coleridge read and paraphrased Garve's essay; see *The Notebooks*, ed. Kathleen Coburn, I (New York: Pantheon, 1957), 1675-76.

*Chapter 3*

1. See C. M. Bowra, *Early Greek Elegists* (1935; rpt. New York: Barnes & Noble, 1960); Georg Luck, *The Latin Love Elegy* (London: Methuen, 1959); Friedrich Beissner, *Geschichte der deutschen Elegie*, 3rd ed. (Berlin: De Gruyter, 1965), pp. 1-12.

2. Beissner, *Geschichte der deutschen Elegie*, pp. 13-45; and Walther Ludwig, "Petrus Lotichius Secundus and the Roman Elegists: Prolegomena to a Study of Neo-Latin Elegy," in *Classical Influences on European Culture. A.D. 1500-1700*, ed. R. R. Bolgar (Cambridge: Cambridge Univ. Press, 1976), pp. 171-90.

3. John E. Clark, *Elégie: The Fortunes of a Classical Genre in Sixteenth-Century France* (The Hague: Mouton, 1975).

4. John W. Draper, *The Funeral Elegy and the Rise of English Romanticism* (1929; rpt. New York: Octagon Books, 1967).

5. Cited in Draper, *The Funeral Elegy*, p. 195.

6. See Beissner, *Geschichte der deutschen Elegie*, p. 81.

7. Martin Opitz, *Buch von der deutschen Poeterei*, ed. Wilhelm Braune, 6th ed. (Tübingen: Niemeyer, 1954), p. 21 (Chap. 5): "In den Elegien hatt man erstlich nur trawrige sachen, nachmals auch buhlergeschäffte, klagen der verliebten, wündschung des todes, brieffe, verlangen nach den abwesenden, erzehlung seines eigenen lebens vnnd dergleichen geschrieben."

8. Opitz, *Ausgewählte Dichtungen*, ed. Julius Tittmann (Leipzig: Brockhaus, 1869), p. 69.

9. Cited in Beissner, *Geschichte der deutschen Elegie*, p. 63.

10. See Draper, *The Funeral Elegy*, pp. 320-21; and Henri Potez, *L'Elégie en France avant le romantisme* (Paris: Calmann Lévy, 1897), pp. 1-85.

11. *Versuch einer Critischen Dichtkunst*, 4th ed. (1751; rpt. Darmstadt: Wissenschaftliche Buchgesellschaft, 1962), pp. 657-68 (II. Teil, 1. Abschnitt, xii. Hauptstück): "Sie soll nämlich in einer natürlichen und fließenden Schreibart abgefasset werden, einen traurigen Inhalt haben, und fast aus lauter Klagen bestehen."

12. Ludwig Christoph Heinrich Hölty, *Werke und Briefe*, ed. Uwe Berger (Berlin: Aufbau, 1966), p. 36.

13. "Elegie auf einen Dorfkirchhof," in *Werke und Briefe*, p. 37. Beneath the title of the first publication (1772) Hölty wrote that his poem was "Not an imitation of Gray, but only an execution of the same idea" (p. 302).

14. Friedrich Matthisson, *Gedichte* (Mannheim, 1787), p. 5. "Elegie auf einem Gottesacker geschrieben" is found on pp. 19-20 of this edition. Matthisson omitted this poem from later editions of his work; hence Beissner, p. 114, mistakenly believes that he used the title "Elegie" only for the "Elegie in den Ruinen. . . ." In fact, he used it four times in this volume. The "Elegie an Sophie von Seckendorf. . . ." quoted below, occurs on pp. 25-29.

15. See Beissner, *Geschichte der deutschen Elegie*, pp. 115-29. For discussions of the characteristics of the elegiac distich in German see Ludwig Strauss, "Zur Struktur des deutschen Distichons," *Trivium*, 6 (1948), 52-83; and Klaus Weissenberger, *Formen der Elegie von Goethe bis Celan* (Bern: Francke, 1969), pp. 15-20.

16. *Klopstocks Gesammelte Werke*, III, 17.

17. Ludwig Gotthard Kosegarten, *Dichtungen*, 5th ed. (Greifswald: UniversitätsBuchhandlung, 1824), vol. 8.

18. "Der Tempel der Freundschaft," in *Gedichte von Friederike Brun*, ed. Friedrich Matthisson (Zürich: Orell, Gessner, Füßli, 1795), pp. 81-83. The volume also contains two brief funeral apostrophes in distichs.

19. In a letter of 25 October 1788 Goethe thanked Knebel for "das Kleeblatt der Dichter." All the relevant passages from letters and reviews concerning the "Römische Elegien" are conveniently reprinted in *Goethes Römische Elegien nach der ältesten Reinschrift*, ed. Albert Leitzmann (Bonn: Marcus & Weber, 1912); here p. 24.

20. Scholars, especially in the nineteenth century, have amused themselves by trying to find an actual Italian model for the girl of the elegies, and various names have been cited with varying degrees of plausibility. See a summary of the evidence in Dominik Jost, *Deutsche Klassik: Goethes "Römische Elegien"* (Pullach bei München: Verlag Dokumentationen, 1974), pp. 19-28. It seems clear from his correspondence that Goethe had various sexual adventures—in his letters to Karl August he refers to them as "Spaziergänge"—during his stay in Italy. Yet it is equally clear that the Roman elegies principally celebrate Christiane Vulpius.

21. Many editions, notably the nineteenth-century ones, print only the twenty poems of the standard text. All twenty-four poems are now most conveniently available in Jost, *Deutsche Klassik*; I cite Goethe's text according to that edition.

22. Letter of 26 October 1794; Leitzmann, p. 28: "die noch über ihre Admissibilität zu urtheilen haben."

23. Letter of 12 May 1795; Leitzmann, p. 28: "anstößige Stellen."

24. Letter of 20 Sept. 1794 from Schiller to his wife Lotte; Leitzmann, p. 50. It is essential in this connection to remember that Schiller was ambivalent toward the notion of "decency"; he saw it as an attitude of a corrupted civilization in contrast to the natural modesty ("Schamhaftigkeit") of nature and culture. See "Über naive und sentimentalische Dichtung," in *SW*, V, 705 and 743.

25. Letter of 5 July 1795; Leitzmann, p. 50: "zwar eine conven-

tionelle, aber nicht die wahre und natürliche Dezenz dadurch verletzt."

26. Letter of 25 March 1797 to Böttger; Leitzmann, p. 55: "Properz durfte es laut sagen, daß er eine glückliche Nacht bey seiner Freundin zugebracht habe. Wenn aber Herr von Goethe mit seiner Italienischen Mätresse vor dem ganzen Deutschland in den Horen den *con-cubitum* exercirt, wer wird das billigen?"

27. Letter of 27 July 1795 from Böttger to Schulz; Leitzmann, p. 52: "die bordellmäßige Nacktheit."

28. Letter of 19 July 1795 from Baggesen to Reinhold; Leitzmann, p. 51: "empören ... die Sittlichkeit, und in Theilen die Sittsamkeit."

29. See the letter of 5 October 1795 to Jacobi; Leitzmann, p. 54.

30. Cited in Böttger's letter of 27 July 1795; Leitzmann, p. 52.

31. For a typical nineteenth-century study see Ferdinand Bronner, "Goethes Römische Elegien und ihre Quellen," *Neue Jahrbücher für Philologie und Paedagogik*, 148 (1893), 38-50, and *passim*. For a sane and realistic appraisal see Georg Luck, "Goethes 'Römische Elegien' und die augusteische Liebeselegie," *Arcadia*, 2 (1967), 173-95.

32. The presence of these three main themes is a commonplace in Goethe criticism; see Trunz's notes in the Hamburger Ausgabe of Goethe's *Werke*, I, 487-92.

33. See Walther Rehm, *Europäische Romdichtung*, 2nd rev. ed. (München: Max Hueber, 1960).

34. Leitzmann, p. 36: "Es läßt sich voraussehen, daß gegen diese Gedichte mit großer Wichtigkeit der Einwurf gemacht werden wird, sie seyen keine Elegien."

35. See Jost, *Deutsche Klassik*, p. 74; and Luck, "Goethes 'Römische Elegien,' " pp. 192-93.

36. Leitzmann, p. 33: "daß seine Sprache ... die treuesten poetischen Nachbildungen der Alten, daß die allein Originalwerke im ächten antiken Styl aufzuweisen hat."

37. Leitzmann, p. 34: ". . . würden sie zwar über den Fremdling aus den germanischen Wäldern erstaunen, der sich nach achtzehn Jahrhunderten zu ihnen gesellt, aber ihm gern einen Kranz von der Myrte zugestehn, die für ihn noch eben so frisch grünt, wie ehedem für sie."

38. Entry for 25 February 1824, in Johann Peter Eckermann, *Gespräche mit Goethe*, ed. H. H. Houben, 21st ed. (Leipzig: Brockhaus, 1925), p. 71.

39. See Jost Hermand, "Schillers Abhandlung 'Über naive und sentimentalische Dichtung' im Lichte der deutschen Popularphilosophie des 18. Jahrhunderts," *PMLA*, 79 (1964), 428-41.

40. *Großes Vollständiges Universal Lexikon Aller Wissenschafften und Künste*, VII (Halle and Leipzig: Johann Heinrich Zedler, 1734), 764-65.

41. Johann Christoph Adelung, *Grammatisch-kritisches Wörterbuch der Hochdeutschen Mundart*, 2nd ed. (Leipzig: Breitkopf, 1793), I, 1787-88: "In weiterer Bedeutung war die Elegie schon bey den Alten ein Gedicht, welches den sanften Empfindungen der Traurigkeit oder Freude, besonders den verliebten Empfindungen einer so wohl glücklichen als unglücklichen Zärtlichkeit gewidmet war."

42. See Klaus R. Scherpe, *Gattungspoetik im 18. Jahrhundert: Historische Entwicklung von Gottsched bis Herder* (Stuttgart: Metzler, 1968).

43. See René Wellek, *A History of Modern Criticism*, I (New Haven: Yale Univ. Press, 1955), 144-46.

44. Moses Mendelssohn, *Ästhetische Schriften in Auswahl*, ed. Otto F. Best (Darmstadt: Wissenschaftliche Buchgesellschaft, 1974), p. 89: "eine Vermischung von angenehmen und unangenehmen Empfindungen."

45. Edmund Burke, *A Philosophical Enquiry into the Origin of our Ideas of the Sublime and Beautiful*, ed. J. T. Boulton (New York: Columbia Univ. Press, 1958), p. 51 (pt. I, section xviii).

46. Mendelssohn, *Ästhetische Schriften*, pp. 137-38: "Dieses ist die Natur unserer Seele! Wenn sie zwo Empfindungen, die sie zugleich hat, nicht unterscheiden kann; so setzt sie sich aus ihnen eine Erscheinung zusammen, die von beiden unterschieden ist, und fast keine Aehnlichkeit mit ihnen hat."

47. Mendelssohn, *Ästhetische Schriften*, p. 139: "Die vermischten Empfindungen haben die besondere Eigenschaft, daß sie zwar so sanft nicht sind, als das reine Vergnügen, hingegen dringen sie tiefer in das Gemüth ein, und scheinen sich auch länger darinn zu erhalten."

48. This point is frequently cited in the secondary studies. See Beissner, *Geschichte der deutschen Elegie*, p. 5; Helmut Prang, *Formgeschichte der Dichtkunst* (Stuttgart: Kohlhammer, 1968), pp. 208-17. It is not impossible that this ambivalence has been detected retrospectively in the classical elegy by critics influenced by eighteenth-century poetics.

49. Thomas Abbt, *Briefe die neueste Litteratur betreffend* (Berlin: Nicolai, 1762), pp. 69-83 (XIII. Theil, 212. Brief, 4./11. Februar 1762); here p. 69: "Man kan nicht immer ohne Unverschämtheit fordern, daß das Publikum sich soll Klagen vorwinseln lassen.—Und wenn es vollends Klagen eines Verliebten sind!"

50. Abbt, pp. 70-71: "Man könte sie überhaupt erklären, als die sinnlichvollkommene Beschreibung unserer vermischten Empfindungen."

51. Abbt, p. 72: "Dem Elegischen Dichter bleiben also nur Empfindungen übrig, die durch die Gegenseitigen schon gemildert sind: Empfindungen, die in der Seele nach und nach entstehen, nicht im Sturm der heftigen Leidenschaft."

52. Abbt, p. 79: ". . . die Seele muß sich in der Gelassenheit befinden, wo ihr weder die bittre Thränen des Leides ausgepresset, noch der tiefe Seufzer der Angst entrissen, noch das röchelnde Schluchzen der Wehmuth abgezwungen wird."

53. Johann Gottfried Herder, *Sämmtliche Werke*, ed. Bernhard Suphan (Berlin: Weidmann, 1877ff.), I, 491, note.

54. *Sämmtliche Werke*, I, 480-82, note.

55. *Sämmtliche Werke*, I, 486, note.

56. *Sämmtliche Werke*, II, 306: "Aus der Mischung also von Unlust, die mit einigem Vergnügen gemildert war, aus ihr ward die erste *Elegie* geweinet."

57. *Sämmtliche Werke*, II, 307: "Nicht Lust und Unlust sind hier vermischt; sondern *sanftere Unlust* durch die *Entfernung gemildert*, so gemildert, daß ich sie *milde Betrübniß* nennen möchte."

58. *Sämmtliche Werke*, III, 23 ("Erstes Wäldchen," 3): ". . . aber niemand verstehe hier unter diesem Namen jenen hinkenden Affen, der sich nach unsern weisen Lehrbüchern der Poesie bloß im Sylbenmaas unterscheiden soll: sondern Elegie sei mir hier die klagende Dichtkunst, die *versus querimoniae* nach Horaz, sie mögen sich finden, wo sie wollen, in Epopee und Ode, in Trauerspiel, oder Idylle; denn jede dieser Gattungen kann *Elegisch* werden."

59. Ibid.; "die Empfindbarkeit des Schmerzes und der Betrübniß."

60. Johann Georg Sulzer, *Allgemeine Theorie der Schönen Künste*, 2nd ed. (Leipzig: Weidmann, 1792), II, 39: "Der wahre Charakter derselben scheint darinn zu bestehen, daß der Dichter von einem sanften Affekt der Traurigkeit oder einer sanften mit viel Zärtlichkeit vermischten Freude ganz eingenommen ist, und sie auf eine einnehmende etwas schwatzhafte Art äußert."

61. J. G. Jacobi, "Ueber die Elegie," *Iris*, I (1775), 96-97: "Jene Wehmuth, und dieses von Thränen unterbrochene Lächeln sind der Innhalt und der Ausdruck der Elegie; einer Lieblings-Gattung von Gedichten für unsre Damen."

62. Jacobi, p. 98: "Und so entsteht bey der armen Verwaiseten eine Mischung angenehmer und unangenehmer Gefühle; der Stof zu einer kindlichen Elegie."

63. Johann Joachim Eschenburg, *Entwurf einer Theorie und Literatur der schönen Wissenschaften*, 2nd rev. ed. (Berlin: Nicolai, 1789), p. 139: "Die Elegie ist ein poetischer, meistens beschreibender, Vortrag gemischter Empfindungen, in welchen sich angenehmes Gefühl mit dem unangenehmen vereinigt, und die daher, schon ihrer Natur nach, sanft und gemäßigt sind."

64. Schiller, *Sämtliche Werke*, V, 720: "Dieser *reflektiert* über den Eindruck, den die Gegenstände auf ihn machen."

65. *SW*, V, 721: ". . . und das gemischte Gefühl, das er erregt, wird immer von dieser doppelten Quelle zeugen."

66. *SW*, V, 728: "Setzt der Dichter die Natur der Kunst und das Ideal der Wirklichkeit so entgegen, daß die Darstellung des ersten überwiegt und das Wohlgefallen an demselben herrschende Empfindung wird, so nenne ich ihn *elegisch*. . . . Entweder ist die Natur und das Ideal ein Gegenstand der Trauer, wenn jene als verloren, dieses als unerreicht dargestellt wird. Oder beide sind ein Gegenstand der Freude, indem sie als wirklich vorgestellt werden."

67. *SW*, V, 728, note: "Daß ich die Benennungen Satire, Elegie und Idylle in einem weitern Sinne gebrauche, als gewöhnlich geschieht, werde ich bei Lesern, die tiefer in die Sache dringen, kaum zu verantworten brauchen. Meine Absicht dabei ist keineswegs, die Grenzen zu verrücken, welche die bisherige Observanz sowohl der Satire und Elegie als der Idylle mit gutem Grunde gesteckt hat; ich sehe bloß auf die in diesen Dichtungsarten herrschende *Empfindungsweise*, und es ist ja bekannt genug, daß diese sich keineswegs in jene engen Grenzen einschließen läßt."

68. *SW*, V, 728: ". . . so darf bei der Elegie die Trauer nur aus einer durch das Ideal erweckten Begeisterung fließen."

69. *SW*, V, 729: "moralische [r] Harmonie."

70. *SW*, V, 730: "Der elegische Dichter sucht die Natur, aber als eine Idee und in einer Vollkommenheit, in der sie nie existiert hat, wenn er sie gleich als etwas Dagewesenes und nun Verlorenes beweint."

71. *SW*, V, 730-31.

72. *SW*, V, 741-44.

73. *Briefwechsel zwischen Schiller und Wilhelm von Humboldt*, p. 224: "Ich will eine *Idylle* schreiben, wie ich hier eine Elegie schrieb. Alle meine poetischen Kräfte spannen sich zu dieser Energie noch an—das Ideal der Schönheit objektiv zu individualisieren, und daraus eine Idylle in *meinem* Sinne zu bilden."

74. *SW*, I, 162.

75. *SW*, I, 203-04.

76. *SW*, V, 730: "Bald durch Leidenschaft, bald durch Abstraktion angespannt, bringt er es selten oder nie zu der ästhetischen Freiheit, welche der Dichter seinem Stoff gegenüber behaupten, seinem Leser mitteilen muß."

77. *SW*, V, 731: ". . . durch Ideen rühren sie uns, nicht durch sinnliche Wahrheit. . . . Unwillkürlich drängt sich die Phantasie der Anschauung, die Denkkraft der Empfindung zuvor, und man verschließt Auge und Ohr, um betrachtend in sich selbst zu versinken."

78. *SW*, V, 735: ". . . nur die Abstraktion hat sie erschaffen, nur die Abstraktion kann sie unterscheiden. Sie sind gute Exempel zu Begriffen, aber keine Individuen, keine lebenden Gestalten."

*Chapter 4*

1. Letter of 20 July 1798 to Goethe; *Der Briefwechsel zwischen Schiller und Goethe*, ed. Hans Gerhard Gräf and Albert Leitzmann (Leipzig: Insel, 1955), II, 115.

2. Letter of 7 December 1796; *Briefwechsel*, I, 270: "ein neues Buch Elegien"; "die Sehnsucht, ein drittes Mal über die Alpen zu gehen."

3. Anyone aware of Goethe's fascination with metrics during this period realizes that metrical reasons alone would fully justify the publication of the poems of "Elegien II" in a group, regardless of other criteria.

4. Letter of 22 June 1796; *Briefwechsel*, I, 167.

5. By analogy, "Die Metamorphose der Tiere" (the companion piece to "Die Metamorphose der Pflanzen") was not included in "Elegien II" because it was written in hexameters.

6. Letter of 14 October 1797; *Briefwechsel*, I, 419: ". . . und ich fühlte ein wundersames Verlangen, jene Erfahrungen zu wiederholen und zu rektifizieren. Ich war ein anderer Mensch geworden und also mußten mir die Gegenstände auch anders erscheinen."

7. See Rudolf Bach, "Begegnung im Zwischenreich: Goethes Elegie 'Euphrosyne,' " in *Goethe*, Neue Folge des Jahrbuchs der Goethe-Gesellschaft, 11 (1949), 134–54. Goethe's elegy has received much praise but surprisingly little critical attention.

8. Letter of 25 October 1797 to Böttiger; cited by Trunz in his notes to the Hamburger Ausgabe of Goethe's *Werke*, I, 502: "Es kann größere Talente geben, aber für mich kein anmutigeres. Die Nachricht von ihrem Tode hatte ich lange erwartet, sie überraschte mich in den formlosen Gebirgen. Liebende haben Tränen und Dichter Rhythmen zur Ehre der Toten. Ich wünschte, daß mir etwas zu ihrem Andenken gelänge."

9. I cite the text according to the Hamburger Ausgabe, I, 190-95.

10. The motif with which the poem begins—the poet's encounter with a deity on a mountain—occurs in other poems by Goethe: notably "Zueignung" (1784) and "Amor als Landschaftsmaler" (1787). The fact that Euphrosyne turns out not to be a deity amounts, in the light of Goethe's earlier uses of the motif, to an ironic inversion of our expectations.

11. Castle, "Das Formgesetz der Elegie," p. 47, arrives at almost the same pattern. I disagree with Castle's observation, however, that almost all Goethe's elegies, including the "Römische Elegien," display a similar pattern (p. 48).

12. Hence I disagree with Klaus Weissenberger, *Formen der Elegie*, p. 155, when he concludes that the "Prinzip der Antithetik" alone can be regarded as "constitutive" for the genre.

13. Abbie Findlay Potts, *The Elegiac Mode: Poetic Form in Wordsworth and Other Elegies* (Ithaca: Cornell Univ. Press, 1967), pp. 36-66, argues that anagnorisis, or "discovery," is the identifying characteristic. Potts of course is talking about the mode rather than the genre since English literature has no closely defined genre of the elegy. "I plan to substantiate from English literature also the hypothesis that, beyond its minor sorrows, elegy is the poetry of skeptical vision and that its most characteristic formal trait is revelation" (p. 2).

14. William James, *The Varieties of Religious Experience* (1902; rpt. New York: New American Library-Mentor Book, 1958), p. 201 (lecture X).

15. Emil Ermatinger, *Die deutsche Lyrik seit Herder* (Leipzig: Teubner, 1925), II, 3-10.

16. *K. L. von Knebel's literarischer Nachlaß und Briefwechsel*, ed. K. A. Varnhagen und Th. Mundt (Leipzig: Reichenbach, 1835-36), III, 471: "die beschwerliche Aufgabe der elegischen Versart in unserer Sprache zu unternehmen."

17. *Nachlaß*, I, 17-32 ("Elegieen"), 89-104 ("Lebensblüthen in Distichen"), and *passim*.

18. See the epigram "Weimar" (*Nachlaß*, I, 72), where Knebel refers to Goethe and Schiller as "zwei holde Gestirn' an dem Himmel" and "dieß Zwillingpaar der Gestirne."

19. *Nachlaß*, I, 22-23.

20. *Nachlaß*, I, 24-26.

21. *Der Briefwechsel zwischen Schiller und Goethe*, I, 387: "er ging auf verschiedene Materien auf eine Weise ein, die Ihre Schule verriet."

22. Letter of 27 June 1797; *Briefwechsel*, I, 352: "Über Produkte in dieser Manier habe ich kein reines Urteil."

23. Letter of 30 June 1797; *Briefwechsel*, I, 353: "Aufrichtig, ich fand in diesen Gedichten viel von meiner eigenen sonstigen Gestalt, und es ist nicht das erstemal, daß mich der Verfasser an mich mahnte. Er hat eine heftige Subjektivität und verbindet damit einen gewissen philosophischen Geist und Tiefsinn."

24. Letter of 30 June 1798; Hölderlin, *Sämtliche Werke* (Kleine Stuttgarter Ausgabe), ed. Friedrich Beissner (Stuttgart: Kohlhammer, 1944-62), VI, 294: "Deswegen darf ich Ihnen wohl gestehen, daß ich zuweilen in geheimem Kampfe mit Ihrem Genius bin, um meine Freiheit gegen ihn zu retten, und daß die Furcht, von Ihnen durch und durch beherrscht zu werden, mich schon oft verhindert hat, mit Heiterkeit mich Ihnen zu nähern.

25. *Sämtliche Werke*, I, 256.

26. Letter of 28 June 1797; *Briefwechsel*, I, 352: "weder durch sinnliches noch durch inneres Anschauen gemalt."

27. *Briefwechsel*, I, 352: "Der Dichter hat einen heitern Blick über die Natur, mit der er doch nur durch Überliefrung bekannt zu sein scheint."

28. See Romano Guardini, *Form und Sinn der Landschaft in den Dichtungen Hölderlins* (Stuttgart: Rainer Wunderlich, 1946), p. 57.

29. *Sämtliche Werke*, II, 73-103. I do not include "Der Archipelagus," which is sometimes counted among the elegies, because it differs from the other elegies so distinctly in meter (dactylic hexameter), organization (strophes of irregular length), and even mood.

30. Bernhard Böschenstein, "Hölderlin und die Schweizer Landschaft als Spiegel der deutschen Literatur vor und um 1800," *Hölderlin-Jahrbuch*, 19/20 (1975-77), discusses the positive revaluation of the Alps in Hölderlin's poetry, and specifically in connection with "Heimkunft"; but he does not link this revaluation to the genre of the elegy.

31. *Sämtliche Werke*, VI, 364: ". . . ich prüfe mein Gefühl, das mich auf dieses oder jenes führt, und frage mich wohl, ob eine Form, die ich wähle, dem Ideal, und besonders auch dem Stoffe, den sie behandelt, nicht widerspreche." For a discussion of Hölderlin's theory of the elegy in the light of this letter see Beissner, *Geschichte der deutschen Elegie*, pp. 173-74; Lawrence J. Ryan, *Hölderlins Lehre vom Wechsel der Töne* (Stuttgart: Kohlhammer, 1960), pp. 229-32; and Jochen Schmidt, *Hölderlins Elegie "Brod und Wein"* (Berlin: De Gruyter, 1968), pp. 16-33.

32. For interpretations of "Menons Klagen um Diotima" see Karl Viëtor, "Hölderlins Liebeselegie," in his *Geist und Form* (Bern: Francke, 1952), pp. 267-91; rpt. in *Hölderlin: Beiträge zu seinem Verständnis in unserm Jahrhundert*, ed. Alfred Kelletat (Tübingen: Mohr, 1961), pp. 161-84; and also Richard Unger, *Hölderlin's Major Poetry: The Dialectics of Unity* (Bloomington: Indiana Univ. Press, 1975), pp. 59-67. Neither interpretation deals with the poem in the context of the elegiac tradition.

33. To this extent Hölderlin's poem exemplifies what Abrams calls "one of the most characteristic Romantic motifs," the *reverdie* or celebration of the regreening earth in springtime. See M. H. Abrams, *Natural Supernaturalism*, pp. 437-42.

34. *Sämtliche Werke*, III, 18: "Wie ein Geist, der keine Ruhe am Acheron findet, kehr ich zurück in die verlaßnen Gegenden meines Lebens. Alles altert und verjüngt sich wieder. Warum sind wir ausgenommen vom schönen Kreislauf der Natur? Oder gilt er auch für uns?"

35. "Fragment von Hyperion," *Sämtliche Werke*, III, 169.

36. See David H. Miles, "The Past as Future: *Pfad* and *Bahn* as Images of Temporal Conflict in Hölderlin," *Germanic Review*, 46 (1971), 95-118.

37. See Julius Petersen, *Die Sehnsucht nach dem Dritten Reich in deutscher Sage und Dichtung* (Stuttgart: Metzler, 1934).

38. "Anmerkungen zum Oedipus," *Sämtliche Werke*, V, 213: "das kalkulable Gesetz."

39. See especially the following essays in vol. IV of *Sämtliche Werke*: "Grund zum Empedokles" (pp. 155-69), "Wechsel der Töne" (pp. 248-50), "Über die Verfahrungsweise des poetischen Geistes" (pp. 251-76), and "Über den Unterschied der Dichtarten" (pp. 277-84). For a thorough discussion of the theory, and particularly its application to the poetry, see Ryan, *Hölderlins Lehre vom Wechsel der Töne*.

40. Letter of 4 December 1801; *Sämtliche Werke*, VI, 455-58.

41. For interpretations of "Brot und Wein" see especially Jochen Schmidt, *Hölderlins Elegie "Brod und Wein"*; and also Richard Unger, *Hölderlin's Major Poetry*, pp. 68-85.

42. See Beissner's notes to the poem in *Sämtliche Werke*, II, 408-09.

43. See Beissner, *Geschichte der deutschen Elegie*, p. 178. In "Elegie" the unnumbered strophes are still quite irregular in length, and in "Menons Klagen" the nine strophes, now numbered, are still not completely regular. But beginning with the 1800 revision of "Der Wanderer" Hölderlin established a rigorously triadic pattern of

eighteen-line strophes, in groups of six or nine, that prevails down to the latest of the elegies.

44. I have taken all the following examples from "Menons Klagen," but precisely the same tendencies are evident in "Brot und Wein" and the other elegies.

45. In this connection see Weissenberger, *Formen der Elegie*, pp. 38-40.

*Chapter 5*

1. *Taschenbuch für Frauenzimmer von Bildung auf das Jahr 1799*, ed. C. L. Neuffer (Stuttgart), pp. 288-89; rpt. in *Hymnische Dichtung im Umkreis Hölderlins: Eine Anthologie*, ed. Paul Böckmann (Tübingen: Mohr, 1965), p. 137.

2. *Musenalmanach für das Jahr 1803*, ed. Bernhard Vermehren (Jena), pp. 132-35; rpt. in *Gedichte 1800-1830*, ed. Jost Schillemeit, Epochen der deutschen Lyrik, 7 (München: Deutscher Taschenbuch Verlag, 1970), pp. 74-75.

3. *Taschenbuch für Frauenzimmer von Bildung auf das Jahr 1800*, pp. 196-203; rpt. *Hymnische Dichtung*, pp. 144-46.

4. *Taschenbuch für Frauenzimmer von Bildung auf das Jahr 1799*, pp. 156-58; rpt. *Hymnische Dichtung*, pp. 146-47.

5. *Der Briefwechsel zwischen Goethe und Schiller*, I, 415.

6. Letter of 23 December 1797; *Schillers Briefwechsel mit Körner*, ed. Karl Goedeke, 2nd ed. (Leipzig: Veit, 1878), II, 285.

7. "Elegien," in *Musen-Almanach für das Jahr 1798*, ed. Friedrich Schiller (Tübingen), pp. 204-15.

8. *Musenalmanach auf das Jahr 1804*, ed. L. A. von Chamisso and K. A. Varnhagen (Leipzig), pp. 106-23.

9. *Musenalmanach auf das Jahr 1804*, pp. 219-21.

10. Ernst Schulze, *Sämmtliche poetische Schriften* (Leipzig: Brockhaus, 1820), IV, 1-73.

11. Johann Peter Eckermann, *Gespräche mit Goethe*, ed. H. H. Houben, 21st ed. (Leipzig: Brockhaus, 1925), p. 278 (entry for 8 April 1829).

12. *Gedichte des Königs Ludwig von Bayern* (München: Cotta, 1829), I, 5-34.

13. Ludwig also wrote a cycle of six "Sicilische Elegien"; *Gedichte*, II, 39-50.

14. *Wilhelm von Humboldts Werke*, ed. Albert Leitzmann (1912; rpt. Berlin: De Gruyter, 1968), IX, 15-17.

15. See Beissner, *Geschichte der deutschen Elegie*, pp. 170–71.

16. *Werke*, IX, 23–46.

17. *Wilhelm von Humboldts Briefe an Johann Gottfried Schweighäuser*, ed. Albert Leitzmann (Jena: Frommann, 1934), pp. 45–46 (letter of 6 April 1808).

18. Walther Rehm, *Europäische Romdichtung*, 2nd ed. (München: Max Hueber, 1960), pp. 193–216; here p. 202. For a further discussion of Humboldt's poem see Beissner, *Geschichte der deutschen Elegie*, pp. 164–66.

19. *Taschenbuch für Frauenzimmer von Bildung auf das Jahr 1800*, pp. 208–09; rpt. *Hymnische Dichtung*, p. 197.

20. *Musen-Almanach für das Jahr 1798*, pp. 155–56; rpt. *Hymnische Dichtung*, p. 221.

21. Siegfried Schmid, *Phantasien* (Erlangen: Schubart, 1803), pp. 251–96; rpt. *Hymnische Dichtung*, p. 223.

22. *Taschenbuch zum geselligen Vergnügen*, ed. W. G. Becker, vol. 11 (1801); rpt. *Hymnische Dichtung*, p. 282.

23. *Musenalmanach auf das Jahr 1804*, pp. 48–53; here p. 52.

24. *Gedichte* (Halle: Renger, 1825).

25. A. W. Schlegel, *Poetische Werke* (Heidelberg: Mohr & Zimmer, 1811), II, 5–23. The volume also contains (pp. 24–40) a second conventional poem in distichs, "Neoptolemus an Diokles" (1800), a long and unframed autobiographical account in the form of a letter from Schlegel's older brother, Carl August, who died in India in 1789 while serving with the British forces. The poem is meant solely as a memorial to a brother who died at the age of twenty-eight, disappointed in his life and frustrated in his ambitions.

26. Friedrich Schlegel, *Dichtungen*, ed. Hans Eichner (München: Schöningh, 1962), pp. 281–85.

27. F.W.J. von Schelling, *Sämmtliche Werke* (Stuttgart: Cotta, 1856–1861), X, 439.

28. Novalis, *Schriften*, ed. Paul Kluckhohn and Richard Samuel, 2nd ed. (Darmstadt: Wissenschaftliche Buchgesellschaft, 1960), I, 403.

29. E.g., *Musenalmanach auf das Jahr 1804*, which even opens with a conventional dedication to the queen in distichs.

30. Ludwig Achim von Arnim, *Gedichte. Zweiter Teil*, ed. Herbert R. Liedke and Alfred Anger (Tübingen: Niemeyer, 1976), pp. 206–209. The edition includes over fifty more previously unpublished poems in distichs—mainly anecdotes, epigrams, and occasional poems.

31. "Geschichte der Elegie"; rpt. in August Wilhelm Schlegel, *Kritische Schriften und Briefe*, ed. Edgar Lohner (Stuttgart: Kohlhammer, 1962-1974), III, 223-43.

32. "Geschichte der Elegie," p. 229: "Die Elegie als ein unauflösliches Gemisch von Leidenschaft und betrachtender Ruhe, von Wollust und Wehmut, einzig gemacht die zwischen Erinnerung und Ahnung, zwischen Fröhlichkeit und Trauer schwebende hin- und herschwankende Stimmung auszudrücken, gewährt in ihrer sorglosen Freiheit den schönsten Spielraum für alle jene süßen Widersprüche, jene zauberischen Disharmonien, welche den Schmerz und den Reiz des Lebens ausmachen, und sie wird daher überall, wo sie in ihrer echten Gestalt auftritt, das Entzücken aller gefühlvollen Seelen sein."

33. "Geschichte der Elegie," p. 241: "Dies ist nun nach der Ansicht der Alten gänzlich unmöglich: denn bei diesen hing der Gattungsname an der metrischen Form, und mit Recht, weil diese, richtig gebraucht, wieder die innere Form der Behandlung bestimmte."

34. "Elegien aus dem Griechischen," *Athenäum*, I (1798), 107-40, esp. pp. 107-11.

35. "Elegien aus dem Griechischen," p. 108: ". . . und ein Dichter, von dem es nie entschieden werden kann, ob er größer oder liebenswürdiger sey, hat zu seinen frühern unverwelklichen Lorbern auch den Namen eines Wiederherstellers der alten Elegie gesellt."

36. "Elegien aus dem Griechischen," p. 110: "klagende Empfindsamkeit."

37. *Schellings Werke*, ed. Manfred Schröter, 3rd Ergänzungsband (München: Beck & Oldenbourg, 1959), pp. 311-12.

38. In this connection see Rehm, *Europäische Romdichtung*, pp. 185-92.

39. A. W. Schlegel, *Kritische Schriften und Briefe*, VII, 18 (letter of 9 November 1795).

40. A. W. Schlegel, *Poetische Werke*, II, 41-66.

41. See, for instance, the representative selection in *Deutsche Epigramme*, ed. Gerhard Neumann (Stuttgart: Reclam, 1969).

42. "Die Natur soll der sichtbare Geist, der Geist die unsichtbare Natur seyn." This famous statement occurs at the end of Schelling's *Ideen zu einer Philosophie der Natur* (1797).

43. In the paralipomena to *Heinrich von Ofterdingen*; in Novalis, *Schriften*, I, 350: "Der Tod ist des Lebens höchstes Ziel."

44. Ernst Moritz Arndt, *Ausgewählte Werke in sechzehn Bänden*, ed. Heinrich Meisner and Robert Geerds (Leipzig: Max Hesse, [1908]), II, 143-45, and III, 51-59.

45. *Ausgewählte Werke*, III, 60-65.

46. Friedrich Rückert, *Gesammelte Poetische Werke in zwölf Bänden* (Frankfurt am Main: Sauerländer, 1868), V, 62-76.

47. Friedrich Rückert, *Gedichte* (Frankfurt am Main: Sauerländer, 1841), pp. 270-78. For the dating and biographical background see Helmut Prang, *Friedrich Rückert: Geist und Form der Sprache* (Wiesbaden: Selbstverlag der Stadt Schweinfurt, 1963), pp. 52-53.

48. First published in *Der Gesellschafter oder Blätter für Geist und Herz* (Berlin, 1823).

49. Cited here according to the text in Karl Immermann, *Werke in fünf Bänden*, ed. Benno von Wiese (Frankfurt am Main: Athenäum, 1971), vol. I, *passim*.

50. See Benno von Wiese, *Karl Immermann: Sein Werk und sein Leben* (Bad Homburg: Gehlen, 1969), p. 115.

51. *Werke*, I, 20.

52. *Werke*, I, 81-83.

53. *Italienische Reise* (entry for 7 May 1787); *Werke* (Hamburger Ausgabe), XI, 296: "Setzt man sich nun dahin, wo ehmals die obersten Zuschauer saßen, so muß man gestehen, daß wohl nie ein Publikum im Theater solche Gegenstände vor sich gehabt."

54. See Rudolf Unger, *Platen in seinem Verhältnis zu Goethe* (Berlin: Duncker, 1903), p. 151.

55. *Die Tagebücher des Grafen August von Platen*, ed. G. von Laubmann and L. von Scheffler (Stuttgart: Cotta, 1896-1900), II, 977-78 (entry for 14 June 1835): "Die hiesige Natur entspricht den schönsten Gegenden am Golf von Neapel; man findet Sorrent und Amalfi wieder und vielleicht noch mehr dazu. Auch habe ich hier eine Elegie und zwei Hymnen gedichtet. . . . Dies alles großenteils im antiken Theater umherwandelnd."

56. August Graf von Platen, *Sämtliche Werke in zwölf Bänden*, ed. Max Koch and Erich Petzet (Leipzig: Max Hesse, [1910]), IV, 101-02.

57. "Taormina," the fifth in Ludwig's cycle of "Sicilische Elegien"; *Gedichte des Königs Ludwig von Bayern*, II, 47-48. In fact, Ludwig's poem does not contain the same landscape allusions as do the passages by Goethe and Platen.

58. *Sämtliche Werke*, III, 159-60.

59. *Sämtliche Werke*, III, 233–34.

60. *Sämtliche Werke*, IV, 195.

61. Erich Petzet, "Schiller in Platens Jugendlyrik," in *Studien zur vergleichenden Literaturgeschichte*, V (1905), Ergänzungsheft, pp. 294–302.

62. Rudolf Schlösser, *August Graf von Platen: Ein Bild seines Entwicklungsgangs und seines dichterischen Schaffens* (Munich: Piper, 1910–1913), I, 149.

63. *Tagebücher*, I (entry for 11 May 1815).

64. The early "Elegien" are printed in *Sämtliche Werke*, VI, 179–202.

65. But note that Heinrich Henel, in his edition of Platen's *Gedichte* (Stuttgart: Reclam, 1968), suggests that specifically these early elegies seem so fully achieved that he is tempted to assign a later date to them (p. 145).

66. Letter of 28 August 1835 to Minckwitz; cited by Max Koch in his Introduction to vol. IV of *Sämtliche Werke* (IV, 13).

67. Heinrich Henel, "Epigonenlyrik: Rückert und Platen," *Euphorion*, 55 (1961), 260–78.

68. Jeffrey L. Sammons, "Platen's Tulip Image," *Monatshefte für deutschen Unterricht*, 52 (1960), 293–301.

69. Schlösser, *August Graf von Platen*, I, 149.

70. Entry for 11 February 1831; Eckermann, *Gespräche mit Goethe*, p. 354: "Daß er in der großen Umgebung von Neapel und Rom die Erbärmlichkeiten der deutschen Literatur nicht vergessen kann, ist einem so hohen Talent gar nicht zu verzeihen."

71. See also the "Römische Distichen" (1841) by Wilhelm Smets; in Joseph Müllermeister, *Wilhelm Smets in Leben und Schriften: Eine Literatur-Studie* (Aachen: Rudolf Barth, 1877), passim. In general, however, the elegiac distich is conspicuous for its absence in the extensive corpus of Rome poetry of the nineteenth century; see *Hellas und Rom im Spiegel deutscher Dichtung: Eine Anthologie*, by Karl Zettel, ed. August Brunner (Erlangen: Palm & Enke, [1907]), II, 3–290.

72. First published in *Taschenbuch aus Italien und Griechenland auf das Jahr 1830*, ed. Wilhelm Waiblinger (Berlin: G. Reimer); rpt. Wilhelm Waiblinger, *Bilder aus Neapel und Sicilien*, ed. Eduard Grisebach (Leipzig: Eckstein, 1879), pp. 1–60.

73. *Hebbels Werke*, ed. Franz Zinkernagel (Leipzig: Bibliographisches Institut, [1913]), I, 187. This poem—"Der Efeu am Grabe der Cecilia Metella"—is highly literary in its implications because the ivy portrayed is growing, as Hebbel well knew, on the tomb on the

Appian Way that provided the background for Tischbein's famous portrait of Goethe.

74. *Werke*, I, 186.

75. Eduard Mörike, *Sämtliche Werke*, ed. Herbert G. Göpfert (München: Hanser, 1958), p. 1317: "gewiß der liebenswürdigste Elegiker unter den Römern."

76. *Sämtliche Werke*, p. 81.

77. *Sämtliche Werke*, p. 220.

78. Here I am in agreement with Weissenberger, *Formen der Elegie*, pp. 46-49, who discusses these two poems in a section entitled "Die idyllische Elegie."

79. *Sämtliche Werke*, p. 75.

80. Jost Hermand, *Die literarische Formenwelt des Biedermeiers*, Beiträge zur deutschen Philologie, 27 (Giessen: Wilhelm Schmitz, 1958), pp. 71-78.

*Chapter 6*

1. Literary history of recent decades, which has interested itself increasingly in the political poetry of the nineteenth century, has largely ignored the Munich school. For good introductions see Emil Ermatinger, *Die deutsche Lyrik seit Herder*, 2nd ed. (Leipzig: Teubner, 1925), III, 160-83; Eduard Stemplinger, ed., *Der Münchner Kreis*, Deutsche Literatur in Entwicklungsreihen, Reihe Formkunst, I (Leipzig: Reclam, 1933); and Fritz Martini, *Deutsche Literatur im bürgerlichen Realismus, 1848-1898*, 3rd ed. (Stuttgart: Metzler, 1974), pp. 237-354.

2. Adolf Friedrich Graf von Schack, *Ein halbes Jahrhundert: Erinnerungen und Aufzeichnungen* (Stuttgart: Deutsche Verlagsanstalt, 1888), I, 24: "[Platen] war unter allen lebenden Dichtern derjenige, der den größten Eindruck auf mich gemacht."

3. *Ein halbes Jahrhundert*, I, 182: "Auch Platen, der jedem Italien-Bereisenden als Begleiter dienen sollte, war immer in meinen Händen."

4. *Ein halbes Jahrhundert*, I, 121: ". . . auf den Stufen des Dionysostheaters zu ruhen, während mein Geist die Szene wieder mit den auf dem Kothurn einherschreitenden Gestalten des Aeschylus und Sophokles, den in weißen, wallenden Gewändern die Thymele umschreitenden Chorsängern belebte."

5. Adolf Friedrich von Schack, *Gesammelte Werke in zehn Bänden*, 3rd ed. (Stuttgart: Cotta, 1897), II, 222-27.

6. *Ein halbes Jahrhundert*, I, 25.

7. *Heinrich Leutholds Gedichte*, ed. Arthur Schurig (Leipzig: Insel, 1910), pp. 47–48: "Fragment aus Sizilien."

8. "Zweite Elegie," in *Gedichte*, pp. 149–51.

9. *Gedichte*, pp. 146–48.

10. "An N. N., Gymnasialprofessor in X.," in Paul Heyse, *Gedichte*, 5th ed. (Berlin: Wilhelm Hertz, 1893), p. 348: "der Moses unsrer Prosodik, / Der in steinerne Tafeln die zehn Gebote des Wohlklangs / Grub. . . ."

11. *Gedichte*, pp. 290–300.

12. *Gedichte*, p. 297.

13. Stemplinger, *Der Münchner Kreis*, p. 140: "Des Abends lesen wir uns unsere Verse vor. Unser Meister, den wir täglich lesen und bis ins einzelne studieren, ist Graf Platen." Around this time Geibel composed a poem in ottava rima entitled "Platens Vermächtnis," in Emanuel Geibel, *Gedichte: Erste Periode*, 54th ed. (Stuttgart: Cotta, 1863), pp. 201–02.

14. "Distichen aus Griechenland," in *Gedichte*, pp. 182–92.

15. *Gedichte*, pp. 222–24.

16. Emanuel Geibel, *Gesammelte Werke in acht Bänden* (Stuttgart: Cotta, 1883), IV, 29–32.

17. *Gesammelte Werke*, V, 103–243.

18. *Gesammelte Werke*, IV, 156–72.

19. *Gesammelte Werke*, V, 49–61.

20. *Gesammelte Werke*, V, 32–48.

21. *Gesammelte Werke*, V, 75–85.

22. *Gesammelte Werke*, V, 86–102. Concerning the composition and biographical background of the cycle see Carl C. T. Litzmann, *Emanuel Geibel: Aus Erinnerungen, Briefen und Tagebüchern* (Berlin: Wilhelm Hertz, 1887), esp. p. 251.

23. On the months at Escheberg see Karl Theodor Gaedertz, *Emanuel Geibel, Sänger der Liebe, Herold des Reiches: Ein deutsches Dichterleben* (Leipzig: Georg Wigand, 1897), esp. pp. 178–92.

24. On Geibel's poetry see Harry Maync, *Deutsche Dichter* (Frauenfeld: Huber, 1928), pp. 117–52; and Walther Killy, *Wandlungen des lyrischen Bildes*, 3rd ed. (Göttingen: Vandenhoeck & Ruprecht, 1961), pp. 94–115.

25. Vischer's discussion of the elegy is included in his Poetics, which was completed in 1857 and which constitutes vol. VI of his *Aesthetik*, ed. Robert Vischer, 2nd ed. (München: Meyer & Jessen, 1923), pp. 252–55 (Paragraph 894): ". . . die Elegie steht also nicht

rein inmitten der idealen Phantasie, sondern sehnt sich von dem Standpunkt der Wirklichkeit nach dem Ideale."

26. Killy, *Wandlungen*, p. 98.

27. See the biography by Anton Bettelheim that constitutes vol. I of *Ferdinand von Saars Sämtliche Werke in zwölf Bänden*, ed. Jakob Minor (Leipzig: Max Hesse, [1908]). For a recent summary of existing views see Robert Mühlher, "Ferdinand von Saar: Ein österreichisches Dichterleben zwischen Vormärz und Moderne," in *Jahrbuch der Grillparzer-Gesellschaft*, 3rd ser., 11 (1974), 11-72.

28. "An Stephan Milow zum 70. Wiegenfeste," in *Sämtliche Werke*, III, 88. Saar also dedicated to Milow an unfinished crown of sonnets entitled "Die Kunst"; *Sämtliche Werke*, III, 44-49.

29. See Saar's ode "Arthur Schopenhauer," in *Sämtliche Werke*, II, 189-90; and Milow's poem "Arthur Schopenhauer," in his *Gedichte* (Stuttgart: Adolf Bonz, 1882), pp. 213-15.

30. *Stephan Milows Gedichte*, ed. Eduard Engel, Moderne Lyriker, 5 (Leipzig: Max Hesse, n.d.), p. 105.

31. *Sämtliche Werke*, II, 188.

32. *Sämtliche Werke*, II, 181.

33. E.g., "An meine beiden Söhne," in *Gedichte* (1882), pp. 282-84.

34. "Eine Antwort," in *Gedichte* (1882), p. 225.

35. *Sämtliche Werke*, II, 180.

36. "Grillparzer," in *Sämtliche Werke*, II, 184-85.

37. "Das Drama," in *Sämtliche Werke*, II, 186.

38. Bettelheim, in *Sämtliche Werke*, I, 116.

39. *Sämtliche Werke*, II, 86.

40. *Sämtliche Werke*, II, 148.

41. *Sämtliche Werke*, II, 224-25; *Sämtliche Werke*, III, 116.

42. *Sämtliche Werke*, IV, 25-69.

43. *Deutsche Elegieen*, Neue, stark vermehrte und veränderte Auflage des Elegieencyklus "Auf der Scholle" (Stuttgart: Adolf Bonz, 1885).

44. *Fallende Blätter* (Kassel: Georg Weiss, 1903), p. 64.

45. *Fallende Blätter*, pp. 74-77.

46. *Fallende Blätter*, pp. 159-63.

47. "Dem Wettkämpfer" (1879), in *Sämtliche Werke*, II, 42.

48. "Im elegischen Versmaß," in *Sämtliche Werke*, III, 72-77.

49. *Sämtliche Werke*, IV, 7-24.

50. The text in *Sämtliche Werke* actually reads: "Ja, hier bereitet sich vor allen in Phasen die Zukunft"—which would seem to be clearly a misprint.

## Chapter 7

1. "Das Gespräch über Formen" (written 1900-1901; published 1905), in Rudolf Borchardt, *Prosa I*, ed. Maria Luise Borchardt (Stuttgart: Ernst Klett, 1957), p. 351: "Wir in Deutschland stehen heute nach den unbeschreiblichen Jahrzehnten, die für alle Zeiten von dem tiefsten kulturellen Stande der Nation nicht zu trennen sein werden, in den Anfängen einer neuen Kultur."

2. "Eranos-Brief" (1924), in *Prosa I*, p. 96: "Das neue Volk des Reiches, entstanden aus der gewaltsamen Absprengung Österreichs vom Gefüge des altständigen Deutschlands . . . hatte keine Geschichte und schrieb sich eine falsche. Es hatte nur eine allerjüngste. Sein Geburtsdatum war der Krieg und die Proklamation in Versailles."

3. "Eranos-Brief," in *Prosa I*, p. 126: "der organische Kulturausdruck der letzten deutschen Universalmonarchie Europas"; "direkter Fortsetzer und Verklärer [der] deutschen Kultur."

4. "Die neue Poesie und die alte Menschheit" (1912), in Rudolf Borchardt, *Reden*, ed. Marie Luise Borchardt and Silvio Rizzi (Stuttgart: Ernst Klett, [1955]), p. 110: "Das tiefste, das seelenvollste und seelenwärmste Volk Europas hat in den Jahrzehnten, in denen es die politische und wirtschaftliche Hegemonie Europas an sich nahm, die geistige Hegemonie Europas sich entgleiten lassen müssen."

5. "Die geistesgeschichtliche Bedeutung des neunzehnten Jahrhunderts" (1927), in *Reden*, pp. 342-43: "Der Riß mitten durch unser Volk, der unsere große Literatur und Poesie, die größte, die wir in geschlossener Entwicklung je gehabt haben, die des zwölften und dreizehnten Jahrhunderts, ihres Volkes beraubt hat . . . ist heilbar. . . . nicht der Poesie Goethes, aber ihrer Auslegung im neunzehnten Jahrhundert, nicht der Klassizität, aber dem Klassizismus entgegengesetzt."

6. See Borchardt's Afterword to his *Ewiger Vorrat deutscher Poesie* (Munich: Verlag der Bremer Presse, 1926), p. 450; rpt. in *Prosa III*, ed. Marie Luise Borchardt and Ernst Zinn (Stuttgart: Ernst Klett, 1960), p. 327: "Es ist ein Irrtum, anzunehmen, es könne einen Dichter im nationalen Vakuum geben."

7. "Schöpferische Restauration," in *Reden*, pp. 230-53.

8. The three elegies—"Saturnische Elegie," "Heroische Elegie," and "Pathetische Elegie" (Göttingen: Privatdruck, 1901-1902)— were subsequently reprinted, along with "Melodische Elegie," in Borchardt's *Jugendgedichte* (1913; Berlin: Rowohlt, 1920). I cite the

poems below according to the text in Borchardt's *Gedichte*, ed. Marie Luise Borchardt and Herbert Steiner (Stuttgart: Ernst Klett, 1957), pp. 106-110 ("Pathetische Elegie"). In a letter to Hofmannsthal (28 May 1901) Borchardt mentions several other elegies that he had written but did not wish to publish. Cf. Hugo von Hofmannsthal / Rudolf Borchardt, *Briefwechsel*, ed. Marie Luise Borchardt and Herbert Steiner (Frankfurt am Main: Fischer, 1954), p. 7. In connection with Borchardt's elegies see Werner Kraft, *Rudolf Borchardt: Welt aus Poesie und Geschichte* (Hamburg: Claassen, 1961), p. 166; Adam Wierzejewski, "Rudolf Borchardt," in *Deutsche Dichter der Moderne*, ed. Benno von Wiese (Berlin: Erich Schmidt, 1965), esp. pp. 201-202; and Weissenberger, *Formen der Elegie*, pp. 75-79 ("Heroische Elegie") and pp. 82-87 ("Melodische Elegie").

9. Rudolf Alexander Schröder, "Einleitung," in *Reden*, p. 10: "von jeder Art der dichterischen Gestaltung . . . noch einmal ein Muster aufzustellen."

10. Borchardt wrote a poem in Greek as the dedicatory epigram to "Das Gespräch über Formen"; rpt. in *Prosa I*, p. 527.

11. Rudolf Alexander Schröder, "Erinnerungen an Rudolf Borchardt," in his *Gesammelte Werke in fünf Bänden* (Berlin and Frankfurt am Main: Suhrkamp, 1952), II, 869.

12. "Die geistesgeschichtliche Bedeutung des neunzehnten Jahrhunderts," in *Reden*, p. 344: "Nichts bleibt als jenes schöpferische Wiedererlebnis der Vergangenheit . . . nichts als uns zu verkehren und wie Herakles in die Unterwelt zu gehen, um die Toten zu holen."

13. "Nachwort" to *Ewiger Vorrat deutscher Poesie*, in *Prosa III*, p. 345: "Die deutsche Poesie ist von derjenigen aller europäischen Nachbar- und Brudervölker dadurch unterschieden, daß in ihr von den ersten Anfängen bis auf den heutigen und wohl den ewigen Tag das Verhältnis des Sterblichen zum Unsterblichen immer wieder aufspringt und fast alle anderen ewigen Relationen des Menschlichen in sich verschlingt."

14. For Borchardt's view of Schiller's poetry see his "Rede über Schiller" (1920), in *Reden*, pp. 168-70. Borchardt refers frequently to Goethe, but see especially his essay "Goethe" (1932), in *Prosa III*, pp. 307-12.

15. *Die Insel*, II/4 (July-Sept. 1901), 59-62, 181-85, 315-18.

16. "Erinnerungen an Rudolf Borchardt" (1947), in Schröder's *Gesammelte Werke*, II, 873.

17. "Erinnerungen an Rudolf Borchardt," p. 864: "Es war das

Gefühl davon, daß schon in jenen Tagen unsre Zeit trotz hallender Parolen, trotz unleugbarer großer Talente eine in unaufhaltsamem geistigen Niedergang begriffene sei."

18. "Erinnerungen an Rudolf Borchardt," p. 864: "Ich hatte mich damals neben der selbstverständlichen Orientierung an Goethe in eine fast abgöttische Verehrung der Antike gerettet."

19. "Nachwort" to his collected poems, in *Gesammelte Werke*, I, 1179: "Frühes Bewußtsein und spätere Erkenntnis der Kontinuität alles echten Geschehens hat mich dahin belehrt, daß die Gattungen und die Themen der Poesie seit ihrem ersten Hervortreten die gleichen geblieben sind."

20. "Nachwort," p. 1177: "Schienen Gedanken oder Empfindungen wichtig genug, um ausgesprochen zu werden, so griff ich aus der Fülle des dem Spätgeborenen zur Verfügung Stehenden die Form heraus, die sich mir anbot, und die zu bemeistern ich mir getraute."

21. I cite "Die Elegien" as they are reprinted in *Gesammelte Werke*, I, 78-137. Schröder omitted from his collected poems (1940) several "elegies" in other metrical forms that he wrote—probably under the influence of Borchardt—before the elegies in distichs: e.g., "Zwei Elegien. I. Fontainebleau II. Michelangelo," in *Die Insel*, II/2 (1901), 105-113; and "Elegien" (twelve poems in iambic trimeter), in *Die Insel*, II/4 (1901), 231-37.

22. "Erster und letzter Besuch in Rodaun" (1929), in *Gesammelte Werke*, II, 824-26.

23. "Der Sänger der Aeneïs" (1930), in *Gesammelte Werke*, II, 163: "den *Georgica*, dem zauberischesten Produkt der lateinischen Literatur."

24. Kurt Berger, *Die Dichtung Rudolf Alexander Schröders* (Marburg: Hermann Rathmann, 1954), p. 122, coins the term "elegische Idylle" to characterize "Der Landbau" and "Tivoli"—a term that is appropriate for the former but not, as I hope to show, for the latter.

25. "Schillers Gedichte II" (1944), in *Gesammelte Werke*, II, 677: "Aber er ist aufs Ganze gesehn kein eigentlicher Elegiker, wenigstens soweit man das nach den einzig uns vollständig erhaltenen Mustern der Gattung, den lateinischen, sagen darf."

26. "Schillers Gedichte II," p. 678: "das eigentlich 'Elegische' . . . die—manchmal zehrende—Süße des Tons, das liebevolle Verweilen auf einer sinnlichen Gegenwart."

27. "Schillers Gedichte II," p. 678: ". . . hebt der 'Spaziergang' an mit einem Landschaftsbild, so innig gefühlt und dargestellt wie kaum etwas ähnliches bei Schiller." In this generous appreciation

Schröder discusses the movement of Schiller's poem: specifically, the walk up the mountain that leads to a view precipitating the viewer's meditations.

28. See Rudolf Kassner's introduction to Rainer Maria Rilke / Marie von Thurn und Taxis, *Briefwechsel*, ed. Ernst Zinn (Zürich: Max Niehans, 1951), I, xxi; cf. also Joachim W. Storck, "Hofmannsthal und Rilke: Eine österreichische Antinomie," in *Rilke heute: Beziehungen und Wirkungen*, II (Frankfurt am Main: Suhrkamp, 1976), pp. 115-67.

29. "Rainer Maria Rilke" (1928), in *Gesammelte Werke*, II, 921.

30. "Erinnerungen an Rilke" (1927), in *Gesammelte Werke*, II, 935.

31. "Rainer Maria Rilke," p. 931: "Man kann nicht sagen, daß seine Not die Not der Zeit gewesen sei; denn sie war eine ungemeine und einmalige, und darin liegt ihr Adel und ihr Wert beschlossen."

32. I cite the *Duineser Elegien* according to Rilke's *Sämtliche Werke*, ed. Ernst Zinn, I (Insel Verlag, 1955), 683-726.

33. For a more detailed analysis of Rilke's metrics see Weissenberger, *Formen der Elegie*, pp. 111-25; and Hermann J. Weigand, "Zu Rilkes Verskunst in den *Duineser Elegien*," *Neophilologus*, 49 (1964), 31-51; rpt. in Weigand, *Fährten und Funde: Aufsätze zur deutschen Literatur*, ed. A. Leslie Willson (Bern: Francke, 1967), pp. 268-88.

34. See Eudo C. Mason, *Rilke und Goethe* (Köln: Böhlau, 1958).

35. R. M. Rilke/Marie von Thurn und Taxis, *Briefwechsel*, I, 59: "Dann ergriff mich mehr und mehr diese Gestalt der kaum zwanzig-jährigen Christiane Neumann, auf deren Hingang Goethe das große Gedicht Euphrosyne geschrieben hat, erinnern Sie's?"

36. *Briefwechsel*, I, 59; ". . . es ist wirklich ein Leuchten um so früh Verstorbene, durch sie bekommt das Totsein etwas Kühnes, etwas Reiches, beinah Berühmtes."

37. See Herbert Singer, *Rilke und Hölderlin* (Köln: Böhlau, 1957).

38. R. M. Rilke/André Gide, *Correspondance 1909-1926*, ed. Renée Lang (Paris: Corrêa, 1952), p. 92.

39. Letter of 6 March 1915 to Thankmar Freiherr von Münch-hausen; in *Briefe*, ed. Karl Altheim (Wiesbaden: Insel, 1950), p. 482.

40. Letter of 24 July 1915 to Norbert von Hellingrath; in *Gesammelte Briefe* (Leipzig: Insel, 1939), III, 396: "Mit besonderer Bewegung und Hingabe"; ". . . sein Einfluß auf mich ist groß und großmütig, wie nur der des Reichsten und innerlich Mächtigsten sein kann."

41. See in this connection also Friedrich Wilhelm Wodtke, *Rilke und Klopstock* (Diss. Kiel, 1948).

42. Letter of 13 November 1925 to Witold Hulewicz; in *Briefe*, ed. Karl Altheim, p. 900: "Der Engel der *Elegien* ist dasjenige Geschöpf, in dem die Verwandlung des Sichtbaren in Unsichtbares, die wir leisten, schon vollzogen erscheint."

43. See in this connection Jacob Steiner, *Rilkes Duineser Elegien* (Bern: Francke, 1962), pp. 200-204. Steiner's study provides the most useful commentary on specific details in the Elegies.

44. Eudo C. Mason, *Rainer Maria Rilke: Sein Leben und sein Werk* (Göttingen: Vandenhoeck & Ruprecht, 1964), pp. 98-100, stresses the development—especially from lament to jubilation—that took place during the years of genesis.

45. *Sämtliche Werke*, II, 94-95.

46. Mason, *Rainer Maria Rilke*, pp. 89-90, assumes that Rilke, who referred to his First Elegy simply as "die Elegie," acknowledged his awareness of the tradition to which the poem belonged.

47. See Kenneth D. Weisinger, "The Structure of Rilke's Seventh Elegy," *Germanic Review*, 49 (1974), 215-39. In this careful analysis Weisinger demonstrates that the Seventh Elegy is composed according to a sophisticated system of encapsulations revolving around a central axis. Weisinger, apparently unaware of Castle's study of "Das Formgesetz der Elegie," does not relate his findings to the elegiac structure of the entire cycle; his analysis receives an even fuller meaning, I believe, when it is seen within that larger context.

48. Georg Trakl, *Dichtungen und Briefe*, ed. Walther Killy and Hans Scklenar (Salzburg: Otto Müller, 1969), I, 530: "Es ist ein so namenloses Unglück, wenn einem die Welt entzweibricht."

49. Letter of 17 November 1913 to Ludwig von Ficker; in *Dichtungen und Briefe*, I, 528: "diese[r] Dreckstadt."

50. Letter of April, 1912, to Erhard Buschbeck; in *Dichtungen und Briefe*, I, 487: "der brutalsten und gemeinsten Stadt."

51. Cited by Ursula Jaspersen, "Georg Trakl," in *Deutsche Dichter der Moderne*, ed. Benno von Wiese (Berlin: Erich Schmidt, 1965), p. 394: "Ich habe kein Recht, mich der Hölle zu entziehen."

52. Herbert Lindenberger, "The Play of Opposites in Georg Trakl's Poetry," *German Life and Letters*, N. S. XI (1958), 193-204; the concept is further developed in Lindenberger's *Georg Trakl* (New York: Twayne, 1971).

53. Ludwig Dietz, *Die lyrische Form Georg Trakls*, Trakl-Studien, 5 (Salzburg: Otto Müller, 1959), esp. pp. 113-41. Dietz, p. 113, surveys representative views of Trakl as an "elegiac" poet. See also Weissen-

berger, *Formen der Elegie*, pp. 99–103, who detects his "elegiac principle" in several of Trakl's poems.

54. See Walther Killy, *Über Georg Trakl* (Göttingen: Vandenhoeck & Ruprecht, 1960), esp. pp. 38–51.

55. See Dietz, p. 114, and Jaspersen, p. 386.

56. See Reinhold Grimm, "Georg Trakls Verhältnis zu Rimbaud," *Germanisch-Romanische Monatsschrift*, N. S. IX (1959), 288–315; and Lindenberger, *Georg Trakl*, pp. 58–80.

57. Dietz, pp. 114–15.

58. Lindenberger, *Georg Trakl*, pp. 90–94.

59. Letter of November, 1913, to Ludwig von Ficker; in *Dichtungen und Briefe*, I, 530: "mein Leben ist in wenigen Tagen unsäglich zerbrochen worden und es bleibt nur mehr ein sprachloser Schmerz, dem selbst die Bitternis versagt ist."

60. *Dichtungen und Briefe*, I, 119.

61. This line exemplifies Trakl's borrowing from Hölderlin; cf. line 6 of Hölderlin's ode "Sonnenuntergang": "Es tönten rings die Wälder und Hügel nach."

62. Weissenberger, pp. 99–103, cites "Stundenlied" and "Jahr" as examples of Trakl's "elegiac principle"; Dietz, pp. 132–41, interprets those two poems as well as "Helian" and "Frühling der Seele."

63. *Dichtungen und Briefe*, I, 141–42.

64. Letter of 8 February 1939 to Hermann Pongs; in Josef Weinheber, *Sämtliche Werke*, ed. Josef Nadler and Hedwig Weinheber, V (Salzburg: Otto Müller, 1956), 423–29.

65. Ibid., p. 425: "Trakl war zu weit fort, sprach zu sehr aus einer jenseitig-dämonischen, ganz im Geheimnis verbleibenden Welt, als daß ich mich hätte in dieser Welt einzurichten vermocht."

66. Ibid., p. 426: "das ans Unheimliche grenzende Vermögen, mit der Sprache alles beginnen und alles vollenden zu können."

67. Ibid., p. 427: "ja, ich übernahm sogar dort zum erstenmale die Gestalt des Engels in meine Dichtung herüber."

68. Ibid., p. 427: "Auch später, als ich auf dem Höhepunkt antiker Beeinflussung, wenn man durchaus will, auch einer Beeinflussung durch Hölderlin stand, habe ich mich nicht gescheut, den Tonfall der rilkeschen Elegie dort anzuschlagen, wo mir das für die Deckung meiner Gedichtinhalte (Auf das Vergängliche) förderlich schien."

69. Rpt. in *Sämtliche Werke*, II (1954), 222–36.

70. Letter of 12 November 1937 to Korfiz Holm; in *Sämtliche Werke*, V, 287: ". . . ich traue es mir zu, die Sonette an Orpheus und

die Duineser-Elegien—nicht sosehr im Formalen, aber in der geistigen Substanz—zu übertreffen. Ich bin ja eigentlich im Nebenberuf
Denker."

71. From a section entitled "Von den Formen" in the volume *Hier
ist das Wort* (1944); rpt. *Sämtliche Werke*, II, 487.

72. Bertolt Brecht, *Gesammelte Werke in 20 Bänden*, werkausgabe
edition suhrkamp (Frankfurt am Main: Suhrkamp, 1967), XVIII, 60:
"Ich richte Ihre Aufmerksamkeit darauf, daß Rilkes Ausdruck, wenn
er sich mit Gott befaßt, absolut schwul ist."

73. *Gesammelte Werke*, X, 849-50.

74. *Gesammelte Werke*, X, 1016. See F. N. Mennemeier, "Bertolt
Brecht als Elegiker," *Der Deutschunterricht*, 23/1 (February 1971),
59-73. Mennemeier, concerned solely with the mode and not the
genre, does not mention the Rilke parody.

75. See Charles W. Hoffmann, *Opposition Poetry in Nazi Germany*,
Univ. of California Publication in Modern Philology, 67 (Berkeley
and Los Angeles: Univ. of California Press, 1962), p. 51; and Theo-
dore Ziolkowski, "Form als Protest: Das Sonett in der Literatur des
Exils und der Inneren Emigration," in *Exil und Innere Emigration*,
Third Wisconsin Workshop, ed. Reinhold Grimm and Jost Hermand
(Frankfurt am Main: Athenäum, 1972), pp. 153-72.

76. Friedrich Georg Jünger, *Sämtliche Gedichte* (St. Gallen: Erker,
1974), pp. 22-41.

77. "Wirkungen Goethes in der Gegenwart" (1938), in Hans
Carossa, *Sämtliche Werke* (Frankfurt am Main: Insel, 1962), II, 946:
"Die herrliche Elegie auf den Tod der jungen Schauspielerin Christiane Neumann dürfte nicht oft einem gläubigeren Herzen begegnet
sein."

78. Ibid., p. 962: "Bekennen wir uns, Gehende wie Kommende,
zum Orden derer, denen alle Länder und Meere der Welt nicht genü-
gen würden, wenn das Reich des Geistes und des Herzens unerobert
bliebe!"

79. "Brief aus Florenz" (1942); in *Sämtliche Werke*, I, 906: "Ach,
jede Reise im Abendland ist heute ein großes Abschiednehmen; nie
wieder wird es uns das Antlitz zeigen, das uns vertraut war. Vom
Chor der schönen Bilder schließen wir uns aus, und wenn diese einst
wieder ans Licht emporsteigen, liegen wir Alten in unseren Särgen;
den Kommenden aber zeigen sie vielleicht ein Medusengedicht."

80. *Sämtliche Werke*, I, 84-88.

81. *Meersburger Elegie* (St. Gallen: Tschudy, 1952). The volume
contains nineteen unnumbered pages of text.

82. *Lombardische Elegie* (Zürich: Arche, 1951), p. 9.

83. "Lebenslauf," in Johannes Bobrowski, *Selbstzeugnisse und Beiträge über sein Werk* (Berlin: Union, 1967), pp. 24-25: "Hauptthema: Der Versuch, das unglückliche und schuldhafte Verhältnis des deutschen Volkes zu seinen östlichen Nachbarvölkern bis in die jüngste Vergangenheit zum Ausdruck zu bringen und damit zur Überwindung revanchistischer Tendenzen beizutragen." In this connection see the discussion of Bobrowski in John Flores, *Poetry in East Germany: Adjustments, Visions, and Provocations, 1945-1970* (New Haven: Yale Univ. Press, 1971), esp. pp. 210-11.

84. "Pruzzische Elegie," written in 1952, first appeared in *Sinn und Form*, VII (1955), 497-500; subsequently reprinted in *Sarmatische Zeit* (Berlin: Union, 1961), the poem was omitted from West German editions of the volume. I cite the poem according to the text in *Sinn und Form*.

85. Eight of these poems, first published in *Das Innere Reich*, X (1943-44), 351-54, are reprinted in Flores, *Poetry in East Germany*, pp. 325-27. On Bobrowski and Klopstock see Flores, pp. 233-54; and Wolfram Mauser, *Beschwörung und Reflexion: Bobrowskis sarmatische Gedichte* (Frankfurt am Main: Athenäum, 1970), pp. 70-86.

86. Interview with Irma Reblitz, in *Selbstzeugnisse*, p. 69: "Erst nach der Gefangenschaft, also erst 1952, als ich schon eine Weile wieder in Deutschland war, habe ich es noch einmal aufgenommen, nun eigentlich sofort in einer äußerlich freien Form—die allerdings für Leute, die von Metrik etwas verstehen, ziemlich deutlich die griechischen Odenstrophen und Versschemata verrät."

87. Here I explicitly disagree with the thesis of Klaus Weissenberger, *Die Elegie bei Paul Celan* (Bern: Francke, 1969), which attempts to link Celan's poetry both formally and thematically to the classical German elegies.

### Chapter 8

1. This controversy has been discussed in many handbooks of literary theory. See, for example, René Wellek and Austin Warren, *Theory of Literature*, 2nd ed. (New York: Harcourt-Harvest Book, 1956), chap. XVII; Ulrich Weisstein, *Einführung in die Vergleichende Literaturwissenschaft* (Stuttgart: Kohlhammer, 1968), pp. 143-62; S. S. Prawer, *Comparative Literary Studies: An Introduction* (London: Duckworth, 1973), pp. 114-19; and Mario Fubini, "Genesi e storia

dei generi letterari," in his *Critica e Poesia* (Rome: Bonacci, 1973), pp. 121-212.

2. *Theory of Literature*, p. 221.

3. While setting is not constitutive for most genres, it clearly belongs to the generic norm of some: e.g., the Sicilian or Arcadian landscape of Theocritan-Vergilian pastoral.

4. Several recent studies of the Bildungsroman have emphasized its self-reflective character; see Martin Swales, *The German Bildungsroman from Wieland to Hesse* (Princeton: Princeton Univ. Press, 1978), p. 4.

5. For an assessment of the achievements and perils of German philosophical idealism with reference to *Bildung* see W. H. Bruford, *Culture and Society in Classical Weimar 1775-1806* (London: Cambridge Univ. Press, 1962), esp. pp. 418-25; George Santayana's sometimes intemperate critique of idealism, which stresses the increasing solipsism of German philosophy in the nineteenth century, implicitly brings out certain parallels to the history of *Bildung* and, by extension, of the elegy. See Santayana, *Egotism in German Philosophy* (New York: Scribner, 1916).

6. For representative attitudes see *Die Gattungen in der Vergleichenden Literaturwissenschaft*, ed. Horst Rüdiger, Komparatistische Studien, 4 (Berlin: De Gruyter, 1974), pp. 1-31 (Jörg-Ulrich Fechner, "Permanente Mutation: Betrachtungen zu einer 'offenen' Gattungspoetik") and pp. 32-62 (Gerhard R. Kaiser, "Zur Dynamik literarischer Gattungen").

7. Our findings would seem to bear out E. K. Bennett's conclusion—in *A History of the German Novelle*, 2nd ed. rev. H. M. Waidson (Cambridge: Cambridge Univ. Press, 1961), p. 160—that "the German genius achieves its finest and most characteristic effects not in the strict observance of the given form, but in straining a form to its utmost possibility—in complete antithesis to the Romance genius, which always achieves its maximum of effectiveness in a complete acceptance of the form."

8. Philipp Mayer, *Theorie und Literatur der deutschen Dichtungsarten: Ein Handbuch zur Bildung des Stils und des Geschmacks*, II (Wien, 1824), 8-13.

9. See Heinz Kindermann, *Das Goethebild des 20. Jahrhunderts*, 2nd ed. (Darmstadt: Wissenschaftliche Buchgesellschaft, 1966), pp. 16-21.

10. For example, in the standard late-nineteenth-century dictionary of familiar quotations—Georg Büchmann's *Geflügelte Worte*—

Schiller is represented with far more quotations than Goethe or any other German writer. See Rudolf Borchardt's "Rede über Schiller" (1920), in his *Reden*, pp. 140-74, which is written with the assumption that Schiller is largely neglected and that, to the extent that his works are known, it is for the wrong reasons. "Er ist von allen großen Figuren der deutschen Geistesgeschichte und der deutschen Literatur derjenige, der am meisten darunter leidet, daß die Vorstellung der Nation ihn in konventionellen Bildern bewahrt" (p. 140).

11. *Prosa III*, p. 341.

12. See Hans Robert Jauss, "Die Partialität der rezeptionsästhetischen Methode," *Neue Hefte für Philosophie*, 4 (1973), 1-46; rpt. in *Rezeptionsästhetik: Theorie und Praxis*, ed. Rainer Warning (München: Fink, 1975), pp. 380-400.

# INDEX

LIBRARY OF CONGRESS CATALOGING IN PUBLICATION DATA

Ziolkowski, Theodore.
    The classical German elegy, 1795-1950.

    Includes index.
    1.   Elegiac poetry, German—History and criticism.
I.   Title.
PT573.E4Z5        831'.04        79-3236
ISBN 0-691-06430-X